John L. Lewis

John L. Lewis

A Biography

ABRIDGED EDITION

Melvyn Dubofsky and
Warren Van Tine

UNIVERSITY OF ILLINOIS PRESS
Urbana and Chicago

© 1986 by the Board of Trustees of the University of Illinois
Manufactured in the United States of America
1 2 3 4 5 C P 5 4 3 2 1

This book is printed on acid-free paper.

Library of Congress Cataloging-in-Publication Data

Dubofsky, Melvyn, 1934–
  John L. Lewis.
  Includes index.
  1. Lewis, John Llewellyn, 1880–1969. 2. United Mine
Workers of America—History. 3. Trade-unions—United
States—Officials and employees—Biography. I. Van Tine,
Warren R. II. Title.
HD6509.L4D8 1986 331.88′33′0924 [B] 85-20116
ISBN 0-252-01349-2 (cloth)
ISBN 0-252-01287-9 (paper)

To Joan and Michelle

Contents

Preface

The story of John L. Lewis can be likened to a prism that refracts and magnifies the history of the American nation and its workers in the twentieth century. His life and career paralleled the forces that pushed Americans from Woodrow Wilson's New Freedom to Franklin Roosevelt's New Deal, into two world wars and a cold war, from the Great Depression to unprecedented affluence, and from national self-assurance to self-doubt. Lewis's active years as a labor leader, moreover, encompassed the rise of the American working class and its labor movement from the background to the forefront of national political and economic struggle. For more than five decades, from 1908 to 1960, Lewis's career in trade unionism reflected oscillations in the American labor movement—rose and fell with the mobilization and demobilization of workers as an independent political and economic force.

When Lewis began his career as a trade unionist in 1908, the American labor movement had just ended its initial and most substantial era of growth, yet trade unionism accounted for less than 10 percent of the nonagricultural labor force, lacked mass membership and power in the enterprises most characteristic of modern industrialism, and scarcely exercised effective national political influence. When Lewis retired in 1960, American trade unionism represented 25 percent of the non-agricultural labor force, claimed its greatest membership in the mass-production, basic industries, and exerted wide-ranging influence on Capitol Hill and in the White House. In the events and developments that propelled the labor movement from the fringes of the economy to its core, that built the movement's membership from just over one million to more than fifteen million, and that transformed it from political impotency to unprecedented power, Lewis could claim preeminence. But Lewis's life illuminates more than the rise of the American labor movement. It exposes several of the dominant themes and tendencies of United States history.

First, Lewis's career is a case study in the myth of the self-made man. From obscure origins as the child of penurious immigrant parents, John L. Lewis rose to fame, power, and wealth. By the mid-1930s, he had become the most powerful labor leader in American history—the first trade unionist to be considered a potential presidential candidate. He conferred with presidents, intimidated congressmen, and socialized with Washington's elite. Individualism and possessiveness personified America's self-made men; Lewis fit the pattern. Self-assertion, pretentiousness, fondness for worldly goods, and social climbing characterized much of Lewis's personal behavior. Paradoxically, however, without the collective strength and solidarity of common folk, Lewis could never have satisfied his more personal, selfish ambitions. His career, fame, and power were rooted in a movement founded on collectivism and solidarity. Few better examples exist of the inherent tension between the self-made man and the society that created him than the life of John L. Lewis.

Second, Lewis's story reveals how trade union leadership evolved from a calling to a career, its exemplars from missionaries to professionals. The first and perhaps second generation of American trade union leaders sacrificed personal security, comfort, and even health to build a labor movement that would, in the future, produce a freer, more equal, perhaps utopian society. Some of their inheritors used the labor movement for personal and organizational aggrandizement. As unions grew larger, more stable, and more powerful, their leaders acquired job security, lush perquisites, and professional life-styles. Lewis's career exemplified that transformation in the American labor movement, as he alternately played the missionary and the professional, the charismatic leader and the rational bureaucrat.

Linked to the transformation of the labor leader's perception of his role was a change in the relationship between trade unions and employers. At their birth and during their formative years, trade unions were protest organizations that represented the workers' claims to economic and political power. Their raison d'être was to protect the workers' interests in an inevitable conflict between employees and employers, labor and capital. Ineluctably, almost imperceptibly over time, trade union behavior shifted away from protest and conflict toward collaboration and accommodation between labor and management. Founded to fight employers in the interest of workers, unions sometimes came to serve capitalism in search of labor peace, higher productivity, and social harmony. No twentieth-century American labor leader preached class struggle more loudly than John L. Lewis—nor practiced class collaboration more cunningly.

As significant as the shifting relationship between labor and management was the relationship between individuals and the state, voluntary associations and coercive public power. During the 1920s (unsuccessfully) and the 1930s (successfully), Lewis sought to use the power of the federal government to strengthen trade unionism and conquer intransigent antiunion employers. At the height of the New Deal, Lewis linked the fortunes of the coal miners' union and the CIO inextricably to the policies and the goals of the Roosevelt administration; the prerogatives of trade unions and the power of the state often seemed indistinguishable. By the end of the 1930s, however, Lewis began to question what he now characterized as an omnipotent, imperial state. As federal actions impinged increasingly on the behavior of individuals and voluntary associations, Lewis feared that American liberties would shrink. He asserted that the omnipotent state and personal liberty were in conflict. Indeed, by the 1940s, Lewis's rhetoric portended an inevitable battle between free men and a coercive state that transcended the irrepressible war between labor and capital.

Related directly to Lewis's fear of the omnipotent state was his perception of the United States' proper role in world affairs. Traumatized by his experiences as a Wilsonian during World War I, Lewis came to believe that the United States could serve the world best by minding its own business. Together with many other prominent Americans frequently dismissed as isolationists, Lewis saw the United States as the globe's brightest symbol of liberty. But he argued that the nation could promote liberty elsewhere only through exemplary domestic behavior, not persistent overseas intervention. Not only would an adventurous, interventionist foreign policy fail to promote freedom abroad or protect national security; it would also inevitably create an imperial presidency, circumscribe individual liberties, and replace the American republic with a vulgar empire. Yet, after 1945 Lewis paradoxically demanded that the government forcefully resist Soviet expansion and supported the cold war at home and abroad.

Finally, Lewis's life and career expose the inseparable relationship between means and ends. A practitioner of the theory that power is the only morality, Lewis used every means at his command to accumulate power: brutality, bullying, deceit, and bluff. Many even have asserted that Lewis's policies as union leader led inexorably to violence and murder, that his favorite means necessarily produced warped ends, and that evil can never create good.

Because Lewis's life and career illuminate the themes cited above and form a vital component in the organizational revolution at the heart of twentieth-century United States history, a biography of Lewis is not only a dramatic and intrinsically exciting life story, it is also, more importantly, a description of the salient social and economic forces that have shaped modern America and an examination of the emergence of a professional, rational, bureaucratic labor movement.

This new edition of a book published in 1977 remains true to the spirit and substance of the original version. No large body of literature or new sources on the subject have become available since we completed our research and writing. Several substantial FBI files on Lewis at the Franklin D. Roosevelt Library and the FBI Building have recently been opened to researchers, but the information in them in no way alters the facts about Lewis's life and career as we originally sketched them.

What we have done in this volume, then, is to try to make the story of Lewis's life accessible to a larger number of readers. We have cut superfluous passages from the 1977 version, eliminated the scholarly annotation, and tightened the prose throughout. We encourage readers interested in full documentation, scholarly controversy, and further research to turn to the original edition, which is fully annotated and includes a lengthy description of sources.

We also remain as indebted as ever to those librarians, archivists, fellow historians, and friends whose contributions we acknowledged in the 1977 edition. To our debts to them, we now add a word of thanks to all of the generous reviewers of *John L. Lewis: A Biography,* whose criticisms have helped to make this what we believe is a tighter and better book. Special thanks is due Chris Burton and Janice Gulker for typing this manuscript and its revisions. Last but not least, this book would not have been possible without the cooperation and encouragement of Richard L. Wentworth, director of the University of Illinois Press, who agreed with us that the life of John L. Lewis should be made available to a new and larger body of readers.

I

From Obscurity to Power, 1880–1920

1

Obscure Origins, 1880–1908

Mention Iowa and an American commonly thinks of rolling prairie, corn, and hogs—a state populated by prosperous farmers. Mention South Wales and an American typically imagines coal, slag heaps, soot, and green valleys turned gray by modern industry's voracious appetite for energy. One thinks of tired, bent, crippled men, young and old, emerging from coal pits at day's end covered from forehead to shoetops with black dust.

Prosperous Iowa and bleak South Wales scarcely seem linked by any common threads of history. Yet in reality the experience of immigration tied together the two disparate landscapes. Sometime in the late 1870s, most probably in 1876, John Watkins, his wife Sarah, and their children settled in the town of Lucas in Lucas County, south-central Iowa. Most likely in that same year, Thomas H. Lewis also arrived in Lucas County. Watkins, then fifty-two years old, and Lewis, twenty-three years old, had left South Wales within a year of each other (1869 and 1870, respectively) to seek better lives overseas. Unrelated and unknown to each other in the old country, Watkins and Lewis linked their lives and families in the new land. In 1878, Thomas H. Lewis married eighteen-year-old Ann Louisa Watkins, the Watkins's eldest child still living at home. And on Lincoln's birthday, February 12, 1880, their first child, John Llewellyn, was born.

What circumstances had brought the Watkinses and Lewises halfway around the globe from South Wales to south-central Iowa? And what were they doing in Lucas County in 1876? It is easier to explain why they left South Wales than how they arrived in Iowa. After 1850, the Industrial Revolution rapidly transformed South Wales. Long an isolated, primitive region of small, self-sufficient dairy and vegetable farmers insulated from the vicissitudes of the commercial grain markets, in the late Victorian era Wales became a primary source of the highest grade "steam coal" and an ideal location for the expanding British iron and steel industry. Industrialism reshaped the Welsh countryside and its social structure. Indigenous and migratory population growth caused proletarians to outnumber peasant farmers. The spread of a cash economy and a substantial rise in land rents compelled many small farmers to become part-time coal miners and drove their male children into full-time work in the pits or iron and steel mills. Enmeshed ever more deeply in the British and world capitalist economy of the late nineteenth century, the Welsh fell victim to capitalism's recurrent crises. Irregular employment, fluctuating prices, low wages, and dangerous work annually drove thousands of Welsh to emigrate overseas—to Australasia, Canada, and, primarily, the United States. John Watkins and Thomas Lewis were among the numerous natives of South Wales who sought a better life abroad.

Yet John Watkins and Thomas Lewis claimed different family origins and came to Lucas in different fashions. Neither Watkins nor Lewis was a typical immigrant. Watkins, who sailed from Swansea with his family in 1869, was older than the ordinary emigrant (forty-six in 1869, an advanced age for a nineteenth-century workingman). Lewis, who left Wales the following year, was younger (sixteen) than the typical male emigrant without family members already settled overseas. And whereas the Watkins family journeyed directly to the United States, Lewis sailed for Australia.

What the Watkins family and the young Lewis did between their departures from Wales in 1869–70 and their arrivals in Iowa in 1876 remains unknown. For John Watkins, who had been a coal miner in Wales, life in the new world probably consisted of a persistent migration from one raw coal camp to another in search of steady work, better conditions, and higher wages. During the 1870s America's coal industry grew rapidly, and skilled Welsh miners were in great demand. Tom Lewis, the son of a small Welsh farmer and himself a part-time coal miner as an adolescent, probably chose Australia in search of land and a rural life. His ambitions apparently frustrated in that British dominion, young Lewis took ship for San Francisco. Precisely when he arrived on the West Coast is unknown, although it could not have been before late in 1872. His life in the United States during the next four years is also unknown. According to an obituary printed in 1919 the *United Mine Workers Journal,* Tom Lewis participated in the gold rush that in 1876 opened up the Black Hills of South Dakota. The same obituary states that in the late 1870s he also worked in the coal mines of Ohio, Indiana, and Illinois. Given the lack of solid evidence on Tom Lewis's peregrinations, however, it seems logical to assume that he traveled directly from the Black Hills to south-central Iowa, a more natural route than a detour back east through Ohio, Indiana, and Illinois. And there in Lucas County, Tom met the Watkins family and his future wife, Ann Louisa.

Still, one may rightly inquire what forces brought John Watkins and Tom Lewis to south-central Iowa, rather than to the coalfields of Pennsylvania, Ohio, or Indiana where most Welshmen dug black diamonds. First, in 1876, Lucas County, Iowa, resembled coal-mining areas back East. The county, in fact, resembled the Missouri hill country just to its south more than the gently rolling Iowa prairie, and its more precious natural resource was a black mineral (coal), not black soil. Indeed, in the Lucas of 1880 and the neighboring hamlet of Cleveland, where John L. Lewis was born and lived as an infant, miners and laborers far outnumbered farmers. According to the 1880 federal census, Lucas had 247 wage workers and only 7 farmers, and Cleveland numbered 125 wage earners (at least 105 of whom listed themselves as miners) to 1 farmer. Not only did wage workers in general and coal miners in particular dominate the local social structure, but the vast majority of local residents also bore Welsh surnames. Thus, in 1880 Lucas-Cleveland, Iowa, was essentially a Welsh immigrant coal-mining community.

Coal was first discovered in the Lucas area early in 1876, probably near Cleveland. Not until the discovery of coal did the area experience substantial population growth. Although local businessmen developed several mines between 1876 and 1880, only one, the Whitebreast Coal and Mining Company located on Whitebreast Creek, proved a success. Its development begun on May 1, 1876, the Whitebreast mine shipped its first coal in October of the same year, and by 1881 it employed three hundred miners underground and sixty craftsmen and general laborers on the surface. From April 1880 to January 1881, the mine produced between 9,069 and 16,667 tons monthly, with production peaking in the late fall; it disbursed a monthly payroll that ranged between $11,531.07 and $23,310.23. The company sold most of its coal directly to railroads and seldom had an excess to sell to local consumers for domestic heating purposes.

Undoubtedly, Watkins and Lewis arrived in Lucas in 1876 to develop the Whitebreast mine and work in it. It was a common practice among mine owners to recruit experienced British miners through extensive advertising in immigrant newspapers and labor journals. It was also customary for miners in newly developed western regions to receive premium wages as an inducement to leave more settled areas.

The type of society and culture that the Welsh immigrant miners established in Lucas seems beyond historical reconstruction. Certainly a substantial number continued to communicate in the Welsh language; according to the 1880 census data, many of them, like John L. Lewis's grandmother, Sarah, reported themselves as illiterate in English. When the folklorist George Korson prepared a children's biography of John L. Lewis, the subject cooperated with the author in an attempt to recreate the milieu of his childhood. Lewis recalled an immigrant community in which organized song festivals in the Welsh language—*eisteddfo-dau*—served as the most popular and cherished group activity. Such festivals were, to be sure, characteristic of first-generation Welsh immigrant life in the United States, but Lewis's reminiscences about life in Lucas are suspect. His family left there while John was still an infant, and when they returned later in the century, the community was no longer predominantly Welsh in character.

The chapel was as important as the pit in the lives of Lucas's Welsh immigrants. Welsh miners founded two of the earliest churches in Lucas and Cleveland. In 1878, Cleveland's residents formed a society of the Congregational Church and erected a place of worship. Two years earlier, another immigrant Welsh group in Lucas had formed a branch of the Reorganized Church of Jesus Christ of the Latter-Day Saints (Mormons). The American environment had thus produced a strange transformation in the religious beliefs and affiliations of Welsh miners and their families. In the old country, the workers were primarily members of the dissenting sects, ordinarily Baptist, Methodist, and Primitive Methodist; in Lucas, Iowa, they affiliated with Congregationalism and, more remarkably, a schismatic Mormon sect.

In the link between Welsh immigrants and Mormonism hangs a strange tale concerning John L. Lewis. According to the 1881 county history, one of the founders of the Mormon church in Lucas was John Watkins, John L. Lewis's grandfather. It seems unlikely that Thomas Lewis, if either a Congregationalist, a typical Welsh dissenter, or, less likely, a nonbeliever, would have courted a Mormon's daughter, especially one who took her father's faith seriously. In the late nineteenth century other Christian church groups ostracized Mormons, and Mormons scarcely associated with "heathens." Is it then possible that John L. Lewis was raised in a Mormon household and that his subsequent rejection of the faith of his mother, whether for theological or opportunistic reasons, explained his lifelong adult silence on matters of religious preference and church affiliation? It is a question well worth posing, because one with a Mormon background would not have risen far in a labor movement dominated by evangelical Christians, Roman Catholics, or outspoken nonbelievers. His mother's Mormonism may also help explain Lewis's distaste for all alcoholic beverages and his generally prudish sexual life as an adult. Perhaps, also, Mormonism influenced Lewis's strange amalgam of individualism (possessive materialism) and communitarianism (trade unionism).

Although it is known that John L. Lewis was born and lived his first fifteen months in Cleveland, not Lucas, it is not known whether he was delivered by a doctor, a midwife, or a family member (the 1880 census indicates no doctor in Lucas or Cleveland). His parents lived in a single-family dwelling that they either owned or rented from the Whitebreast Company. Although evidence suggests that by 1881 most miners owned their homes, Lewis asserted in 1940 and also 1941 that he had been born in a company house.

The family milieu in which Lewis formed his first images of external reality also seems impenetrable. One suspects, but there is no proof, that his parents and grandparents spoke Welsh more often than English among themselves and their friends. (As late as 1900 his father remained an alien.) Tom Lewis worked a long day in the mines and probably returned home too exhausted to spend much time with his only child. But in 1880 he was unemployed for three months — likely the late spring slow season for coal mining — and may have then showered attention and affection on the infant John L. Ann Louisa, apparently a gregarious, generous, and affectionate young woman with long, deep-red hair, remained at home. In a mining town, few opportunities except for domestic service attracted females outside the home. Ann Louisa also likely spent much time with her own mother, who lived only a mile away in Lucas.

More than affection likely bound daughter to mother. Grandmother Sarah Watkins was, in 1880, fifty-one years old — a woman who had borne twelve children, less than half of whom had survived infancy and childhood. Perhaps old and worn beyond her years, Sarah had to care for a household consisting of her coal-mining husband; an eighteen-year-old son who also mined; a five-year-old daughter; an eleven-year-old son (put to work in the mines); and four male boarders, three of whom were crippled. Sarah certainly needed Ann Louisa's assistance to care for such a menage. It is thus quite likely that John L. Lewis as an infant encountered death (conversation about Sarah's deceased children and the parents of the Watkins's adopted son). He also saw human frailty revealed in the crippled bodies of the three boarders. In a sense, the Watkins's household and its Lewis appendage resembled a modified extended family, but it is questionable how much security, comfort, and affection such a network provided its members.

John L., his mother, and his grandmother spent most of their time at home. When employed (usually nine months of the year), the men occupied themselves beneath the ground. Aside from home and work, Lucas-Cleveland offered few diversions to its residents. The thirsty

Cleveland dweller could escape to one of the two saloons in Lucas. But for Welsh chapel types, whether Congregationalist or Mormon, saloons were forbidden territory. Cleveland boasted one general store patronized primarily by miners; Lucas, as befit a town three times larger (981 residents to Cleveland's 380) possessed a larger business district. Children of school age could attend either of the one-room ungraded schools taught by the two local teachers, one in Lucas and the other in Cleveland. For their parents, church services and socials beckoned.

Coal miners had one other diversion—and a notable one. The largest single structure in Cleveland, a two-story hall, the lower floor of which served as the schoolhouse, was built and financed by the miners. Yet the impressive building did not signify a work force far advanced in the mechanics of trade unionism or collective action. Not until February 1881 did the local miners establish an aid society to assist members in distress (by then mutual-benefit societies had had a long tradition among British workers), and the Miners' Hall still lacked a library or reading room—features prominent in almost all late nineteenth-century union facilities.

Lucas, however, claimed a branch of the era's preeminent national labor organization: the Knights of Labor, Local Assembly No. 850. Probably founded in 1878 or 1879, L.A. 850 was led in 1880 by one Daniel W. Jones, most likely a Welshman. Between February 1881 and May 1882, the records of the Knights of Labor indicate no affiliate in Lucas. L.A. 850 either discontinued paying dues to national headquarters or went out of existence, perhaps to be replaced in 1881 by the miners' benefit society.

During the period in which L.A. 850 became moribund, Tom Lewis moved his family away from Lucas; in July 1882 a second son, Thomas A., was born in Beacon, Iowa, a small town about seventy miles northeast of Lucas. Only a few miles from Oskaloosa, Beacon was surrounded with small towns whose names were redolent of Welsh anthracite patches in northeastern Pennsylvania. Moreover, Mahaska County, in which Beacon was situated, was one of Iowa's primary coal producing centers.

During the Lewis family's absence, L.A. 850 rejuvenated itself, becoming by July 1882 the largest Knights of Labor local assembly in Iowa. Their organization's rejuvenation and size may have led the local coal miners to engage in the almost legendary protracted strike against the Whitebreast Coal Company. This was the labor conflict that the legend of John L. Lewis, as repeated in nearly every biography and sketch of the man, tells us that Thomas H. Lewis led—refusing to surrender and consequently suffering blacklisting as a result of his radical militancy. Yet precisely when the strike occurred, what caused it, how long it lasted, and how it was ended remain unknown. Neither the records of the Knights of Labor, the United States Bureau of Labor Statistics reports on strikes in the United States, nor state of Iowa official sources report a strike in Lucas-Cleveland in 1882. And the one local newspaper, the Chariton *Democrat-Leader,* whose 1882 issues survive, contains no references to a strike in Lucas or Cleveland.

But the *Democrat-Leader* does report singularly interesting news about Lucas coal miners in 1882. In 1880 the mine labor force had been all white and mostly Welsh immigrant in composition. By March 1882 Afro-Americans were at work in Cleveland's mines. What brought the blacks to the Lucas area, how many there were, and how long they remained cannot be discovered from the available evidence. That blacks were working in the area's mines before any strike is certain, and that they were employed in the Whitebreast mine is even more certain; in May 1882 the *Democrat-Leader* reported the death of a Negro miner in the Whitebreast shaft. It also seems reasonable to assume that the local white miners perceived the blacks as a threat to their economic security and wage levels, which is perhaps why mine owners employed Afro-Americans. In fact, by October 1882, the *Democrat-Leader* reported that racial antagonism in Lucas had become intense.

Yet, despite the Chariton newspaper's warning of an impending race war in Lucas, no such untoward event occurred. Nor apparently did local miners strike against the Whitebreast Coal Company. On all fronts, withdrawal seemed to characterize the behavior of the miners. Their Knights of Labor local assembly collapsed when during 1882 the national organization suspended sixty-four members of L.A. 850 and expelled another sixty-seven. Unable to force the black workers to leave Lucas, to alter company labor policy, or to salvage their labor organization, white miners like Tom Lewis may have simply decided to seek work elsewhere. Late in 1882 the senior Lewis, after a brief return to Lucas-Cleveland, again moved his family away from the area.

The infant John L. Lewis was jolted with several shocks during 1882. First, his mother gave birth to a second child, a sibling rival for parental affection. Second, John observed his father's behavior during a crisis, one that may have been precipitated by racial conflict, and that also perhaps heightened tension in the household. Third, twice in the same year, John was wrenched away from the familial and physical world that had sheltered and nurtured him since birth. For the next fifteen years, as John passed from childhood to adolescence to early adulthood, his family moved persistently among the towns and cities of central and southern Iowa.

John L. Lewis's life between the ages of three and seventeen seems almost a closed book. The few references that Lewis made about those years to associates, journalists, and biographers cannot be verified through historical sources. What can be pieced together from a variety of diffuse sources reveals a pattern common for late nineteenth-century working-class families, particularly familes of coal miners. Perhaps the most typical feature of working-class life was spatial mobility. Upwardly mobile workers sought better neighborhoods; frustrated workers fled the rent collector and sought better jobs elsewhere. And coal miners, of course, necessarily moved when the mine in which they worked was depleted. The fact that the Lewis family moved repeatedly between 1882 and 1897 did not distinguish it from other American working-class families.

The economics of Iowa coal mining also explain the persistent residential mobility of the Lewis family. In Mahaska County, where the family lived more than once after leaving Cleveland, work was good, although according to one report, "the operators rule, as it were with martial law and to the extent that the men dare not even express their opinion, should they differ from those of their employers." In Lucas, the operators ruled with an iron hand; according to the same source, "everything is lovely and the goose hangs high. The wages per ton are just what the operators are a mind to make it, and the men have to submit to just such treatment as the company, through their bosses see fit to deal out to them regardless of justice." The Des Moines district, however, where the Lewises lived much of the time between 1888 and 1897, was booming by 1887, and miners earned decent wages with steady work. Moreover, by January 1887, Des Moines area miners seemed sufficiently organized to act collectively to resist a wage cut.

With several exceptions, both the sort of work Thomas Lewis did and his family's place of residence between 1883 and 1897 appear obscure. At the birth of their third child, George, in 1885, the Lewises lived either in Cedar Mines, Monroe County, a small town east of Lucas, or in Cedar, Mahaska County, a more substantial coal-mining region. Still later, when John was old enough to do the family shopping (certainly by 1889), the Lewises lived in Oswalt, about twenty-five miles northeast of Des Moines. Oswalt was so small that John did the family shopping in Colfax, a mile south, a larger although still small Iowa farm town that he reached by train. From Oswalt the family moved to Oskaloosa, a small city by national standards yet large for south-central Iowa.

One must wonder what sort of employment other than coal mining Tom Lewis found in such small towns. Could he have been a farm laborer as well as a miner? To be sure, his Welsh origins were agrarian, and he undoubtedly had worked on the Lewis family farm. Moreover, larger Iowa farms customarily needed steady, if not year-round, laborers, and smaller farms always needed hired hands during the cultivating, haying, and harvesting cycles. Demand for coal miners declined precisely when the need for farm labor rose. This was also the sort of work that younger male children, John and Thomas, for example, might be expected to share at an early age.

By the mid-1890s, the Lewises had apparently settled in Iowa's largest city and its capital, Des Moines. There the senior Lewis claimed to have been employed by the city police department, and an 1894 studio photograph does show Thomas H. Lewis and two mates posed in Des Moines policemen's uniforms. Coal mines also operated just outside the city, and it is possible the father still took occasional employment in the pits. John L. Lewis, when revising his own official autobiography in 1964, asserted that he had attended high school for three and a half years, obtaining all but his diploma. If he indeed attended high school, it would have been in Des Moines, where he also sold newspapers to supplement the family's income, defended his younger brothers in street fights, and played amateur baseball. By then, 1894–97, John had developed into a strapping working-class youth of more than average height—extremely broad in the shoulders, wide in the girth, and with a handsome face topped with stunning, wavy auburn hair.

What else can be said about the Lewis family between 1883 and 1897? Working-class families, especially among coal miners, tended to be larger than those of the upper classes. The Lewises proved no exception to this rule. Between 1882, when John's first brother, Thomas, was born, and 1894 Ann Louisa Lewis gave birth to six other children, four of whom survived infancy (George, b. 1885; Alma D. (Dennie), b. 1889; Howard, b. 1891; and Hattie, b. 1894). Spaced approximately two years apart, the births represented maximum fertility for Ann Louisa and suggest that the deceased infants were born either between Thomas and George (1882–85), George and Alma D. (1885–89), Howard and Hattie (1891–94), or after 1894. The birth pattern also indicates that throughout the years during which the Lewises moved persistently, Ann Louisa always had an infant at her breast or underfoot. Without help from the older children, Ann Louisa would have faced a staggering household burden.

One can only imagine the domestic routine in such a home and in a climate such as Iowa's—blazing hot in the summer and freezing cold in the winter. The typical coal miner's home was no more than a shack rented from the local coal company. Framed in clapboard and roofed with tar paper, it lacked central heating, indoor plumbing, and electricity. Water would be drawn from an outside well, and family members would relieve themselves at a primitive outdoor privy. A coal-burning cookstove heated the home in the winter, boiled its water, and cooked its food; in summer it probably made the kitchen-living area the most uncomfortable in the home. When Tom Lewis was fortunate enough to work in the mines, Ann Louisa would have to rise before dawn, start a fire in the stove, and prepare breakfast and a dinner pail for her spouse. As dawn broke and the senior Lewis departed for another day's work, Ann Louisa would awaken the older children, cook their breakfasts, and prepare them for school. Later, but still early in the morning, she would tend to her preschool-age children. Part of the late morning and early afternoon, she might have free time to visit neighbors, shop at the local store, wash, sew, or simply relax. Before long, however, Ann Louisa would have to prepare for the return home of children and husband. Water had to be drawn from the well, heated on the stove, and set in a metal washbasin so that Tom Lewis could bathe and wash the coal dust from his body. Supper, meantime, had to be prepared, cooked, and served. After supper, the household had to be tidied, and the next day's supply of water and coal brought into the kitchen. Family members would then straggle off to bed (the growing family probably never shared more than two bedrooms).

The impact of family expansion and household routine on John L. Lewis can only be surmised. At first, the presence of male siblings probably produced rivalry, not burdens, because John was too young to assist his mother in household chores. Never especially close to Thomas, John developed an intense relationship with the next four children—George, Dennie, Howard, and Hattie. One might assume from this pattern of sibling relationships that by Dennie's birth in 1889 John had begun to assume responsibilities in the household that grew greater after the subsequent births of Howard and Hattie. Certainly, during his adult years, John L. Lewis evinced singular concern for his siblings' welfare, protecting them from their own foibles, employing them in good jobs, and even providing them with homes.

What else might reasonably be said about John L. Lewis's childhood and adolescence? We might surmise that his connection with Welsh culture and language became attenuated. The Lewises lived in towns and cities not dominated by Welsh immigrants and used the language of their English-speaking neighbors; the children chose typical American-born Iowans as playmates. This meant a childhood and adolescence that separated Lewis from the culture of his parents, introduced him fully to American mores, and transformed him by age seventeen into an acculturated second-generation American.

Whatever the Lewis family did between 1883 and 1897, they returned to Lucas County in the latter year. By then, however, the area's character had been altered. No longer did coal dominate the local economy, nor did the Welsh far outnumber other groups. The number of producing coal mines had increased, but by 1900 farmers clearly surpassed miners in local number and significance. Lucas scarcely included any miners among its residents, and despite a substantial number of miners, Cleveland was no longer a company town or the residence solely of miners and their families.

The factors that brought the Lewis family back to Lucas are unclear. Perhaps Ann Louisa desired to be close to her parents, both of whom were by then octogenarians, and to enable John and Sarah Watkins to see more of their grandchildren. Perhaps Tom Lewis had lost his job in Des Moines and had chosen to move his family into the home that his father-in-law owned in Cleveland while he and his older boys sought work in the coal mines, which were likely to expand production as the national economy boomed after four years of severe depression. Perhaps a new opportunity beckoned Thomas Lewis back to Lucas County.

Again the absence of records and sources makes it impossible to draw firm conclusions about the Lewis's life from 1897 to 1901. The only firm surviving evidence raises more questions than it answers. The 1900 federal census lists the Thomas H. Lewis family as residents on a farm in Whitebreast Township (the rural section beyond Cleveland); the senior Lewis reported his occupation as farmer, and the three oldest boys—John, Thomas A., and George—were listed as farm laborers. And Tom Lewis rented the farm. Because the census was taken in June, it might present a misleading picture of life for the Lewis family. Perhaps they, like many American miners of that era, dug coal during the winter and farmed during the warmer months.

Several scraps of evidence link John L. Lewis to the mines. Writing to Lewis in 1966, an old acquaintance from Lucas enclosed a photograph of the old Big Hill Mine, where, he observed, Lewis had mined coal as a young man. The Lewis Papers at the State Historical Society of Wisconsin also contain photographs of the mines Lewis worked in as a young man and references to his days in the pits. Equally interesting, former United Mine Workers president John P. White asserted in a speech delivered June 1, 1924, on John L. Lewis Day in Lucas County "that Mr. Lewis was the first recording secretary of the first local union organized in Lucas County." And in August 1941 the *United Mine Workers Journal* printed a photograph of the original 1901 charter of Local Union No. 1933 of Chariton, Iowa (the Lucas County seat), which listed John L. Lewis as its secretary.

Aside from farming and working in the mines from 1897 to 1901, John L. Lewis apparently performed as an amateur actor in talent shows at the Lucas Opera House. He also managed the facility and brought in traveling companies to perform *Uncle Tom's Cabin, St. Elmo, East Lynn,* and medicine shows.

By the age of twenty-one, then, John L. Lewis had experienced a varied existence. He had lived in hamlets, small towns, and Iowa's largest city; attended one-room, ungraded, rural schools and an urban secondary school; peddled newspapers on city streets, worked the soil, dug coal, performed in amateur theatricals, managed a small-town theater, and served as a trade union officer. He seemed a young man of many talents and interests, a typical small-town striver, yet a person whose future promised no spectacular accomplishments. In 1901, however, a restless aspect of John's personality would also reveal itself.

For most of his formative years John L. Lewis had been saddled with unchildlike responsibilities. As the oldest child in a large but poor family, he had had to assist his mother with the housework, tend the younger children when asked, and do a variety of chores. In adolescence he had worked first part-time and then full-time in order to supplement family income. But by 1901 he could more freely and easily choose his own path in life. By the time that Ann Louisa bore another child, Raymond, in October 1900, the youngest daughter, Hattie, although in school, was old enough (seven) to assist with household chores. The older boys, Tom and George, could work full-time and add substantially to family income.

In finally choosing to exercise his independence, John L. Lewis made the break with his family as complete as possible. He departed the household for the Rocky Mountain West and remained away for five years. More surprising than his flight from the family and pursuit of personal autonomy was his relinquishment of the union post to which he had just been elected. In seeking a new future, John L. Lewis had apparently rejected a career in trade unionism.

Precisely what Lewis did in the West remains subject to conjecture. At various times he claimed to have worked in gold, silver, lead, and copper mines from Montana to Mexico. It would not have been surprising if he had also labored on the railroad and general construction gangs. He also hinted that he had been a member of the Western Federation of Miners, the most militant labor union of its era (1893–1907), although no records prove or disprove the claim. Yet when reminiscing among family members about his western experiences, Lewis never spoke about work in the hard-rock mines. Instead he told colorful stories about his many "business" ventures.

A plethora of tales have accumulated concerning Lewis's western hegira, most of which are unverifiable. The most dramatic story concerns Lewis's involvement in the 1903 disaster at the Union Pacific Railroad Company's coal mine in Hanna, Wyoming. Passing through the area by chance, Lewis arrived in time to assist a rescue team in carrying out the torn, charred bodies of 234 miners. "The descent into the mine that had become a charnel house was for Lewis a descent into hell," writes his biographer Saul Alinsky, "but what ripped his emotions to shreds was the sight of the numb, mute faces of the wives now suddenly widows of the men they loved. It was at Hanna, Wyoming, that John L. Lewis was baptized in his own tears." This is a dramatic story certainly, although it cannot be documented.

The importance of those five years in shaping Lewis's life will probably never be known. "I would say," Lewis allegedly told Alinsky, "that those five years did more to shape my feelings and my understanding of how people behave than anything else in my experience. Those five years were probably one of the most important parts of my life." If so, they scarcely helped Lewis in forging a permanent, secure identity or purpose in life. He returned to Lucas at the end of 1905 no surer of what he wanted to do in the future than when he had left, no wealthier, if perhaps wiser, and scarcely a success. And now he was in his mid-twenties, an age by which most successful men had chosen their occupations, professions, or careers.

Back in Lucas among family and acquaintances, John settled into his prewestern routine. He entered the mines again, and later claimed that in 1906 members of the Lucas County miners' union chose him as their delegate to that year's convention of the United Mine Workers (UMW). If Lewis played an active role at the convention, or even attended it as a delegate, no records disclose his contribution to the miners' cause. Once again, moreover, work in the mines and election to union office failed to convince Lewis that his future lay in the labor movement.

John still toyed with amateur theatricals and managed the local "opera house." He also joined the Lucas Lodge of the Masons, and in 1907 he was elected junior warden. Indeed, in 1907, as John L. Lewis associated himself with Lucas's solid citizens, ventured into a business partnership, and participated in town politics, he appeared more the striving bourgeois citizen than the emerging proletarian leader.

He also married in 1907. On June 5, he married Myrta Edith Bell, the oldest child in a family of seven children. The Bells had moved to Lucas from Ohio between 1884 and 1887. The head of the family, John C. Bell, practiced medicine and belonged to the American Medical Association. He earned enough income to purchase a home and to send his oldest children, Myrta and her sister Florence, to Drake University in Des Moines for summer sessions. Dr. Bell was one of Lucas's most respected citizens—a member of the prestigious Presbyterian Church and the leader of the most influential men's club, the Masons.

On the surface, the Bells appeared to be everything the Lewises were not. They traced their lineage back to the colonial era, claimed superior educations, practiced prestigious professions (medicine for the father and teaching for the eldest daughters), and belonged to what passed for a Lucas elite. For John L. Lewis, marriage into the Bell family represented a firm step up the American social ladder.

But why did Myrta, throughout her life exceedingly concerned about social status, choose to marry a coal miner and the son of immigrant parents? Eligible males may have been scarce in a town the size of Lucas, especially for a young woman (not so young, however, in terms of a first marriage) as demure, reserved, and withdrawn as was Myrta Bell. For such a woman, most of whose peers had probably already married, John L. Lewis may have seemed a prize well worth the pursuit. He was handsome, outgoing, obviously talented, and patently ambitious. By 1907 he had outgrown life as a coal miner and proved it, as we will see, by his other activities. Perhaps it is best to consider the union of John L. Lewis and Myrta E. Bell as a marriage of convenience and mutual advantage.

Theirs was not a tempestuous or passionate courtship of two love-struck postadolescents. If John L. Lewis was only a year or two older than the typical male at first marriage, Myrta Bell was fully five years older at first marriage than the typical female. By age twenty-seven, John had experienced many environments and forms of work; he was a mature adult who had fashioned his own identity. Myrta, too, by age twenty-seven, after more than seven years of teaching experience, was a mature, self-sufficient adult.

The marriage of two such mature individuals renders suspect the myths that have flowered concerning Myrta's influence on John L. Lewis. According to Alinsky and other biographers, Myrta "organized Lewis's reading habits and introduced him to Dickens and to Homer and other classics. She encouraged his interests, guided him, and loved him. Myrta Bell was to become the most important single force in the life of John L. Lewis." She also, it has been alleged, taught her husband diction, voice inflection, and effective speech mannerisms.

The facts of John L. Lewis's life before marriage suggest otherwise. In 1907 he was not putty in his wife's hands, a malleable material that could be shaped in any form Myrta desired. Rather, he was an individual who had completed all but the final term of secondary school (quite an accomplishment for the 1890s), practiced his speech and language on the stage of the Lucas Opera House (where he also became acquainted with the classics and not-so-classics), and knew that impressive classical allusions could be drawn from *Bartlett's Familiar Quotations* and the even more familiar Bible. Later in life he evinced no deep interest in literary classics, preferring instead military history, western adventures, formula mysteries, and what became his favorite magazine in the 1950s and 1960s, *American Heritage.*

If John L. Lewis remained malleable in 1907, it was by his own choice and his continuing failure to select a "career." Indeed, in his pursuit of occupational success, 1907 dealt Lewis two more severe blows. First, local voters rejected his bid for the Lucas mayoralty, more probably a loss of prestige rather than material benefits. Second, and more important, Lewis failed in business. Sometime in 1907 he and a man named Brown opened a grain and feed business in Lucas. Their venture was ill timed, for 1907 was a year of bank failures, a national financial panic, and an ensuing economic recession.

A failure in politics and business less than a year after his marriage, John L. Lewis seemingly had reached a career dead end. Restlessness, frustration, or a combination of both led Lewis to make the biggest decision of his life. In the spring of 1908, he chose to pursue a career in trade unionism, a choice from which he never thereafter deviated and which, within a decade, brought him unalloyed success.

Sometime between April 4 and June 25, 1908, John and Myrta Lewis left Lucas, Iowa, for Panama, Illinois—a company town recently developed in the central Illinois coalfield. A short time later, John's parents, his five brothers, and his two sisters also moved to Panama.

2

The Road to Power, 1908–19

The young man who arrived in Panama, Illinois, in the early summer of 1908 resembled and differed from the typical American coal miner. Twenty-eight-year-old John L. Lewis was the son and grandson of coal miners. Like the children of most miners, he had experienced an unsettled youth as the Lewis family moved frequently from one small Iowa town to another. And like other miners' sons, the young Lewis had left the household from 1901 through 1905 to seek work far from home, in his case in the coal and nonferrous mines of the Rocky Mountain West.

Why, then, did the young husband of a thoroughly middle-class, status-conscious wife choose to move from a small Iowa village to a newly developed, raw west-central Illinois company town? Why did Lewis, the frustrated politician-businessman and sometime-thespian, return to the pits and seek a career in the labor movement? Satisfactory answers to these questions will probably never be found, yet the available facts enable us to draw several logical inferences.

Prosaic reasons probably best explain Lewis's selection of Panama. First, and perhaps foremost, the Lewises moved as an extended family group. John's parents, as well as his five brothers and a sister, accompanied John and Myrta. Finding employment for a male family group of six miners was no mean task, especially in the recession year of 1908 when coal-mine employment declined. Panama provided a solution, because it was the site of a mine first developed in 1906. Indeed before the sinking of a shaft in 1906 by the Shoal Creek Coal Company (named for the creek on which the town was situated), Panama did not exist. When the Lewises moved there in the summer of 1908, Shoal Creek's Panama Mine No. 1 was the largest in Montgomery County and, out of some two thousand mines, the thirty-first largest producer in the state.

Geography also played a part in Lewis's migration. The main railroad lines east from Lucas provided excellent service to Springfield, Illinois, the state capital and in 1908 itself a coal-mining community, situated about thirty-five to forty miles north of Panama. Springfield, moreover, was the headquarters for District 12 and a vortex of UMW political machinations.

Although economics and geography best explain the Lewis family's move to Panama, John's desire for a career in trade unionism had some influence. Yet Lewis would not have settled in Illinois simply in order to improve his political prospects in the union; the state was a bitter cockpit of intraunion politics, one in which eager candidates regularly annihilated each other. When Lewis arrived in Illinois, District 12 numbered many prominent union politicians including John H. Walker, Frank Hayes, Duncan MacDonald, Frank Farrington, Adolph Germer, and William Sneed. Lewis was scarcely in a position to challenge any of them for power, and he did not do so. Instead, he attached himself to some of the more prominent figures in the union and used their influence to gain preferment.

Panama introduced Lewis to a variety of ethnic types. A county history published in 1918 observed of the village: "It is a mining town of some 1,500 population, largely composed of those of foreign birth, who do not as yet assimilate well with our native people." Scattered bits of evidence indicate that Italian immigrants may have been the dominant ethnic group.

The Lewis family, however, was not in Panama to learn from the immigrants; it was there to use them. In Lucas, the Lewises had been only one among many Welsh families; elsewhere they might have been one among a majority of English-speaking mining families. But in Panama they were a tightly knit English-speaking family of Protestant background set down amidst a mass of non–English-speaking Catholic immigrants. And the UMW then was run by men of British origins and Protestant connections; even the Irish Catholic union leader proved the exception at the uppermost levels of the union hierarchy. In the world of union politics, new immigrants deferred to English-speaking leaders, who, in turn, appointed the immigrants to UMW positions that they might never have won in contested elections.

Beyond jobs in an expanding coal mine and the chance to serve as English-speaking leaders to an immigrant population, Panama had little to offer the Lewis family, especially Myrta. Aside from its coal mine, it included a post office, a bank, a lumberyard, several stores, and, in the words of the county history, "several places where booze may illegally be obtained, interfering to some extent with the security and stability of the town and clouding the future prospects for growth and permanency." Panama apparently failed to provide the Lewises with a home of their own. As was typical in a new mining village that would not have existed except for coal, John and Myrta lived in a company house, as did the other family members.

Life in Panama did not separate John and Myrta from their family and friends in Iowa. They visited regularly with the Bell family and probably also with John's maternal grandparents. Such trips were especially frequent during the summer months, when coal mines cut production and travel was easier. John and Myrta maintained their links to Lucas well into the mid-1920s and only severed them completely in the mid-1930s after the death of Myrta's father.

The six Lewis men (Raymond was too young) wasted no time entering union and town politics. Within a year of their arrival, John's brother, Thomas, served as a Panama police magistrate, and John had been elected president of UMWA Local 1475, which by the end of 1910 was among the ten largest locals in Illinois. From that beginning the Lewis family extended its reach ever deeper into union, town, and state politics. When John resigned his local union presidency in 1911 for a more prestigious position in the labor movement, a younger brother succeeded him in office. As John thrived as a trade unionist, his younger brothers also pursued successful careers. The police magistracy proved only a start for Tom. In June 1916 he was elected president of Local 1475 and, most remarkably, at the same time also apparently acted as manager of the Shoal Creek Coal Company's Mine No. 1. In July 1917 he assumed office as a state mine inspector, one of the ripest political plums available to UMW members. Younger brother Dennie in 1916 became financial secretary of the Panama local, a position he retained until conscripted for military service during World War I.

The Lewis men also enriched themselves at the expense of the union treasury. Long after John L. had left Panama Local 1475, the officials of District 12, at the urging of several discontented Panama miners, investigated the Lewis family's stewardship. The two auditors appointed by the state officials uncovered a pattern of corruption and embezzlement whereby Tom and Dennie Lewis as well as their father maintained a dual set of books, issued illegal checks, and forged checks to double the expenditures legally approved by the local union. Between September 1916 and July 1918, the auditors estimated that Thomas A. Lewis and his father tapped the local treasury for $631.66, and Dennie for $255.71. The auditors described the Panama scandal as "one of the widest conspiracy cases in the United Mine Workers on record."

Throughout the crisis engendered by the scandal, which did not erupt until 1918, a UMW election year, the Lewis family stood together. Brother George offered the local full restitution for the embezzlements of his father and two brothers—and he made good on the offer. John, then acting vice-president of the UMW and engaged in his first race for national union office, never criticized his kin publicly. He insulated himself from connection with the scandal and never suffered from its impact.

Indeed, by 1918 John L. Lewis had become too adept a bureaucrat and wily a union politician to involve himself in cheap financial chicanery, or if he did so, to keep records of the transactions. As we have seen, Lewis lost no time in becoming president of Local 1475. He lost less time entering district and international union politics, where he quickly showed a talent for choosing winners. In Illinois he immediately associated himself with John H. Walker, a popular union leader of Scots extraction and a socialist who was then president of District 12, later would serve as president of the state federation of labor, and was admired by American Federation of Labor (A.F. of L.) president Samuel Gompers. During the 1909 UMW election John threw the support and votes of his large Panama local to the winning slate: Tom Lewis of Ohio District 6. A year later he campaigned for John P. White against the incumbent Lewis and endorsed William Green for secretary-treasurer; again Lewis was on the winning side.

Whenever possible, Lewis used the influence, votes, and power he controlled in the large union local to inveigle patronage appointments from UMW superiors rather than run for office and face a union electorate. Lewis built a political machine from the bottom up. Beginning with the support of family members, Lewis gained control of a large local union and then used his local power to gain preferment from district and international union officials.

Lewis's first union appointment resulted from his efforts on behalf of John Walker and William Green in 1909. One of the worst mine disasters in state history occurred that autumn in the small nothern Illinois town of Cherry, a tragedy that erased the lives of almost the entire local adult male population. In the aftermath of the disaster, District 12 intensified its lobbying campaign in Springfield for improved mine safety laws, and John Walker chose Lewis as one of his new lobbyists, appointing him a District 12 legislative agent. In his new position, John ingratiated himself further with Walker and established links to state politicians.

As legislative agent, Lewis continued to involve himself deeply in UMW politics. UMW elections were customarily sordid affairs in which charges and countercharges of fraud flew about recklessly and in which electoral results seldom passed unchallenged. As William Green reminded Lewis on December 21, 1910, there was a distinct possibility that the national UMW convention scheduled for January 1911 would declare President John White's recent victory fraudulent. "I say this," wrote Green, "because as you well know the cry of fraud will be raised and every method resorted to in order to continue control of the organization. It is highly important that our friends prepare for this contest and try to have the local unions represented by men who will not permit such action to be taken." Lewis thus saw to it that he represented Panama Local 1475 at the 1911 convention.

Although he remained largely in the background as a convention delegate, the few times Lewis took the floor revealed his political acumen. First he moved that William Green be seated as a delegate when challenges arose disputing the secretary-treasurer's credentials. Later, toward the end of the convention, Lewis again demanded the floor, this time to defend Samuel Gompers against the allegations of a black UMW delegate who accused the A. F. of L. leader of charging that Negroes were not far enough removed from slavery and barbarism to act as good union men.

As the 1911 convention ended, Lewis could take pride in what he had accomplished in a brief Illinois union career. John Walker, one of the state's most popular labor leaders, admired Lewis, and the UMW's highest elected officers, White and Green, owed him a political debt. Moreover, Lewis's defense of Gompers during the convention did not pass unnoticed.

By the spring of 1911, Lewis could also take pride in the growth of his family. Early in 1910, a daughter, Mary Margaret, was born to the Lewises, and only a year later, on April 14, 1911, a second daughter, Kathryn, was born. From his marriage in 1907 until Kathryn was six months old, John acted the proper family man. Aside from brief trips to district headquarters in Springfield, he remained at home with Myrta. A growing family, however, suggested to a man as ambitious as John that it was time to seek a position more important and more remunerative than that of a common coal miner, local union president, or state legislative agent. And for a person as cunning as Lewis, opportunities in the labor movement beckoned.

In the autumn of 1911 Lewis obtained the position he wanted. Gompers needed a special agent to represent the A.F. of L. in the territory of New Mexico, where organized labor was actively campaigning for the adoption of a "progressive" state constitution with some of the most advanced protective labor provisions in the nation. Lewis seemed an ideal candidate; he came from the nation's largest union, he had worked in the coal and metals mines of the American West, and he had some experience as a lobbyist. He also came highly recommended. John P.

White informed Gompers that in Lewis he would "secure the services of a valuable young man, who is well balanced in every respect and has a large grasp upon the affairs of the organized labor movement." Endorsements from John Walker and William Green also supported Lewis's candidacy.

On October 21, 1911, Gompers offered Lewis a three-month appointment as a special A.F. of L. organizer in Santa Fe, New Mexico, with the promise that a permanent position would follow. Two days later, Lewis accepted the appointment and promised to arrive in Santa Fe on the twenty-fifth. Gompers granted his new agent a salary of $5 per day for a six-day week, hotel expenses not to exceed $2.50 daily, and full railroad expenses; Lewis also received a $150 advance.

Lewis's new position represented a substantial improvement in material status. His $5 daily wage was more than even the most skilled miner could earn in 1911 and considerably more than local union officials received. The A.F. of L. job also included steady employment— a prospect beyond the reach of most American wage earners in 1911, especially coal miners. Lewis's basic annual salary (he soon received the permanent appointment which he held for six years) of $1,560 was nearly double that of the average wage earner and, with expenses added, amounted to a sizeable annual income. The appointment, moreover, brought Lewis into contact with the most influential man in the labor movement, Gompers, and with a host of trade union officials across the nation.

Lewis's new position also entailed sacrifices, the most obvious of which were his family and home lives. From his initial assignment in New Mexico in October 1911 until his resignation from the A.F. of L. in February 1917, Lewis seldom had the opportunity to be at home with his wife and young daughters.

Two travel diaries, one for 1912 and the other for 1915, hint at the flavor of Lewis's routine as an organizer. In 1912, he traveled through the industrial Midwest, the deep South, and the Southwest on organizing forays. He also visited A.F. of L. headquarters in Washington. At most, he spent twenty-nine or thirty days at home with his family in Panama. The year 1915 proved a little better. Lewis organized mostly in Pennsylvania, Ohio, and West Virginia, and he moved Myrta and the children to a rented home in Pittsburgh. Still, he was away from home for more than half the year. Like a traveling salesman, the pre–World War I labor organizer seemed forever on the road.

Some years later Lewis would express what it meant to be a labor organizer in the early decades of the twentieth century. During the 1919 UMW convention Lewis sought to still complaints about the manner in which the union appointed its organizers. "The life of an organizer is not a bed of roses," he told the delegates. "Our field workers are laboring in fields remote from their homes in the non-union or partially organized sections, where we demand their constant attention to their duty and the application of their entire time to the work of organizing the unorganized. They are privileged to return home at stated intervals to visit their families and renew their home associations, but are asked to spend no unnecessary time in such a manner." And so, Lewis proceeded, the corps of organizers constantly changes as some men discover how unsatisfactory is such an employment and such a life.

Yet Lewis retained his position as an A. F. of L. organizer for a full six years, a period when he was regularly absent from home and during which his daughters grew from infancy to childhood. While Lewis traveled, Myrta bore the full responsibility for raising the girls, a task rendered more onerous by a brief residency in Pittsburgh, away from family and friends. Not until Mary Margaret and Kathryn were of school age would John rejoin the household on a regular basis and then move it to Springfield on a street occupied by other members of the extended Lewis family.

What precisely did Lewis do during his years as an A.F. of L. organizer? What did he gain by sacrificing home, family, and local and district union offices? How did his association with Gompers affect his subsequent rise to power in the UMW?

Lewis's employment with the A.F. of L. had many advantages for a man eager to rise in the labor movement. First, it enabled Lewis to escape temporarily from the savage political infighting that in the UMW ruined the prospects of many rising young labor leaders. Yet organizing for the A.F. of L. allowed Lewis to maintain his contacts among coal miners and indeed to win new friends and allies in outlying coalfields in West Virginia, Alabama, and New Mexico. Second, Lewis widened his contacts within the labor movement. A typical week in 1912 saw him confer regularly in Indianapolis with Frank Duffy, secretary-treasurer of the United Brotherhood of Carpenters and Joiners; address local machinists; and speak to "scab" mechanics. He also gained first-hand knowledge of the jurisdictional conflicts that plagued A. F. of L. affiliates and consumed so much of Gompers's time. Third, Lewis benefited tangibly from his association with Gompers, whose influence and patronage within the labor movement were unrivaled. Fourth, Lewis learned how to deal with and serve important political leaders and the vital role of state and national politics to organized labor. In short, Lewis's employment with the federation proved an ideal apprenticeship in labor movement bureaucracy and politics.

Organizing for the A.F. of L. in the years before World War I also had its heartaches and frustrations. Nothing depressed Lewis more than his lack of success in organizing mass-production workers in the Pittsburgh-Wheeling-Cleveland industrial triangle. When he was not mediating jurisdictional disputes, circulating among coal miners, or addressing union gatherings, Lewis devoted his time to trying to organize glassworkers, steelworkers, and electrical industry employees in Pennsylvania, West Virginia, and Ohio. He achieved some success among the more skilled glassblowers and pottery workers but failed miserably in attempting to bring trade unionism to steelworkers.

His failures as an organizer notwithstanding, Lewis had several substantial triumphs during his A.F. of L. years. Success, of course, crowned his first assignment for the federation when New Mexico voters adopted the labor-endorsed state constitution. Lewis proved so skillful politically in New Mexico that during the 1912 presidential election the chairman of the Democratic National Committee asked Gompers to assign Lewis to campaign in the Southwest on behalf of Woodrow Wilson.

Wilson's victory in 1912 involved the A.F. of L. and Lewis more deeply in Democratic and national politics. The A.F. of L. in particular and workingmen in general formed an important element in the Wilsonian coalition and as such were regularly consulted by the new administration on a variety of matters. In 1916, for example, President Wilson through Secretary of Labor William B. Wilson sounded out Gompers for labor's reaction to Judge John H. Clark of Cleveland as a possible successor to Charles Evans Hughes on the Supreme Court. Gompers immediately asked Lewis to investigate Clark's qualifications. He carried out his assignment with dispatch. A month later, Lewis returned an extremely negative report on Clark, who was not appointed to the Supreme Court. Later that same year Gompers asked Lewis to check the credentials of a possible appointee to the federal court for the Western District of Missouri. This time Lewis, whom Gompers now referred to as one of his organization's "most trusted representatives," submitted a favorable recommendation. Although the available evidence is scanty, it seems certain that Lewis did considerable political work for Gompers and the A.F. of L.

Gompers considered Lewis an able organizer qualified for highly confidential assignments. But precisely how close a relationship the two men established is open to question. For several reasons, it is unlikely that Gompers and Lewis maintained a father-son, teacher-student relationship. First, Lewis's travels left him as little time to be with Gompers as to be with his wife and children. Meeting together only once every several months and sometimes less frequently, and then only on official A. F. of L. business, Lewis and Gompers had little opportunity or reason to form a deep personal relationship. Nor did Lewis have much occasion to chaperone Gompers during the latter's recurrent bouts with the bottle.

Indeed their relationship was so distant in some respects that once in 1917 Gompers apparently confused John L. with a different Lewis. And as far as learning from the old master was concerned, the same limitations apply. They were simply not together enough, Lewis was too egotistical to play the willing pupil to any teacher, and Lewis learned more than enough about the labor movement from six years of fieldwork.

Yet Lewis perhaps had a closer relationship to Gompers than most A.F. of L. organizers. The old man referred to the younger man in salutations as "Dear Friend John" or "My Dear Lewis." Gompers several times asked Lewis to travel with him, and Lewis accompanied Gompers, at the latter's invitation, on a speaking tour of Indiana and Illinois in 1916. The A.F. of L. president also assigned Lewis to especially delicate and confidential tasks—the political work noted above as well as a special assignment for two months with President John P. White of the UMW. But one might also argue that this relationship was founded on strict business and political considerations.

In the years during which Lewis served the A.F. of L., the United Mine Workers formed the largest single bloc of votes within the federation. The Secretary of Labor, William B. Wilson, was an ex–UMW official and a supporter of John White. For Gompers, ever the pragmatic labor politician, it paid to cultivate the mine workers' union. Lewis came to the A.F. of L. with the most important credentials: the blessings of John White, William Green, and John Walker. Considering the tight network of relationships built among present and former UMW officials, Lewis's place on the A.F. of L. payroll added to Gompers's influence with Labor Secretary Wilson. John White and the UMW also benefited from the Lewis appointment. The miners' union remained during the years 1911–16 an organization wracked by factionalism. For those in command, it always paid to have friends in Washington among A.F. of L. and government officials. A kind word from Gompers, a firm decision by the A.F. of L. executive council, a patronage job from William B. Wilson could strengthen UMW incumbents and weaken insurgents. Gompers and Lewis thus formed a relationship based on business not pleasure, union politics not friendship, and one that would later ease Lewis's rise to power in the UMW.

Throughout his A.F. of L. years, Lewis never neglected the coal miners and their union. He spent considerable time in the mining districts of West Virginia and quite regularly circulated among the miners of Illinois and Indiana. A.F. of L. business also took him frequently to Indianapolis, national headquarters for the UMW. Lewis, moreover, continued to meddle in internal UMW politics. In February 1912, only four months after assuming his A.F. of L. position, Lewis published a pseudonymous broadside aimed at his UMW enemies. Signing himself "Juvenal Gordon," the actual author used a literary style and phrases indelibly associated with John L. Lewis. "Gordon" accused former UMW president Tom Lewis and perennial District 12 candidate Duncan MacDonald of enriching themselves at union expense. "Darkness would be on the face of the earth and the voice of the organization, like that of Rachel in the Wilderness, would be heard in wails and lamentation," if the Tom Lewises and Duncan MacDonalds held office. "Jowl by cheek," "Gordon" charged, did MacDonald "sit at luxury-laden tables with the dissolute sons and the butterfly daughters of the idle and vicious rich, with captains of industry and malefactors of great wealth. Royally was he entertained. . . . Merrily he tripped through Folly's halls." In 1912, John L. Lewis, already the master of sarcasm, invective, and the purple passage, posed as the ally of UMW radicals, combating class collaborationist officials who supped at capitalist tables. "Yours for the ultimate and complete economic emancipation of the downtrodden proletariat and the triumph of working class principles," pledged "Juvenal Gordon."

Lewis did more than compose pseudonymous leaflets criticizing his union enemies for class collaboration. He also engaged in electoral shenanigans worthy of the most cunning big-city boss. John H. Walker, who had given Lewis his initial boost up the union ladder, experienced Lewis's ingratitude. In 1915 Walker challenged White for the union presidency and in the ensuing bitter campaign for votes, Lewis backed the incumbent White. Lewis contributed a series of forged telegrams, purportedly sent by Walker, appealing to employers for financial support in the race against White. Lewis knew in 1915, as he had known in 1912, that the most deadly charge one could make against a miners' union official was class collaboration; nothing angered the rank and file so much as the thought of being "sold out." White triumphed, and Lewis received his reward.

On the last day of December 1915, Gompers assigned Lewis to assist President White of the UMW in thwarting union militants and insurgents. White promptly put Lewis to work. At the UMW convention, which met in Indianapolis from January 18 to February 1, 1916, Lewis played a decisive role. He served as chairman of the resolutions committee, and he also presided over the convention during the debate over the committee on officers' reports; these were posts that gave him substantial authority during heated floor debates. Lewis proved a strong, decisive convention chairman—one who was well versed in parliamentary procedure and adept at avoiding the personal, ad hominem type of argument common at UMW conventions. Committed to defending the White administration, Lewis spoke as a realist on all intraunion and external political issues. On policy resolutions that ranged from old-age pensions to union solidarity to hostility to the National Guard to racialism in the labor movement, Lewis pleaded for moderation.

On every score the 1916 convention, so ably chaired by Lewis, sustained the White administration. In turn, White wasted no time in showering good fortune on his younger supporter. In the summer of 1916, White appointed Lewis to the wage scale committee charged with negotiating a new contract for District 5 miners in western Pennsylvania. In the last week of July Lewis served as chairman of a special convention that reorganized District 5, bringing to the district presidency Philip Murray, a man with whom Lewis would be associated for the next quarter of a century and the man who would become Lewis's most loyal union lieutenant.

Obviously satisfied by his rising stature in the UMW, in 1916 Lewis ran as a candidate in an international election for the first time in his career, seeking to be a UMW delegate to the 1917 A. F. of L. convention. That contest tells us a good deal about Lewis's standing among coal miners. Thirty-eight men, including the most prominent and respected leaders of the UMW, contested for the five delegate positions. Only eight candidates received more votes than Lewis, but their margins were enormous: White and Frank Hayes polled more than 100,000 votes; John Mitchell and William Green received more than 90,000 and John Walker, then Lewis's most bitter enemy, garnered 85,359 to Lewis's 48,672.5. Frank Farrington, who would challenge Lewis for control of the union in the 1920s, also outpolled Lewis by a wide margin. Yet those whom Lewis bested included such prominent union men as Alex Howat, Tom Kennedy, Phil Murray, William Mitch, and Robert Harlin. The final results revealed, then, that Lewis, although not the most popular of candidates, had considerable rank-and-file support.

Lewis's role in the 1916 UMW international elections produced a plethora of rumors. White won reelection by less than nine thousand votes out of almost two hundred thousand cast in a hotly contested race with John Walker (52 per cent to 48 percent). Walker was a man consumed by his desire to obtain the union presidency and one unable to concede that he might lose a fair election. He preferred to believe that he was a victim of conspiracy and that the prime conspirator was his former Illinois ally, John L. Lewis. In November 1916, Walker complained to Gompers that Lewis had been abusing his A.F. of L. position by campaigning for White among coal miners. Lewis immediately denied Walker's allegations, contending instead that it was a case of the pot calling the kettle black. In a letter dripping with sarcasm, Lewis alleged to Gompers that Walker, in fact, had sought the former's support in the union election; Lewis then asked: "Is it possible that . . . Walker is considering this matter with the biased judgment of one frantically scrambling for office and has worked himself into a mental attitude wherein he believes that all who are not 'electioneering for him' are 'electioneering against him'?" Lewis swore that he had abided by and would continue to abide by the A.F. of L. policy concerning noninterference in the internal affairs of affiliates, and he suggested that his desire to do so "will, of course, be greatly strengthened by the knowledge that my ever vigilant friend, Mr. Walker, with his sensitive ear attuned to catch the slightest discordant note, stands ready at all times to aid and assist by keeping a constant super-vision over me."

Lewis's denials and sarcasm notwithstanding, circumstantial evidence suggests that Lewis was active in the 1916 union election. It is scarcely likely that he polled almost fifty thousand votes without some effort on his own behalf; and it is even less likely that he failed to influence the substantial bloc of votes cast by his old Panama local. White's action soon after his reelection also gives the lie to Lewis's denials. On January 23, 1917, White appointed Lewis international statistician for the UMW, a post that was customarily a sinecure but one for which White and Lewis now had different plans. Lewis thus formally entered the UMW hierarchy in the same manner he earlier had joined the A.F. of L.— by patronage appointment.

Lewis assumed the statistician's post on February 1, 1917, a particularly opportune moment in trade union history. Since the initial upsurge of modern American trade unionism in the years 1897–1903, the labor movement—the UMW included—had lost momentum. Employer resistance, judicial decisions, and economic recessions retarded the further growth of trade unionism. Between 1904 and 1915, the membership of the A.F. of L. and the UMW grew more slowly than during the previous decade. The coal miners fastened their union more securely in the states composing the Central Competitive Field (western Pennsylvania, Ohio, Indiana, and Illinois), a collective bargaining unit established by the operators and the union in 1898, and in several outlying western states (Iowa, Missouri, Kansas, and Oklahoma) but experienced much less success in the southern Appalachian states of West Virginia, Virginia, Maryland, Kentucky, Tennessee, and Alabama. A recession beginning in 1913 and deepening into a depression by early 1915 threatened to deal trade unionism further setbacks. But the European war, which had erupted in late summer 1914, stimulated the American economy. Production boomed, factories and mines operated overtime, workers enjoyed a sellers' market, and trade unionism advanced aggressively.

As 1916 passed into 1917, the pace of labor militancy quickened.

Millions of workers walked off their jobs. Scarcely an industry or a region remained untouched by labor discontent. In 1917–18, the UMW added more members, absolutely and relatively, than it had from 1904 through 1916. By Armistice Day, 1918, the UMW claimed more than four hundred thousand members and was by far the nation's largest trade union.

The mine workers for the first time began to win substantial collective bargaining agreements in the southern Appalachian fields and in some of the other outlying districts. Before, but especially after, the nation entered the war in April 1917, the Wilson administration wooed labor leaders. Federal officials, including the president, promised to promote "legitimate" trade unionism (meaning the A.F. of L. variety) if trade unionists endorsed the war effort. And in 1918 the government made good on many of its promises. Never before had organized labor in America appeared so successful, nor had it wielded so much influence in "official" Washington. Lewis and the mine workers, moreover, were at the center of the wartime labor vortex.

Lewis's travel diary for 1917 and reports in the UMW *Journal* indicated his widening role in the miners' union. His travels now took him on a different circuit in which he did new things. He traveled more frequently between Springfield, Illinois (his new family residence) and UMW headquarters in Indianapolis and also often visited New York City and Washington, D.C. His trips to coal-mining districts involved UMW, not A.F. of L., business, and they concerned collective bargaining more than public speaking. By mid-1917 Lewis served as a key UMW negotiator and Washington lobbyist. Throughout 1917 Lewis labored to make himself indispensable to fellow union officials, coal miners, operators, and government leaders.

John White granted Lewis a singular opportunity to publicize his accomplishments and to trumpet his name within the union. In late summer 1917 Lewis became business manager of the UMW *Journal* as well as international statistician. As administrator of the union paper, Lewis followed precedent; wherever possible, he featured the accomplishments of the incumbent officers and his own "prominent" role in bringing them about. The *Journal,* after all, existed more to convey the union leaders' position on issues than to enlighten coal miners—and John L. Lewis would not break precedent.

Lewis's growing influence in the labor movement in the summer of 1917 followed conventional lines. In June, along with such prominent UMW figures as John White, Frank Hayes, William Green, and John Mitchell, Lewis served as a member of the wartime coal production committee's labor delegation. And Lewis used his influence with Gompers to win patronage jobs for several of his supporters in the UMW.

Even greater gains awaited Lewis—not, however, before family tragedy intervened.

Since the birth of his first daughter in 1910, Lewis had been most prominent in the family by his absence from home. The year 1917 proved no exception to the rule. June, July, and August saw him at home infrequently and then most often only for a day. When he finally rejoined his family for an extended visit, it was the result of personal tragedy. As was her custom in the late summer, Myrta had returned to Lucas with the children, where during the first week in September Mary Margaret became seriously ill with typhoid fever. By September 6, Lewis's seven-year-old daughter had died; on September 8, she was buried in Lucas.

The impact of Mary Margaret's death on the Lewis household remains shrouded in mystery. In the biographical data that the Lewis family later fed to inquisitive journalists and putative biographers, accurate facts were rarely given concerning either the birth or death of Mary Margaret. That the death of her firstborn daughter profoundly affected and depressed Myrta Lewis has been attested to by a sister-in-law, who also recalls that John was grief-stricken by the tragedy. Six-year-old Kathryn probably experienced a loss as great, or greater, than her mother's. Mary Margaret's death must also have been related to John and Myrta's decision to have another child, because only fourteen months later, on November 25, 1918, the Lewis household increased again to four members with the birth of a son, John L. Jr.

Unlike the female members of his family, John could compensate for his daughter's death by immersing himself more deeply in union affairs. On September 18, 1917, less than two weeks after the funeral, Lewis returned to UMW headquarters in Indianapolis and spent most of the next six weeks there and in Washington. Those six weeks proved a decisive period in Lewis's emergence as president of the mine workers. Political bargaining in Washington among Gompers, Labor Secretary William B. Wilson, and President Woodrow Wilson led to John P. White's appointment as a permanent member of the wartime Federal Fuel Board and labor adviser to fuel administrator Harry A. Garfield. White promptly resigned his UMW presidency and, under the union's constitution, Vice-President Frank Hayes automatically succeeded to the highest office. White and Hayes, in turn, appointed Lewis acting vice-president, a position that required international executive board confirmation. Contrary to John Brophy's assertion that members of the IEB opposed Lewis's appointment, the board approved his promotion unanimously, prompting Lewis to scribble these words in his travel diary for Thursday, October 15, 1917, the day White announced his own resignation: "Our ship made port today." Indeed it had, for without once winning election to an international union office, Lewis had become the UMW's second-ranking official.

As vice-president, Lewis had wider latitude for action than the post customarily allowed. President Hayes proved himself ineffective and alcoholic. Lewis gladly filled the administrative vacuum. It was Lewis who most often represented the union during delicate negotiations with coal operators and federal officials. And it was Lewis, not Hayes, to whom Gompers turned when he wanted a prominent labor leader, one who "was true blue," to guide a party of British trade unionists visiting the United States to promote Allied wartime unity. As Hayes's drinking habit worsened and he fell victim to despondency, Lewis, in effect, ruled the UMW. Still, Lewis bided his time before seeking the presidency in his own right.

Despite Hayes's alcoholism, he remained a popular figure among the rank and file, and Lewis knew it. Thus in the 1918 union election Lewis chose to remain as Hayes's running mate—an especially wise choice, in view of the fact that Lewis obtained only fifteen nominations for the presidency from union locals compared to Hayes's 714 and John Walker's 295. In the vice-presidential race Lewis had a clear field, receiving 773 nominations to his closest contender's 89. In fact, Walker's running mate in the election, Thomas Kennedy, chosen to add anthracite voting strength to the ticket (Kennedy was a leader in Anthracite District 7 of northeastern Pennsylvania), obtained only 23 nominations and, as Lewis gloated, not one in "Illinois, Indiana, Ohio, Western and Central Pennsylvania and all of the Southwestern districts and the Northwestern fields, including Alabama, Tennessee, Kentucky, and West Virginia, although my erstwhile friend, Mr. Walker, had made all possible efforts to secure the nominations for him in Illinois." In the event, the Hayes-Lewis ticket swept the field.

Less than a year after his successful race for the vice-presidency Lewis became the UMW's acting president, once again achieving high union office without contesting an election. In one of the many letters filled with paranoid charges of corruption and conspiracy written during the 1918 campaign, John Walker accurately prophesied the future. "Just as soon as the election is over," he wrote a friend on December 4, 1918, "if by any hook or crook they [Lewis, K.C. Adams, Al Hamilton] can steal it, I expect they will depose him [Hayes]. Lewis will go in the position and another henchman of Al Hamilton's will be appointed Vice-President, and the organization will then be completely in control of the most unscrupulous corruptionists that ever represented crooks, trying to destroy the labor movement and prevent the progress of common humanity."

Aside from Walker's comments about crime and corruption, the remainder of his prophecy came true. In the spring of 1919 Hayes traveled to Europe on a joint A.F. of L.–UMW mission to discuss postwar reconstruction with British and Continental labor leaders, leaving Lewis home to serve as the UMW's acting president. In Europe, Hayes's alcoholism worsened. After his return to the United States in midsummer 1919, Hayes proved unable physically to administer the union. Lewis thus ran the UMW unofficially until January 1, 1920, when Hayes, citing ill health, formally resigned from office. Lewis then became acting president and promptly appointed Philip Murray as acting vice-president. Murray was a longtime Pittsburgh area associate and acquaintance of Al Hamilton.

Indeed Lewis may have achieved his position using the methods suggested by Walker, Farrington, and others. But he had also proved himself by 1919 an exceedingly able union official, one who in many respects was a far better administrator than his predecessors or contemporaries. During the war years no other UMW official proved so adept at negotiating union contracts in hitherto nonunion districts or at improving existing contracts. No other union official had superior contacts in Washington or presented the union's case more effectively before government agencies and administrators—certainly not Frank Hayes or William Green. During the January 1918 UMW convention, the first one at which Lewis served as an international officer, he gave a virtuoso performance. His reports to the delegates were remarkable for their detailed statistics, thorough content, and complete knowledge of the economics of coal and risks of mining. Despite considerable rank-and-file hostility to the Washington agreement of October 1917, which increased miners' wages substantially but penalized them monetarily for unauthorized strikes, Lewis masterfully elicited overwhelming delegate support for the UMW administration.

Lewis may have used cunning and even corruption to fight his way to the top, but he also earned his command of the UMW. In 1919 the miners' union had no more impressive figure. Gompers looked to Lewis as one of the nation's most responsible trade unionists and implored him to serve as labor representative to President Wilson's 1919 Industrial Conference. No UMW leader handled raucus convention delegates more diplomatically and more authoritatively. Nor could any union member match Lewis's oratory. By 1919 he had already mastered two different but equally effective styles of public speaking. When emotion and sentiment were needed, Lewis had at his command an ample supply of carefully prepared and rehearsed biblical and Shakespearean allusions that enthralled union delegates. Never at a loss for words even during the most tempestuous debates, he mastered the caustic comment and the ad hominem argument. He also changed pace with consummate skill. When the time came to defend a new contract or to analyze the economics of coal mining rather than to cut down a union rival, Lewis marshaled facts and figures with the best of economists. Indeed, he early used eminent economists for advice, and during the war years he built a relationship with the academic economist and reformer W. Jett Lauck that would influence all the UMW's economic proposals over the next three decades.

Yet Lewis did not reach the top without personal sacrifice. For almost nine years he had lacked a close family life. His daughter, who died at the age of seven, probably spent at most a year of her short life in her father's presence, and his younger child, Kathryn, later intensely possessive of her father, had an early childhood equally devoid of a paternal presence. On the road and in strange towns, Pullmans, and hotel rooms where Lewis spent most of his time between 1911 and 1919, he enjoyed few of the diversions popular among his traveling trade union contemporaries. The saloon, the ball park, and the opposite sex failed to attract the vigorous, physically handsome man then in the prime of his life. All Lewis's energies, all his desires, seemed to be sublimated in a single-minded drive to dominate the mine workers' union and become the most influential figure in the American labor movement.

Travel, family tragedy, and an apparently lonely existence left few overt scars on John L. Lewis. In 1919 he seemed a vibrant, tireless, and attractive man, a perfect specimen of robust good health. Wavy dark auburn hair topped a leonine face that featured penetrating blue eyes, a fine aquiline nose, a firm full mouth, and remarkably bushy eyebrows that lent Lewis a singularly sensuous and mysterious appearance. The most conventional, conservative dark blue and gray suits draped broad shoulders, an immense chest, and stout legs. Not quite six feet in height but in excess of two hundred pounds, John L. Lewis's body showed the first signs of corpulency but not the least indication of age. A powerful trade union had found a leader of commanding physical stature.

By midsummer 1919, Lewis had achieved a part of his great ambitions. He was acting president of the nation's largest and, perhaps, most militant trade union. With four hundred thousand members and union contracts covering coalfields from Alabama to Montana and from northeastern Pennsylvania to Washington state, the UMW seemed a labor colossus able to paralyze the American economy.

3

The Testing and the Triumph, 1919–20

World War I ripped apart the fabric of the Western world. Bolshevik revolutionaries ruled Russia; the German Empire, scarcely half a century old in 1919, stood in ruins; the ancient Hapsburg Empire and its more recent offspring, the dual monarchy of Austria-Hungary, had vanished, the victims of wartime defeat and Czech, Serbian, Croatian, Rumanian, and Bulgarian nationalists. In 1919, communists seized power in Bavaria and Hungary, and in the streets of Berlin militant German leftists, the Spartacists, fought pitched battles with returned troops and city police backed by a reformist Social Democratic government. On the plains of western Russia and eastern Poland, Leon Trotsky's Red Army waged full-scale war with Polish nationalist forces. In Italy workers seized factories, and in Great Britain, the Labour party, which had replaced the Liberals as the nation's second party, proclaimed its program for a postwar socialist order. Wherever one looked in 1919 one witnessed radical turmoil and masses in motion. A new world seemed to be in the making.

In the United States, too, workers and their spokesmen dreamed of a new, better, and more equal society. In the midst of the war, Sidney Hillman, immigrant leader of the men's clothing workers, proclaimed labor's new goals. "What labor is demanding all over the world today," he asserted, "is not a few material things like more dollars and fewer hours of work, but a right to a voice in the conduct of industry." By 1918 Hillman was fired by messianic dreams as he related to his daughter: "Messiah is arriving. He may be with us any minute—one can hear the footsteps of the Deliverer—if only he listens intently. Labor will rule and the World will be free."

American workers in 1919 acted vigorously to reshape society. The year began with a general strike in Seattle, which initiated an unprecedented wave of labor unrest. More than four million workers struck in 1919, a number never before reached and not to be exceeded until 1946. Early in September in Boston even the police walked off the job, and later that month more than three hundred thousand iron and steelworkers left work in the first mass strike to affect that basic industry. Union membership by year's end soared to more than five million.

As American radicals awaited an imminent revolution, conservatives grew anxious. Typically, Warren G. Harding wrote in the autumn of 1919: "I am really more anxious about the tranquility of our country, than I am about personal or party success. I really think we are facing a desperate situation. It looks to me as if we are coming to a crisis in the conflict between the radical labor leaders and the capitalistic system under which we have developed this republic. . . . I think the situation has to be met and met with exceptionable [sic] courage." Much to Harding's subsequent relief, the Wilson administration acted decisively, causing the Ohio Republican to concede that President Wilson, "in spite of his illness . . . may be considerably more sane than some of us have been willing to believe."

Harding's anxieties had been triggered in October 1919 by an impending national strike of soft-coal miners. Long one of the most militant affiliates of the A.F. of L. and a union with a substantial socialist membership, the United Mine Workers could scarcely remain immune to the labor unrest sweeping the nation. Moreover, internal union politics and external economic conditions intensified militancy among coal miners. Wartime increases in wage rates lagged behind inflation, and after the basic Washington wage award of October 1917, coal miners' wages fell further behind prices. Increased wartime coal production had brought miners steadier employment and greater job security than normal. Protected by the marketplace on one hand and federal benevolence on the other, the mine workers' union built its membership and widened the geographical scope of its collective bargaining agreements.

Internally, however, the union had problems. Its president, Frank Hayes, lacked the authority and the ability to run the organization. Almost as soon as he had been elected president in December 1918, Hayes found himself under attack by a number of putative successors. Furthermore, Hayes's vice-president, John L. Lewis, sought to grasp the union power steadily slipping through Hayes's palsied fingers. The various pretenders to Hayes's UMW throne maneuvered to enlarge their union constituencies and in so doing promised rank-and-file miners higher wages, shorter hours, and greater union influence in the industry.

But the 1917 Washington agreement bound the UMW not to renegotiate the basic contract before the war officially ended or April 1, 1920, whichever came first. Although an armistice had been signed in

November 1918, the victorious allies in September 1919 had not implemented final peace terms. Legally, then, the coal miners' union was caught in a dilemma: If, in 1919, neither the operators nor the Federal Fuel Administration voluntarily met the UMW's wage demands and a strike ensued, it would pit the miners not simply against their employers, but also against the federal government.

Yet union leaders and their rivals had to satisfy the rank and file's insistence on higher wages. Thus, in March 1919, President Hayes convened a national policy committee meeting in Indianapolis to discuss the possible termination of the Washington wage agreement and the restoration of peacetime labor conditions. During the policy committee's sessions, the more extreme demands carried as aspiring union politicos outdid each other in bidding for rank-and-file support. Among the more important union goals set in March were the achievement of a six-hour day and five-day week, the nationalization and democratic management of all the coal mines in the United States, and the appointment of an officers' committee to draft a bill for presentation to Congress providing for nationalization of the coal mines.

The means to achieve such ambitious aims, however, were left ambiguous. Unsure as to when a peace treaty would be ratified, Hayes and the policy committee equivocated. President Hayes concluded that the basic agreement "shall not be disturbed until a special International Convention is held." Whether such a convention would be called before or after the formal ratification of a peace treaty was left open.

Through the summer of 1919, while strikes fanned the flames of labor discontent, UMW leaders restrained dissatisfaction among coal miners. Drinking more heavily, President Hayes rapidly lost control of affairs and John L. Lewis administered the UMW from its headquarters in Indianapolis.

By 1919, Lewis's new role, heightened status, and increased income was reflected in the way he lived. He now spent considerable time with his family. Indeed, for the first time since they left Lucas, John and Myrta had a real home of their own. In 1917 Lewis had purchased a large and typically Victorian-style three-story frame house on a wide, tree-lined street in a respectable Springfield neighborhood. He also had purchased two other houses in the same neighborhood for his parents and sisters. John's younger brothers simultaneously established households in Springfield, thus reuniting the Lewis clan. The move made it possible for Kathryn to attend the Springfield public schools regularly and for Myrta to enjoy the company and assistance of her in-laws while John was away from home.

Lewis's desire to become a homeowner, to assist his parents, and to be close to his brothers and sisters is certainly understandable. His decision to live in Springfield rather than Indianapolis makes less sense. His 1919 travel diary suggests Lewis's greater attention to family affairs. Seldom before the coal strike crisis of October and November was he away from home for extended periods of time during 1919. In fact, the diary records constant trips between office and home, Indianapolis and Springfield. Why, then, did Lewis live in Springfield when he administered the UMW from Indianapolis? Why did a man who apparently felt guilty about his absences from the family in the years 1911–18 and about the death of his firstborn child endure regular train trips between two cities and lonely nights in hotel rooms in preference to being at home with Myrta and the children? What aspect of Lewis's personality demanded such an existence? Perhaps during his years as an organizer he had grown accustomed to absence from the family; perhaps Myrta's oppressively bourgeois character, her accumulation of fragile antiques, and her excessive cleanliness irritated him; perhaps he feared, because of guilt about his daughter's childhood death that if home and office were in the same city he might tend to spend more time with his family at the cost of his union career and soaring ambition.

Whatever the motivations, Lewis drew a sharp line between home and career, family and business. It was as if the two aspects of Lewis's life required totally different personalities and to intermingle them would diminish his dual roles as father-husband and union leader. The union role necessitated public presence, cunning, excessive selfishness, and low ethics; proper family life demanded privacy, personal warmth, cooperative effort, and a firm moral code. Only by keeping the two roles in separate, even airtight, compartments could Lewis play them simultaneously and successfully.

The manner in which Lewis reorganized his life-style in 1919 also had enormous impact on his future family and union relations. Kathryn now saw her father more regularly. One could imagine that when Lewis was at home he tried to compensate for past neglect of his surviving daughter; one can also surmise that Kathryn became intensively possessive of her father and that his still-frequent departures from home upset her. This singular relationship between father and daughter to which the elder carried guilt and the younger brought possessiveness in the 1930s and 1940s caused no end of trouble for Lewis.

And what of his infant son, John Jr., born in November 1918? Obviously the son accepted his father as a regular presence in the home, whose absences were no more common than his appearances. Yet the intensity of the relationship between father and daughter must have increasingly irked John Jr., who built a circumspect relationship with his father and ultimately elected to follow the profession of his maternal grandfather, medicine, whereas Kathryn chose a trade union career.

Family tragedy also once again stalked Lewis's rise in the union hierarchy. His appointment as acting vice-president had been preceded only a month earlier by his daughter's death; on February 27, 1919, a month before Lewis assumed command of the UMW from a debilitated Frank Hayes, his father, Thomas, died.

During the summer of 1919, with formal ratification of the peace terms no closer to achievement than the previous winter, coal miners chafed at the restraints under which they labored. Consumer prices soared while wages remained frozen at levels fixed in October 1917. Miners, moreover, were still bound by the wartime clause in their contract that penalized them financially for wildcat walkouts. Yet despite legal restraints and the penalty clause, miners, especially in Illinois and Kansas, spontaneously laid down their tools. Union left-wingers and ambitious office seekers eager to ride rank-and-file militancy into high office encouraged "spontaneous" strikes.

That summer Lewis commanded a powerful but undisciplined union army. If coal miners failed to improve their working conditions either through collective bargaining or government award, they threatened to strike under insurgent commanders. Unless Lewis acted decisively, his troops might desert him and follow his union rivals. If he lost control of the miners and failed to improve their contract, the odds favored Lewis's defeat in the December 1920 UMW election. Lewis's political enemies believed that they had placed the acting president in an impossible predicament. In a public newsletter and a subsequent private interview with a Bureau of Investigation secret agent, K. C. Adams analyzed political machinations inside the UMW. Lewis's enemies, observed Adams, "sought to build a sentiment among the men for wage increases, reduction in hours and other betterments so unreasonable in makeup that Lewis's failure to achieve them in wage negotiations with the operators would sound the death knell of his political future."

In this perilous situation Lewis established his claim to union leadership. First he split his union opponents; next he directed a strike against mine owners and federal officials; and finally he won for coal miners substantial improvements in their basic contract. His handling of the 1919 strike led many coal miners to agree with K. C. Adams that "no other leader in their ranks possesses the daring and ability of Lewis."

Well aware that he would lose control of the UMW and popularity among coal miners unless the 1917 agreement was revised, Lewis induced the union's executive board to call the special convention recommended by the March policy committee report. On September 9, 1919, more than two thousand UMW delegates gathered in Cleveland to discuss their union's future. This was the first convention at which

Lewis presided as the UMW's chief officer, and it proved the stormiest in many years. Debate focused primarily on the issue of a strike, but other issues also embroiled the convention. Ethnic and racial tensions aggravated the customary conflict between district officers and international officials over district autonomy. And candidates for the UMW presidency used the special convention to maneuver for power.

On the issue for which the convention was specifically called into session — contract negotiations — Lewis mixed militancy with caution. In his formal presidential report to the delegates, Lewis declared that the union should not be penalized for the Senate's failure to ratify the peace treaty. Because the coal miners had demonstrated their good faith and met their moral responsibilities for more than two years and because the actual fighting had been over for a year, Lewis recommended that the convention rule the 1917 Washington agreement officially terminated no later than November 1, 1919. If mine operators refused to renegotiate the Central Competitive Field contract on the terms demanded by miners, Lewis recommended a national bituminous strike. Other aspects of his report, however, disclosed caution. Lewis explained that he had delayed wage negotiations until the fall in order to conduct them at the most propitious time — a period when coal production rose, demand increased, and miners had steadier work. Circumspection also led Lewis to temporize on the policy committee's call for nationalization. Because the question was so complicated and fraught with grave implications, union officers, he asserted, lacked the time to prepare a proper plan for congressional action.

The convention granted Lewis full authority in contract negotiations. As proposed by the scale committee, the body charged with drawing up all union contract demands, the delegates voted to ask for a 60 percent wage increase applied to day labor, tonnage rates, yardage, and dead work. They also demanded the six-hour day at the face, the five-day week, and the abolition of the automatic penalty clause. If these demands could not be achieved through collective bargaining, the delegates authorized Lewis to call a general strike of all bituminous miners in the United States on November 1, 1919.

Only three days after the special convention adjourned, representatives of the union and the mine operators from the Central Competitive Field met in Buffalo. The union-management negotiations, which began September 26 in Buffalo and resumed on October 9 in Philadelphia, were doomed to failure. On the one side, UMW representatives had been instructed to seek wage and hour demands that were absolutely unacceptable to the operators; on the other side, the operators felt no compulsion to bargain seriously and expected the federal government to enforce the 1917 agreement. Lewis thus used the negotiations more to demonstrate the recalcitrance and miserliness of the operators than to achieve his union's demands. "In God's name," he pleaded, "we expect some consideration to be given those 452,000 human souls [the miners] who are asking for bread and have been given a stone."

The breakdown of collective bargaining thrust the federal government into the situation just as the mine owners expected. Secretary of Labor William B. Wilson wired John L. Lewis and the chairman of the operators' negotiating committee, Thomas T. Brewster, to meet jointly in his Washington office. Wilson also requested that Lewis postpone any strike order until after the Washington conference. In their response to Wilson's request, the union and the operators exposed their basic strategy. Replying for the Central Competitive Field operators, Brewster agreed to confer with the secretary and the UMW provided: (1) the union promised to respect the existing contract to its legal termination; (2) the union rescinded the existing strike order effective November 1 and allowed miners to work pending negotiations; and (3) the present eight-hour day, six-day week remained in effect. Lewis could scarcely promise to rescind the strike order for the union, especially when the operators had refused to bargain about material issues. To cancel the strike not only would have left the miners impotent to redress their grievances, it would also have rendered Lewis's position in the UMW politically untenable. Yet to reject federal overtures would leave the UMW at the mercy of employers supported by federal power.

The disputants thus cooperated in Labor Secretary Wilson's last-minute efforts to avert a conflict. From October 21 to October 24, union and management representatives met with Secretary Wilson in Washington. The operators refused to negotiate unless the UMW rescinded its strike order, and union officials felt such negotiations to be pointless if miners surrendered their only effective weapon. In a final effort to block a strike, Secretary Wilson read a letter from President Wilson appealing to the miners and operators to settle their differences peacefully or "to refer the matters in dispute to a board of arbitration for determination, and to continue the operation of the mines, pending the decision of the board." Placed in a dilemma by the president's letter, union officials agreed to reopen negotiations but refused to call off the strike or accept binding arbitration. At that, the operators walked out of the conference, terminated all bargaining, and expected that the federal government would smash a miners' strike.

The next day, October 25, President Wilson played the operators' trump card. In a public statement demanding that the union rescind its strike order the president labeled the impending miners' walkout as "not only unjustifiable but unlawful."

Lewis learned of the president's statement while on his way home to

Springfield. Intercepted by reporters at a train stop in Bloomington, Illinois, Lewis was asked to respond to Wilson's plea. "I am an American, free born, with all the pride of my heritage," he replied with customary aplomb. "I love my country with its institutions and traditions. With Abraham Lincoln I thank God that we have a country where men may strike. May the power of my government never be used to throttle and crush the efforts of the toilers to improve their material welfare and elevate the standards of their civilization."

The reporters who interviewed Lewis in the parlor car claimed to find him perusing the *Iliad* and *Odyssey*. Amazed to discover a labor leader reading classical literature, the journalists probed for an explanation. Lewis responded: "The world is about the same now as it was then." This offhand reference to continuities and cycles in human history reflected, more than the reporters then realized, Lewis's essential view of human nature and social dynamics.

Lewis's reaction to the president's statement expressed another salient aspect of the man's personality. On October 26, 1919, as he would do numerous times in the future when faced with serious crises, Lewis withdrew into total isolation, cutting himself off from friends, associates, and public. Arriving home in Springfield late on the twenty-sixth, he shut off all external communications and left word with the swarm of reporters still pursuing him that he was not to be disturbed before 11:00 a.m. the next day.

In the privacy of his home Lewis decided not to retract the UMW's strike order. To be sure, he had no choice in the matter. Coal miners had waited too long for wage increases to defer them pending arbitration. Moreover, in 1919—with millions of workers on strike and rebellion in the air—one could scarcely expect militant coal miners to behave as the president and the mine operators desired. Not surprisingly, the UMW's executive board, meeting on October 29, rejected Woodrow Wilson's plea and resolved to call the miners out on November 1.

That same day, October 29, a letter from President Wilson's secretary, Joe Tumulty, to William B. Wilson suggested Lewis's and the coal miners' dilemma. Learning of the UMW executive board's decision, Tumulty stated why he thought the union and the miners must not strike. "I am sure," he wrote, "that many of the miners would rather accept the peaceful process of settlement . . . than go to war against the Government of the United States." Suddenly an economic struggle between workers and employers had been transformed into a political conflict between labor and the state; a private battle in which compromise was ordinarily the rule had become a public crisis in which the rule of law had to prevail. This change in the terms of battle boded ill for Lewis and the coal miners.

Lewis soon received the bad news. On October 31, Attorney General A. Mitchell Palmer applied in federal district court in Indianapolis for an injunction against the strike. Without hesitation, Judge A. B. Anderson issued an *ex parte* temporary restraining order against the UMW and set a full hearing for November 8. That same day, October 31, the federal government put its troops on alert in the West Virginia coalfields and dispatched Bureau of Investigation secret agents to Indianapolis.

Actually, federal officials expected not to use all the coercive weapons at their command. An injunction had been secured, federal troops placed on alert, and secret agents dispatched primarily to frighten union leaders into accepting federal arbitration. Even before resorting to these weapons, cabinet members urged Samuel Gompers to intercede with Lewis, which the A.F. of L. leader did. Writing to Lewis on October 29, Gompers pleaded: "I urge that the situation be courageously faced and an endeavor made by all means to avert the strike if possible, or at least postpone it pending the opportunity for negotiating an agreement." The same day Palmer sought his injunction, he also assured Gompers that if the UMW postponed the strike President Wilson would appoint a five-man commission to adjust the dispute and render an award retroactive to November 1, 1919. At the end of the strike's first week, Palmer still promised to delay legal action—that is, the full hearing before Judge Anderson—if Lewis called off the strike.

Lewis had plotted his strike strategy weeks before the walkout commenced. He had offered mine operators and federal officials good reasons to deal with him instead of other union leaders. "Lewis is not a socialist, bolshevist, labor party man or government ownership advocate," assured his friend K. C. Adams. "He has never been a blind follower of any alleged reform or reformer. He does not belong to the 'whoop 'em up' variety of labor leader. . . . There never was at the head of any labor organization a man so thoroughly soaked in practicality.

Militancy for the miners, moderation for employers and government officials—that was the Lewis formula in 1919. In the future also he would often portray himself as a conservative counterweight to more radical labor leaders and rebellious rank and filers. In return for thwarting radical influences, Lewis, however, expected to receive substantial material gains for the men he represented.

The basic disparity in power between coal miners and government quickly emerged. The miners held one weapon: the power to strike and thus eventually to paralyze a society dependent upon coal for heat, energy, and transportation. But even that weapon's effectiveness was diluted because not all miners were union members, nor did all mines operate under union contract. The government's weapons were many and less diluted. Courts stood ready to serve injunctions; troops prepared to assist operators to reopen their mines with strikebreakers; spies in-filtrated all levels of the union, tapped telephones, and intercepted cables; immigration authorities threatened to deport alien UMW members and strikers; and newspapers and magazines supplied with artfully leaked information concerning the strike, fueled a blatant antiunion propaganda campaign.

On November 8, Lewis experienced the first heavy blow in the government's effort to end the strike. Judge Anderson issued a temporary mandatory injunction that gave officers of the UMW until 6:00 p.m. on November 11 to withdraw and cancel their original strike order. Anderson's injunction barred all aspects of strike action, and it named eighty-four UMW international and district officers. It was the most sweeping injunction issued against a major union since the Pullman boycott of 1894, when federal court orders had effectively thwarted the strike of Eugene V. Debs's American Railway Union.

Faced with the prospect of swift legal action and the imprisonment of all the UMW's officials unless the strike was canceled, Lewis convened an emergency meeting of his union's executive board on November 10 in Indianapolis to discuss how to respond to Anderson's injunction. Press reports hinted that Frank Farrington and Alex Howat led a more militant faction that preferred to defy the injunction and challenge the government, but that conservative influences seemed likely to dominate. The reporters proved prescient; at 4:10 a.m. on November 11 the executive board voted at Lewis's behest to comply with the injunction under protest.

Although Lewis canceled the strike, with few exceptions miners stayed home, which is probably what Lewis expected and which, as he desired, compelled the government to make the next move in the crisis. Himself a politician, Lewis knew what to expect from federal officeholders. Elected public officials, like union officials, sought votes and rarely alienated potential constituents. Considering how important organized labor had been to the Democratic party in 1912 and 1916, Lewis rightly suspected that Wilsonians would hesitate before breaking a strike. To a degree, he was correct.

Labor Secretary Wilson made a final effort to effect a compromise solution. His department's Bureau of Labor Statistics prepared a careful study of the relation between prices and wages in three key coal-mining towns. Armed with this information, Secretary Wilson proposed an agreement based on the Bureau of Labor Statistics' recommendation of a 31 percent wage increase.

But just as Lewis recognized the realities of national politics, so, too, did the mine operators. If Democratic officials weighed organized labor's political influence, they also evaluated the sentiments of the vast majority of nonunion voters. To accept William B. Wilson's recommendation of a 31 percent wage increase implied a substantial rise in the selling price of coal. Because the cost of coal in 1919 bulked large in the typical householder's budget, a government-authorized rise in retail prices might cost the Democrats votes. Several federal officials certainly believed so. Using his own set of price-wage figures, federal fuel administrator Harry A. Garfield calculated that miners' wages had fallen only 14 percent behind prices and that operators could make up the difference without raising prices. Garfield's opinion undercut Secretary Wilson's contentions as well as the 20 percent increase the operators had already offered the miners. President Wilson's support of his fuel administrator gave Garfield, in the words of Labor Secretary Wilson's advisers, "veto power over any results arrived at in the negotiations between the Secretary of Labor and the operators and miners."

This indeed being the case, after two weeks of negotiations in Washington in which the UMW agreed to bargain on the basis of a 31 percent wage increase and the operators refused to offer more than 14 percent, the union representatives and the operators ended their conferences on November 28 no nearer agreement than at the start. Most miners still remained at home, coal production had not yet reached 50 percent of prestrike levels, UMW officials faced the prospect of being cited for contempt, and federal officials played consumer politics.

When negotiations collapsed again, federal officials hastened to act decisively. The government offered the operators up to one hundred thousand federal troops to protect those miners willing to resume coal production and declared martial law in Wyoming. Justice Department agents and Immigration Service officials intensified their repressive tactics, and on December 3 Judge Anderson cited eighty-four UMW officers for contempt of court, placing all international, district, and local officers in Indiana under arrest until $5,000 bonds were provided for local officials and $10,000 for the others.

But once again Democrats preferred compromise to repression. On December 6, in a move designed by cabinet members, an ailing President Wilson invited Lewis and William Green to Washington to confer with Palmer and Tumulty. Wilson's advisers warned Lewis that the government would yield only to superior forces. Yet they also stressed that the president had authorized them to pledge that if the miners returned to work on the basis of an immediate 14 percent wage increase pending hearings by a presidentially appointed bituminous commission, Wilson would guarantee just and fair consideration of the miners' demands for wage increases, shorter hours, and improved working conditions.

With the new federal proposal in hand, Lewis and Green returned to Indianapolis for a special meeting of the district presidents, the UMW executive board, and the union scale committee. To help Lewis make the case for President Wilson's proposal, Labor Secretary Wilson wired the UMW leader on December 8, urging him to accept the proposed terms because the strike "threatens the very foundation of our social life." Secretary Wilson asked Lewis to read the telegram to the UMW board members, and he also released it to the press. For three days the union officials debated the government's proposal, and in the end they decided unanimously that "while protesting in our hearts against what we believed to be the unjust attitude of the government, we decided to submit to the inevitable." On December 11, Lewis formally asked the strikers to return to work with the knowledge that they had won an immediate 14 percent increase in wages and that within sixty days the president's commission would undoubtedly hand down a retroactive award substantially increasing wages, lowering hours, and improving conditions. To insure that the leaders' decision satisfied the membership, Lewis scheduled a reconvened international convention for January 1920 to vote on the proposed settlement.

Years later Lewis would be criticized for selling the miners out in 1919 and particularly for his comment on December 7, "I will not fight my government, the greatest government on earth." Radicals and communists especially asserted that Lewis's weakness in 1919, when the UMW was powerful and miners exceedingly militant, presaged the union's rapid decline in the 1920s. Had he defied the injunction, rejected the president's proposals, gone to jail, become a martyr to labor's cause, goes the radicals' version of UMW history, the history of American labor during the 1920s might have been far different. Had the miners remained on strike, the government would have forced the operators to concede to union demands, and the UMW and organized labor in America would have entered the 1920s a rising instead of declining power in society. Perhaps.

Lewis, it might be argued, had a far better case than his critics. As Lewis told his union's reconvened convention in January 1920: "What would it have availed to have a convention with every officer incarcerated and any other men who assumed to take our places as officers finding themselves confronted with the same obstacles?" Second, all of the UMW radicals shared Lewis's perception of reality in December 1919; John Brophy, Frank Farrington, Alex Howat, and Robert Harlin all signed the call for the strike's termination, and not one voted against the December 10 decision.

Other factors buttressed Lewis's position. Never did the strikers curtail all coal production, and anywhere from one-quarter to one-third of the nation's coal was produced in nonunion mines. Before the strike was officially ended, coal production approached 50 percent of normal levels. Miners may indeed have been militant in 1919, but they were also deeply patriotic, and once the strike became a conflict between union and government, union leaders realized that many miners might return to work. Most miners distinguished between the state and capital, public officials and private employers, and they expected equity from the federal government.

Lewis did what he had to do in December 1919, what circumstances and the realities of power demanded. Had he been more radical and less conservative, more idealistic and less opportunistic, he probably would have acted similarly. Ultimately the 1920 reconvened convention and the presidential commission's arbitration award justified Lewis's decision to terminate the strike.

Lewis, however, could not rest once the immediate crisis passed. He prepared for the reconvened union convention scheduled to open on January 5, 1920, in Columbus, Ohio, and to present the UMW's wage claims to President Wilson's Bituminous Coal Commission.

As more than 1,900 UMW delegates convened in Columbus during the first week of January 1920, the battle lines within the UMW hardened. For three days the delegates vigorously debated Lewis's decision to terminate the 1919 strike under the proposed arbitration agreement. Acting President Lewis, pleading for cooperation with the government, regularly took umbrage at delegates who fired what he characterized as "insulting questions" at the chair. Harlin and Farrington led the opposition, which impunged Lewis's courage, implied that the UMW leader had practiced "class collaboration," and called upon the delegates to reject President Wilson's "compulsory" arbitration commission. The opposition busily built its platform for the December 1920 UMW election in which Harlin, Howat, Farrington, and John Walker would unite to challenge Lewis.

By January 1920, however, Lewis had created a smooth-running union machine. His loyal lieutenant, Phil Murray, delivered the votes of western Pennsylvania's miners; Van Bittner led a West Virginia delegation loyal to Lewis; Tom Kennedy, two years previously John Walker's ally and running mate, had joined the Lewis team and brought with him the support of northeastern Pennsylvania's anthracite miners; and Secretary-Treasurer William Green provided legitimacy and strength in Ohio's vital District 6.

Lewis also used his brilliant rhetoric. In a major speech defending the strike's termination and the acceptance of President Wilson's settlement terms, Lewis overwhelmed the delegates with emotionalism, sarcasm, anecdotalism, and patriotism. He appealed to the delegates to understand the plight of a union leader. "We have felt the weight of our burden," sighed Lewis. "We have paced the floor at night into the wee small hours of the morning, when the men and women of our organizations were peacefully sleeping in their beds wondering what we could do." And what did we leaders receive for our pains? The most terrible attacks, hate letter after hate letter, threats upon our lives. "We were insulted in conference, we were insulted in the streets, we were insulted on trains and in hotels. Ye gods! Such concentrated fury was never visited upon any helpless set of men in such an unjustifiable way!" Lewis also appealed to the delegates' common sense. He reminded them that as a result of his leadership in the 1919 conflict, the "lamentations of no widow can be heard . . . and the wails of no fatherless child can assail our ears." And finally, he informed the delegates, "We are Americans. I shall never lead any organization but an American organization. . . . I think we have the greatest nation of any on earth; I think we have the greatest people of any in the world. I am proud of the traditions of our country."

Swayed by Lewis's rhetoric and held in line by Murray, Bittner, and Kennedy, the convention delegates overwhelmingly approved their leader's handling of the 1919 strike. By a vote of 1,639 to 231 the UMW voted to accept President Wilson's settlement terms and to abide by the award of the Bituminous Coal Commission. Lewis had survived the first major crisis of his union career and could look forward with optimism to the December 1920 UMW election.

For an American labor leader in 1920, however, things were never so simple as they seemed at first glance. With the assistance of Labor Secretary Wilson, Lewis won a substantial wage package from the coal commission in February 1920; tonnage men, the bulk of the miners and union members, received an increase of 27 percent, and day men gained a 20 percent raise. Already earning less than the tonnage miners, day men chafed at an award that left them even further behind. Lewis's rivals used the discontent of some miners to precipitate spontaneous strikes and to undercut the acting president's authority. But in the summer of 1920, Lewis, through negotiations, won a $1.50 daily wage increase for non-tonnage soft-coal miners. As a result of the increase, UMW bituminous dayworkers had won a basic wage of $7.50, by far the highest in the history of American coal miners, and a rate for which Lewis took full credit.

Lewis's triumphs at the bargaining table brought no surcease from internal UMW politics. His rivals, who asserted that they wanted to "get honest, competent men put in charge of our organization," left no dirty trick or canard untried in their campaign against Lewis. They resurrected and exaggerated the 1917 Panama scandal, even charging that the Lewis family had enriched themselves at the expense of widows and orphans. John Walker referred to Lewis as without "a drop of red blood in his veins. He is a sneak, a treacherous hound in my judgment, cowardly, every atom of him." And Walker once again implied that the UMW was controlled by Al Hamilton of Pittsburgh, whose crowd would go to any extremes including murder to prevent their candidates from being defeated in the union election.

Lewis's union enemies selected their candidates for office wisely. For president they offered Robert Harlin of Washington state, a man with few known enemies and one widely associated with the popular demand for nationalization of the mines; for vice-president, they ran Alex Howat, well known for his enemies within the union but more admired among the rank and file for his courage and militancy. The machinations of his foes led Lewis in October 1920 to inform an old friend: "I am kept so busy with my enemies that I scarcely have any time to give my friends. We have, of course, a tremendous fight in our organization between the orderly, constructive element and the disorderly, destructive element. I am undaunted in the fight, however, and expect the ship of state to maintain its stability and remain afloat."

Lewis's optimism flowed from his control of the levers of union power. For every dirty trick his rivals played, Lewis could counter with an ingenious interpretation of union law. In the miners' union, unlike the federal government or American state governments, the constitution meant what the president said it did, and the only court of appeal was the international executive board, more often than not simply the president's own hand-picked tribunal. Lewis first exercised his power of constitutional interpretation to eliminate rivals for office. For example, in the spring of 1920 Lewis ruled John Walker ineligible to stand for election as a UMW delegate to the A.F. of L. convention because Walker was an officer of the Illinois State Federation of Labor and hence not a UMW member.

Successful in eliminating one opponent, Lewis became more audacious. In the fall of 1920 he attempted to rule Robert Harlin's candidacy for the presidency illegitimate. Citing a clause in the UMW constitution that required a candidate for office to have had five years of practical experience as a miner, Lewis declared Harlin ineligible because the latter had entered the United States in 1907, been elected to union office in 1910, and thus had at most three years practical work as a miner. This time, however, Lewis's tactic failed, and its failure illuminated his audacity. Harlin remained a candidate for president partly because as the author of the constitutional clause in question his interpretation of its meaning was hard to challenge, and partly because he could prove that he had worked as a miner in England for almost two decades before emigrating.

What Lewis could not accomplish with constitutional interpretations, he achieved with publicity and money. The union journal, edited by Ellis Searles, Lewis's handpicked editor, denied space to the rival slate for office, banned all "political" news from its columns, and advertised the union leadership's contributions to the welfare of coal miners. Finally, the union's organizers, appointed and paid by Lewis, served their master loyally.

Lewis had built his union machine too well for his enemies to wreck. Not only did he have firm allies inside the UMW; influential public officials and the most prominent mine owners also preferred Lewis to his rivals. Phil Murray secured western Pennsylvania; Tom Kennedy did likewise for anthracite; Ohio District 6 fell in line; the Alabama and West Virginia miners showed their appreciation for Lewis's financial and moral support; and William Mitch of Indiana, a recent addition to the team, provided Lewis with a slender electoral majority in the Hoosier state. The final results gave Lewis a better than sixty thousand vote margin over Harlin, although Murray beat Howat by only eleven thousand votes. Except for Illinois, long the core of anti-Lewis sentiment, the administration slate carried the vital Central Competitive Field and the southern Appalachian area, the most productive coal-mining regions. The opposition's electoral strength centered in the outlying western United States and Canadian districts, areas of lesser importance in the industry and in union affairs.

In January 1921, Lewis had finally attained the UMW presidency in his own right. An imposing public figure, he possessed a voice that more than matched his physical stature. Having mastered the imperatives of public speaking in the pre-microphone age, Lewis's voice alternately bellowed and modulated, crooned and cursed. He charmed and cajoled his audiences, entertained and taught them, agitated and pacified them. So fine was his voice modulation, so smoothly could Lewis change moods, that listeners became hypnotized by him and cheered platitudes, inappropriate classical allusions, and outright solecisms. For Lewis, speech was an instrument to sway audiences, not enlighten them. And he used that instrument impressively.

The union Lewis commanded was also imposing. No other labor organization in the United States was as large or as publicized. The only industrial union that functioned in a major industry, the UMW was a power in the land. In 1921 coal reigned supreme as a source of energy, and miners possessed the potential power to paralyze society through a strike. As a consequence, Lewis stood in the front rank of labor leaders; only Gompers had greater public recognition and, perhaps, esteem.

II

Trade Union President, 1921–32

4

A President and His Union, March 1921–March 1923

John L. Lewis's first two years as president of the United Mine Workers of America were filled with success. Republican leaders wooed him, businessmen flattered him, and editorialists praised him. In 1921 Lewis even challenged Gompers for the presidency of the A.F. of L. Despite a postwar economic depression (1920–21) that sapped union strength and deflated wages, Lewis preserved the UMW as the nation's largest trade union.

Beneath the glittering surfaces of Lewis's success, however, lay faults. Fundamental flaws soon appeared in the economy of coal, the structure of the UMW, and the policies of John L. Lewis. The 1921 depression, from which the nation rapidly recovered, prefigured the future for coal miners and their union. And the UMW's apparent victory in a 1922 coal strike actually undermined the stability of the mine workers' union. Lewis's own oscillations between moderation and radicalism, "business unionism" and "reform unionism," class struggle and class collaboration, failed to advance his union.

By the end of the 1920s Lewis had become famous as the nation's most eminent labor Republican, a reputation only partly deserved. Lewis had carried a tradition of Wilsonianism to the 1920s. For seven years, from Woodrow Wilson's initial bid for the presidency in 1912 until the coal strike of 1919, Lewis had cooperated politically with Democratic leaders. Wilsonianism, however, collapsed in the wake of postwar disillusionment, and Lewis turned against Wilson and the Democrats. The government's role in the 1919 coal strike rankled the UMW leader and remained a persistent sore point. But Lewis did not campaign actively for Warren G. Harding in 1920, nor did he play a substantial role in national Republican politics.

Harding's brief tenure in office provided Lewis no obvious influence.

The labor leader received only one recorded recommendation for appointment as secretary of labor, and Lewis himself recommended no candidates for that post or any other cabinet position. Republicans, nevertheless, recognized Lewis's stature as head of the nation's largest trade union and, together with Gompers, usually invited him to serve on honorific committees that required broad-based public membership.

One federal committee on which Lewis served revealed his differences with the Republican leadership and suggested the continuity of his beliefs on government involvement in economic affairs from the 1920s through the New Deal of the 1930s. By the autumn of 1921, economic decline and high unemployment had become critical political issues. Urged to act by Secretary of Commerce Herbert Hoover, in September President Harding invited representatives of industry, labor, and the public to Washington the following month for a special conference on unemployment. Hoover, the mastermind of the conference, planned to prove the Republican administration's determination to reduce unemployment. He preferred to rely on a combination of voluntary action by industrialists to increase private investment (and hence employment) and state and municipal spending for public works. Hoover's program to combat unemployment received an unenthusiastic response from labor's delegates, including John L. Lewis.

Publicly, Lewis advocated direct government credits to the unemployed, the creation of a compulsory employer-financed unemployment insurance system, and nationalization or stringent government control of coal mining. Responding to employer demands for wage deflation as the solution to unemployment, Lewis observed that he would gladly accept "wage deflation" if business tolerated "profit deflation." "It is the duty of employers," he intoned, "to let the public know the real truth, that excessive profits and not labor costs are responsible for the maintenance of unwarranted prices." During private sessions Lewis apparently broached more far-reaching proposals for direct federal intervention in the economy.

Labor politics offered Lewis a more attractive arena in which to exercise his talent and ambition. The presidency of the UMW afforded him potential control of the largest single bloc of votes cast at A.F. of L. conventions and great influence with Gompers. But a precedent set in the prewar years awarded the UMW's seat on the A.F. of L. executive council to the union's secretary-treasurer, not its president. Hence William Green, not John L. Lewis, sat on American labor's most prestigious executive committee. Lewis might have demanded Green's seat, but such a request would have precipitated an open break with Green, a popular figure in the UMW, when Lewis's grip on the presidency was shaky. Political realities foreclosed Lewis from demanding a seat on the executive council. As much an egotist as a realist, Lewis instead chose to gamble recklessly, to contest Gompers for the presidency of the A.F. of L.

The militancy that had stirred American workers since 1916 had not abated in 1921. Many of the larger national trade unions, the coal miners among them, still demanded the creation of an independent labor party and the nationalization of such vital industries as railroads and mining. Since organized labor's setbacks in 1919, Gompers, however, had drifted toward a conservative position. Many of the younger, radical members of the A.F. of L. chafed under Gompers's leadership and desired more militant officers.

In May and June 1921 John L. Lewis presented himself as a radical alternative to Samuel Gompers. Acting cautiously, Lewis privately sought the A. F. of L. presidency. Until the A. F. of L. convention opened on June 21 in Denver, Lewis remained silent and allowed rumors to circulate. Sometime earlier, however, Lewis decided that he could indeed defeat Gompers; on June 20, 1921, he publicly declared his candidacy for the A.F. of L. presidency. He had also chosen a political strategy by then. Counting on the substantial bloc of votes cast by eight UMW delegates, Lewis planned to add the support of those unions committed to nationalization, such as the railway workers and machinists; those unions represented by socialists, such as the ladies' garment workers and brewery workers; and his old Indianapolis friends the carpenters, whose leaders detested Gompers. To solidify left-wing support, Lewis endorsed nationalization of the railroads and coal mines and also the establishment of federal old-age pensions and unemployment insurance. Moreover, he coordinated his campaigning at the convention, a process the *New York Times* described in a report of June 21 as "hot electioneering," through two UMW left-wingers, John Brophy and Adolph Germer.

Lewis's candidacy posed the first effective threat since the 1890s to Gompers's command of the A.F. of L. Gompers thus used all his political wiles to thwart his opponent. First, he and his lieutenants hinted to convention delegates that the antilabor Hearst papers were behind Lewis's challenge. Second, Gompers used his patronage power within the labor movement and among Washington politicians to hold wavering delegates in line. Third, and most important, Gompers split the UMW's own delegation. Three bitter enemies of Lewis—Frank Farrington, Alex Howat, and John Walker—were among the eight UMW delegates at Denver, and Gompers won the support of all three, a fact that undermined support for Lewis among many uncommitted delegates. The three UMW delegates preferred Gompers, the candidate of labor conservatism, to Lewis, the putative radical challenger. Yet the difference between Gompers and Lewis was perhaps more apparent than real, and the *New York Times* may have been correct when on June 23 it commented editorially that both Lewis and Gompers were "labor conservatives," although the former was "an unknown quantity."

The split in the UMW delegation, the ILGWU's majority vote for Gompers, and the incumbent president's fine-tuned poltical machine defeated Lewis. He polled only one-third of the total vote cast, losing most of the railway department support he had counted on and picking up most of his votes from the machinists' union, the carpenters, and the dwindling band of socialists. In defeat, Lewis appeared magnanimous, at least publicly, thanking the delegates who had voted for him and applauding the independence and integrity of those who had originally promised their support but then exercised the privilege of changing their minds. Gompers returned the magnanimity, as befit a man who still had to deal with the leader of the largest affiliate of the A.F. of L. In September Gompers asked Lewis to accompany him on the train trip from Indianapolis to Washington for President Harding's unemployment conference.

What had been the result of Lewis's bid for the A.F. of L. presidency, and why had Lewis challenged Gompers in 1921? Answers to those questions do not come easily, but enough information is now available to clarify the record. Lewis's assertion that he never electioneered for a single delegate vote at the A.F. of L. convention is plainly untrue. Suggestions that Lewis made the race as a publicity gambit are equally suspect. Lewis was not averse to publicity, but he was too astute to risk a resounding personal defeat for a few newspaper lines. His defeat, moreover, had negative organizational as well as personal ramifications; it widened rifts within the UMW and stimulated new threats to Lewis's still-insecure tenure as union president. Only the conviction that he had a real chance to win explains Lewis's decision.

But why would he trade the presidency of the largest and most powerful trade union in the nation, a position he had just won, for the A.F. of L. presidency? Prestige was a consideration never absent from Lewis's calculations. He was a striver, a climber, a man driven by ambition and perhaps eager to compensate for his lowly social origins by achieving parity with America's economic and political elite. Interestingly, on his passports during the 1920s Lewis listed his occupation as "executive," rather than labor leader or trade union official. The presidency of the A.F. of L., a post that involved considerable honorific association with presidents, governors, and even chambers of commerce, conferred more prestige and status on its occupant than the leadership of the UMW. It is also conceivable that in June 1921 Lewis had premonitions of the UMW's bleak future. The presidency of the A.F. of

L., in that case, offered him a chance to escape from a future fraught with internecine union struggles and economic tragedy for American coal miners.

From 1910 to 1920, the bituminous coal industry had experienced extraordinary economic growth, reaching a productive peak in 1918. High wartime prices and an insatiable market for coal brought marginal mines into operation and led operators to develop properties in previously underdeveloped regions, especially in the southern Appalachians. The coal strike of 1919—which reduced stockpiles—and the economic needs of postwar Europe prevented a collapse in the market for American bituminous. But after 1919, foreign demand for American coal diminished. Overproduction glutted domestic markets, and the soft coal industry in the United States slumped, a decline aggravated by the postwar depression of 1920–21.

The economics of coal posed a myriad of problems for the UMW. Operators sought to stimulate per capita productivity either through intensive labor discipline or the substitution of machines for men. In either case they discharged miners. Even more threatening to the UMW was the growth of productivity in nonunion mines in West Virginia, Kentucky, and Alabama.

The relatively high cost of coal also caused such major coal consumers as the railroads, the steel industry, and public utilities to introduce more efficient methods of fuel consumption. Moreover, oil and natural gas competed for the domestic heating and light industrial markets. In August 1921, John L. Lewis would have to have been blind to miss seeing the economic disease that blighted bituminous: too many mines and too many miners producing too much coal.

Events in Alabama and southern West Virginia delivered the initial shocks to the UMW. Alabama coal operators had refused in November 1919 to accept President Wilson's compromise settlement and subsequently proved equally adamant in declining to implement the award of the president's coal commission. Instead, they slashed wages to prewar levels, endured UMW–sanctioned strikes, and smashed the union. Lewis's unswerving support failed to save Alabama UMW District 20 from extinction.

During the war years the UMW, for the first time, had succeeded in organizing the Fairmont and Kanawha coalfields in northern and central West Virginia, but union organizers had had little success in the southwestern counties of Logan, Mingo, and McDowell. In the immediate postwar years some of the nation's largest coal companies, including subsidiaries of U.S. Steel, the Consolidation Coal Company, and the

Island Creek Company, developed properties in southwestern West Virginia primarily to escape high union wages and restrictive work rules. The mines of Logan, Mingo, and McDowell counties captured markets from the unionized operators of the Central Competitive Field.

Financed by UMW headquarters, the leaders of West Virginia District 17, C. Frank Keeney and Fred Mooney, determined to unionize Mingo and Logan counties. Their resolute effort to organize the nonunion mines met with equal determination by nonunion employers to keep the UMW out and resulted in what Winthrop D. Lane, a contemporary journalist, called a *Civil War in West Virginia.*

The summer 1921 labor civil war in southwestern West Virginia brought two contending armies into the field—one unit composed of six thousand armed miners and their sympathizers and the other consisting of two thousand well-armed private detectives and county deputies. It also prompted the governor to ask President Harding for federal assistance. Harding dispatched 2,150 regular army troops and a light bombing squadron to West Virginia. Military intervention temporarily curbed violence in Logan and Mingo counties; it also terminated the UMW's effort to organize the region's coal mines.

Legal actions initiated by nonunion coal operators also crippled the UMW. Ever since the union signed its first contract in 1898 with employers in the Central Competitive Field, open-shop operators had charged that the UMW was engaged in a "criminal conspiracy" to restrain trade by denying nonunion miners the right to work. That had been one of the claims made by West Virginia operators in the *Hitchman* v. *Mitchell* case (which the Supreme Court decided against the union in 1917). After the war ended, West Virginia operators returned to the legal offensive. From Judge A. B. Anderson's federal district court in Indiana and in numerous state courts in West Virginia, the operators secured injunctions that prohibited UMW organizers from approaching nonunion mining properties or proselytizing among nonunion miners. By the early 1920s, judges had ruled it a crime for the UMW to attempt to organize nonunion mines in most parts of southwestern West Virginia and eastern Kentucky.

Where miners already belonged to the union and mines operated under union contract, employers found other legal weapons to use against the UMW. An Arkansas coal company—the Coronado Company—that had been the victim of a UMW strike and ensuing property damage brought suit not against individual miners charged with criminal action, but against the UMW, which, the owners charged in court, should be held responsible for violence and property losses during strikes it sanctioned. The case, which the UMW fought all the way to the Supreme Court, imperiled the union's existence. If the UMW could be held financially liable for strike damages, coal operators could "tax" the union out of existence. In a politic ruling, the Supreme Court denied the Coronado Company its full damage claims, thus saving the UMW a huge financial penalty, but the court majority implied that where sufficient evidence existed a trade union could be held liable for the actions of individual members or strikers, even when they acted without explicit union orders. It also declared that strikes aimed at organizing nonunion mines interfered with the movement of coal in interstate commerce and hence could be enjoined under the terms of the Sherman Antitrust Act, thus further crippling any chance the UMW had to organize nonunion Appalachian mines.

Even when the coal miners' union won favorable decisions in court, it suffered grievous losses. In 1920 the UMW expended more than $150,000 in legal expenses; the following year the cost of legal assistance soared to almost $460,000; and in 1922 the union expended nearly $223,000 for attorneys and legal costs. Only once during the entire decade of the 1920s did the UMW's legal costs drop substantially below $100,000 annually.

Legal battles and the costs of the West Virginia organizing campaign left the UMW in perilous financial condition. In June 1921 Secretary-Treasurer William Green informed Lewis that for the period from February to May 1921, union expenses exceeded revenues by $108,627 and that the organization had only a bare minimum left in its checking account. Worse yet, most of the UMW's recent expenditures had been financed by a special assessment of nearly $700,000, of which little remained to be collected. Moreover, added Green, the depression in the mining industry had caused union membership to fall to its lowest level in more than a year.

Green's report only hinted at the union's economic predicament. From January 1920 through December 1922, three years during which a nationally sanctioned coal strike occurred only in the last year, the UMW expended more than $2 million annually on strike relief. In 1920 strike payments represented 54.3 percent of all union expenses; the next year, 52.6 percent; and in 1922, 54 percent.

His union's financial plight vexed Lewis. He had increased his salary once from $3,000 to $5,000, and in 1921 he proposed that it be raised to $8,000. Lewis had implemented or recommended similar salary increases of almost 200 percent over a two-year period for other international officials. With the UMW's expenses now exceeding its revenues, Lewis's salary requests seemed excessive, and he knew it. But rather than reduce the salaries of union officials or postpone recommending a second round of increases to the 1921 convention, Lewis cut the union's field staff drastically and on June 28, 1921, suggested (in reality, commanded) that every international officer and field worker donate their July salary to the union.

Financial difficulties seemed minor compared to the other problems Lewis faced as union leader. More immediately threatening was the depression in soft coal and the bituminous operators' insistence on wage reductions. Unionized employers asserted that high wages made it impossible for them to compete successfully for markets with nonunion operators and that they must have the right to negotiate competitive state or district contracts in place of the basic Central Competitive Field agreement. Yet union miners, unable to live adequately on current earnings, resisted wage reductions. Lewis found himself caught between harassed operators and a restive union rank and file.

To compound Lewis's predicament, federal authorities shared the coal operators' perception of economic realities. A Labor Department agent saw only one solution to a depressed market: The union and the operators must voluntarily reduce "inflated" wage rates before April 1, 1922. Commerce Secretary Herbert Hoover agreed that high wages for union miners caused irregular employment and that, in his words, "we are . . . in a most vicious circle of trying to support an overplus of mines and miners at a cost . . . to the public." Hoover suggested that wage reductions would solve part of the problem by inducing miners to seek work elsewhere, stabilizing employment for the remaining union miners, and reducing the cost of coal for consumers.

Precisely how Lewis personally felt about government diagnoses of the ills that beset soft coal is impossible to discern, but militancy prevailed in September and October 1921, when UMW delegates met in regular convention, and in February 1922, when they reconvened in special session to consider contract demands for the upcoming negotiations. By overwhelming majorities, convention delegates favored nationalization of the coal mines and the creation of an independent national labor party. In February 1922 the UMW delegates stripped equivocal language and compromise proposals from the scale committee's recommended contract demands. Delegates substituted insistence on the six-hour day underground for the committee's proposed eight-hour day and the word *demand* for *recommend* in asking for weekly wages and abolition of the wartime strike penalty clause. Lewis found himself under constant attack by militant delegates who, for example, rejected by a substantial majority their president's proposal for substantial salary increases. Farrington, Harlin, Howat, and Walker sparked the anti-Lewis floor sentiment and almost stole the convention from Lewis's control. On one key vote cut to the heart of Lewis's power in the union during the 1922 reconvened session, he won only 51.5

percent of the delegate votes and gained his slender majority primarily because of patronage and funds he controlled as president.

The UMW rank and file held Lewis captive on nearly all matters concerning negotiations with employers for a new agreement in 1922. Yet, when conflict came, Lewis artfully could play a role that he relished: commanding general of a union army engaged in total war during which any criticism of his leadership could be characterized as treason.

With a national coal strike now inevitable, Lewis acted as the personification of labor militancy. In a letter sent to the officers of sixteen railway unions on February 1, he invited them to meet with UMW officials in order to plan a common front against employers' demands for wage cuts. And on February 21 and 22—at a meeting in Chicago attended by fifteen railway unions including the four largest and UMW officials—those in attendance agreed to unite miners, railway workers, and longshoremen (as in the British Triple Alliance) "for closer co-operation of our forces which will operate to more effectively protect the union workers in wage struggles." Lewis, who dominated the meeting, served as its chief speaker and hogged its press releases, but outlined no precise program of allied labor action. He even denied that plans had been set for a sympathetic rail strike on April 1 to coincide with the UMW walkout.

What then was Lewis up to? His prestrike strategy encompassed three immediate objectives. First, the proposed American "Triple Alliance" and the fighting rhetoric that accompanied it stimulated morale among UMW militants and assured them that Lewis intended no surrender to the mine operators. Second, the possibility of the railway unions uniting with the coal miners might impress employers with the futility of a coal strike and cause them to accede to the UMW's primary demands before the April 1 negotiating deadline. Third, the threat of joint strike action by what newspapers estimated as an alliance of more than two million union workers was intended to trouble Washington officials, specifically Hoover and Harding, who, in their anxiety to avert industrial crisis, would urge operators to meet the union's demands.

Yet when the *New York Times* observed editorially on February 3 that Lewis "may just be bluffing," the editors were more astute than they realized. Later in the month the paper's editors proved even more perceptive when they noted that the February 22 Chicago agreement "is a rather dry sop to the radical workers in the mines" and prophesied the UMW's future with startling clairvoyance. "Coal overproduction," the *Times* editors suggested, "doubtless induces a feeling that the miners' cause is lost."

Bluff was indeed intrinsic to Lewis's strike strategy, but coal operators and government officials refused to be misled. On April 1, 1922, he thus led the largest coal miners' strike in United States history. Not only did all the miners in the unionized bituminous fields walk out, but many of the major nonunion fields—especially Somerset, Fayette, and Westmoreland counties in Pennsylvania—also struck, as did the 155,000 anthracite miners of northeastern Pennsylvania, whose contract had also expired on March 31. More than six hundred thousand coal miners left work on April 1 or shortly afterward in a struggle that was to determine the future of the UMW for the next decade.

Bluff, militancy, and florid language punctuated Lewis's behavior during the strike's early stages. Called before the House Labor Committee on Monday, April 3, Lewis read a four-hour statement in which he used the threat of mine nationalization as a club to pressure the operators into agreement. In June, the editor of the union journal, Ellis Searles, published an article in the *Review of Reviews* that argued that, because of the managerial deficiencies of mine operators, Congress must regulate the bituminous industry as it did transportation and that a government commission of mines comparable to the Interstate Commerce Commission be immediately established.

Lewis's threats may have impressed the miners and the public—but not the operators. A Republican administration and a Republican Congress were unlikely to enact radical legislation, and an administration in which one of the most influential cabinet members, Secretary of the Treasury Andrew Mellon, was himself a major investor in bituminous mines would scarcely assist the UMW. Although the Harding administration's reaction to the crisis in coal, as expressed primarily by Commerce Secretary Hoover, favored neither miners nor operators, it was a neutrality that in effect benefited employers. The president, Hoover, and Labor Secretary James J. Davis considered themselves conscientious public servants whose primary duty was to insure consumers an adequate supply of coal at equitable prices. President Harding especially thought that the coal miners shared administration concern for the public welfare and that only autocratic and radical union leaders favored a strike.

From the day the coal strike began to the moment it ended, the Harding administration maneuvered to insure the public an adequate supply of coal. It acted on the initial assumption that the industry's surplus capacity and production from nonunion mines would offset any loss of output resulting from the strike. Lewis complained bitterly to Hoover about the latter's efforts to insure a sufficient supply of nonunion coal, and he warned the commerce secretary that such a policy endangered union coal operators (as well as the UMW), who would never regain markets lost to nonunion competitors. But Hoover and Lewis simply talked past each other, using the same English language to convey contradictory interpretations of reality. In a letter to Lewis, the commerce secretary assured the union leader that the government was absolutely neutral in the conflict. "The administration," Hoover pledged, "is not injecting itself into the strike; it is trying to protect the general public from the results of the strike."

Fortunately for the miners, Lewis had a firm grip on the economics of coal. Fortunately for Lewis, the miners showed more determination and solidarity than operators or federal officials expected. Throughout April, May, and June the strikers held fast. They paralyzed production in the Central Competitive Field and kept it to a trickle in the hitherto nonunion fields of Pennsylvania and West Virginia. Faced with legal injunctions, arrogant company guards, and summary evictions from company housing, the strikers in the nonunion fields carried on. During the spring and summer, UMW–financed and administered tent colonies sheltered thousands of strikers. As coal inventories disappeared and nonunion production failed to satisfy current demand, a major winter fuel crisis loomed.

By June 1922, the shortage of coal had passed from a potential crisis to a real one; soaring prices for the scarce commodity stirred consumer resentment and induced northern operators to offer a settlement to the union; moreover, an impending strike on the nation's railroads scheduled for July 1 threatened to remove nonunion coal from the market. Something had to be done—and quickly.

Unable to bring union and operators together, on July 9 Harding broached his own strike solution, one obviously concocted by Hoover. The president proposed that miners resume work immediately at the March 31 wage level pending the appointment and decision of a federal arbitration commission that would fix permanent wage levels. The commission would establish a temporary wage scale to prevail from August 10 until March 31, 1923. The part of the proposed solution most dear to Hoover required an exhaustive federal inquiry into coal mining aimed at a complete reorganization of the industry.

Neither operators nor union leaders at first understood what Harding's plan entailed. The promise of an arbitration award attracted the interest of the operators; the suggestion of a national agreement and a reorganization of the industry intrigued Lewis. A few days later, however, at a lengthy meeting on July 15 of the UMW's policy committee, members found substantial loopholes in the president's plan. Harding had linked fact-finding and arbitration; the union position, as defined by Lewis, favored a full inquiry into all aspects of the coal industry but rejected arbitration and any change in wages or conditions before the completion of the federal investigation. Lewis thus informed the president that the UMW policy committee had decided to reject his settlement proposal.

Lewis's message confirmed Harding's belief that the union was more recalcitrant than the operators and that it was responsible for protracting the strike. Hoover undoubtedly shared the president's sentiments, for in an unsigned and uninitialed memorandum concerning the July 9 settlement proposal (one which he obviously had prepared), the commerce secretary included the words: "Order men to return to work." The president issued almost such an order when, during a July 17 conference with mine operators, he advised them to resume production regardless of the UMW and offered federal troops to protect company property. Indeed, the next day, July 18, he wired the governors of all coal-producing states, ordering them to protect coal mines and advising them that federal troops had been placed on the alert for strike duty.

Just as Lewis had originally hoped to bluff the operators into submission and the government into complicity with the union, Harding intended to bluff the strikers, if not their leaders, into returning to the pits. Threatened by nonunion labor on the one hand and military intervention on the other, the strikers, Harding calculated, would surrender. But just as mine operators had called Lewis's bluff, the union called Harding's, and the president was scarcely prepared in July 1922 to use regular army troops to break a strike.

Harding's proposal of July 9 and his statements of July 17 and 18 scarcely stimulated coal production. Operators and governors in the well-organized northern districts would not resume production on a nonunion basis and risk open, violent confrontations with strikers. Simultaneously, the railroad shopmen's strike that began on July 1 reduced shipments from the nonunion mines. Coal disappeared from the marketplace, and with summer ending, its price soared. Mine owners could now both afford union wages and earn substantial profits, precisely what Lewis expected.

By the end of the first week in August, the outlines of a strike settlement emerged. "Matters are such," Lewis wrote on August 4, "that the present situation cannot endure indefinitely and I expect the coal operators to capitulate in the near future at least in substantial numbers. The strike is won insofar as wages are concerned and it only remains to devise some procedure which will enable us to realize upon our victory." Lewis's beliefs were apparently based on a secret understanding he had reached at a conference in Pittsburgh with operators from the Central Competitive Field. Whatever the precise details of the secret Pittsburgh agreement, the conference revealed to Lewis divisions among the mine operators, which he relied on to achieve his goals. The Pittsburgh meeting was followed by bargaining sessions beginning on August

7 in Cleveland. Operators representing Districts 2 and 5 in Pennsylvania and District 6 in Ohio joined Lewis in Cleveland; the Illinois and Indiana operators' associations boycotted the sessions.

Lewis's bargaining strategy was simple, and, as usual, his was the only voice that spoke for the union. Once a number of mines resumed production under union contract, he reasoned, the recalcitrant operators, fearful of losing markets and profits to their competitors, would also sign with the UMW. By August 15 Lewis won a tactical victory: Operators controling about sixty million tons of production and employing one hundred thousand miners in seven states contracted with the union on the basis of the status quo ante. During the next four weeks, other northern and western operators rushed to sign up with the union; by mid-September, Lewis had reached agreements covering nearly all the prestrike union mines. "It was a triumph of comparative unity," wrote Heber Blankenhorn, "over inherent disorganization."

Lewis celebated the settlement as a great victory for the UMW. In a period of wage deflation and labor intensification, he had preserved 1920 wage rates and job conditions until April 1, 1923. "The miners may well be termed," he proclaimed, "the shock troops of the American labor movement, and this controversy their industrial Verdun."

The preservation of existing wage rates in the 1922 agreement notwithstanding, Lewis's and his union's losses were many. For the first time since 1898, the UMW failed to sign the operators of the Central Competitive Field to a single agreement. That, however, was the least of the union's losses. Nonunion production in West Virginia, Kentucky, and Alabama remained untouched and thus free to chip away further at the markets for union coal. And Lewis also deserted the nonunion miners of Somerset, Fayette, and Westmoreland counties in Pennsylvania, who had joined the strike, resisted to the bitter end, and refused to return to work when the August agreements excluded them.

By the summer of 1921, the UMW's expenses exceeded its revenues — a financial situation worsened by the 1922 strike. In order to meet strike expenses, which exceeded $1 million, union officers sold $550,000 worth of UMW securities, borrowed $50,000 from the Brotherhood of Locomotive Firemen, and, in a singularly strange deal borrowed another $200,000 from the Harriman National Bank of New York on the personal notes of William Green and John L. Lewis.

The 1922 settlement divided rather than united the UMW. In the wake of Lewis's strike "victory," mutinies erupted among the rank and file. The aftermath of the strike also demonstrated the hollowness of Lewis's militancy. Before the miners walked out, he had raised publicly the specter of a labor triple alliance among coal miners, railroad workers, and longshoremen. After the miners returned to the pits, but while the railroad shopmen remained on strike against the most notorious federal antilabor injunction in history, Lewis repudiated sympathetic strikes in support of the shopmen.

Lewis also rejected militancy and labor solidarity within the miners' union when it concerned action, not words. Many of the operators who signed with the union in August and September ran nonunion as well as union mines. John Brophy of District 2 maintained that strikers should not return to work until their employers signed for *all* their properties, including those that had been hitherto nonunion. But Lewis insisted otherwise; in his eagerness to weaken operator resistance at the Cleveland conference, he had promised mine owners that he would not demand agreements covering their nonunion properties. And when union members, on their own volition as happened in District 2, refused to return to work until their employers also signed for nonunion mines, Lewis ordered them back.

Lewis's mismanagement of the 1922 strike and settlement, his critics then and later asserted, matched his betrayal of the miners during the 1919 strike. His enemies maintained that by ordering union men back to work before nonunion strikers achieved recognition Lewis had broken union solidarity. "Why a man so forceful and astute as Lewis was in many ways, should have made this colossal blunder can only be explained," surmised Brophy, "by some fatal defect in his character." Hindsight would prove that the "colossal" blunder of deserting the nonunion miners in 1922 guaranteed the collapse of the UMW later in the 1920s by leaving the coal industry a house divided.

Such criticism of Lewis and his policies would have been just had he been negotiating from a position of strength. The solidarity and militancy exhibited by coal miners during the strike of 1922 was indeed remarkable, but so was the resistance of the largest mine operators. The 1922 strike scarcely touched the nonunion fields of West Virginia, Kentucky, and Alabama; in Pennsylvania's nonunion fields, operators, led by the steel industry and its captive mines, refused to recognize the union; and in the outlying western fields of Kansas, Oklahoma, and Washington, among others, antilabor laws and governors partially broke the strike. Lewis realized that the federal government in 1922, as in 1919, would not allow the strike to reach a point that threatened a consumer crisis, and the Harding administration was less sympathetic to labor than Wilson's. Beset by external economic and political liabilities, Lewis commanded an organization split internally. As he informed Adolph Germer early in August, during the strike he had had to overcome "opposition from people within our ranks" as well as "tremendous obstacles" externally.

Because Lewis understood that too many miners were producing too much coal and that the American labor movement was growing weaker, he was pleased to come away from the 1922 strike with the preservation of the status quo ante. For Lewis, the 1922 settlement represented a substantial victory against overwhelming odds; for the UMW and the coal miners, however, it presaged decline.

If economic circumstances and political realities made Lewis cautious in his negotiations with mine owners during and after the 1922 strike, his manipulation of the mine nationalization question disclosed his autocratic tendencies. Ever since 1916, UMW conventions had voted in favor of nationalization of the nation's coal mines, and John L. Lewis had approved nationalization in principle, raising only pragmatic, political reservations. Yet when John Brophy sought in April 1921 to have material printed in the UMW *Journal* that discussed District 2's plan for nationalization, editor Ellis Searles responded: "I do not believe it to be the mission of the United Mine Workers' *Journal* to publish propaganda. . . . The *Journal*['s] . . . columns should not be used for the purpose of attacking its [UMW] policies." A most peculiar response indeed, considering that Searles was John L. Lewis's mouthpiece, that nationalization was official UMW policy, and that Lewis had even sanctioned it in principle. Stranger things were to follow.

At the September–October 1921 UMW convention, delegates adopted, without a dissenting vote, a resolution endorsing nationalization of the mines. In response to President Lewis's comments about the complexities of the issue, however, the delegates accepted his suggestion that the union appoint a mine nationalization committee. On October 5, the last day of the convention, John Brophy submitted a memorandum that Lewis approved granting the following duties and powers to the nationalization committee: (1) it was to devise a practical policy of nationalization; (2) it would make occasional reports before its final completed nationalization treatise; (3) the international union would bear the committee's expenses; and (4) the committee would complete its work promptly. Lewis requested only that the committee, once established, do nothing publicly that might create the impression that nationalization was a scale (contract) demand on the operators or release publicity before the 1922 labor-management negotiations. Two days later, October 7, in a letter officially appointing Brophy; Christ J. Golden, president of District 9 in Pennsylvania's anthracite area; and William Mitch, secretary-treasurer of District 11 (Indiana) as the nationalization research committee, Lewis charged them with "formulating a detailed practical policy to bring about the nationalization of the coal mines and to aid in the dissemination of information among our members and the public and the crystallization of sentiment for the attainment of such end." He further assured his three appointees that he "will be glad to co-operate with each of you gentlemen in the fullest possible way."

Lewis's promise of complete cooperation proved misleading. Ellis Searles closed the *Journal*'s columns to proponents of nationalization. Members of the nationalization committee also had to go outside the UMW for information, materials, and even funds. Brophy obtained support from prominent members of the Socialist party, the Workers' Education Bureau, the Bureau of Industrial Research, and the League for Industrial Democracy (left-wing reform groups located in New York City). Their interest in the mine workers enabled Brophy to publicize nationalization in the pages of the *New Republic* and *Nation.*

Never personally enthusiastic about nationalization, Lewis grew more leery as New York intellectuals poked their fingers into his union pie. Early in January 1923 he informed Brophy that the union had yet to discuss or approve a specific nationalization plan, that it was thus misleading for the committee to release information in the name of the UMW, and, finally, that it would be unwise for committee members to appear before the United States Coal Commission. At a three-hour meeting with members of the nationalization committee on January 21, Lewis berated them for their contacts with leftists and their efforts to publicize nationalization outside the UMW. Lewis's criticism led Christ Golden to resign. Shortly afterward, Ellis Searles unleashed a newspaper blast at the Bureau of Industrial Research and the League for Industrial Democracy. Searles accused Brophy's friends of being "Greenwich Village reds" seeking to "butt in on the affairs of the miners' union" and of being "parlor coal diggers, who might better be designated as gold diggers, [and] represent nothing." In response, Norman Thomas, on January 29, addressed an open letter to John L. Lewis. "To favor nationalization but to forbid public discussion of concrete plans," Thomas wrote, "reminds me of the old nursery rhyme:

> Mother may I go out to swim?
> Yes, my darling daughter,
> Hang your clothes on a hickory limb
> But don't go near the water."

A day after the appearance of Thomas's letter, Lewis reacted. Writing to William Mitch, Lewis asserted that in his October 7, 1922 letter appointing the nationalization committee he had never meant to suggest that committee members were free to publicize their plans before the mine workers had approved them. Mitch took his cue from Lewis and reminded Brophy that publicizing the issue outside the UMW had been wrong, that a Republican administration in power made nationalization inopportune, and that even in Europe, nationalization was no longer a "live issue." Lewis praised Mitch's "excellent judgment." Controversies concerning the UMW should not be aired publicly, Lewis wrote on February 10, 1923.

With mine nationalization a dead issue by mid–February 1923, the possibility of a soft-coal strike in 1923 ended by an agreement of January 24, and the UMW not scheduled to hold another convention until January 1924, Lewis took a well-earned vacation. On February 24, 1923, he and Myrta sailed from New York on board the S. S. *Celtic* for a six-week combined vacation-business trip to Great Britain.

Lewis left Philip Murray in charge of the UMW. A letter from Murray to Lewis dated March 15, 1923, in which the acting union president tried to humor his "boss," reveals better than any other extant document Lewis's conception of how best to run an efficient trade union. Murray, to be sure, advised the Lewises not to rush home, to rest fully while they had the opportunity, because they were unlikely to have another one soon. "The only thing that your friends in the office and I fear," wrote Murray jocularly, "is the possibility of your returning home with spats, cane, and a monocle." Murray's strained humor also cut to the heart of Lewis's conception of union politics. Our friends in charge of the constitutional department, joked Murray, "have been making rulings having for their purpose the preservation of the principles as laid down by yourself. It goes without saying that these rulings not only protect the interests of the organization, but also protect our friends." All joshing aside, Murray assured his absent chief that UMW affairs were running smoothly and that "if any of these district officers peep their heads up, I will do just as you would do, — kick them out of the organization, then revoke their charters." Finally, Murray expressed what he considered to be his boss's estimate of such militants as John Brophy. "Your close-up of British nationalization," he suggested to Lewis, "will give you an appreciation of the nuts who are leading the movement for nationalization on this side of the ocean."

5

Emerging Labor Statesman, 1923–24

By the spring of 1923 John L. Lewis had traveled far from his obscure origins. His parents had left Wales in 1869 and 1870 as part of the post–Civil War wave of British emigrants who took advantage of reduced steamship rates and steerage passage to better their fortunes overseas. A half-century later John Lewis reversed the route of his parents, but he traveled first-class, saw his name in the society column of the *New York Times,* and on his passport described his occupation as "executive."

A career in trade unionism had thus far been good to Lewis. As a third-generation UMW official he could treat the labor movement as a career, not a calling or a mission. First-generation union leaders in the United Mine Workers and elsewhere received minimal salaries, bare expenses, little secretarial assistance, and no security of tenure; in most cases, they fell from office as easily as autumn leaves. Second-generation UMW leaders typically bettered themselves through the labor movement. John Mitchell gained national repute, hobnobbed with the business elite, counted prominent politicians among his friends, and, at his death, left behind a not inconsequential estate. Mitchell's successors in the presidential office also improved themselves materially. Tom Lewis became a well-paid official of a West Virginia mine owners' association, and John P. White served first as a federal official and then as a business executive. By the time John L. Lewis entered office his predecessors had established a pattern of union careerism. Presidents were well paid, received elastic expense arrangements, employed extensive secretarial staffs, and traveled first-class. They attended formal dinners in tails and white ties. If they had not in fact been admitted to full membership in the corporate-political elite, they tried to imitate its life-style.

Union business still took Lewis away from home—the three-story house he maintained on West Lawrence Avenue in Springfield. The journey between his home and UMW headquarters in Indianapolis became routine in the 1920s, yet it was now not unusual for Lewis to bring secretaries home with him so that official business could be transacted in Springfield as well as Indianapolis. Collective bargaining and political lobbying carried Lewis to New York, Philadelphia, and Washington where he stayed at the finest hotels: the Ambassador, Roosevelt, and Waldorf-Astoria in New York; the Bellevue-Stratford in Philadelphia; and the Willard in Washington. His wife often accompanied him, as did other members of his immediate family, especially his closest brother, George. During the summer, daughter Kathryn traveled with her father frequently, although the child of the family, John L. Jr., usually remained at home.

Family support proved essential to Lewis's existence. Most family members cared for each other in time of trouble, and aunts and uncles tended Kathryn and John Jr. when John L. and Myrta traveled during the school year. Most members of the Lewis-Bell clan earned their livelihoods directly or indirectly through the UMW. Those family members Lewis did not place directly on the union payroll obtained positions through union influence. Brother Dennie's job with the State Mine Inspection Department resulted from the mine workers' political influence in Illinois. And brother-in-law Floyd C. Bell became cashier of an Indianapolis bank that Lewis served as president.

The Lewis family during the 1920s developed a distinctly haut bourgeois life-style. Photographs of John L. Lewis (and they were becoming increasingly numerous by this time) show him in the finest tailored and conservatively cut dark business suits with vest, gold chain, lightly starched white collar, and silk tie. Myrta dressed demurely but stylishly and wore a luxurious mink coat in winter. Lewis also began to purchase and drive expensive Cadillac roadsters. Lewis's 1926 travel diary, for example, contrasts starkly with his earlier ones. Where heretofore the diaries recorded the costs of constant railroad travel and Pullman berths, the 1926 book consisted entirely of entries estimating the cost of fuel, tires, and tune-ups for Lewis's Cadillac. In the 1920s Myrta developed her life-long passion: the acquisition of antiques. Beginning with the Lewis's 1923 visit to Britain and the purchase of seventeenth- and eighteenth-century English antiques in Swansea and Cardiff, Myrta dealt regularly with antique dealers on two continents. In 1928, when coal miners were fortunate to average $30 a week in wages, Myrta spent $35 for one English sterling silver soup ladle (nineteenth century) and $16.50 for one "fine old spoon." Later she accumulated Waterford compotes, French porcelain, Chippendale furniture, and Oriental rugs.

While Myrta collected antiques, John accumulated prestigious country club memberships. On December 1, 1922, he became a lifetime member of the Congressional Country Club in Washington, his membership certificate signed by the club's president, Herbert Hoover. And in 1926 the directors admitted him to a lifetime membership in the Army, Navy, and Marine Corps Country Club, also in Washington. Lewis, however, was neither a golfer nor a social drinker, and his country club memberships obviously were primarily for the status they conferred, not the leisure activities they offered. Lewis's primary outdoor interests were deep-sea fishing off the Florida coast and hiking and trail riding in the high mountains of Colorado and Wyoming. Later in life, when his income made it possible, he purchased a vacation home on Pine Island off the Florida Gulf Coast and became a regular summer visitor to a resort in the Jackson Hole area of Wyoming that catered to wealthy business executives.

Outside the large family circle to which he was close and devoted, Lewis lacked intimate friends. Phil Murray, who served him faithfully and well for a quarter of a century, never entered John L. Lewis's charmed social circle. The diaries and correspondence of other Lewis associates in the UMW and CIO suggest a similar social distance between them and their boss. Like a corporate executive patronizing his employees, the best that Lewis could do was to take Phil Murray, Tom Kennedy, and Jett Lauck on a fishing trip for a day. When Lewis was in Indianapolis during 1920–23, he seldom spent time away from the office with fellow members of the UMW. Instead, he joined a steady evening poker game that included "Big Bill" Hutcheson, president of the carpenters' union; Dan Tobin, president of the teamsters; and officials from other unions with Indianapolis headquarters. Lewis's attitude toward colleagues is best revealed in a story told by R. J. Thomas, who, in 1937, had just been elected president of the United Auto Workers. Immediately after the election, Lewis advised Thomas: "Well, look. I think it's all right for a man in your position now to have some recreation but don't let them [UAW associates] get too close to you. By coming close to you they will become contemptuous and they won't give you the proper respect. If you play poker, and you live out in Detroit, play with your neighbors or somebody. Don't play with anybody in your official capacity."

Lewis followed his own rules of social etiquette religiously. He kept fellow officers of the UMW at a distance, practiced regal aloofness, and acted to the union as a king to his court. Lewis reserved his friendship for business executives, high public officials, and other members of the American elite. They dined with the Lewises on a reciprocal basis, and he charmed them with well-told stories and stimulating conversation. The Herbert Hoovers, the Gardner Jacksons, the Harrimans, the Cyrus

Chings, corporation executives in general—they were the type of people John L. Lewis cultivated. Cyrus Ching, a United States Rubber Company executive and later a prominent federal labor mediator, described Lewis as "a brilliant conversationalist," the "soul of courtesy... a typical southern gentleman." Nonflamboyant in private conversation, Lewis, according to Ching, had a dry, keen sense of humor, one that enabled him to swap stories for seven consecutive hours with George Love, a leading coal company executive, as Ching laughed ceaselessly.

During the 1920s Lewis established a particularly close business and personal relationship with the Harriman family. Not only did Jacob Harriman, president of the Harriman National Bank, extend a substantial line of credit to the UMW during the 1922 strike, but he also personally telephoned President Harding to plead the union's case. Lewis, for his part, deposited UMW funds in Harriman's bank and sought to obtain other union business for his banker friend. Harriman regularly extended credit without collateral simply on the basis of Lewis's personal signature. For example, W. Jett Lauck, the UMW's economic adviser and Lewis's personal tax and real estate consultant, financed his own many—and mostly unsucessful—real estate ventures through loans obtained from the Harriman National Bank on the signatures of Lewis and Phil Murray. Averell Harriman occasionally invited Lewis to polo matches in which the former played. And Lewis, the trade union leader and miners' spokesman, felt no embarrassment appearing at the matches attended largely by members of New York's "400."

Lewis's relationship to the world of banking went considerably beyond his acquaintance with Jacob Harriman. In September 1923 Lewis agreed to become president of the United Labor Bank and Trust Company of Indianapolis (capitalized at nearly $1 million) and demanded "a salary commensurate with the character of the institution and the degree of responsibility involved." He also suggested that the bank's organizers appoint his brother-in-law, Floyd C. Bell, cashier and a member of the board of directors at an annual starting salary of $4,000 to $5,000, to rise when business increased. In his letter of acceptance, Lewis enclosed two separate personal checks for $1,100 in payment for ten shares of bank stock each for himself and Floyd Bell in order to qualify them for their executive positions.

The reasons for establishing a labor bank and appointing Lewis as its president seem obvious. Three of the largest labor unions in the nation—the miners, the teamsters, and the carpenters—and many smaller ones had their national headquarters in Indianapolis. Unions, moreover, maintained an enormous cash flow as dues receipts trickled in and benefits poured out. A bank fortunate enough to become a depository for union funds gained substantial economic advantages, which is what the directors of the United Labor Bank likely expected from Lewis's bank presidency during the 1920s.

Lewis not only assimilated a haut bourgeois life-style from his associations with the nation's economic and political elite, he also absorbed their ideological values and their imperious business practices. A man who had flirted with radicals and radicalism from 1917 to 1922 became by 1923 "the scourge of the reds." The elected leader of a putative union democracy, he increasingly practiced autocracy in his administration of the UMW.

At the height of the red scare from 1918 to 1919, Lewis and his union were among its most notable objects. By 1923, however, as fear of radicalism abated, Lewis entered the battle against the red and the rebellious. In January 1923, the UMW international executive board officially condemned bolshevism and radicalism. In June of the same year, during the annual tri-district (anthracite) convention in Scranton, Lewis, finding himself under attack by union militants led by one Rinaldo Cappellini, resorted to red-baiting. Aware that William Z. Foster's son-in-law, Joseph Manley, was among the observers at the convention, Lewis launched a tirade against communism, calling Foster, Manley, and their ilk "industrial buzzards" and ordering them to go to their "beloved Russia."

In September 1923 Ellis Searles prepared a UMW "White Paper" on the Bolshevik threat to the American labor movement, which was subsequently printed as an official United States Senate document. In the paper, Searles alleged that Soviet Russia was financing a campaign led by William Z. Foster and his Trade Union Educational League (TUEL) to disrupt responsible trade unions, subvert the A.F. of L., and capture American labor for bolshevism. Years later businessman George C. Moore wrote to Lewis: "No one seems to recall that you alone for ten years were the only bulwark against Communism penetrating the United States, when it was a true menace . . . and . . . that you were the obstacle to the recognition of Russia."

Despite the intense criticism from insurgents that he endured from 1920 to 1926, Lewis ran the union as he pleased. Secretary-Treasurer William Green, the only official whose tenure in office preceded that of Lewis, lacked the power to challenge the union president. On two separate occasions in 1923 and 1924 when Green acted in accord with the union constitution, past practices, and precedents, Lewis berated him. In May 1923 Lewis curtly informed Green, "I would be very glad to have you accommodate your bookkeeping arrangements . . . so as to square with the rulings of the President's office." Green promised to conform with Lewis's wishes. In 1924, when Green again cited past union precedent and procedure as a basis for his action, Lewis raised the superior standard of presidential authority and interpretation.

Lewis's management of union finances offered abundant evidence of his cavalier approach. Between 1922 and August 1924, Lewis authorized Ellis Searles to spend more than $19,000 in union funds, of which more than $12,000 was expended in the form of bribes to obtain information or influence people in the interest of the UMW. None of Searles's expenditures was billed or receipted, nor was Secretary-Treasurer Green allowed to record them in the union's books. When Green complained of such unethical practices, Lewis replied: "I have discussed the matter with him [Searles] and am entirely satisfied that his expenditures were legitimate and that the organization received full value therefrom." When Green refused to accept Lewis's explanation and demanded a personal meeting with the president, Lewis again asserted that he possessed the authority to sanction Searles's activities for the union. Yet Lewis, always eager to avoid written records of activities such as Searles's, notified Green: "I see no reason . . . to discuss the matter through the instrumentality of correspondence. I will be glad to discuss the matter with you personally at any time."

The union journal also remained the exclusive property of Lewis. Not even district officers could get their material printed without Searles's permission, and Lewis relied on the editor to exercise his judgment in the UMW president's interests. When William Mitch, secretary of Indiana District 11 and by 1923 a firm Lewis supporter, pleaded with the president to order Searles to publish articles written by Mitch, he got nowhere. Lewis referred him back to Searles, and the editor announced that *Journal* policy foreclosed its use for Mitch's purposes. A frustrated Mitch simply let the whole matter drop. Considering Mitch's treatment in the matter, one can surmise how Searles treated Lewis's declared rivals and critics and why union insurgents found it so difficult to maintain contact with the rank and file.

In some instances power inadvertently fell into Lewis's lap. During the 1920s union failures enhanced Lewis's authority. Union stability insured district vitality, and prosperous, successful districts zealously guarded their autonomy against international incursions. When union districts declined, whether because of internal factionalism, incompetent officials, or employer resistance, their autonomy vanished. District 17 in West Virginia, for example, never recovered from the "civil war" of 1921. By 1924, district officials faced financial ruin. In mid–June 1924, unable to pay their debts or even meet current operating expenses, President Frank Keeney, Secretary-Treasurer Fred Mooney, and all the other West Virginia union officials filed an appeal asking the international executive board to assume the administration of District 17.

Effective June 16, Lewis suspended the autonomy of District 17, appointed Percy Tetlow its new president, and assigned Van Bittner to administer the unionized northern half of the district. The previous summer, the Nova Scotia, Canada district had lost its autonomy as a consequence of political divisions within the district between communists and anticommunists. Before the decade ended, other outlying union districts would lose their autonomy, or whatever had remained of it.

The years 1923–24, however, were not without frustrations for Lewis. Most of his problems flowed from the economics of the coal industry and his negotiations with operators. His ability to influence the economics of coal mining and the attitude of employers was far less than his authority to control the UMW. Soft-coal mining remained an economically prostrate industry throughout the prosperity decade. And hard-coal, or anthracite, mining, the one stable element in the industry, carried its own burdens for Lewis and his union.

The economics of anthracite differed from that of bituminous. A handful of companies controlled by coal-carrying railroads dominated hard coal—an industry limited geographically to three counties in northeastern Pennsylvania. Not only did competition among operators scarcely exist, but the market for anthracite was also far more stable than that for bituminous. Hard coal, unlike soft coal, was used primarily for domestic heating purposes. Consequently, the demand for anthracite fluctuated more in relation to the thermometer than to the barometer of industrial activity, as did the demand for bituminous. However anthracite had its own problems; by the 1920s its era of growth terminated as new homes increasingly used natural gas and fuel oil for domestic heat.

On the surface, anthracite was the one secure element in the UMW situation. Almost all the miners were union members, some 155,000 in all, and scarcely any nonunion hard coal entered the market. As union membership slipped elsewhere, hard-coal miners became an increasingly large proportion of UMW membership. They also formed a solid bloc of voting support for Lewis at UMW conventions, and, not infrequently, the votes from the three anthracite districts (numbers 1, 7, and 9) provided the UMW administration with its margin of victory. Lewis thus could scarcely neglect the interests of anthracite miners, nor could he leave them insecure and less well paid than soft-coal miners.

General labor peace had prevailed in the anthracite region from the strike of 1902 until the summer of 1922, when the hard-coal miners struck for five months. In 1923 conditions remained much as they had been since the basic settlement of 1902. In anthracite, unlike bituminous, the union lacked both closed-shop contracts and the dues checkoff.

Wage rates varied considerably even among union miners, and day-workers earned from $4.20 to $5.60 daily compared to the $7.50 minimum in unionized soft coal.

In 1923 anthracite operators still fought most of Lewis's demands. Unwilling to cut profits or lose customers, the operators balked at wage increases. They resisted the closed shop and the dues checkoff even more strongly. They feared that to concede the closed shop and the checkoff in the anthracite mines would undermine the open shop on the railroads, which they also operated. On the issue most important to union officials—union security—and the one most important to miners—higher wages—little room for compromise existed, and a hard-coal strike seemed likely when the 1922 agreement expired on September 1, 1923.

An autumn hard-coal strike posed inescapable political ramifications. Unless householders in the Northeast could obtain coal before election day in November, they might vote against incumbent Republicans. Consequently, the Coolidge administration and the various state governments in the northeastern anthracite-consuming states sought to pressure the operators and the union into agreement, with Coolidge and Governor Gifford Pinchot of Pennsylvania assuming the lead. Coolidge requested the United States Coal Commission to speed its investigations of the industry and come up with a settlement satisfactory to operators and miners; Pinchot urged the operators to raise wages and provide union security through a voluntary dues checkoff.

Negotiations between Lewis and the operators dragged on through July and August 1923 without success. More concerned about union stability than about improving conditions for the miners, Lewis proposed that the operators sign a long-term contract (three or four years) maintaining current conditions. The operators, however, preferred not to bind themselves for an extended period during which the market outlook for their product seemed bleak. Yet the more rapidly fall and the November elections approached, the more eager public officials became to formulate a settlement, especially as the union issued orders to anthracite miners to strike beginning September 1.

The UMW strike order precipitated a final frantic round of negotiations among union officials, operators, the United States Coal Commission, President Coolidge, and Governor Pinchot. The site of the bargaining moved from New York to Philadelphia and, finally, to Harrisburg. In his new style, Lewis left New York on August 27 with his wife, two children, brother George, personal secretary, and entire office staff to establish headquarters at the Bellevue-Stratford Hotel in Philadelphia. Falling victim to a cold, Lewis, ever concerned about his health, remained in his hotel room while Philip Murray represented the union in the bargaining conferences that brought a settlement at Pinchot's Harrisburg executive office.

After a strike that lasted only five and a half days, Governor Pinchot announced on September 7 the terms of his compromise settlement. The new two-year anthracite agreement included a 10 percent wage increase for day and tonnage miners; a voluntary system of dues checkoff in which union delegates, not management, collected the money; and the promise of only marginal increases in the retail price of anthracite.

Although an apparent triumph for Lewis, the UMW, and the hard-coal miners, the 1923 agreement, in fact, left the primary causes of the strike unresolved. Operators still rejected the closed shop, they had not agreed to equalize wages, and despite the 10 percent wage increase, anthracite miners still earned less on an hourly basis than their brothers in bituminous or than other industrial laborers whose work was safer. Another strike, this time a longer and more costly one for the union and the miners, would have to be waged to resolve the outstanding grievances.

Meantime the crisis in soft coal, which first emerged during the depression of 1920–21, had worsened rather than abated by 1923. More than ever it was now apparent that the bituminous industry alone could not solve the problem of too many miners in too many mines producing too much coal. Nonunion fields, moreover, continued to capture markets from the higher-cost unionized fields. Because wages represented almost 70 percent of the cost of coal production, union contracts that required high daily and tonnage rates placed organized mines at a competitive disadvantage compared to nonunion mines, which could adjust their wage levels to price fluctuations for coal. But even nonunion mines and nonunion miners suffered from the industry's surplus capacity.

Lewis saw no easy escape from the dilemma of bituminous coal. To continue current labor practices meant higher unemployment in the union fields and a declining UMW membership. The alternative of bringing supply into closer accord with demand for coal also posed a threat to the union. Reduced supply could be achieved only by shutting down at least one-third of the operating mines—those considered to be marginal or high cost—and hence causing considerable unemployment among coal miners. Whichever alternative Lewis chose, the result would be a reduced membership for the UMW.

Lewis personally preferred a total reorganization of the soft-coal industry. Throughout the 1920s he and Jett Lauck discussed privately their plans to stabilize the coal industry by consolidating production into fewer, more efficient units; restricting competition in marketing and pricing; and liberating the coal industry from the antitrust laws.

The Lauck-Lewis program for coal proposed to reward employers who provided miners with steady work by requiring operators whose mines had irregular employment patterns to pay substantial financial penalties into an unemployment insurance fund. Theoretically, more efficient production by fewer and larger firms would enable operators to pay higher wages, offer steadier work, protect profit levels, and insure consumers against sharp price rises. Lewis's and Lauck's proposals to stabilize the coal industry required an active role by the federal government never before contemplated in peacetime. On the one hand, federal officials had to allow operators to divide markets and fix prices in violation of antitrust legislation; on the other hand, the federal government had to act positively to protect union operators from nonunion competitors and use its power to protect the UMW in the nonunion fields.

Some operators in the northern fields favored Lewis's program for soft coal, and almost all northern operators desired protection against Appalachian nonunion competitors. As one central Pennsylvania operator, F. E. Herrimann, wrote to Lewis in July 1923: "Many operators—both 'outlaws' [nonunion] and inlaws—are wishing more power to your union." But no prominent federal officials, among whom the most significant was Herbert Hoover, desired to implement the UMW program because it implied far too much government regulation of a private enterprise. Hoover, like Lewis, wanted to stabilize the bituminous coal industry, encourage economic consolidation, stimulate efficiency, and reduce competition; but the commerce secretary also wanted to restrain union power by protecting the nonunion mines.

Aware that the UMW lacked the strength in 1923 to endure another national coal strike and that such a conflict would likely destroy both the UMW and the unionized operators, Lewis worked behind the scenes with friends in industry and government to avert a walkout. Two Pennsylvania operators—F. E. Herrimann, president of the Clearfield Bituminous Coal Corporation, a New York Central Railroad subsidiary, and Rembrandt Peale, chairman of President Wilson's Bituminous Coal Commission—acted in December 1923 as private intermediaries for Lewis in discussions with northern operators about a new contract with the union. That same month Lewis met Herbert Hoover, two prominent New York City financiers, and chief Associated Press correspondent Melville Stone at a private dinner arranged by George G. Moore, a utilities and coal capitalist, in the latter's suite at the Ambassador Hotel in New York. For two hours Lewis and Hoover discussed the economics of soft coal and the best way to avert a strike in 1924. Both men agreed that only a protracted period of industrial peace could save the soft-coal industry from economic ruin by offering the larger, more efficient operators a chance to drive marginal competitors out of business.

In the final weeks of December 1923 and throughout January 1924, Lewis and Hoover worked feverishly to arrange a new agreement between coal operators and the union. Lewis cultivated his supporters among the employers and also won union endorsement for his aims; Hoover urged recalcitrant western Pennsylvania operators, especially those associated with the industrial empire of his cabinet colleague Andrew Mellon, to bargain with the UMW.

As the conference in Jacksonville, Florida—which had been provided for in the January 1923 agreement—approached in February 1924, Lewis's and Hoover's industrial diplomacy appeared successful. On February 4, Lewis reported to the commerce secretary that at the recently adjourned UMW convention, despite being "somewhat hampered by the ultra-radical influence which hovered around the . . . convention [we put through our program] without amendment of any character." What the convention in fact did was to authorize Lewis "to secure the best agreement obtainable from the operators in the Central Competitive Field on the basis of no reduction in wages" for a four-year period (April 1, 1924 to March 31, 1928), with the agreement to be subject to membership ratification. Hoover did his part, obtaining commitments from western Pennsylvania operators to join the bargaining in Jacksonville.

Jacksonville worked out precisely as Hoover and Lewis had planned. A week after the conference opened on February 19, operators and union negotiators reached agreement on a new three-year contract that preserved existing terms. That same day the UMW's international policy committee approved the agreement and recommended that it be applied to all the outlying union districts. And the next day Hoover advised President Coolidge to compliment Michael Gallagher, chairman of the coal operators' committee, and John L. Lewis for carrying through "the undertakings that each of them made with me [Hoover] in December last" and for maintaining constructive peace in the industry. On February 20, the commerce secretary also informed Lewis that "I believe you have worked out one of the most statesmanlike labor settlements in many years."

Publicly, thereafter, Lewis and Hoover seemed to form a mutual admiration society. The union leader echoed the federal official's political philosophy. "I am not one," proclaimed Lewis, "who believe[s] that enactment of arbitrary legislation will prove to be a panacea for every maladministration of industry or that economic law can be set aside by the sweep of a legislative pen." Referring specifically to the coal industry, Lewis added: "We must give economic laws free play.

. . . It is the survival of the fittest. Many are going to be hurt, but the rule must be the greatest good for the greatest number." Hoover voiced his opinion that "Mr. Lewis is more than a successful battle leader. He has a sound conception of statesmanship of long-view interest to the people and the industry he serves."

Privately, however, Lewis and Hoover failed to agree in March and April 1924 concerning the commerce secretary's more detailed plans for economic stabilization of bituminous coal mining. Despite Lewis's paeans to private enterprise, the free market, and the law of supply and demand, he realized that the UMW could survive only through federal regulation of the coal industry. Hoover, on the contrary, preferred government to stimulate private enterprise, not control it. Soon the two leaders would be in open conflict over the meaning and implementation of the Jacksonville agreement. But in the spring of 1924 the future of bituminous coal appeared sufficiently secure for the Commerce Department to observe in its annual report: "The coal industry is now on the road to stabilization."

By the summer of 1924, Lewis's power in the UMW and his influence outside had peaked. When nominations came due in August for election to international union office, not a single challenger for the presidency emerged. Yet secure as Lewis's position seemed, he still evinced signs of paranoia. "My leisure moments have been very few of late as is usually the case," he apologized to K. C. Adams, "my friends always suffer in order that I can devote myself to the affairs of the organization and give some attention to my several enemies."

Politically, Lewis acted as the nation's most eminent labor Republican. In April, Jacob Harriman laid before President Coolidge John L. Lewis's claim to the Republican vice-presidential nomination. During the summer Republican officials appointed Lewis a member of the Advisory Committee of the Republican National Committee, and Lewis publicly endorsed the incumbent president, largely because, as he wrote to K. C. Adams, "I judge that President Coolidge will be re-elected." After Coolidge's reelection, Cleveland mine operator Joseph Pursglove, speaking for himself and several bankers and steelmen associated with the Mellon interests, asked Lewis if he would be interested in becoming secretary of labor. And delegates to the 1924 A.F. of L. convention endorsed Lewis for the secretaryship. But the UMW president played coy, discouraging an open interest in the cabinet office. Lewis's coyness probably flowed from his realization that he lacked effective influence with the Coolidge administration.

If Lewis had limited political influence, his standing among some coal operators remained remarkably high. Several of the union operators in the fall of 1924 considered establishing a powerful new owners' association, with Lewis as its chief executive officer. Joseph Pursglove, who originally broached the suggestion to Lewis in February 1924 at Jacksonville, still felt in November that Lewis would be the ideal man to head an operators' association. On November 18, 1924, he asked Lewis directly if he would accept such a position. "I do not think it appropriate," replied Lewis on November 27, "that I should have anything to do with the formation of a coal operators' association and naturally am not open to suggestions for employment by such an organization."

As 1924 ended, Lewis was about to win his final major trade union triumph of the 1920s. Shortly after the A.F. of L. convention adjourned in late November 1924, the aging Samuel Gompers took seriously ill. On December 3, the A.F. of L. president died, and with him ended an era in American labor history. With the A.F. of L. presidency now apparently more readily within his grasp than it had been in 1921, Lewis instead urged William Green's claim to the position. Why? Lewis probably realized that the most influential members of the A.F. of L. executive council, as imperious in their behavior as he was, preferred not to have another strong executive succeed Gompers. A regular poker partner of Dan Tobin and Bill Hutcheson, two of the three most influential A.F. of L. members, Lewis obviously knew that they would not tolerate him as their superior in the labor movement. And all the members of the executive council apparently shared the estimate of Lewis held by Gompers's longtime personal secretary, Florence Thorne: "Lewis was impatient with differences of opinion, and he wanted to tell people what to do rather than argue it out with them."

Green, however, appeared a perfect candidate. Already a member of the executive council, he represented the nation's largest trade union. Where Lewis was imperious in his relations with others, Green was deferential; where Lewis ignored the opinions of others, Green always preferred to compromise rather than carry his own position.

Green's triumph also served Lewis's aims in two important respects. First, it removed a troublesome official presence from the UMW. Alone among international officials in the years 1919–24, Green had challenged Lewis's interpretations of the union constitution and his administrative practices. Second, Lewis assumed that Green would simply act as a surrogate president of the A.F. of L. Despite their past differences concerning UMW policy, Green, in the end, had always deferred to Lewis, and Lewis saw no reason why such a relationship should not persist. An entrepreneur friend of Lewis's once referred to Green and Murray as Lewis's "pair of canaries." Just as rumors had circulated in 1919 and afterward that Lewis had used a sexual scandal involving Green to remove the latter as a challenger for the UMW presidency, stories passed among A.F. of L. executive council members that sexual improprieties by their new president placed him in Lewis's power. Whatever the truth of the matter, there is little doubt that Lewis expected Green to be his man and that until the dramatic break between Lewis and the A.F. of L. in the years 1935–37, Green did indeed serve the interests of the UMW president.

With Green rising to the A.F. of L. presidency, Lewis could appoint his own secretary-treasurer, and he chose Thomas Kennedy of District 7 in Pennsylvania, whose appointment solidified Lewis's strength in the anthracite districts. For the next seventeen years, until Lewis and Murray split in 1941, Lewis, Murray, and Kennedy formed the unshakable triumvirate that dominated the United Mine Workers. And when Lewis finally retired as union president in 1960, Kennedy succeeded him.

In late 1924, then, John L. Lewis stood on the top of the trade union world. He and his handpicked associates ruled the United Mine Workers, and a Lewis man headed the A.F. of L. The Jacksonville agreement of February 1924 protected the UMW in its northern strongholds for a three-year period and maintained high wage levels for union miners. His standing with the Coolidge administration was unsurpassed among trade unionists. Herbert Hoover, the strong man of the cabinet, served, so Lewis thought, as a means of transmitting his ideas. Financial journals, bankers, and many northern coal operators praised Lewis as a labor statesman—the one American labor leader who grasped the reciprocal relationship between capital and labor and who devoted himself to harmonious labor relations. So prominent a public figure had Lewis become that the citizens of Lucas County, Iowa, invited their most famous native son home in the summer of 1924 to join them in a gala celebration in the county seat of Chariton on John L. Lewis Day.

6

Union Tyrant:
Mastering the Opposition,
1921–27

The United Mine Workers, like most American trade unions, had originated as a confederation of autonomous local and regional organizations. For most of the UMW's first three decades, from 1890 to 1920, the union had functioned as a decentralized institution in which effective administrative authority existed at the district level. However much international officials, the president included, dominated the process of collective bargaining, they nevertheless were as much the servants as the masters of district officials. The most powerful district presidents chaired the union's major policy committees and established the bargaining parameters within which the president negotiated with employers. Moreover, electoral coalitions among the largest northern districts determined the fate of international officers, which is why in the UMW, as in most American trade unions before World War I, the president lacked secure power. Even John L. Lewis maintained his authority by the barest majority during his first two years in office.

If Lewis inherited a decentralized union structure, he grappled with a complex national economy. Not only did the largest coal companies operate mines in several union districts, but improved means of transportation also widened the scope of competition for markets among producers. More than ever before, nonunion coal competed with union coal, and wage bargains struck in the Central Competitive Field affected the outlying districts. As long as district officials retained the authority to negotiate about working conditions not covered by the Central Competative Field agreement, neither unionized operators nor international officials could relax.

The dialectical relationship between a decentralized union and a national economy created conflicts. When the autonomous districts flourished, as did District 12 from 1910 to 1930, the power of the international union over its members ebbed. International, or presidential, authority waxed only insofar as district power waned. But the districts would only relinquish or diminish their autonomy if faced with financial or structural ruin. Ironically then, Lewis achieved undiluted authority to negotiate binding national agreements with employers only as the number of union members he represented declined at a rapidly accelerating rate. Put simply, Lewis's personal power in the UMW during the 1920s rose in proportion to the decline in his union's actual strength and influence. For John L. Lewis, that was the cruelest of ironies: to struggle so hard and so ruthlessly for union power only to clutch the shattered shell of a labor organization.

Lewis approached internal organizational problems in much the same opportunistic manner as he dealt with the union's external relationships. Personal alliances were broken as easily as they were formed. The anti-red hysteria that won for Lewis the plaudits of businessmen and Republican politicians could also be used—and effectively, at that—to tarnish union opponents. Less principled rivals could be captured with the lure of an international sinecure, unintelligent or politically clumsy opponents could be ridiculed and led to destroy themselves, the principled and the adroit could be ruthlessly purged and even physically abused. Because Lewis's internal rivals were more divided among themselves than his external "opponents" in business and politics, he functioned more ruthlessly within the union than outside, and his political cunning produced success rather than failure.

Lewis had been president of the UMW less than a year when his opponents formed an anti-Lewis coalition. Elected president in December 1920, Lewis would preside over his first convention in September 1921, the initial opportunity for his rivals to challenge Lewis's authority in the UMW. It was an opportunity, moreover, eagerly awaited by his challengers, among whom the most notable and influential were Frank Farrington and John Walker of District 12 (Illinois) and Alex Howat of District 14 (Kansas). Walker personified the union's old guard socialists, men of high principle and rectitude. Howat, at his best, exemplified the militancy, flavor, and courage of rank-and-file miners. Farrington, in contrast, copied Lewis's opportunistic and entrepreneurial style of union leadership; the District 12 president allied himself to Illinois Republicans, nestled up to the coal operators, and simply envied Lewis's place in the union. United solely by their hostility to Lewis, whatever its motivation, these men in 1921 represented powerful tendencies in the UMW.

For several reasons Howat appeared the most vulnerable of Lewis's rivals. First, he led a smaller, weaker UMW district that had fewer than twelve thousand members and depended on support from the international and bargaining gains won in the Central Competitive Field negotiations. Second, Howat had few sympathizers, if any, among the coal operators and numerous enemies among Kansas and federal government officials. Third, few of Howat's allies in the UMW trusted him, partly because of his weakness for alcohol and partly because he tended to act before he thought.

Howat's bumptious behavior in Kansas, especially his endorsement of wildcat miners' strikes frequently in violation of contract, led Howat into persistent conflict with operators, Kansas public officials, and Lewis. So common were miners' walkouts in Kansas that during the postwar wave of antiradical hysteria, the state passed an industrial court law that effectively outlawed strikes and mandated compulsory arbitration of labor disputes — a policy that was an anathema to the entire American labor movement, Lewis included.

Despite the Kansas law that banned strikes and a 1920 contract between District 14 and the Southwestern Coal Operators' Association that the UMW guaranteed, Howat, as district president, endorsed local strikes. This meant that District 14 was constantly involved in litigation in Kansas courts and that Kansas operators regularly threatened to sue the UMW for not compelling Howat to implement contract terms. Whatever the reason for a local strike, Howat posed as the defender of the rank and file and, if need be, as an imprisoned martyr to its cause. He transformed all disputes between miners and operators into a clash between the union and the unjust Kansas industrial court law, between freedom and tyranny. Lewis, on the contrary, distinguished between strikes banned by law and by contract, and he used that distinction to destroy Howat and to seize control of District 14.

The 1921 UMW convention constituted the first significant challenge to Lewis's tenure as union president. From September 20 to October 5, 1921, more than two thousand delegates debated Lewis's internal union policies and struggled for mastery within the UMW. As delegates argued about the relative authority of district versus international officials, about the sanctity of contract versus the rights of working miners, debate turned angry, words spilled over into physical force, and violence loomed.

The tempestuous behavior of delegates to the 1921 convention flowed from the strength of Lewis's opponents and the importance of the issues debated. The year 1921 witnessed the consummation of a working alliance among Howat, Farrington, Walker, and Robert Harlin. Had they been able to add John Brophy and William Mitch to their coalition, they might well have defeated Lewis on a climactic roll call vote that determined Howat's future. But Lewis proved sufficiently adept in September 1921 to curry favor among Brophy, Mitch, and other UMW left-wingers by satisfying their desire for nationalization of the coal mines. Lewis also proved an expert at framing the convention debate in terms that buttressed his own position.

Lewis first tangled with Frank Farrington. The District 12 president, raising the standard of "district autonomy" to defend his unaccounted expenditure of $27,000, argued that districts should be free to operate as they pleased. Lewis had a ready riposte to this line of argument. To allow districts to go their own way, he replied, would precipitate a process of union disintegration as subdistricts and then locals challenged superior authority on the basis of autonomy. Moreover, to carry the principle of autonomy to its logical conclusion would vitiate the trade union principle that an injury to one is the concern of all. Lewis commanded general delegate support against Farrington because few miners, radicals especially, sanctioned the manner in which Farrington administered District 12.

After defeating Farrington's challenge, Lewis turned to the more serious and divisive Howat-Kansas question. If Farrington matched Lewis in egotism, intrigue, and opportunism, Howat far surpassed both in appealing to rank-and-file delegates and coal miners. Where Lewis and Farrington ingratiated themselves with operators and politicians, Howat gloried in the role of class warrior, the man who would risk prison before selling out workers to their employers or public officials. Where Farrington used the principle of district autonomy to excuse misallocation of union funds, Howat spoke in favor of union solidarity and warned delegates that to surrender the rights and traditions of Kansas miners ultimately threatened the security of miners everywhere. Howat assured the convention that he had sanctioned the strikes at the Dean and Reliance mines because employers had unilaterally altered work traditions, and unless the coal miners' prerogatives were defended in Kansas, operators would also change customs in Oklahoma, Illinois, Iowa, and other districts. Which policy was preferable, Howat asked the convention, Lewis's collaboration with operators or his own defense of the coal miners' rights?

Lewis refused to debate Howat about coal miners' customs or prerogatives. Instead he instructed delegates that the union protected its members best through the instrument of a binding contract with employers and that Howat's methods in Kansas violated the sanctity of contract. If Kansas tactics spread elsewhere, Lewis implied, operators would sign no contracts with the UMW, and miners would one day "have no pledges to conform to." Unless miners met their obligations, he advised, the UMW had no future. On that note, Lewis asked delegates to cast their votes for or against the executive board's decision to suspend Howat and the officers of District 14 for refusing to order striking miners back to work.

The ensuing roll call vote disclosed how well Lewis had estimated his own strength. Delegates from only four out of twenty-seven union districts cast a majority of their votes against the suspension of Howat, and of the four districts, only Illinois 12 represented substantial size and influence. Lewis amassed more than 60 percent of the delegate votes, a remarkable triumph when one considers the coalition formed by Howat, Farrington, Walker, and Harlin.

Howat's suspension once again stimulated Lewis's union rivals to build an antiadministration coalition. District 12 leaders immediately pledged Howat financial and moral support, and four of them visited the Kansan in prison.

Van Bittner, whom Lewis had dispatched to Kansas to assume control of District 14, reported back in early November concerning the complicated local situation and how he was using every weapon at the international's disposal to adjust matters satisfactorily and see to it that "the influence of our friend, Howat and his regime has gone forever."

In a step in violation of a specific clause in the UMW constitution, Howat went to court seeking an injunction to restrain Lewis from suspending District 14 officials. Foreclosed by law from judicial relief in Kansas, Howat took his case to a Missouri circuit court where, on January 14, 1922, the judge ruled that because Howat had violated both union law and a legal contract with coal operators, the international executive board had been justified in suspending him from office. "No man or set of men," declared the Missouri judge, "can violate and defy the Kansas laws and at the same time get relief from the courts of equity of a sister state."

Frustrated in court, Howat again appealed to the UMW rank and file. The union constitution provided an administrative appeals process that Howat ignored because of Lewis's domination of the UMW hierarchy. Instead he intended to carry his grievance directly to the membership when the union met again in special convention in February 1922. Howat believed, with good reason, that additional district leaders and delegates would vote in his favor at the reconvened convention. Clearly, if Lewis's suspension of Howat went unrepudiated, then other district presidents might in the future be vulnerable to similar autocratic punishment. That, at least, was how Howat assumed other district officials would interpret Lewis's action, and he was not far from wrong.

When the UMW delegates reconvened on February 14 in Indianapolis, they found themselves once again confronted with the Lewis-Howat conflict instead of the impending struggle between miners and operators. A convention called solely to discuss collective bargaining and strike plans spent almost all its time debating the Kansas controversy.

In the interim between October 1921, when the original convention had adjourned, and February 1922, when it reconvened, Howat had gathered substantial additional delegate support, so much so that Lewis allowed Howat to address the convention although the Kansas insurgent lacked convention credentials. Howat acted the militant in his speech to the delegates. He explained that the Kansas difficulties arose from his stouthearted opposition to an unjust state labor law that imposed tyranny on coal miners, and that he considered "it an honor to be condemned and vilified by the corporation press of this country." Unless the delegates endorsed his appeal, Howat warned, "in time to come this is going to be a one-man organization."

Lewis, too, proved true to tradition in defending himself against Howat's charges. If Howat proved his courage by fighting employers and politicians, Lewis demonstrated his own fearlessness against dangerous enemies. "Day by day, mail after mail," he intoned dramatically, "I have been receiving letters telling me that if I presumed to preside over this convention, telling me that unless I resigned as President of the United Mine Workers it had been decreed in secret conclave I would die." Lewis swore that he would stand fast against this "organized plot of terrorism." Having proclaimed his own courage, Lewis appealed to the delegates' sense of solidarity and union loyalty. On the eve of an impending conflict with employers, Lewis warned, the union "army is now asked to halt and wash out its dirty linen." "Are you going to stop now," he asked, "and become embroiled in a controversy that will only serve to expose your weaknesses to your foes?"

Lewis's plea to the delegates for solidarity went unanswered. For five days they indeed proceeded to wash their dirty linen in public, to shout, and to slug each other. Allan Haywood, then an anti-Lewis delegate from Illinois, at one point charged the press table, cursed, and threatened reporters. Howat's disputed Kansas delegation raced up and down the aisles creating a tumult as it instigated other delegates to heckle Lewis and Vice-President Murray.

Balloting on the question of whether or not to reconsider the suspension of Howat, the UMW delegates divided right down the middle. Howat retained his voting strength in the Illinois delegation, by far the largest at the convention, and picked up support from John Brophy in District 2 and in the southwestern (Oklahoma, Arkansas, and Texas) and western (Montana, Wyoming, and Washington) delegations. Lewis won his largest majorities in two of the anthracite districts, the declining southern Appalachian districts, and Kansas, whose official delegation he now controlled. Out of the 4,028 votes cast, Lewis secured a bare majority of 51.5 percent to his opponent's 48.5 percent. Considering that many of the votes were cast by phantom Appalachian locals, Kansas delegates representing the international administration rather then local miners, and delegates on the international payroll, one can perceive how tenuous was Lewis's control of the UMW in February 1922. A handful of votes cast the other way might have ended Lewis's power in the union, and had his opponents been united in a positive alliance rather than a negative coalition of convenience, they might indeed have won enough votes to handcuff Lewis.

The closeness of the vote explains the bitterness that preceded it and the tumult that followed. Lewis, as customary in a time of crisis, withdrew into a shell. Instead of acting as convention chairman during the roll call or even casting his own delegate vote, he spent most of the decisive day at his office clearing away routine work. The vote itself failed to quiet the acrimony in union ranks, as the convention adjourned on February 18 in the words of one newspaper report, "amid wild disorder, with hundreds of delegates howling like madmen, bewailing the defeat of Alexander Howat." Howat, moreover, refused to accept defeat, vowing that "they can't keep me down . . . I am in the fight to a finish. John Lewis will never get away with this deal that he has handed me."

Lewis kept affairs in the Southwest tightly in his grip and again sent Van Bittner from western Pennsylvania to Kansas in order to quell the insurgent forces. As usual, international funds and patronage flowed to anti-Howat men in the southwestern coalfields. The more frustrated Howat became, the more he erred in his policies. Howat's clumsiness notwithstanding, he remained a threat to Lewis's union power throughout the 1920s because he served the purposes of other influential Lewis rivals.

The year 1922 was not only the year that saw the resolution of the Howat-Kansas struggle and the combined bituminous-anthracite strike; it was also an election year for the UMW, and Lewis's foes were busy organizing their alliances and counteralliances. Farrington continued to engage in an acrimonious correspondence with Lewis and to lay various Byzantine political schemes. Pennsylvania insurgents, unhappy with the terms of the emerging 1922 bituminous settlement, planned to nominate an anti-Lewis ticket for union office.

Aside from Farrington, the central figures in the 1922 union election were Tom Stiles, an editor and publicist for District 2; Powers Hapgood, a young Harvard graduate, son of a socially prominent Indianapolis family, coal miner, and leader of the nonunion Somerset County, Pennsylvania, strikes; and John Brophy, president of District 2. The three

Pennsylvanians were united by radicalism, commitment to union democracy, and personal rectitude. Eager to build an anti-Lewis coalition,
Hapgood and Stiles wired Brophy, who was in Cleveland for the 1922
negotiations with operators, for his advice. "International officers will
have no opposition in coming election as it is impossible to defeat any
of them," advised Brophy by return wire. "It is your duty to use every
effort to cooperate with present international officials in the prosecution
of this strike. It is no time for men to talk about naming a ticket."
Only later did Hapgood and Stiles learn that their telegram to Brophy
had been intercepted by a Lewis agent, who dispatched the return
telegram signed Brophy. By the time the deception was uncovered, it
was too late to field a viable opposition candidate.

Although opposition to Lewis inside the UMW intensified after the
1922 election, his rivals continued to slay each other. The rising dissatisfaction among coal miners with Lewis's union policies prompted
William Z. Foster, a leader of the American Communist party and
founder of the Trade Union Educational League (TUEL), the party's
labor arm, to seek support among UMW members. Committed to
boring from within existing trade unions and antipathetic to all forms
of dualism, Foster's TUEL sought to create "progressive" cells, or blocs,
that would eventually capture control of "legitimate" unions. For Foster,
the UMW seemed the most desirable of targets; in 1923 it was not only
still the nation's largest union, but it also had a tradition of rank-and-
file militancy and political radicalism. Militants and radicals, moreover,
chafed under the cautious but autocratic Lewis leadership. To seize on
rank-and-file dissatisfaction with Lewis, Foster called a meeting of the
Progressive International Conference of the United Mine Workers of
America to convene in Pittsburgh on June 2 and 3, 1923. Foster's
venture into the arcane world of coal miners' politics inadvertently
assisted John L. Lewis in the latter's struggle to achieve hegemony within
the UMW.

For every anti-Lewis union leader that Foster attracted, he repelled
one. None of the UMW officials that Foster vexed was angrier than
Frank Farrington. A conservative by instinct and a Republican by
choice, Farrington presided over the most radical of all the union districts. Customarily criticized by such socialists as Adolph Germer, John
Walker, and Duncan MacDonald, Farrington now worried about communist influence in Illinois. Consequently, he realized the impossibility
of fighting Lewis and communists simultaneously, and he chose to make
peace with the lesser of the evils: John L. Lewis. On May 21, 1923,
Farrington informed Lewis that unless "real believers" in the UMW
united, destructive elements would gain control and "the Red Flag will
be our standard, or else demoralization and division in the ranks . . .

will prevail." Further correspondence in late May and personal conferences early in June produced a Lewis-Farrington coalition aimed
against union radicals.

The Pittsburgh conference also split Lewis's Pennsylvania critics.
Among the participants at the conference were Powers Hapgood and
a second delegate from District 2, both of whom attended without the
approval of District President Brophy. Although the Pittsburgh conferees
had resolved to work within the UMW and to reject dual unionism,
Brophy, like Lewis, distrusted all communists and considered them by
definition to be dual unionists. He also suspected that Lewis would
characterize all participants in the Pittsburgh conference as dual unionists, apply constitutional sanctions against them, and thus split and
scatter progressive miners. That prospect combined with Brophy's utter
weariness from six years of ceaseless intraunion strife motivated him
to resign from District 2 leadership.

Brophy proved a good prophet indeed, for on July 11, 1923, Lewis
ordered him to discharge Hapgood and the other District 2 delegate in
attendance at Pittsburgh from union office because they, along with all
other participants in the progressive conference, had "treacherously
consort[ed] with the avowed enemies of our organization and participate[d] with them in their sinister and reprehensible activities." Pessi-
mism overwhelmed Brophy, who had decided as a member of the IEB
to fight Lewis's expulsion of alleged "dual unionists" but who nevertheless believed that in a year or two Lewis would crush all communists
and radicals inside the UMW.

The red-baiting of Hapgood, Howat, and other UMW men who
attended the Pittsburgh progressive conference temporarily left many
of Lewis's rivals in a state of shock. But they recovered quickly and
reorganized themselves to provide a substantial challenge to Lewis's
union leadership at the January–February 1924 coal miners' convention.
Behaving as opportunistically as their hated opponent, the insurgent
miners formed an alliance of traditional UMW left-wingers, communists, and anti-Lewis conservatives. Early in the convention this alliance
won a majority voice vote repudiating Lewis's right to appoint union
organizers and field officials. Whereas in the past insurgents customarily
demanded roll call votes after suffering defeats in oral balloting, in 1924
Lewis resorted to the roll call device and caused a convention uproar
when he announced that his power to appoint officials had been upheld
by a vote of 2,236 to 2,106. For the next hour the insurgents whistled,
stamped their feet, demanded a recount, raced up and down the aisles,
and engaged in fistfights.

The 1924 mine workers' convention ended as tumultuously as it had
begun. Lewis adjourned the session on Saturday, February 2 amid wild

disorder as rival factions struggled for physical possession of the platform. Defeated in yet another delegate vote, Alex Howat leaped to the stage only to be thrown off bodily; for the next fifteen minutes his supporters labored unsuccessfully to push Howat back up on the platform while Lewis's men formed a solid wall of opposition. In a final gesture to demonstrate his authority in the union, Lewis called his wife to his side for an impromptu reception on the auditorium's stage.

Never again after 1924 would Lewis preside at a UMW convention during which a substantial number of delegates challenged his power. Other threats to Lewis's hegemony in the union would arise—and for many of the same reasons—but they would pose far less danger to his rule. Indeed, each effort by insurgents to curtain Lewis's power resulted, ironically, in the expansion of the UMW president's authority. By 1930, Lewis would fashion a union whose constitution granted the chief executive autocratic power.

In the mid-1920s only one UMW district—No. 12 in Illinois—remained partially independent of Lewis. After Howat's defeat at the 1924 convention, the authority of the international union ran unchallenged throughout the Southwest. John Brophy's resignation as president of District 2 in 1923 led to his replacement by men much more susceptible to Lewis's influence. Frank Farrington of Illinois stood as the solitary obstacle to undiluted union power for John L. Lewis. If Frank Farrington could be made to disappear, reasoned Lewis, District 12 would become more amenable to international union discipline.

Farrington, however, could scarcely be red-baited or accused of promoting dual unionism. After all, he had allied with Lewis in 1923 to save the UMW from the "reds," and no more conservative or business-oriented trade unionist existed anywhere in the American labor movement. Unable to use his customary ploys, Lewis resorted to even more devious tactics.

The precise mechanics of Lewis's plan to purge Farrington remain something of a mystery. Certain facts, however, may be inferred from the actual course of events. Like Lewis, Farrington enjoyed the good life—fine clothes, fast cars, ample food, and association with corporate executives—and needed the income to buy it. Like Lewis, he also desired union power, a prospect beyond his reach by 1925–26. Unable to replace Lewis as UMW president, Farrington elected the good life. Before Lewis, nearly every top UMW official had eventually entered the employ of the coal operators as a labor relations executive with a high salary. Farrington proved true to that old UMW tradition by signing a contract on July 1, 1926 with the largest coal operator in Illinois—Styvesant "Jack" Peabody of the Peabody Coal Company—to serve as labor adviser for a three-year period beginning January 1, 1927, at an annual salary of $25,000 (three times Lewis's and five times his own union salary). The contract included a pledge from Farrington disclaiming all future office in District 12. Under the terms of the then-secret contract, Farrington would have his money, Peabody under-the-table influence in District 12, and Lewis one less union rival.

With the contract in his pocket and his future financially secure, Farrington left for a grand tour of Europe. While abroad, however, Farrington unexpectedly decided that he would take the money from Peabody and still serve as District 12 president. "The more I think of it," he wrote to Peabody on August 1, "the more firmly I am convinced that I can do the operators more good by continuing as president of the Illinois miners and I wish you would not make known the fact that I have signed a contract to work for you until we can talk it over."

Farrington's repudiation of his pledge to resign from union office led to a strange denouement for the Illinoisan. In late August John L. Lewis, who had the most to lose from Farrington's change of mind, made public the terms of the secret contract and demanded that Farrington either resign as president of District 12 or that the Illinois district executive board dismiss him from office. On August 30 Farrington resigned his district presidency and went to work for Peabody Coal as its labor consultant. Thus did Lewis remove his District 12 rival and forever taint his reputation among coal miners.

Not a single district official now threatened Lewis's authority. Had collective bargaining triumphs coincided with Lewis's political successes, his power might have gone unchallenged. But just as Lewis vanquished one union rival after another, the UMW lost one contract after another, and its membership and income declined sharply. Union setbacks prompted old and new critics of Lewis's leadership to seek a change in the administration of the UMW.

A group of trade union radicals and their sympathizers began to meet in the summer of 1926 to discuss plans to revitalize the UMW. At a meeting at John Brophy's home in Clearfield, Pennsylvania during the July 4 weekend, Powers Hapgood, Albert Coyle, left-wing editor of the Locomotive Engineers' *Journal,* and Art Shields, a communist journalist, discussed a plan to defeat Lewis in the December UMW election.

In the weeks that followed, Hapgood served as a link between Brophy and such communists as Jay Lovestone and William Z. Foster, who were eager to put a ticket into the field against Lewis. At Hapgood's insistence, the communists agreed to withdraw their own candidates if Brophy sought the UMW presidency. In August, Brophy took the leap, issuing an open letter criticizing Lewis's administration of the UMW and promising to organize the nonunion fields and, as his later campaign literature would stress, "Save the Union." The heart of Brophy's campaign policy encompassed aggressive organizing in the nonunion fields, nationalization of the coal mines, and the creation of a labor party—goals in harmony with communist policy.

Lewis could not and did not fight Brophy on the issues. By 1926 he had few organizing triumphs to proclaim, and no intelligent miners' leader dared publicly repudiate nationalization or a labor party. Instead, Lewis resorted to time-tested tactics. Searles closed the columns of the union journal to any news of the Brophy campaign, a host of minor officials appointed by Lewis and paid from the international treasury campaigned for him in the far-flung union districts, and, finally, Lewis red-baited Brophy, whose alliance with the communists made him an easy target. As usual, Lewis reduced every question to personalities and conspiracies.

Once again a purloined letter figured prominently in Lewis's strategy, this time correspondence between Albert Coyle and Powers Hapgood that discussed the communist role in Brophy's campaign. Setting the stage well by saving the Coyle-Hapgood letter for the October 1926 A.F. of L. convention, Lewis appeared on the platform as the central character in a trade union drama that pitted Americans against "reds." Reading from the Coyle-Hapgood letter, which discussed several prominent communists, Lewis pointed his finger at the convention gallery and at W. Z. Foster, "the arch priest of communism in the United States," who made annual visits to Russia to make his reports and receive his orders. "Never has a convention of the American Federation of Labor," reported the *New York Times,* "witnessed such an excoriating attack on communist attempts to 'bore from within and seize, control, and wreck the American labor movement' as marked today's session."

Lewis's campaign tactics not only assured his victory by a wide margin over Brophy, a triumph Brophy and his supporters later claimed was stolen at the ballot box, but they also once again divided the leftist opposition internally. In the spring of 1927, Hapgood, reflecting on what had happened to the insurgent campaign, lamented: What if the communists were friendly? "Must they always be told to go to hell and their cooperation refused in certain things in which every honest progressive believes merely because we differ from them in ultimate revolutionary ideology?"

Fresh from his victory over Brophy, Lewis turned the January 1927 UMW convention into a complete rout of union progressives. Among other actions, the convention raised President Lewis's salary by 50 percent to $12,000, barred communists from union membership, and eliminated from the constitution's preamble the phrase that miners were entitled to the "full social value of their product" and substituted instead the words "an equitable share of the fruits of their labor." Other convention actions exemplified Lewis's unchallenged authority. For the first time since the UMW was founded in 1890, the president's report to the delegates, in effect the union chief's state of the union address, was most notable for its brevity and lack of substantive information. Delegates ceded the IEB the right to levy assessments on union members without time limit—a right never before granted the international officials. Lewis, his fellow officers, and a majority of the delegates scrubbed the UMW clean of all taint of radicalism. Lewis repudiated nationalization of the coal mines and praised Hoover's program of voluntarism as the solution to the coal industry's ailments. The resolutions committee recommended against the recognition of Soviet Russia. By a large majority the delegates resolved to endorse the A.F. of L.'s nonpartisan political policy of rewarding labor's friends and punishing its enemies. So complete was Lewis's domination of the convention that a new rule denied delegates the right to amend a report or resolution until after it had been voted on. Insurgents were so scarce at the 1927 convention that for the first time in Lewis's tenure as president they lacked the strength to obtain roll call votes on crucial questions.

Lewis's behavior as convention chairman personified his autocratic power. To delegates who questioned him about Howat's status in the union, Lewis replied: "It does not make any difference what you think. The chair has ruled." When Howat himself asked for the right to speak, Lewis responded: "You will not, and you will sit down." When several delegates asked why the union had never released the full tabulation on its 1926 election, Lewis asserted that he did not feel like spending $10,000 just to please one communist miner (John Watt). In the same speech, he referred twice to "John Brophy and all his slimy friends." Shortly afterward, when Powers Hapgood asserted his right to be seated and speak as a delegate, Lewis ruled that Hapgood was not a member of the union and added: "Any man who thinks he can abuse the privilege of the convention and come here and defy the chairman . . . or the convention rules is merely a fool." Then, turning directly to Hapgood, Lewis observed: "If I hear another word from you you will be ejected from the convention and conducted to the street."

Lewis reserved his choicest rhetoric for Brophy, who had had the temerity to seek the union presidency. Because Brophy was also rash enough to criticize Lewis's policies and state that the union had lost power and members, Lewis accused him of having committed treason by providing the operators with information detrimental to the coal miners. "In the days when people were besieged in a walled city and a soldier got upon the top of the wall and called to the enemy that the people were weak," Lewis narrated, "they merely took his life and threw him off the wall to the dogs below. Here in these modern days we tolerate the lamentations of the timid and we even tolerate at times the words of a traitor . . . [but] I say . . . that the man who stands upon this platform and mouths mutterings of consolation to the enemies of this Union is nothing more nor less than a traitor."

Lewis carried the internal struggle directly against his critics. Lewis sympathizers entered Hapgood's hotel room during the convention and brutally beat the young insurgent. To Brophy's demand for a full tabulation of the 1926 union election results, Lewis responded that Brophy was simply pursuing the policy set by William Z. Foster and the communists. Any union members sympathetic to Brophy or the "Save the Union Campaign," which survived Brophy's electoral defeat, found themselves labeled as "reds" and expelled from the UMW as dual unionists. In May 1928 Lewis ordered the Nanty-Glo Pennsylvania union local to which Brophy belonged to oust the union critic for acting as dual unionist. By July 1928 any UMW member who failed to follow the Lewis line faced expulsion.

By the year 1928, then, Lewis had perfected the instruments of his union power: press, purse, and patronage. Ellis Searles edited the UMW *Journal* to suit Lewis. Granted the right by the 1927 convention to assess dues without fixed time limits, Lewis had won the additional financial resources needed to assure international union dominance over the scattered districts. William Green had long since departed as secretary-treasurer, and his successor, the deferential Tom Kennedy, lacked the will to challenge Lewis's cavalier style of spending union funds. At the 1927 convention, moreover, for the only time during the 1920s, no substantial group of delegates disputed Lewis's right to appoint international organizers, auditors, and fieldworkers—the men responsible for carrying Lewis's influence to the rank and file; the issue never even came to a vote.

The perfect union autocrat by 1928, Lewis ironically saw his external influence in ruins. Everywhere he turned during that final year of America's prosperity, Lewis was at a loss. His corporate and Republican party allies deserted him by the droves. Operators, who had once praised Lewis as a labor statesman and even weighed hiring him as director of an employers' association, now refused to deal with him or his union. Politicians, who hitherto had sought his advice and encouraged his political ambitions, now rejected Lewis's proposals to save the coal industry, and Herbert Hoover refused even to consider him for appointment as secretary of labor. It is to this aspect of Lewis's failure as union leader in the 1920s that we now must turn our attention.

7

The Collapse of the Union, 1925–28

By the late 1920s the bituminous coal industry was a disaster area. Domestic production of bituminous declined steadily, falling in 1927 nearly 60 million tons below the 1920 level. So, too, did the size of the labor force, dropping between 1920 and 1927 from more than 700,000 miners to approximately 575,000. Yet a persistent surplus of labor forced the typical miner to work only 142 to 220 days a year, ordinarily closer to the lower figure. This meant that despite the high minimum daily union wage of $7.50, hundreds of thousands of coal miners earned less than an adequate annual income.

Four states—West Virginia, Pennsylvania, Illinois, and Kentucky—produced about 70 percent of the United States' supply of soft coal, and in three of those states the UMW had been shattered by the end of 1925. Only Illinois—a state with relatively large, mechanized, efficient mines and with markets partially protected by economic geography—remained a union stronghold. Unionized operators in Pennsylvania, Ohio, and, to a lesser extent, Indiana could not compete successfully for markets with nonunion operators in Kentucky, West Virginia, or their own states. Consequently, union operators either went out of business or hired nonunion miners.

The UMW's financial records, officers' reports, and convention proceedings attest to the organization's decay. After the 1924 convention, the president, the vice-president, and the secretary-treasurer kept silent about membership trends. To maintain the fiction of a large, healthy union, the UMW continued, even after its membership had fallen below one hundred thousand, to pay per capita dues to the A.F. of L. on a paper membership in excess of four hundred thousand. In 1927 the union expended more than $1,500,000 on relief, and the following year more than $3 million. So little remained in the UMW treasury that in the two succeeding depression years of 1929–30 the union spent a total of $38,500 on aid to the unemployed.

In February 1924, President Coolidge, Commerce Secretary Hoover, the nation's press, and especially the financial journals had hailed John L. Lewis as a labor statesman. Such praise had been occasioned by the Jacksonville agreement of 1924 from which everyone theoretically benefited. Union operators were freed from annual strikes, the UMW won long-term security in its Central Competitive Field strongholds, and consumers gained a steady supply of "cheap" coal.

Economic realities promptly dashed the hopes of northern operators, UMW leaders, and federal officials for stability in the soft-coal industry. Union producers lost sales to operators who paid wages 30 to 50 percent lower than the union scale. Companies that met the price of competition from nonunion mines often did so only at the cost of losing money. By the summer of 1924 soft-coal operators, especially in Pennsylvania and Ohio where the competition for markets was fiercest, began to demand revisions in the Jacksonville wage scale. "Some operators," Lewis informed K. C. Adams in August, "are still muttering about the necessity of modifying the Jacksonville agreement. I shall do my best to prevent their dreams in this respect from coming true."

By early 1925 the union operators' desire for a general downward revision of the wage scales spread west into Indiana and Illinois. Commerce Secretary Hoover, an architect of the Jacksonville agreement, allegedly informed Lewis at a conference in mid–February 1925 that the union wage scale was "uneconomic." Such advice was neither pleasing nor news to Lewis who, according to *Cushing's Survey,* a business newsletter, bluntly informed Hoover: "You got me into this mess; it's up to you to help me out. You dictated the Jacksonville scale; it's up to you to end it."

But there seemed to be no alternative to the Jacksonville agreement for either Lewis or Hoover. How, asked *Cushing's Survey* on February 19, could Hoover offer the operators a compromise "without handing to them a club and extending to them an invitation to beat Mr. Lewis' brains." Lewis, to be sure, could not confess his own weakness, request a wage revision, and suffer repudiation by his rank and file. Nor could Hoover repudiate the Jacksonville scale without harming his own party's political credibility among coal miners and other organized workers. Lewis thus reaffirmed to operators his determination not to revise the Jacksonville scale, and Hoover remained silent.

Union operators had only one choice under the circumstances, and they took it. On March 10, 1925, Secretary of Labor James Davis reported to President Coolidge that mine operators had started to transfer many of their operations to nonunion properties, that employers in the outlying districts had openly repudiated the Jacksonville agreement and cut wages 25 to 40 percent, and that most union mines might close after April 1. The operator's intention, concluded Davis, was to starve the miners and their union into submission to a reduced wage scale.

Lewis expected some of the ills that beset the soft-coal industry. A gambler by instinct, he had decided to suffer small immediate losses in order eventually to enjoy immense gains. The Jacksonville agreement, he believed, would drive hundreds of inefficient mines and perhaps two hundred thousand surplus miners out of the trade. Lewis's courageous public commitment to a high wage scale temporarily pleased rank-and-file miners even as they lost their jobs. "Before we started this fight," Lewis told a *New York Sun* reporter in May 1925, "we measured our own strength and that of our opponents. We expect losses, perhaps heavy losses, but we are confident of victory in the end."

Lewis's gamble depended for success on two variables he failed to control. First, he assumed that the more efficient unionized northern mines, as a consequence of their higher productivity and lower union labor costs, could easily compete for markets with nonunion properties that he believed to be inefficient and labor intensive. Second, he expected the federal government to enable union operators to share information about costs, prices, and markets without fear of prosecution under antitrust laws; he also assumed that the Interstate Commerce Commission would revise freight rates to favor union over nonunion coal. And he expected the Coolidge administration to defend the UMW. From its position of strength in the largely mechanized northern mines, the UMW would appear so powerful, Lewis informed the *Sun* reporter, "that there will be no coal miner in the country willing to stay outside the union ranks." But few northern union mines outside of Illinois could compete with their nonunion Appalachian competitors, and federal officials seemed more concerned about consumers and coal operators than the needs of the United Mine Workers. For Hoover, Davis, and Coolidge, indeed for almost all federal officials, the nonunion mines served to insure consumers a steady supply of coal and acted as a restraint on potential union monopoly.

Events in West Virginia and western Pennsylvania soon ruined Lewis's strategy. The UMW president had committed all his organization's dwindling resources to a struggle to retain the northern West Virginia coalfields for the union. Still, disaster befell the West Virginia coal miners, whose union membership declined in two years from 75,000 to 10,000 — 7,500 of whom survived on union benefits. A similar collapse in union membership followed in western Pennsylvania, where the two largest companies — Consolidation Coal and Pittsburgh Coal — repudiated the Jacksonville agreement, cut wages across the board, and broke off relations with the UMW. From these two giant companies, the open shop spread across the Pennsylvania coalfields, leaving the UMW by the fall of 1925 with a corporal's guard of members in the state.

Lewis reacted by publishing a book, *The Miner's Fight for American Standards*. Published in the early summer of 1925, the book distilled Lewis's knowledge of the coal industry, revealed his values, and promoted his solution to the ills of soft coal. Nothing in the book would have surprised coal miners or operators—it was not written for them. Instead, it was intended to win public favor for Lewis's program and influence federal officials to rescue the union from its economic predicament. Not surprisingly, Lewis personally sent a copy to Herbert Hoover.

The extent to which Lewis wrote any large portion of the volume remains subject to doubt. Throughout his career in the labor movement, Lewis relied on a stable of ghostwriters to prepare his speeches, essays, and, one might assume, book. Three men in particular—Ellis Searles, K. C. Adams, and W. Jett Lauck—composed the bulk of the material that appeared under Lewis's name. Lauck probably wrote the sections of *The Miner's Fight* that analyzed the economic relationship between the soft-coal and railroad industries. K. C. Adams perhaps filled the book with its purple passages. But the tone was vintage Lewis.

The book can only be understood in relation to the collapse of the Jacksonville agreement and the dominant values of Calvin Coolidge's America. It was, to be sure, a propaganda piece for middle-class Americans who believed with their president that the business of America was business. The book assured its readers that the United Mine Workers was neither new nor revolutionary—that it was an American institution founded on American characteristics. "When the United Mine Workers of America declares that it will take no backward step, this great union," proclaimed Lewis, "speaks in unison with the heart beats of America, and puts into economic language the very essence of the American spirit." Free enterprise, he reassured citizens vexed by trade unionism, guarantees the ultimate prosperity of all by encouraging each man to better his own condition. Trade unions and corporations serve the system as phenomena of capitalism that share an economic aim: gain. Lewis asked every thinking businessman and American to support the UMW "because it proposes to allow natural economic laws free play in the production and distribution of coal." The Jacksonville agreement, Lewis suggested, had subjected the mining industry to "the law of supply and demand" and thus was working an economic cure through elimination of marginal mines.

Lewis then turned to the book's real subject matters: the preservation of the Jacksonville agreement, the maintenance of high wage rates, and the total unionization of the coal industry. This part of the work, most likely written by Jett Lauck, actually rejected classical economics and its most important tenet: the law of supply and demand. Now Lewis informed readers that free competition in the marketplace must not be allowed to drive down wage rates and that any voluntary reduction in union rates would only induce further cuts in nonunion mines, igniting a cycle of ever-decreasing wages. The American system, felt Lewis, was based on expensive labor, not cheap labor—labor that could earn enough to purchase the products of American industry and provide the economy with an immense domestic market. "Those who seek to cheapen coal by cheapening men," he wrote, "seek to reverse the evolution of American industry. It cannot be done." Wage reductions, he concluded, not only would harm the domestic economy, but they would also retard the process of reorganization in the coal industry by allowing marginal high-cost, low-wage mines to remain in production.

Not a fool, Lewis realized that his commitment to high wages depended on total unionization of the industry. Hence the UMW president demanded that the federal government join with the miners' union in extending the protection of the American Constitution and American law to the remotest corners of the country—especially West Virginia, Kentucky, Alabama, and western Pennsylvania—because "what Lincoln once said of the nation applies with poignant force to the coal industry today: It cannot live 'half slave [nonunion] and half free.'"

Because Lewis desperately needed Hoover's support, he filled his book with concepts dear to the heart of the commerce secretary. The UMW, Lewis promised Hoover, "is as practical as the most efficient business man or production engineer, and its atmosphere is fatal to glittering generalities." Employers and unions must cooperate voluntarily, suggested Lewis, to eliminate the inefficient and unscientific, to discharge their social duties successfully, and to provide profits without exploitation. Only when "cooperative capitalism" replaced "competitive capitalism" would the nation's basic industries achieve stability and dependability. Lewis, like Hoover, looked forward to the day when businessmen, federal officials, and trade unionists could function cooperatively and use their ingenuity and modern science to create a harmonious corporate society based on high wages, mass consumption, and steady profits.

Lewis never retreated from certain ideas that he expounded so forcefully in his 1925 book. American civilization, he always believed, was founded on high wages achieved by substituting capital for labor, machinery for human hands. A high-wage, mass-consumption economy in turn necessitated total unionization of the labor force. Lewis knew that unscrupulous employers abounded and were quick to cut wages in order to increase their profits. Only if "responsible" employers, public officials, and labor leaders allied to promote trade unionism throughout the economy could twentieth-century enlightened capitalism be safeguarded from retrograde nineteenth-century capitalism.

Much to Lewis's chagrin, his book and his ideas met a hostile response. The critic of archaic capitalism found himself accused of being an antiquarian labor leader. "Lewis," wrote the author of a special *New York Times* feature on labor leaders after Gompers in June, 1925, "though only 45 years old, represents the older type of labor executive, autocratic, more aggressive than penetrating, unreceptive to the newer principles, a protagonist of simple unionism." Still worse, Hoover kept silent about *The Miner's Fight,* federal authorities failed to guarantee the Jacksonville agreement, and the United Mine Workers continued to decay.

Unable to sustain his cause through propaganda, Lewis resorted to threats of economic warfare. On June 30, 1925, speaking to delegates to the tri-district anthracite convention, he accused the Pennsylvania Railroad, the Consolidation Coal Company, the Pittsburgh Coal Company, and the combined Rockefeller-Mellon interests of a conspiracy to break the Jacksonville agreement and threatened a national coal strike unless operators implemented the 1924 contract.

Primarily concerned with the collapse of his union in the soft-coal fields, Lewis plotted to use its strength in anthracite to pressure federal officials. By the summer of 1925, anthracite remained the UMW's only stronghold outside of Illinois. A strike by hard-coal miners, he assumed, would create a crisis in the densely populated northeastern states, which relied on anthracite for domestic heat, and cause problems for incumbent politicians, primarily Republican, at the November elections. Lewis apparently offered the anthracite operators a long-term contract that preserved existing conditions provided they introduced the checkoff (a demand that cost no money); yet he was not unhappy when employers rejected his proposal.

For almost two months, beginning on July 9, a joint conference of operators and miners negotiated in Atlantic City. While Lewis bargained with the employers, his wife and the children enjoyed the sand, sun, and sea. By early August, when federal mediators joined the deadlocked conference, Lewis's strategy had emerged. Because anthracite operators refused to accept any of the union's demands and insisted that they be submitted to binding arbitration, Lewis prepared for a long strike. Simultaneously he demanded that federal officials act against soft-coal operators who had violated the Jacksonville agreement. Lewis thought it only fair that the same federal influence applied to secure the original 1924 agreement be exerted to have it respected. Demanding federal intervention in soft coal, Lewis rejected it in anthracite.

In that frame of mind, Lewis left Atlantic City in mid-August for headquarters in his favorite Philadelphia hotel, the Bellevue-Stratford, a site closer to the anthracite fields. For another two weeks he went through the motions of seeking labor peace, but on August 24 he advised K. C. Adams: "The region will shut down on September 1st." And so it did, as 150,000 hard-coal miners answered their union's strike call and began what would be the longest strike in the history of the anthracite industry. Lewis made it clear that the federal government could not influence the anthracite negotiations unless it entered them with its hands cleansed by the act of publicly reprimanding those bituminous operators who had violated the Jacksonville agreement. Lewis used a mass meeting in West Virginia to remind federal officials of their obligation to the UMW. The industry has a right to expect, he observed, "that the moral influence and power of those same government officials" who promoted the Jacksonville agreement "be utilized to preserve the integrity of the agreement and to maintain . . . the tranquility of the coal industry."

Hoover now clearly feared that the UMW president desired to drag the administration into the bituminous controversy. "Mr. Lewis's personal attitude toward you is not cordial," one colleague informed Hoover. "He evidently expected that you would urge the operators to observe the Jacksonville agreement." In fact Lewis expected that Hoover and President Coolidge would urge Treasury Secretary Andrew Mellon, whose brother's company, Pittsburgh Coal, had initiated the repudiation of the 1924 agreement in western Pennsylvania, to act in the matter. But no one in the Coolidge administration intended to satisfy Lewis.

Confronted by a stalemate in anthracite, where the operators still demanded arbitration, and stymied in Washington, Lewis made public his case for federal intervention in bituminous. On November 22 he released to the press a letter addressed to President Coolidge demanding that the administration enforce the Jacksonville agreement. The letter appeared in the newspapers before Coolidge received it.

Lewis's action stimulated cabinet discussion among Hoover, Mellon, and Davis, and President Coolidge. The results scarcely gratified Lewis. As drafted by Hoover and amended by Davis for Coolidge's signature, the official federal reply to Lewis's letter of November 22 denied that the administration had been a party to the Jacksonville agreement. It deplored any breach of contract by operators but observed that "the government not being a party to contracts has no status in enforcement." Yet the government paradoxically warned Lewis that if his union struck to enforce contracts, it would violate a binding agreement and "be a fatal blow at most collective bargaining." Federal officials suggested that Lewis take his grievance to court. Hoover also personally insisted that the UMW accept arbitration to settle the anthracite dispute. Hoover honestly but wrongly believed that Lewis would support the proposals because "he has a sense of responsibility of his group to these questions."

Lewis's frustration now broke through as he remarked to a newspaperman about President Coolidge's forthcoming statement: "No man can rebuke me with impunity." Although perhaps only the reaction of a tired man and hardly a threat to the president, the comment disclosed Lewis's deep feeling of hurt. Hoover's suggestion that Lewis go to court infuriated the labor leader. Every lawyer the union consulted advised that no law favors the union. Unless prompt federal action saved the union, operators' repudiation of the contract would "spread like a rotten spot in an apple until the whole Jacksonville agreement is consumed." Yet Lewis was helpless. Deserted by his allies among Republican officeholders and his former admirers among coal operators, he could not retard the UMW losses in soft coal.

With what little strength he and his union retained, Lewis fought to the bitter end in anthracite. Relying on complete loyalty among the hard-coal miners, Lewis vowed to hold them out indefinitely, and he warned the operators that "they cannot break this strike." At the end of November an informant told Hoover: "The men may cuss their leaders . . . and the women become sorer than they are now, but there is nothing to indicate revolt or break." From late November until a settlement was achieved in mid-February, Lewis held fast to secure a compromise agreement suggested by Governor Gifford Pinchot that included a five-year contract based on existing wages, voluntary arbitration that might raise but not lower wages, and a voluntary checkoff. The operators, for their part, continued to insist on binding arbitration of all questions in dispute.

Drained by four and a half months of industrial warfare, anthracite operators and miners declared a truce in mid-February. Exercising his singular flair for the dramatic, Lewis signed a new contract with the anthracite operators on his forty-sixth birthday, February 12, 1926. At the Bellevue-Stratford Hotel in a flower-filled room that included a huge birthday basket of roses sent by W. W. Inglis, chairman of the Anthracite Operators' Negotiating Committee, Lewis showed reporters a birthday gift, a copy of Carl Sandburg's *Life of Lincoln,* inscribed: "The Lincoln of Labor." Sighing with relief at the achievement of a strike settlement, he remarked: "Some birthday!" Actually, except for promising anthracite miners five years of fixed wages, the 1926 agreement offered little else. Yet this minimal achievement in collective bargaining was the one bright element in an otherwise gloomy scene for the UMW and John L. Lewis.

Even this one bright spot soon darkened. Markets lost by anthracite coal during the long strike were never recaptured. Between 1926 and 1930 anthracite production declined almost 25 percent. By February 1929 an article in the *Nation* correctly noted, "anthracite . . . is a critically sick industry. A pall of gloom hangs over the sections of Pennsylvania which are dependent on the mining of coal."

In the year 1926 Lewis faced only bleak prospects. A Bureau of Mines survey based on the conditions in the soft coal industry as of December 31, 1925, showed that 65.3 percent of all soft coal produced came from nonunion mines and 61.3 percent of all miners worked without a union contract. Only his personal philosophy "that events run in cycles and that circumstances repeat themselves" sustained Lewis times that must have tried a union leader's soul.

With the future in doubt, union representatives and operators assembled on February 15, 1927 in Miami to negotiate a new contract. On the opening day, despite intense heat that wilted many a collar, John L. Lewis, reported a newspaper correspondent, "a picturesque orator with his heavy mane of reddish hair and thundering voice—a massive figure of a miner—spoke for more than a hour." Lewis could have orated for ten hours and it would have made no difference, because operators and union delegates engaged in a dialogue of the deaf. The union negotiating team had been instructed by the 1927 UMW convention to secure the best possible contract based on no reduction in wages. Employers, however, refused to bargain about any other issues until the union acceded to a downward revision of the Jacksonville wage scale and accepted the principle that wages should be automatically adjusted to changing prices for coal. Neither party to the conference being willing to compromise the issue of wages, the Miami meeting adjourned indefinitely on February 22, and the operators, the union, and federal officials planned for a nationwide soft-coal strike set for April 1, 1927.

The 1927 strike, caused because the UMW had no alternative to its enunciated policy of "no backward step" on wages, ruined the miners' union everywhere outside of Illinois and Iowa. Already extinguished in West Virginia, Kentucky, Virginia, Maryland, Alabama, and most of central Pennsylvania, the union struggled to hold on in western Pennsylvania and Ohio. In western Pennsylvania, coal companies evicted striking miners from their company homes, cut off credit at company stores, used private armed guards and state police to turn mine towns into fortresses, and imported strikebreakers by the thousands—including many black miners from Tennessee and Alabama, whose arrival intensified local bitterness.

His union army a tattered remnant by the fall of 1927, Lewis sought external assistance. He had no choice; the UMW had lost its economic muscle as the 1927 statistics of soft-coal production revealed. Despite the strike, the Labor Department reported that "the coal now in sight and to be produced this year will equal the total production for 1925 and surpass the total production of 1921, 1922, 1924." At Lewis's urging, A.F. of L. President William Green convened a special convention in Pittsburgh to assist the UMW. Attended by more than three hundred A.F. of L. representatives including the federation's most influential leaders, the conference resulted in a resolution to call upon all international unions to send money, materials, and organizers to assist the strikers; to instruct the A.F. of L. executive council to confer with President Coolidge about the "intolerable situation" in Pennsylvania; and to appoint a committee to remonstrate with the governor of Pennsylvania about the role of the state police in breaking the strike. At a time when mine operators violated civil liberties wholesale, the A.F. of L. delegates beseeched coal miners to observe the law "and to pay no heed to power assumed by those who are unauthorized under the law to limit, circumscribe, or repress, their rights as citizens."

Just as pleas to coal miners to obey the law exposed the American labor movement's flaccidity in the face of repression, so, too, did the request of labor leaders that the Coolidge administration mediate the coal strike reveal obsequiousness. On November 17, Green, fellow executive council members, and Lewis called on Coolidge, who shunted them off to his least influential cabinet member, Labor Secretary James J. Davis. A second conference with the president on November 21 proved equally fruitless.

Lewis now found himself in a completely new situation. In the past, especially during the coal strikes of 1919 and 1922 and the negotiations preceding the Jacksonville agreement, it had been federal officials and, to a lesser extent, mine operators who urged public mediation or arbitration. Then an affluent, large, and stable UMW played the reluctant guest at government-sponsored bargaining sessions. Now Lewis acted the ardent suitor, wooing federal officials with every wile at his command. Rejected by Coolidge and neglected by Hoover, Lewis relied on Labor Secretary Davis to serve as matchmaker for a new relationship between an ardent union and a frigid operators' group.

On December 9, 1927, Davis telegrammed all the coal operators and UMW officials in central and western Pennsylvania, northern West Virginia, and Ohio asking them to attend a conference on December

13 at his office. Speaking for his union, Lewis accepted the invitation with alacrity. But the largest mine operators either sent no response or rejected Secretary Davis's invitation. A second and third telegram from Davis to the operators elicited no better response. Consequently, the December 13 conference proved farcical. A full UMW delegation, including Lewis, Murray, and Kennedy, assembled in Davis's office. Only eleven operators (compared to fifteen union men), mostly from smaller companies, attended. Three days of separate meetings among federal officials, union men, and operators, as well as joint sessions, led nowhere.

After his conference adjourned on December 15, Davis learned further from operators why they declined to bargain with the UMW. If Lewis knows any other way to unionize Pennsylvania and Ohio other than through the wage cut proposed by operators at the Miami conference, wrote F. E. Taplin, "I would like to have him tell me how it can be done." There is simply no way, he concluded, that union wages can exceed nonunion rates by 50 percent when nonunion mines provide the nation with all the coal it needs. A large operator linked to the steel industry, John A. Topping, informed the secretary that his proposal for a conference had come too late, "as there are now too many non-Union men employed in Union fields to make *any conference on wages with Lewis and his crowd practical,* as no employer is going to take back Union miners and displace non-union workers."

By 1928 the UMW was in a headlong race to oblivion. By spring 1928 the UMW scarcely existed anywhere in the Appalachian fields; Pennsylvania and Ohio had gone the way of West Virginia, Kentucky, and Alabama. From a high of more than five hundred thousand bituminous members in 1921–22, the UMW membership had fallen to perhaps eighty thousand by mid-1928, two-thirds of whom were in only one district: Illinois. And even in District 12, its last soft-coal stronghold, the UMW was in retreat. Not only did Lewis surrender completely the union's policy of refusing to negotiate separate district agreements in the Central Competitive Field, but he also relinquished his edict of "No backward step." Those districts, such as District 12, that still had agreements to renegotiate on April 1, 1928, were advised to accept the best terms offered. "Under the circumstances confronting us," Lewis informed Jett Lauck on July 26, 1928, "we had no alternative than to amend our policy." By then, however, Lewis had little to save, for his organization as an effective trade union was dead everywhere except Illinois.

Having outlasted all his union rivals by 1928, Lewis was bereft of external influence. One hope remained—the election of Herbert Hoover as president, and to that objective Lewis committed himself in the 1928 election campaign. On the evening of October 17, Lewis appeared on a national radio network under the auspices of the Republican National Committee, to deliver a major address for Herbert Hoover. In his speech, Lewis linked Hoover to the economic program expounded in *The Miner's Fight*. In his five years as Secretary of Commerce, Hoover had, Lewis informed his listeners, established a "new economic order" in which higher wages, greater consumer power, and a rising standard of living created a domestic market that insured prosperity. "Industry and trade," Lewis asserted, "must be released from the restrictions of the anti-trust laws so that the maximum economies in production and distribution may be made possible." Now government must enable employers to introduce coordinated industrial planning and work toward the elimination of unemployment, "a necessary condition to the permanent prosperity of modern industry and of the country as a whole." To continue the "economic revolution" begun in 1923 and insure the elimination of poverty itself, American voters must, intoned Lewis, elect Herbert Hoover as the next president of the United States. Republicans were so pleased with Lewis's radio address that they published it in pamphlet form under the title *Hoover's Tonic Safest for Industry* and distributed it widely among workers.

The UMW president expected compensation for his endorsement of Hoover. As president, Hoover could, reasoned Lewis, urge Congress to pass legislation that would stabilize the soft-coal industry, foster the industrial cooperation that operators refused to provide themselves, and mandate a place in the system for organized labor. That prospect, however, offered only a long-term solution to Lewis's predicament.

Lewis, ever the opportunist, saw a quicker way to turn failure into success. As soon as the presidential election was over, Lewis eagerly campaigned for appointment as secretary of labor. Working through Dan G. Smith, chairman of the Republican party National Labor Committee, Lewis contacted congressmen, senators, bankers, and businessmen on his own behalf. By mid-January Hoover was deluged with telegrams and letters recommending that Lewis be appointed secretary of labor. Among the more prominent backers of the UMW president were W. Averell Harriman and E. N. Foss, former governor of Massachusetts. When Lewis heard no news by the end of January 1929, he instructed Jett Lauck to seek a private interview with Hoover concerning the cabinet position.

Lewis's campaign had been in vain, for he had completely misread Hoover. Thinking himself the labor leader closest to the economic, political, and social ideas of the new Republican president, Lewis expected the appointment. Hoover, however, had other ideas about John L. Lewis, as the president-elect revealed to an industrialist friend troubled by rumors that Lewis might be appointed secretary of labor. "You need have no fears in the direction you mention," Hoover assured his friend.

The plight of the UMW and the American coal miner in 1928 presaged the fate of the nation under Herbert Hoover. As affluent Americans celebrated the victory of "the Great Engineer," coal miners vainly sought work, burdened local relief agencies, and, sometimes, starved. As the universe of the American coal miner collapsed, his union and its leader watched impotently.

The economic circumstances that shattered Lewis's union, turned his corporate allies into enemies, and reduced his political influence had no apparent impact on his private or family life. Lewis continued to live well, maintain three homes in Springfield, drive a large Cadillac, and support an extended family on the payroll of the union and the Indianapolis bank he headed.

Myrta, too, suffered no diminution in what had become her accustomed standard of living. Lewis's wife and children traveled with him during the summer, although they ordinarily returned to Springfield for the school year, where Kathryn and John Jr. attended the local public schools. As a teenager Kathryn developed the traits that made her life so burdensome. She was enormously overweight, bore little attraction for the opposite sex, felt uncomfortable among female companions, and lived increasingly in a world bounded by her family and her father's career. Aside from occasional newspaper photos showing him at play on the beach at Atlantic City, John Jr. remained the family's invisible member, seldom mentioned by his father, and, unlike his older sister, totally shielded from his father's trade union universe.

Lewis was very much a man of the American 1920s. Not only the president of a prosperous bank, according to a business newsletter of February 1925 he was also "one of the wisest small traders that ever takes a flier in the stock market. His success . . . shows that he knows economics far better than do nine out of ten coal operators. And, he is making more money for himself today than are ninety-five out of a hundred operators."

Had Lewis desired merely a substantial income, a prosperous family, and influential associates, he might have been pleased with his status in 1929.

8

The Nadir, 1929–32

Life worsened for coal miners after November 1929 as economic depression paralyzed the entire nation. With rising unemployment and a shrinking consumer market, railroad traffic diminished, steel mills cut production, and utility companies transmitted less power. In a marketplace already glutted with soft coal, national depression spelled disaster for mine operators and their employees.

By 1932 average hourly earnings for soft-coal miners had fallen to fifty cents, and in the following year almost one-third of the nation's mines paid their workers less than $2.50 a day. In the absence of the union and its checkweighman, mine managers in effect reduced wages by crediting miners with less tonnage than they produced. Miners who rebelled at company exploitation heard the footsteps of the "barefoot man" whom folklorist George Korson learned about. "There's a barefoot, hungry man outside waiting for your job," miners told him.

The plight of the union paralleled the fate of the coal miner. By 1932 little remained of what had once been the proudest trade union in the United States. Unionism had been erased as a functioning institution from the coalfields of West Virginia, Virginia, Maryland, Kentucky, Tennessee, and Alabama. Pennsylvania, which once included more than one hundred thousand members in its two primary soft-coal districts, counted less than fifteen hundred. Ohio's hitherto prosperous District 6 had lost nearly its entire dues-paying membership. The outlying districts of Iowa, Missouri, Kansas, Oklahoma, Montana, Wyoming, New Mexico, and Washington counted their members by the hundreds. And the gem of the union, Illinois District 12, as we will see, had been shattered by corruption, purges, provisionalism, insurgency, open rebellion, and dual unionism.

How the union paid its international officers and met its other financial obligations seems miraculous. The total union payroll declined by more than $200,000 between 1920 and 1930, with the greatest decrease coming after 1924. In 1929 and 1930 the union practically ceased financial aid to striking and unemployed miners, such expenditures falling from more than $3 million in 1928 to just over $17,000 a year later. Between $50,000 and $60,000 was saved simply by not calling the regular convention scheduled for 1929 and by postponing indefinitely all future conventions.

Yet Lewis cut expenditures shrewdly. Few of the cuts diminished the union president's authority or patronage. Reductions in manpower, materials, and miscellaneous expenses occurred proportionately more at the district than the international level. Economy, in this instance, perpetuated and enlarged the power of the union president. So, too, did the spread of provisionalism among the decaying union districts as Lewis appointees replaced elected district officers. Districts without dues-paying members, in West Virginia, Kentucky, Tennessee, and Alabama among other states, existed only by virtue of funds and officials dispatched to them by Lewis; Lewis's appointees also served as convention delegates and always voted with the administration. Yet Lewis's economic and administrative adjustments to depression barely kept the UMW alive.

Although the international union administration survived from 1929 through 1933, the UMW could do little to protect the American coal miner. Lewis's loss of mastery and the collapse of his union induced fresh challenges to his power from opportunistic union careerists, old UMW left-wingers who romanticized the union's pre-Lewis past, and militant communists. Paradoxically, rather than checking Lewis's influence in the union, in the end these challengers enhanced the UMW president's power. Opponents who sought to restore trade union democracy instead hastened the establishment of a more perfect union autocracy.

The most significant challenge to Lewis's authority came from Illinois District 12, the last bastion of union strength for coal miners and the one district over which the UMW president lacked complete control. District 12 officials demanded autonomy in their relations with international officers and, as the spokesmen for more than two-thirds of the UMW's dues-paying membership, represented a real threat to Lewis's power. John H. Walker, Frank Farrington, and Adolph Germer retained considerable influence in District 12, and such other critics of Lewis as John Brophy, Powers Hapgood, and Alex Howat also intrigued in Illinois. As the UMW declined, critics blamed Lewis. "For downright blundering, mad, unreasoning, stupid, destructive, and disloyal leadership," Farrington asserted in a privately published pamphlet, "Lewis's action has never been equalled by any leader in the organized labor movement of America."

Lewis found swift and certain means to strike back at his critics in Illinois. Corruption and chicanery among officials of one of the Illinois subdistricts—No. 9 in Franklin County, the most productive coal county in the state and the union's largest subdistrict—gave Lewis his opportunity. On June 14, 1929, ostensibly acting at the request of Franklin County miners, Lewis suspended Subdistrict 9's officers, appointed his own men in their place, and established a provisional administration under the direct supervision of the international office.

Lewis next moved against District 12 officials. Early in September 1929, Lewis summoned two of the suspended subdistrict officers to his union's Indianapolis headquarters and obtained from them a confession linking District 12 officials directly to the alleged corruption in Franklin County. With this confession in hand, Lewis purged Harry Fishwick and other elected District 12 officials. On October 10, 1929, Lewis suspended the charter of District 12, removed its officials, and replaced them with a provisional administration responsible solely to himself.

District 12's elected leaders promptly fought back. They went to court to enjoin Lewis from establishing a provisional district, and they recruited prominent allies. John Brophy, inactive in union affairs since his defeat in the 1926 UMW election and his subsequent banishment, returned to the struggle. By November 1929, according to William Mitch, coal miners in his own state of Indiana were in a fever heat of turmoil, and the popular thing was to denounce union leaders. The turmoil in the miners' union was intensified by an Illinois state court decision that in January 1930 ruled in favor of District 12 and prohibited Lewis from establishing a provisional government and removing elected officers without adhering to the UMW's constitutional rules concerning the filing of formal charges and hearings.

Meantime, Farrington and Howat and such other enemies of Lewis as Walker, Brophy, Germer, and Oscar Ameringer sought control of the existing United Mine Workers. The UMW insurgents plotted at a secret meeting in Chicago attended by all the above and Sidney Hillman, president of the Amalgamated Clothing Workers of America, a trade union that itself had originated as a result of an internal organizational schism. The strategy they chose paralleled the action taken by Sidney Hillman's union fifteen years earlier. Instead of deciding to found a new miners' union, they accused Lewis of violating the UMW constitution and leading an illegitimate organization. They asserted that because Lewis had not held an international union convention in 1929 as mandated by the constitution, the UMW lacked an international constitution and officers empowered to call conventions or administer union rules. Lewis's challengers thus called their own convention to reestablish the "true" United Mine Workers of America.

At their Chicago conclave, the insurgents wisely chose a slate of prospective officers. Howat was slated for the vice-presidency, a position carrying visibility but not power. For the two primary administrative posts, president and secretary-treasurer, the insurgents selected John H. Walker and John Brophy. Walker could be charged with neither personal ambition nor selfish motives, because he had to relinquish his secure and prestigious office as president of the Illinois Federation of Labor in order to serve the insurgent coal miners.

The UMW insurgents' strategy seemed ingenious. Rather than commit the sin of dual unionism, they claimed to be rescuing the real United Mine Workers from the usurper John L. Lewis and his corrupt machine. They chose three candidates for international office, two of whom, Walker and Brophy, appeared selfless; and before establishing their own UMWA at a convention scheduled to meet on March 10, 1930, in Springfield, Illinois, the insurgents offered a compromise to John L. Lewis. They suggested that Lewis join with them in convening a special convention attended only by delegates representing active locals, whose credentials would be screened by a committee appointed by the A.F. of L. executive council; that William B. Wilson and William Green serve as the convention's presiding officers; that a firm of certified accountants audit the books of the international union and District 12; and that officers responsible for any irregularities found should resign. If Lewis accepted those conditions, the insurgents promised to postpone their convention scheduled for March 10 and to seek instead a harmonious solution to the union's internal difficulties.

Lewis planned no compromise with his opponents. Instead, he looked forward to routing them. No sooner did insurgents issue their call for a convention to meet on March 10, in Springfield, than Lewis called his own UMW convention for Indianapolis on the same day.

On March 10, 1930 one of the strangest moments in American trade union history occurred. Two groups of delegates meeting in separate conventions in the respective capital cities of Indiana and Illinois each asserted the right to represent the legal, legitimate United Mine Workers of America. One convention, that called by John L. Lewis in Indianapolis, proceeded in clockwork fashion and completed its business faultlessly. The other convention degenerated into chaos.

The Indianapolis convention saw Lewis in absolute control of his troops. And why not? As Lewis afterward informed Jett Lauck: "It was an excellent convention. Our enemies were all gathered in one boat at Springfield, which in many respects is not a bad situation." Lewis's defenders in Indianapolis devoted the first five days of their convention to endorsing the UMW president's actions in Illinois. Delegate after delegate from District 12 charged the deposed Illinois officials with corruption, excoriated the insurgents as traitors, and threw mud at anyone who dared criticize John L. Lewis. They listened attentively as Lewis characterized the Illinois insurgents as "a little band of malcontents . . . a rag-tag and bobtail element who . . . are muttering in their biers" and linked them to Frank Farrington and communism. And delegates applauded vigorously when Lewis advised them that only one question lay at the heart of the Illinois controversy. "No man in our union," he proclaimed, "can be greater than the law of this union. It is axiomatic that he must, like all others, abide by the laws, and after all, when you get down to the real heart of the question that is what it amounts to today." Delegates agreed overwhelmingly with their president that the District 12 officials had been legally and constitutionally wrong to disobey Lewis's rulings.

The Lewis delegates devoted the remaining five days of their convention to transforming the UMW into a constitutional autocracy. The delegates authorized the president to interpret the UMW constitution and to exercise unrestrained executive power between sessions of the international executive board. They also expanded the president's prerogative to expel union members for fomenting dualism; to revoke the charters of districts, subdistricts, and local unions; and to create provisional governments in their places.

Lewis closed the convention with an unusually powerful, brief oration. He assured the delegates that their union remained "a tremendous moral and economic force in the affairs of the coal industry and . . . the nation." The labor leader proudly proclaimed to the miners that he had "pleaded their case from the pulpit and the public platform, in joint conference with the associated operators of the country, before the bar of state legislatures, in the councils of the President's cabinet, and in the public press of this nation—not in the quavering tones of a feeble mendicant asking alms, but in the thundering voice of the captain of a mighty host, demanding the rights to which free men were entitled." Then, in an ironic peroration, Lewis confessed his personal impotency to the men who had just granted him autocratic power. "As an individual," he observed, "my opinion and my voice is of no more consequence in our world of affairs or in the coal industry . . . than the voice or the opinions of any passerby upon the street. It is only when I am able to translate your dreams and aspirations into words which others may understand that my tongue possesses any strength or my hand has any force."

Disunity wracked the insurgents in Springfield. Even before their convention opened on March 10, their careful plans when awry. Howat threatened to withdraw from the anti-Lewis movement if he was not chosen president, and his radical sympathizers pledged to withhold financial and moral endorsement if the new organization failed to choose militant leaders. Rather than experience a split, the two most active Illinois insurgents, John Walker and Adolph Germer, built a new slate. Walker withdrew in favor of Howat, a concession intended to elicit support from miners in the Southwest, rank-and-filers everywhere, and eastern socialists; Germer agreed to accept the vice-presidency; and Walker replaced John Brophy as secretary-treasurer-designate.

But preconvention compromises failed to instill harmony among the insurgents. Their hunger whetted by Walker's withdrawal in favor of Howat, the radicals sought to substitute Powers Hapgood for Germer, a demand that intensified dissension. Worse, the Springfield delegates engaged in a fractious floor struggle over the seating of Frank Farrington. After two days of debate, the majority supported Farrington, a decision that angered Walker, Germer, and especially Brophy, who noted: "I can't see that tying themselves up to Farrington would be any better than being tied to Lewis." Indeed, Brophy promptly decided "not to cooperate with a movement that gives Farrington a clean bill of health and that opens wide the door of its inner councils to him."

A union civil war followed immediately upon the adjournment of the two miners' conventions. Lewis entered the internecine struggle as the constitutionally autocratic leader of an organization that was in complete control of anthracite coal, firmly in command of all the bituminous fields except Illinois, and endorsed by the A.F. of L. The insurgents and their Reorganized United Mine Workers of America (RUMWA) began the battle with no substantial strength outside of Illinois.

Yet the insurgents posed a threat to Lewis for six months and perhaps longer. The RUMWA started with a significantly larger paper membership in Illinois than the Lewis UMW—at least 65 percent (perhaps 85 percent) of the state's miners to Lewis's remainder. But both organizations had fewer dues-paying than total members. Because Illinois had numbered more than two-thirds of the UMW's total membership before the split and held the only contract with operators, the insurgents' numerical dominance in District 12 provided them with considerable strength. From the first, they aimed to use District 12 as a club with which to smash the Lewis organization.

The greatest advantage that Lewis exercised in the civil war flowed from splits among his rivals. Although Farrington scarcely figured in the RUMWA, Lewis and his spokesmen persistently associated the insurgents with Farrington and, by implication, with class collaboration and corruption. Furthermore, Alex Howat unconsciously served Lewis better than he led the RUMWA. Eager to play the role of radical labor leader, Howat, much to the dismay of Germer and Walker, sought advice from such leftists as A. J. Muste and Tom Tippett. The more Howat associated with alleged communists and eastern urban "intellectuals," the more Lewis red-baited the insurgents, accusing them of seeking to "bolshevize" the mine workers and of subjecting workers to the influence of effete New York left-wing bohemians.

His flirtation with the political left proved the least of Howat's deficiencies as an insurgent union leader. Much worse was his administrative bungling and his thirst for hard whiskey. While Germer and Walker labored to hold Illinois and gain allies elsewhere in the coalfields, Howat spent most of his time away from the decisive arena of struggle either in local taverns or in Kansas among his idolators.

Lewis cunningly assisted his enemies as they cannibalized each other. He threw all his resources into the struggle in Illinois. The union *Journal* slandered the insurgents; union funds flowed to Lewis supporters in Illinois; Phil Murray and Van Bittner traveled through the coalfields carrying Lewis's message; William Green declared the insurgents dual unionists, had John Walker purged from the Illinois State Federation of Labor, and closed the state labor movement to RUMWA locals; Lewis's brothers, George and Dennie, used their political influence in the state to strengthen loyalists and punish rebels; and Lewis's allies used force and violence against the insurgents.

The decisive struggle between Lewis and the insurgents materialized not in the streets with fists and guns but in Illinois courtrooms with writs and injunctions. Insurgents had won the first legal battle back in October 1929, when an Illinois judge enjoined Lewis from suspending the charter of District 12 and deposing its elected officers. For more than a year afterward the legal battle seesawed back and forth as Lewis sued to deny the insurgents the right to use the name UMW for their organization (thus RUMWA) and his opponents secured writs citing Lewis et al. for violating the original October 1929 injunction.

The climactic legal decision occurred in February and March 1931 in the Dixon, Illinois, courtroom of Judge Harry Edwards. Judge Edwards, in a temporary decree of February 13 that he made final on March 6, suggested a compromise solution to the intraunion controversy. It was one that in effect handed Lewis a victory. To Lewis's dissatisfaction, Edwards ruled that the UMW president had illegally established a provisional administration in District 12 in October 1929; that the officers elected by the Illinois miners in December 1930, including John Walker as District 12 president, were entitled to hold office; and that miners had paid their dues to the RUMWA in good faith and could not be reassessed by Lewis's UMW. To the frustration of the insurgents, however, Edwards decided that the Indianapolis UMW was the legal miners' organization; that Lewis, Murray, and Kennedy remained the legitimate international officers; and that District 12 must accept as binding the constitution, rules, and regulations of the Lewis UMW. In return for offering the Illinois miners a measure of district autonomy, Judge Edwards asked them to dissolve the RUMWA.

Lewis seemed well satisfied with the results of the year-long legal imbroglio. The insurgents found little to celebrate in Edwards's decree. Walker and Germer had prepared in advance to quit the struggle in the event of an adverse ruling. Within days of Judge Edwards's final edict, Walker and Germer disbanded the RUMWA, turned over to Lewis the complete financial and organizational records of District 12, and abided by the law. For them the larger struggle was over, and all that remained was a secondary effort to preserve District 12 from absolute domination by Lewis.

Many left-wingers and also rank-and-filers were left aghast by Walker's and Germer's hasty and complete surrender. They wondered why, as Norman Thomas put it in a letter to Germer, "a fight such as you waged must be dropped at one unfavorable or partly favorable decision?" In truth, Walker and Germer accepted the legal ruling because it saved them from publicly confessing their own failure.

After a year of bitter and sometimes violent internecine conflict in Illinois, the insurgents claimed twenty-six thousand members (a substantial loss from their initial asserted following of seventy-five thousand miners) to Lewis's sixteen thousand—an actual increase for Provisional District 12. In Kansas, all of whose members Howat promised to deliver to the RUMWA, the insurgents counted sixty-five dues-paying members, and there were fewer than two hundred in the neighboring states of Oklahoma and Missouri. In West Virginia they ended up with fewer than three hundred dues-paying members, and in Ohio, twenty-two members. The insurgents lacked any following among Pennsylvania miners. The whole financial burden of the RUMWA, Germer confessed, fell on the Illinois miners, who could no longer carry the burden.

Good and substantial cause partly explained Germer's and Walker's surrender. But other less honorable and unspoken reasons underlay their decision. Fearful that communists were gaining inordinate influence with Howat, who relied heavily on the noncommunist A. J. Muste and Tom Tippett for advice, Walker and Germer, both old-guard socialists who since 1919 were more anticommunist than anticapitalist, decided that compromise with Lewis was necessary. And as their base of support among coal miners withered, they had to choose among a slow death, coalition with Muste (independent of the communists but to the left of the socialists), or compromise with Lewis. In the event, much as they despised Lewis, Walker and Germer considered Muste, whom they falsely linked to communism, a greater evil.

Thus the first round of the Illinois coal miners struggle ended in March 1931, when a legal ruling, financial problems, and anticommunism drove Germer and Walker into Lewis's arms. At an international executive board meeting on June 12, 1931, Lewis gloated that he had emerged from the Ilinois conflict with his union hegemony secure. He asked board members to take pride in a new long-term anthracite contract that guaranteed existing wage rates and to look forward with optimism to the day when the cycle of history swung from depression to prosperity. He also reminded board members of the trauma their union had just endured. Thankfully, the UMW had preserved itself against treason, it had "lived through its winter of discontent . . . [and] emerged as a solvent, functioning business institution."

Lewis's optimism initially seemed premature. In July 1931, Illinois miners at the Orient mines in West Frankfort began a wildcat strike. When Lewis went there on July 26 to urge the miners to return to work, they greeted their president with catcalls, boos, and hisses, and they stopped him from speaking. Then in 1932, when District 12's contract came up for renegotiation, insurgency reappeared in Illinois. Unable financially to sustain a strike, in early July, District 12 officials accepted a $5 wage, still the highest in any of the coalfields. But on July 11 the Illinois miners voted overwhelmingly to reject the new contract. Additional conferences between union officials and operators resulted in a renegotiated contract that provided a six-hour day and promised to spread employment among more miners. On August 2, 1932, Lewis, in an official notice to Illinois miners, advised them to ratify the contract. Unless they did so, Lewis warned, their wage rate would not be $5 but would decline to the abysmally low level "now being paid the distressed mine workers in Kentucky, West Virginia, and Ohio. Lest he who would destroy, consider the price of such destruction."

The impending election on the revised contract boded ill. Communists, followers of Muste and of Howat, and plain malcontents urged Illinois miners to reject a wage cut. In some locals, according to John Walker, rebellious leaders allowed only negative ballots to be cast. But the referendum suddenly took a strange turn. On the morning of August 10, a Lewis lieutenant, one Fox Hughes, took the ballots from the official union auditors, who subsequently reported that they had been robbed. Claiming that a state of emergency existed in District 12 because of the theft of the ballots, Lewis declared the revised agreement ratified. This incident gave birth to the following bit of doggerel:

> John L. Lewis blew the whistle;
> John H. Walker rang the bell;
> Fox Hughes stole the ballots,
> and the miners wages went to hell.

The Illinois election was not a case in which John L. Lewis autocratically usurped the authority of district officials. Walker, in fact, signed the revised contract, urged Illinois miners to ratify it, and never criticized Lewis's August 10 action.

Many rank-and-file Illinois miners, however, did not share their district president's sentiments. Lewis's declaration of a state of emergency and his arbitrary ratification of the Illinois contract stimulated a new wave of rebellion in District 12. In several coal-mining communities, especially in Macoupin County and the surrounding East St. Louis–Belleville area (once the Germer insurgent stronghold), Illinois miners declared their independence from the Lewis UMW and formed a dual miners' union: the Progressive Mine Workers of America. If the progressive miners did not pose as great a threat to Lewis's authority as the Howat-Germer-Walker insurgency, they demonstrated far greater staying power.

The Progressive rebellion shattered John Walker's influence among Illinois miners. Committed to enforcing the 1932 contract, Walker fought the Progressives and bankrupted District 12 in the process. With his members slipping away to the dual union and his treasury empty, in February 1933 Walker turned to Lewis for salvation, asking the UMW president to assume control of District 12 and to establish a provisional administration. From one of the most dedicated enemies, Lewis thus obtained what he most desired: absolute dominion within the UMW, as the last powerful autonomous district became an administration satrapy.

By early in 1933 Lewis had become an absolute ruler, the master of an empty empire. First weakened by the collapse of the soft-coal industry, brought to a terminal stage by the Great Depression, and reduced to impotency by the 1930–31 Illinois miners' civil war, the UMW seemed an anachronism.

Despite hard times, massive unemployment, and poverty—perhaps because of them—American coal miners behaved as few other workers did in the early stages of the Great Depression. They struck. In 1931 a total of 113,808 coal miners walked off the job, compared to the previous year's 46,877. The 113,808 striking miners remained idle for almost 2.2 million man-days (compared to 1930's 999,937 man-days), or 32 percent of the time lost to strikes in all American industries combined. The following year, 1932, the number of miners on strike slipped to 83,211, but the number of man-days lost rose to more than 6 million, or 58 percent of the time lost to all American industries.

The UMW and John L. Lewis had few links to the renewed militancy among coal miners. In 1931 and 1932, Lewis was too involved in his battle with the Illinois insurgents and in Washington politics to devote attention to industrial strife in the coalfields. Leadership of the 1931–32 mass coal strikes slipped into other, more radical hands, and the leaders of the coal strikes posed a final threat to Lewis's dominion in the miners' union.

One of the major 1931 strikes flowed directly from Lewis's conflict with District 12 and the creation of the RUMWA. Among the founders of the RUMWA was C. Frank Keeney, a former district president (No. 17) in northern West Virginia and a former socialist. In the summer of 1931 Keeney called his West Virginia miners out on strike. Local law officers in 1931 still served the coal companies, the governor assisted the operators; and employers evicted miners from company houses and replaced them with strikebreakers protected by armed guards. The defeated and depressed West Virginia miners drifted back to work, left the state, or subsisted on minimal relief allotments. Keeney's defeat left West Virginia coal unionism, or what little remained of it, in the grip of John L. Lewis's provisional District 17.

American communists represented a second challenge to Lewis's influence among coal miners and proved as eager as Keeney to lead strikes. At the end of the 1920s, communist trade union policy shifted toward combating rather than "boring from within" existing labor movements. After the defeat of Brophy and Lewis's repression of the "Save the Union Movement" in 1927–28, communist trade unionists gave up all hope of capturing the UMW. Instead, at a conference in September 1928 in Pittsburgh they formed a separate dual organization, the National Miners' Union. In 1931 officials of the National Miners' Union led strikes in western Pennsylvania, eastern Kentucky, and Ohio. They organized mass marches by unemployed miners, their wives, and children; challenged local and state law enforcment officials; and, for more than a year, kept the three coalfields in turmoil. In all three regions, and especially Harlan County, Kentucky, bloodshed and death marked the National Miners' Union strikes, and by the end of 1932 the communists had as little to show for their efforts as Frank Keeney did. Depression defeated communists just as it frustrated UMW insurgents and John L. Lewis.

On almost every front from 1930 through 1932—economic, political, and personal—Lewis suffered defeat or frustration. Rejected by his political allies and beset by enemies inside the UMW throughout 1930 and 1931, Lewis suffered yet another family tragedy. In March 1931 his younger brother, George, the sibling closest to him, died unexpectedly. For more than ten years George had served his older brother loyally as the UMW's legislative and political agent (Springfield and Washington lobbyist, in other words). According to close associates of Lewis, his brother's death caused the UMW president to cry openly and honestly and thereafter to dwell on health and death. Lewis's fixation on death is understandable considering that close family members had died at three critical moments in his trade union career: In October 1917, his daughter, Mary Margaret; in September 1919, his father, Thomas; and now in 1931, his brother, George.

In the spring of 1931 Lewis sublimated his depression over family loss and his fixation about death to union business. He once more turned to Washington and to Herbert Hoover for salvation. In June he appealed to Hoover to bring the operators and miners together in a national conference to save the bituminous industry from total disaster. Several operators now shared Lewis's belief that the decline of the miners' union had harmed rather than benefited northern bituminous coal, and they also urged federal action. "It must be admitted," F. E. Taplin, president of the North American Coal Corporation, wrote to the president, "that the situation is even worse than when we dealt with the union. . . . Personally, I would much prefer to deal with the United Mine Workers than with these ruthless, price-cutting, wage-cutting operators who are a detriment to the industry." But Taplin, like Lewis, realized that the UMW lacked the strength to organize all the coalfields, and the mine operator, like the union leader, looked to Hoover for a solution. "Please think this over carefully," he asked the president, "and let me know what comments you have to make of a constructive nature that will benefit the industry."

Hoover, however, proved as uneager as Harding and Coolidge before him to involve presidential prestige in the insoluble economic dilemma of bituminous coal. The president instead suggested that the union and the coal operators take their problems to the secretaries of labor and commerce, William Doak and Thomas Lamont, respectively, both of whom refused to act.

Lewis and the coal miners were not alone in the summer of 1931 in learning that Hoover and the Republicans had no solution for the depression. As Jett Lauck wrote to Lewis at the end of August, "all classes—labor, employers, white collar, congressmen, bankers . . . want a leader, if he has a sound and constructive policy." Lauck suggested that Lewis be that leader, that the UMW president "take the field for the revival and stabilization of the soft coal industry" by demanding that Hoover call a special session of Congress to pass the union's coal stabilization bill and adopt an emergency plan to control production and stabilize prices in all industries under government boards composed of employers, organized labor, and the public. Aware, to be sure, that Hoover was unlikely to adopt such a policy, Lauck proposed an intensive political and public relations campaign, for "I am sure that *now* affords an opportunity which will never occur again for generations. You could take the leadership of the whole constructive movement—all classes of organized labor . . . farmers, bankers, businessmen, and industrial leaders . . . a movement of real industrial statesmanship and accomplishment which you would start and lead to success."

Here in embryo was the program of Franklin Roosevelt's first "hundred days"—but with Lewis cast in the role of the statesman who would offer the nation industrial planning, labor-management cooperation, stimulation of the domestic economy, and a cure for depression. "You are a Shakespearean scholar," Lauck flattered his putative national savior, "and you know that 'There is a tide in the affairs of men which taken at ebb leads on to victory,' or words to that effect." Lewis, indeed, claimed to be a student of Shakespeare, and he certainly believed in the tides of history; but he was also cautious, cunning, and opportunistic. "The suggestions have a distinct appeal," he informed Lauck, "but we would undoubtedly encounter substantial obstacles in the way of attainment of the desired objectives. . . . It is debatable," Lewis concluded, "that I could undertake, with propriety, to act as a spokesman for industries other than coal."

Although Lewis apparently disregarded his adviser's most ambitious ideas, some of Lauck's concepts had begun to germinate in the union leader's mind. In his 1931 Labor Day speech, Lewis warned that unless the nation's political leaders took immediate action to combat depression, the United States faced radical changes. "Those in high places who rest serene in the thought that cycles must have their fling," he continued, "will soon have to go into action or face action which might bring radical changes in our recognized system of commercial enterprise."

A month later, in October 1931, Lewis consented to Lauck's proposal to have the UMW president appear at a congressional hearing scheduled by Senator Robert LaFollette to consider national economic planning and stabilization. "It is the occasion," noted Lauck, "I think, we have been waiting for." Throughout the remainder of October and all of November, as the LaFollette hearings were postponed, Lauck and Lewis discussed the details and substance of the latter's public statement. They also planned to publicize their policies and the incipient movement for national economic planning with the assistance of Louis Stark, the *New York Times* labor reporter and the man they selected as an outlet for well-timed news leaks.

More important to Lewis, however, than leadership of a national political movement was congressional legislation to stabilize the coal industry. From December 1931 through March 1932 Lewis lobbied intensively for passage of his union's bill. Lauck and Searles won Labor Secretary Doak's endorsement and the support of congressmen. And

Lewis, by late February, thought he had gained the approval of several large coal operators for passage of the Davis-Kelly Bill, as the union's proposed law was known. "I find a good deal of sentiment for the bill in a private way," Lewis informed Lauck, "and some [operators] said they were exercising their private influence, but they are hardly in a position as yet to come out in the open. I am hopeful that some of the seeds I planted may produce results later."

Whether Lewis, in fact, had influenced the operators or he had instead misunderstood their position on federal legislation is an open question. By 1932 most bituminous operators desired some sort of federal legislation to liberate coal from the antitrust laws and to sanction price-fixing and joint marketing arrangements. The UMW's bill provided that much, but it also mandated that coal operators respect their workers' right to organize and bargain collectively with them in good faith. In the event, then, most coal companies opposed the Davis-Kelly Bill, President Hoover never endorsed it, and it died in congressional committee.

Surprisingly, Lewis publicly endorsed Hoover's reelection in 1932. By November 1932, however, Lewis was likely playing both sides of the political fence. In the late spring or early summer of 1932, he had privately informed a Roosevelt emissary that most labor leaders, himself included, "will support the democratic nominee unless Mr. Hoover withdraws. . . ." He also promised to work behind the scenes for Roosevelt's election.

Lewis by 1932 had rejected absolutely what Jett Lauck referred to as Hoover's "old rugged individualism." Lewis had been stirred by Lauck's dreams and by the possibility of more radical solutions to the nation's crisis. Although Lewis rejected Lauck's more ambitious political schemes, the labor leader, long a believer in the cyclical theory of history, perceived that in 1932 a new cycle was about to begin—that now was the time to ride a rising political tide to victory.

The election of 1932 over, Lewis forsook Hoover and Hooverism. Now he, Lauck, and the UMW lobbyists in Washington looked to the new president and the Democratic leadership in Congress for action. That a new chapter was about to begin in Lewis's personal history became evident at the November 1932 A.F. of L. convention. Now he criticized the labor barons who dominated the federation and who offered unemployed workers the principle of voluntarism instead of bread. Compulsory government-financed unemployment insurance must come, Lewis asserted, for "it is inevitable that the die-hards among those opposed to the principle will have to modify their position [opposition to all government welfare programs] or be defeated." He also battled unsuccessfully to enlarge the A.F. of L. executive council from eight to twenty-five members so that more affiliates would be represented, especially those linked to the mass-production industries, which lacked an effective voice in the federation.

Well before Franklin Roosevelt entered office in March 1933, Lewis expressed the social and economic philosophy indelibly associated with the later New Deal. Ever since the mid-1920s he had demanded that the federal government intervene more directly in private enterprise by stabilizing the soft-coal industry under public control, promoting the interests of the UMW, and stimulating a high-wage, mass-consumption economy. The time had come, Lewis informed the Senate Finance Committee in February 1933, to free industry from the grip of the investment bankers, to control prices and production in the national interest, to stimulate mass purchasing power among those who labored for wages and salaries, and to offer wage and salary earners direct participation in the management of industry. Just as the violent miners' strikes of 1931–32 were precursors of the labor upheaval of the Roosevelt years, Lewis's speeches and public statements in late 1932 and early 1933 presaged the New Deal reforms and the industrial union rebellion against the A.F. of L. in 1935 and 1936.

Mr. and Mrs. Lewis and daughter, Kathryn, after visit to the White House, 1923–24. (State Historical Society of Wisconsin, Miller Photo, Photograms, N. Y.)

At a press conference during the Flint sit-down strike, January 28, 1937. (The Archives of Labor and Urban Affairs, Wayne State University)

Addressing a union rally in Detroit, April 7, 1937. (The Archives of Labor and Urban Affairs, Wayne State University)

A trophy from Lewis's favorite sport: deep-sea fishing. (State Historical Society of Wisconsin)

In the garden of his Alexandria, Virginia home. (State Historical Society of Wisconsin)

With Kathryn's bulldog, Socrates, 1936. (State Historical Society of Wisconsin)

As a debonair Washingtonian, 1941. (State Historical Society of Wisconsin)

In the living room of his Alexandria home, 1953. (State Historical Society of Wisconsin)

At Monticello in good company: Samuel Eliot Morison, Harvard historian; J. Russel Wiggins, *Washington Post* managing editor; and Lewis, 1954. (State Historical Society of Wisconsin; photo by Bob Tenney, Charlottesville (Va.) *Daily Progress*)

III

Years of Glory, 1933–40

9

Rebirth of a Union,
1933–34

March 4, 1933, the day of Franklin Delano Roosevelt's inauguration as president, dawned gray and wet in Washington, D.C. Nature reflected the mood of a nation, whose banks had closed the previous day and in which thirteen to fifteen million men and women were jobless. American capitalism seemed dormant; the future of democracy itself appeared problematic. Some citizens toyed with the idea of ceding autocratic authority to the nation's chief executive. "Even the iron hand of a national dictator," lamented the Republican governor of Kansas, Alfred M. Landon, "is in preference to a paralytic stroke."

Sensing the mood of the nation, Roosevelt promised swift action: "We must act, and act quickly." Warning that it might become necessary for him to assume powers ordinarily exercised only in wartime, he assured Americans that they had nothing to fear but fear itself. Roosevelt implored citizens to cast away their anxieties and to join with him in a program of action.

John L. Lewis knew precisely what he wanted from the new president. By 1933 Lewis had already concluded that only federal intervention could revitalize an ailing soft-coal industry. Now the labor leader and his advisers refashioned those plans to nationalize the coal industry into a proposal to reform the entire national economy—a program in which the federal government compelled industry to function collectively, eliminated destructive competition, insured stable employment, inflated wage rates (and hence consumer demand), and granted organized labor full participation. What the United States needed, asserted John L. Lewis, was the New Deal.

Lewis's testimony on February 17, 1933, before the Senate Finance Committee, presaged the substance of the New Deal. Lewis demanded the creation of a board of emergency control composed of representatives from industry, labor, agriculture, and finance, which would have plenary emergency power to reduce the hours of labor, guarantee the right of collective bargaining, stabilize prices, and implement national economic planning. Some may criticize this proposal as the beginning of a dictatorship, conceded Lewis, but "it is the form of procedure resorted to . . . during the crisis of World War, when the enemy was three thousand miles from our shore. Today the enemy is within the boundaries of the nation, and is stalking through every community and every home, and, obviously, this proposal is the most democratic form of internal regulation that can be devised to deal with our economic and industrial collapse."

Lewis wasted little time in discovering whether Franklin Roosevelt agreed with his prescription for economic recovery. On Monday, March 27, John L. Lewis, Phil Murray, Tom Kennedy, Van Bittner, and Ellis Searles met with President Roosevelt and secretaries of labor and interior Frances Perkins and Harold Ickes, respectively, to discuss federal stabilization of the coal industry. Although Lewis refused to comment to reporters after the meeting and the president issued a noncommittal public statement, behind the scenes presidential advisers busily laid the foundation for a reorganization of the economy along the lines suggested by Lewis in February.

Among the more influential of the administration's economic advisers was the UMW's own consultant, W. Jett Lauck. President Roosevelt's "brain trusters," especially Rexford Guy Tugwell and Raymond Moley, came from the same academic and institutional milieu as Lauck; their intellectual predispositions were identical, their values were similar, and their proposals for national economic planning were simply the UMW's coal industry plan writ large. Lauck influenced the planning sessions that formulated the National Industrial Recovery Act (NIRA) and particularly the incorporation into it of Section 7a, the clause that guaranteed workers the right to "organize unions of their own choosing" and to bargain collectively with their employers.

As ultimately presented to Congress, the NIRA exempted industry from prosecution under the antitrust statutes if enterprises eliminated competition by stabilizing prices and allocating markets. In return for exemption from antitrust legislation, businessmen had to adopt presidentially sanctioned codes that established minimum wage and maximum hours, eliminated child labor, and recognized the right of workers to organize unions and bargain collectively.

Roosevelt's recommendation that Congress enact the NIRA ignited a legislative and public struggle reminiscent of the conflict over federal coal legislation from 1928 to 1932. Just as the mine owners earlier had sought relief from antitrust laws and the right to stabilize prices and

allocate markets among themselves but balked at accepting trade unionism as the price for cartelization, most American industrialists in May
and June 1933 favored the passage of NIRA—but without its labor
clause, Section 7a. In the press, on the radio, and before congressional
committees, industrialists and labor leaders clashed concerning how to
save the economy. Free us from antiquated antitrust regulations, let us
handle labor unencumbered by costly union practices said industrialists,
and we will restore employment, productivity, and prosperity. Guarantee
workers the right to organize and compel employers to bargain in good
faith with trade unions asserted labor leaders, and the labor movement
will secure the high wages and steady employment that industrialists
had failed to deliver.

When by overwhelming majorities Congress passed the National Industrial Recovery Act on June 16, Section 7a remained intact, providing
what Lewis proclaimed as the greatest single advance for human rights
in the United States since Abraham Lincoln's Emancipation Procla-
mation. For organized labor, Section 7a substantiated Harold Ickes's
description of the impact of Franklin Roosevelt's first hundred days in
office. "It's more than a New Deal," said the Interior Secretary. "It's a
new world. People feel free again. They can breathe naturally. It's like
quitting a morgue for the open woods." And none felt freer nor breathed
more easily than American coal miners.

That Lewis desired the incorporation of Section 7a into the Recovery
Act is indisputable; that he lobbied unstintingly for its passage is without
question; but that he envisaged Section 7a, in the words of Saul Alinsky,
as the means "to fertilize the egg of the CIO" and organize *all* the
nation's mass-production workers is legend. In the spring of 1933 different thoughts and objectives were uppermost in the mind of John L.
Lewis. Organization of the nation's mass-production workers, the timid-
ity of the A.F. of L.'s leadership, and the necessity for a new national
labor federation may have been ideas germinating in the deepest recesses
of Lewis's imagination. But Lewis remained too much the realist to
plan an unprecedented organizing campaign in the mass-production
industries and a potential rift in the labor movement when the great
mass of the nation's coal miners remained unorganized and his own
union was barely solvent. Before Section 7a could become the Magna
Carta for all unorganized industrial workers, Lewis first had to attend
to his own union's immediate needs.

While labor leaders and employers fought in Washington to obtain
an industrial recovery program satisfactory to their respective interests,
rank-and-file workers, coal miners included, seemed quiescent. Few
symptoms of the discontent that had swept through the coalfields in
1931 and 1932 lingered; American workers again appeared as lethargic

as they had been early on during the Great Depression. From one Appalachian coalfield a UMW member reported in February 1933 that "as far as West Kentucky is concerned there is no sign of organization. Now . . . you could not organize a *baseball team.*" A week later, an Illinois District 12 miner observed: "Things are in a bad way. . . . The future is not bright."

Yet by June coal miners seemed liberated—their lethargy transformed into militancy, their indifference to the UMW replaced by fierce union loyalty. On June 23, precisely one week after the passage of NIRA and Section 7a, Van Bittner reported from West Virginia that the UMW's current organizing campaign was like a dream, too good to be true. "We expect to be practically through with every mine in the state and have every miner under the jurisdiction of our union by the first of next week." Northern West Virginia had been completely reorganized, and the southern counties of Logan and McDowell, where the UMW had never functioned, were fast being conquered. Referring to southern West Virginia, Bittner exulted: "That field is completely organized and unbounded enthusiasm prevails among the miners and their people." What happened in West Virginia repeated itself in other coalfields. Begun on June 1, the UMW's organizing campaign was practically completed by July 1—August 1 in some of the more recalcitrant antiunion districts. Neither wage increases instituted by coal companies nor the establishment of company unions retarded the UMW advance.

John L. Lewis's role in the revitalization of the UMW and the reunionization of the coalfields was central yet tangential. It was salient to the extent that his political influence led to the enactment of Section 7a and that afterwards he gambled his union's slender financial resources on an intensive organizing campaign. It was tangential in the sense that coal miners seemed to organize themselves in June and July 1933, even in the absence of UMW funds and organizers. Organizers such as Van Bittner did not have to plead with miners to join the union; all they needed to do was sign up recruits as fast as they appeared. In fact, the accomplishments of Roosevelt's first one hundred days were more important than any speech or action by John L. Lewis in motivating coal miners to rebel against their employers and the conditions of their existence.

Equally important, the initial New Deal reforms left coal operators paralyzed. With minor exceptions, few coal companies openly resisted their workers' unionization, not because they now favored trade unions, but because the policies of the Roosevelt administration confused them. The UMW did its job so quickly, one observer noted, "that organizations were established before the mine owners woke up." Some mine owners, moreover, perceived the New Deal reforms and the unionization of the miners as an opportunity to resurrect a declining industry. Northern operators, unable to compete with lower-cost southern mines, favored the UMW as an instrument to equalize wage rates, and they saw the New Deal's economic recovery program as a means to control prices, allocate markets, and rationalize an otherwise anarchic industry.

Organization of the miners was only a first step in Lewis's campaign to restore UMW influence, improve working conditions, and, ultimately, build a powerful national labor movement. Once the mass of miners enrolled in the UMW, he sought to negotiate contracts with coal operators. Here Lewis encountered serious obstacles. Caught unaware by the UMW's lightning organizing campaign and the miners' alacrity to join the union, nonunion operators now regrouped to resist further UMW advances. Traditional open-shop operators in the South and the captive mines (those owned and operated by the steel industry) everywhere refused to bargain with the UMW, discharged union militants, and attempted to crush the UMW before Roosevelt approved the NIRA code of fair competition for the bituminous coal industry, which would penalize employers who refused to bargain collectively in good faith. Particularly in southwestern Pennsylvania, the captive coal companies refused to recognize the UMW or bargain with labor. To recognize trade unionism in the mines, they feared, would set a precedent that might open the iron and steel industry to organized labor.

In July and August 1933, however, coal miners were in no mood to tolerate employer resistance. Throughout the summer militant miners, acting on their own, walked out of the pits in wildcat strikes aimed at achieving union recognition. Rank-and-file impatience with the tedious process of negotiating a code for the coal industry under the NIRA led Lewis to develop a seemingly contradictory but effective bargaining strategy. On the one hand, the UMW president, eager to remain on good terms with the Roosevelt administration and to mollify operators, kept a tight lid on action in the coalfields. Lewis repeatedly urged miners to sit tight, remain at work, and allow their leaders "to bring home the bacon." On the other hand, Lewis knew that if the coal miners in fact sat tight and worked diligently, operators would be less likely to bargain seriously with the UMW or to offer the union the terms it desired. Negotiations then underway in Washington to establish NIRA codes for the steel and auto industries revealed to Lewis labor's inability to extract concessions from employers whose workers were neither effectively organized nor able to paralyze production. Lewis thus acted as the moderate in his relations with the Roosevelt administration and the coal operators while a militant union rank and file threatened rebellion from below.

Early in August UMW representatives, coal operators, and federal officials began hearings on a code of fair competition for the bituminous coal industry. Two factors strengthened Lewis's position in the negotiations. No labor leader seemed to command more respect in the nation's capitol, as evidenced by his appointment on August 5 by President Roosevelt to serve as a member of the Labor Advisory Board under the NIRA. Lewis also established a close personal relationship with General Hugh S. Johnson, the director of the National Recovery Administration (NRA)—the agency created to administer the NIRA. The friendship between Lewis and Johnson was particularly crucial during the negotiations to write a coal code, because Johnson chose to intervene directly, often, and sometimes inopportunely, in the bargaining between coal operators and union officials.

The start of the bituminous industry hearings found employers and union far apart. Lewis's demands were numerous, fundamental, and costly. He sought an agreement that would cover the southern Appalachian fields as well as the old Central Competitive Field; a uniform national minimum daily wage of $5 (many southern mines were then paying as little as $1.50); the six-hour day, six-day week; the right to check off union dues and for miners to select their own checkweighmen; the prohibition of noncash wage payments and compulsory company houses and stores; the elimination of child labor; and the creation of equitable grievance procedures.

Divided about whether or not to deal with the UMW, the coal operators united in their insistence, as stated by their chief negotiator, Charles O'Neill, that they could not pay higher wages. On August 9, the first day of hearings in Washington, O'Neill said that operators would gladly unite to set prices and allocate markets but would absolutely reject any legal requirement that employers must deal with labor. The next day, Lewis, speaking for his union, warned that the future welfare of the United States, if not the whole Western world, depended on the results of the code hearings. The NIRA, he stressed, "offers . . . not only a way out, but the only way out."

As industry and union representatives quarreled in sultry Washington offices, coal miners and mine managers fought a real industrial war in western Pennsylvania and other coalfields. Lewis had little direct influence in Pennsylvania. The miners, especially those who walked out of the captive pits, followed the leadership of insurgents like Martin Ryan and acted without orders from the UMW hierarchy. Indeed, most of the Pennsylvania strikers looked more to Franklin D. Roosevelt than John L. Lewis for salvation. Assurances from Roosevelt that if the men returned to work, coal operators would deal with the union and adopt an industrial code caused the strikers temporarily to end their walkout in mid-August.

But when negotiations between employers and UMW officials brought no resolution to the dispute over code terms and General Johnson complicated matters by suggesting he might "clarify" the meaning of Section 7a — a public statement that led southern nonunion operators to believe the general would sanction the open shop and company unions — miners took matters into their own hands. Louis Stark wired Roosevelt on August 23 that "hell" was about to break loose in the coalfields.

Stark's warning that "seething discontent in the [coal] fields may break out worse than ever. From coal it will spread to steel and autos" had to vex the president. Yet Roosevelt also must have been pleased by Lewis's attitude, as characterized by Stark. "Lewis is holding tight. He knows that if the conflagration starts it may be disastrous for everybody." The key to peace, advised Stark, echoing Lewis's analysis of the coal situation, "is an agreement between the union and the southern operators."

Other influential presidential informants buttressed Lewis's strategic campaign to win presidential sanction for the UMW. On September 5, Gifford Pinchot informed Roosevelt "that if we have a prolonged general soft coal strike, bang goes Recovery." He also assured the president that coal miners trusted Roosevelt as the worker's friend, indeed worshipped him, and believed fervently that "you are working to get them recognition of the United Mine Workers of America."

Lewis's strategy had its intended effect on Roosevelt, motivating the president to intervene directly in the code negotiations. On the evening of September 6, a day after he received Governor Pinchot's warning, Roosevelt invited UMW officials and leading coal operators to a private conference at the White House. At that meeting the operators' representatives spoke first, asserting that they had already eliminated an open-shop clause from the proposed coal code, would never accede to the closed shop, and were morally compelled to protect the liberty of nonunion miners. To which Lewis asked: Where are the nonunion miners?

As the operators described a code more notable for its complexities than for its concessions to labor, Roosevelt observed: "The contract you suggest and your contract are drafted in an English that 9/10th of the miners can't understand — they simply won't read it." Roosevelt then asked that he personally be allowed to draft a supplementary statement encompassing the operators' aims that would say in plain words "that a man shall have the right to work without being a member of a union." Weasel words, observed Roosevelt, "always add difficulties and finally land us in an endless mess."

Although the operators balked at the president's suggestion, Lewis, the only voice that spoke for the UMW, promised that the "United

Mine Workers will accept your good offices, Mr. President." For the remainder of the conference Lewis and Roosevelt harmonized their positions, the president urging the operators to compromise and the labor leader offering revisions in the UMW's original demands. "You get that contract written up tomorrow," urged the president as he bid his guests goodnight, "and if you've anything else on your minds, just let me know."

But a week after the White House conference, the UMW and the coal operators were no closer to agreement. On September 12 Pennsylvania miners, once more acting more militantly than their leaders, voted to strike the next day unless a satisfactory code was written. And once again Governor Pinchot urged President Roosevelt to act, for "one more outrage . . . might easily plunge the whole area into tumult and riot." Faced with the threat of a coal strike in Pennsylvania—one likely to spread throughout the bituminous fields—Roosevelt pressured UMW officials and operators to remain in daily bargaining sessions, weekends included.

Lewis's strategy brought the UMW handsome dividends. Using rank-and-file rebelliousness to pressure both operators and the president, Lewis won for his union the first code written under the NIRA that awarded organized labor substantial concessions and a role in its implementation. The bituminous coal code, as approved by President Roosevelt on September 21, granted the UMW what it had fruitlessly struggled for since its founding in 1890: a contract that covered all the major soft-coal producing districts—Pennsylvania, Ohio, West Virginia, Virginia, eastern Kentucky, and Tennessee—with supplemental agreements that covered Indiana and Illinois. Although Lewis failed to win uniform wage rates, the remaining differentials had been narrowed.

Other benefits flowed to American coal miners as a result of the bituminous coal code. Statutory law now guaranteed them the eight-hour day, five-day week, the right to choose their own checkweighmen, and the abolition of wage payment in scrip and of the requirement to trade in company stores and live in company houses. The code outlawed child labor (defined as under age seventeen) and granted miners a grievance procedure culminating in arbitration. Although the UMW failed to win the union shop, it did gain the right to compel employers to check off union dues from the payroll. In a comment as apt as it was witty, *belle-lettrist* Howard Brubaker observed in the *New Yorker:* "the defeated mine-owners agreed to all things that deputy sheriffs usually shoot people for demanding." More revealing, a northern mine operator immediately wired Lewis: "I want to congratulate you on getting a code . . . which puts the United Mine Workers in every bituminous mine in the country which I am sure will do more to stabilize the . . . coal industry than anything which has been done in its history."

The political relationship between John L. Lewis and Franklin D. Roosevelt that secured coal miners rights that had eluded them for almost half a century was caught in songs composed by black and white southern miners. In Trafford, Alabama, Uncle George Jones sang:

> In nineteen hundred an' thirty-three
>   when Mr. Roosevelt took his seat,
> He said to President John L. Lewis,
> "In union we must be."
>
> Hooray! Hooray!
>   Fer de union we must stan',
> It's de only organization
>   Protects de laborin' man.
> Boys, it make de women happy,
>   Our chillun clap deir hands,
> To see de beefsteak an' de good po'k chops,
>   Steamin' in dose frying pans.
>
> When de President and John L. Lewis
>   Had signed deir decree,
> Dey called fer Mitch an' Raney—
> Dalrymple made de three:
> "Go down in Alabama,
>   Organize ev'ry laborin' man,
> Spread de news all over de lan':
>   We got de union back again!"

And in McDowell County, West Virginia, they sang:

> Some people don't know who to thank,
>   For this "State of McDowell" that's so free;
> Give part of the praise to John Lewis,
>   and the rest of it to Franklin D.

However much truth miners' songs revealed, they failed to give sufficient credit to the role of rank-and-filers. Without coal miners' loyalty to trade unionism and their willingness to walk out of the pits repeatedly, neither John L. Lewis nor Franklin D. Roosevelt could have compelled operators to acquiesce in the September 21 agreement. It was the militant behavior of coal miners, not the tough language and sharp bargaining of John L. Lewis, that threatened Roosevelt's plans for industrial recovery. However astute Lewis may have been during his negotiations with operators, his achievements would have been minimal had miners not occasionally "blown the lid." Lewis, moreover, knew this. He realized that his bargaining achievements derived from the power exercised by masses of angry workers. Alone, Lewis was impotent as a labor leader; backed by hundreds of thousands of loyal followers ready to struggle for their rights, he wielded real influence. "We [labor leaders] would be just as other people, as the man on the street, if it were not for the fact that back of us is the great force of the workers for whom we can speak in relation to their hopes and aspirations, and the attention we get, the favorable attention . . . comes as a result of the fact that *back of us is organizaton"* (emphasis added).

The September 21 agreement placed the United Mine Workers in the strongest position in its history. The miners' union had finally won a contract that guaranteed it recognition and stability in the hitherto nonunion southern Appalachian fields. But one exception — and a glaring one — remained to the UMW's triumphant conquest of the coalfields. The captive mines refused to recognize the miners' union or bargain with it.

Although the captive mines produced only about 8 percent of the nation's soft coal and did not market their output commercially, their existence as bastions of the open shop threatened the security of the miners' union. Lewis remembered well how after World War I, when the UMW had achieved its peak membership, those Pennsylvania operators most closely associated with the iron and steel industry had fought the UMW and precipitated the breakdown of the Jacksonville agreement. Lewis never doubted his union's ability to dominate smaller operators and independent coal companies, but he feared the economic power symbolized by an alliance among Wall Street investment bankers, major railroads, and mass-production industries (the Morgan-Rockefeller-Mellon-Dupont nexus — the economic royalists repeatedly condemned by the presidents of the miners' union and of the United States). If the UMW tolerated the open shop in the captive mines, commercial operators might demand similar arrangements. Moreover, the possibility always existed that the steel companies and their Wall Street allies might in the future lead a campaign reminiscent of the antilabor crusades of the 1920s, to eliminate the UMW from the coal industry.

Lewis pursued precisely the same strategy to organize the captive mines as he had applied against the commercial coal operators. A whirlwind organizing campaign succeeded in enrolling most of the captive miners in the union before employers realized what had happened. Lewis again relied on a militant rank and file to threaten the president's plans for economic recovery. And he alternately "kept the lid" on his miners' behavior and allowed them to explode rebelliously until the resultant pressures forced Roosevelt to wrench from reluctant employers a limited victory for the UMW and the first substantial breach in steel's hitherto impregnable antiunion wall.

As the commercial mines fell before the UMW onslaught in September 1933, the captive mines beat a strategic retreat. On September 21, the owners of the captive mines agreed to comply with the terms of the Bituminous Coal Code and to maintain as favorable hours, wages, and working conditions as those prevailing under the agreements between commercial coal operators and the UMW. On September 29 President Roosevelt approved the agreement, and on October 1 the captive mines implemented the new working conditions.

Yet the captive mine operators refused to relinquish arbitrary control of their labor force. A policy statement issued on September 27 by United States Steel covering labor relations for its coal mining subsidiaries specified "that if request is made to sign a Union scale or an Agreement with the Union, statement can be made that same cannot be done."

The Frick Company's refusal to bargain with the UMW precipitated another crisis in the coal industry. A telegram from Gifford Pinchot to President Roosevelt advised that "unless you [Roosevelt] can force Taylor to recognize union at least seventy five percent of entire Pennsylvania bituminous field will be out tomorrow and the rest by Wednesday or earlier. Rank and File miners complaining they are being kidded. Era of good feeling is over. Looting of food stores has begun. ... It seems a shame," lamented the governor, "that pigheaded obstinacy of handful of men should force this calamity upon us and endanger your whole recovery program."

Precisely as Lewis had expected, the militancy of Pennsylvania's miners and the threat that they posed to the New Deal's recovery program induced Roosevelt to intervene forcefully in the captive mines dispute and, more important, to assist the UMW. During an October 7 White House conference and in a subsequent letter to the operators on October 9, President Roosevelt persisted in defining the phrase "working conditions" to encompass negotiations with the union and the dues checkoff. The operators offered a small concession: They agreed to check off dues for any miner who voluntarily requested it. Yet they refused to negotiate with union representatives and insisted that they would deal only with individuals, not labor organizations.

Wisely remaining in the background during the dispute, Lewis allowed Murray to represent the union and Roosevelt to manipulate the operators. In this instance the president did not disappoint Lewis. Roosevelt appreciated Lewis's and Murray's moderation—their appeals to the miners for restraint. Irked at the obstinacy of the captive mine owners, on October 18 Roosevelt berated them. He told them that their collective bargaining policy was hypocritical and that he was at a loss to understand how their insistence on negotiating with individual employees was "consistent with your agreement [to] enter into negotiations at once, in good faith, with representatives of their workers."

Unable to sway the president or to resume full production at their strike-plagued mines, on October 30 the operators finally accepted a presidential compromise. The UMW promised to call off its strike on November 6, and the companies pledged to implement the terms of the Appalachian agreement and to accept the principle of the checkoff. The thorny issue of union recognition was left in abeyance. The UMW and the operators agreed to abide by the results of representation elections, to be conducted by the National Labor Board (NLB), in which miners would select collective bargaining representatives with whom employers would negotiate a contract. In the event that no settlement was achieved through collective bargaining, the NLB would resolve the issues in dispute.

In late November the NLB conducted representation elections at the captive mines. Except at the Frick properties, the UMW won substantial majorities among the miners, who voted for slates consisting of Lewis, Murray, Kennedy, and the respective district officials. Out of thirty such elections, the UMW won twenty, tied one, and lost nine—the defeats almost all coming in Fayette County, Pennsylvania, the stronghold of the Frick Company, where wages were highest, company unions firmest, and repression most common. Afterward, however, the steel companies failed to execute collective bargaining agreements with the UMW, which resorted to the National Labor Board for relief.

Hearings conducted by the NLB in January 1934 revealed the steel companies' steadfast recalcitrance on the issue of union recognition and the UMW's inability to conquer the captive mines even with presidential support. The companies' attorney, Nathan Miller, former governor of New York, asserted during the hearings that the NIRA did not require employers to bargain with unions. Thus when an agreement was finally reached in mid-January 1934, the captive mines signed it with the individuals elected by the miners—Lewis, Murray, and Kennedy—not with the UMW as an organization, and the NLB declined to rule whether such an agreement constituted legal union recognition.

The first clash between Lewis and the nation's leading industrialists had ended with the most crucial issues unresolved. Compelled to hold representation elections, to check off union dues, and even to bargain with union representatives, the steel operators nevertheless refused to concede the principle of union recognition. Having succumbed temporarily to political and economic pressures, they intended in the long run not to allow unions to dilute company authority. Guided by the Frick Company, operators hardly bargained in good faith, schemed to replace independent labor organizations with company unions, and discharged their most militant union employees.

If Lewis had breached steel's hitherto impregnable antiunion walls, his union's penetration scarcely shattered the fortress of the open shop. Indeed, in late 1933 and early 1934, Lewis watched workers in steel, autos, and other mass-production industries suffer successive union defeats. And as President Roosevelt and his advisers repeatedly favored employers over trade unionists, Lewis became convinced that the Morgan-Rockefeller-Mellon-Du Pont financial elite had lost none of its economic and political influence.

Simultaneous with his triumphs in the coalfields, Lewis extended peace feelers to his former left-wing critics. In October 1933 Lewis recommended that William Green appoint Adolph Germer, long-time District 12 insurgent, old-guard socialist, and advocate of industrial unionism, as a voluntary organizer for the A.F. of L. The same month Lewis, at the urging of Phil Murray, met with John Brophy in Washington and restored his former foe to good standing in the UMW. That a new phase was about to begin in the career of John L. Lewis was revealed in the labor leader's comment to Brophy during their reconciliation. "I suppose," observed Lewis, "our differences in the past were largely ones of timing."

In the autumn of 1933 Lewis expressed publicly his desire to build a more powerful labor movement. At the October 1933 A.F. of L. convention, he demanded that the organization's executive council be expanded from eight to twenty-five members in order to represent better the full spectrum of the labor movement and allow a voice to mass-production workers. His proposal defeated by a delegate roll call vote of 14,133 to 6,410, Lewis clashed verbally—and almost physically—with Dan Tobin, president of the teamsters' union and the most outspoken critic of industrial, or mass-production, unionism.

Lewis further reaffirmed his commitment to the mass-production workers at the January 1934 UMW convention. He recommended that the A.F. of L. relinquish the claims of craft unions in the mass-production industries and allow industrial unions to emerge in the interest of a more comprehensive form of labor organization. The inability of mass-production workers to benefit from the NIRA and the failure of the craft unions to aid them necessitated new policies for the American labor movement. "Without question the problem of organizing the workers in . . . automobile, steel, rubber, lumber, electric and other industries is of paramount importance to American labor. There is imperative necessity by the American Federation of Labor of a sound and practical policy that will meet the requirements of modern industrial conditions."

But before Lewis could transform the structure of the American labor movement, he had loose ends to tie up in his own industry. As 1933 passed into 1934 and Roosevelt's New Deal entered its eleventh month of experimentation and innovation, the UMW had yet to conquer such obdurate antiunion regions as Harlan County, Kentucky, equalize wages between north and south, or gain miners the material improvements that their revived power justified. For years, as Edward Wieck reported, coal miners had waited patiently for better times. "How long they will wait for better conditions, how long it will take them to rebel when better conditions and wages are not forthcoming," Wieck concluded, "it is impossible to say. But . . . the United Mine Workers must be able to deliver, or they will be pushed aside."

Lewis heard his miners' angry voices, and he meant to deliver what the rank and file demanded. When negotiations commenced between the UMW and the Appalachian coal operators in Washington on the last day of February 1934, Lewis expressed his union's extensive demands, relating them to the aims of the New Deal as well as to the material needs of America's coal miners. The time has come, proclaimed Lewis, to end the baseless and inequitable wage differentials between districts and to establish uniform wage levels. Trust the New Deal, the NRA, and its coal code, he assured operators, and prices for coal will be set high enough to cover increased wages and still produce a profit. Lewis argued that coal's economic recovery necessitated cooperation with the UMW, President Roosevelt, and the New Deal. Miners' wages not only must be equalized, but they must also be increased substantially he warned, because the New Deal's effort to revive the national economy depended on high wage levels and expanded consumer purchasing power.

Northern operators proved willing collaborators with Lewis and the UMW. The coal code had saved them from financial ruin, and Lewis's demand for wage equalization promised them further competitive benefits. But southern operators refused to make further concessions. Southern West Virginia operators early on left the 1934 Appalachian Joint Conference, and Alabama mine owners never attended. And those southern interests remaining in the conference fought hardest against the UMW's demands. Not until the early morning of March 31—described by the UMW *Journal* as "the last minute on the last day before the expiration of the old contract between operators and miners"—did the operators make substantial concessions to the UMW. Rather than risk a nationwide coal strike on the following day and the likelihood of presidential intervention on behalf of the miners, southern operators joined with their northern colleagues in accepting a new Appalachian joint agreement with the UMW to run from April 1, 1934 to March 31, 1935.

The 1934 agreement granted the UMW a substantial victory. Miners won the seven-hour day, five-day week and a narrowing of wage differentials; $5 became the basic daily minimum wage in all the large northern districts and $4.60 the minimum throughout the South. The union also won complete recognition, the full dues checkoff (meaning, in effect, the establishment of the union shop, insuring that all workers in union mines would have to join the union), and the right to discipline militant union members and wildcat strikers. So complete was Lewis's victory that even a majority of the Harlan County operators signed the new agreement, and in a separate arrangement, southern West Virginia mine owners accepted terms. Only Alabama's operators refused to respect the 1934 Appalachian agreement.

What Lewis failed to win through union power he obtained through federal intervention. Almost immediately, Lewis requested Hugh Johnson to make the new contract's terms part of an amendment to the September 1933 bituminous coal code, a process that would apply the revised wages and working conditions to all soft-coal producers. Johnson promptly announced hearings scheduled for Washington on April 11 to amend the bituminous coal code in order to encompass the seven-hour day, five-day week and a rise in minimum daily wages in southern Appalachian mines from $3.40 to $4.60. Not unexpectedly, the Alabama operators rejected the amendments and vowed to obtain a legal injunction against implementing them.

Marshaling his evidence carefully, presenting detailed statistics on comparative living costs and wage levels, and defending the right of southern workers to a decent existence, Lewis shattered the operators' case for a lower southern cost of living, especially for black miners who composed half or more of their labor force. Black coal miners lived more poorly than their white brothers and tolerated a lower standard of living, Lewis proved, not because their needs and standards were more primitive, but because they had no choice. Racism not only depressed black wage levels, but it also compelled black miners to pay more than whites for identical housing. Operators had no answer to Lewis's statistical presentation, and, as the UMW president expected and Johnson promised, the bituminous coal code was amended as Lewis recommended.

The UMW was now secure for at least a year if not longer in the nation's commercial soft-coal mines. Government-sanctioned and union-approved wage rates and working conditions covered miners from northeastern Pennsylvania to Alabama, from eastern Ohio to Washington state. In the vast majority of coal mines covering more than 90 percent of working soft-coal miners, Lewis won contracts that provided union recognition, the checkoff, and the union shop.

The year-long struggle to build labor influence with Franklin D. Roosevelt and to reorganize the coalfields under the NRA had taken its toll physically on John L. Lewis and also on Phil Murray. Lewis's apparent physical vigor and vitality cloaked a constitution vulnerable to collapse. His resistance to respiratory infections weakened by his early years in the mines and later years of ceaseless travel, Lewis was immobilized by the common cold. Apparently fatigued by the feverish and protracted negotiations that resulted in the last-minute agreement with mine operators on March 31, 1934, Lewis became ill and left Washington to recuperate at the Fort Sumter Hotel in Charleston. Writing to Phil Murray from the hotel on May 6, Lewis joked: "Am still a little below par, but improving. Am up and around and eating with enthusiasm. Meals on the American plan. One tries to eat his way right down through the menu." Rejuvenated by his retreat from union affairs, Lewis offered Murray advice. "Am sorry, indeed, that you are ill— Hope you are much improved. Trust you will take plenty of time to get well. Stay away from the downtown office. . . . Things seem to go just as well when we are both taking time out. Let us therefore, says I, take more time out."

Lewis soon had another opportunity to "take more time out." No sooner had he returned to Washington than Secretary of Labor Frances Perkins appointed him as one of the American labor delegates to the upcoming International Labor Organization meeting in Geneva. On route to the meeting, Myrta and John celebrated their twenty-seventh wedding anniversary on June 5 aboard the S.S. *President Roosevelt,* where the captain entertained them at dinner. In Paris the Lewises were flooded with dinner invitations from wealthy American expatriates, businessmen, and diplomats, as well as foreign officials. Lewis even appeared as the featured guest at a reception held by the American Chamber of Commerce in Paris. Throughout his month-long European trip, Lewis spent more time with diplomats, foreign dignitaries, wealthy exiles, and socialites than with the labor leaders he met in Geneva. Myrta used the occasion to add expensive additions to her gallery of antiques. Picture postcards that the Lewises mailed to their family and friends suggest that Myrta and John made the most of their journey.

Lewis returned to the United States in midsummer 1934 ready to open a new chapter in his own career and in the history of American trade unionism. The labor lamb who had laid down with corporate wolves from 1924 to 1932 was about to become the union lion who roared at industrialists and congressmen. The man who in 1933 seemed "merely a labor boss of the most conventional kind," "a big-bellied, oldtime labor leader . . . an autocrat, per capita counter, egotist, power seeker" was about to become the idol of labor radicals, social reformers, and militant workers. The labor leader characterized by A. J. Muste in October 1934 as an "essentially reactionary" and obsequious follower of the Roosevelt administration would soon win a reputation as a radical and eventually become the labor movement's bluntest critic of Franklin D. Roosevelt.

10

The Challenge,
July 1934–October 1935

While John L. Lewis vacationed in South Carolina and toured the European continent, American workers rebelled. In Toledo, Minneapolis, and San Francisco, strikers, police, and troops waged a bloody class war. Ohio National Guardsmen with fixed bayonets cleared Toledo's streets of strikers. A violent confrontation between teamsters and police in Minneapolis's main square left sixty-seven persons wounded—two fatally. And in San Francisco, the deaths of two strikers and the presence of state militia armed with machine guns and armored vehicles ignited a citywide general strike.

More significant than the violence associated with the three conflicts was the reality that all erupted independently of the American Federation of Labor and under militant radical leadership. Strikers in the three cities acted without A.F. of L. authorization and sometimes against the federation's wishes; in Minneapolis and San Francisco they won more complete victories for trade unionism than "legitimate" A.F. of L. unions had achieved in 1933 and 1934.

Signs of labor unrest also flared among other workers. Auto workers either flooded A.F. of L. federal labor unions in late 1933 and early 1934 or joined several independent labor organizations especially active in the Detroit area. Eager to improve working conditions, gain job security, and build an industrial union encompassing all employees in the industry in March 1934 auto workers threatened a nationwide strike. Only presidential intervention averted the walkout.

Similar stories repeated themselves in the steel, rubber, aluminum, and other mass-production industries. Mass-production workers by the thousands enrolled in newly chartered federal labor unions or flooded old lodges of such established unions as the Amalgamated Association of Iron, Steel, and Tin Workers. Wanting action and immediate gains, the new union members demanded solidarity—industrial unions that encompassed all workers in a single industry regardless of skill, job classification, or earnings, not craft unions that parceled them out among many varieties of labor organizations. But in steel and rubber as in autos, A.F. of L. leaders refused to charter unrestricted industrial unions, advised against militant action, feared the power of employers, and deferred to President Roosevelt's desire for industrial peace. By the summer of 1934 the initial gains by organized labor in the mass-production industries had been completely dissipated.

Even where A.F. of L. affiliates acted vigorously in 1934, the results proved disappointing. In June, the United Textile Workers of America inaugurated a general strike in the textile industry that spread from Maine to Alabama and involved between three and four hundred thousand workers. Employer resistance crushed the textile workers' union and its strike. For millions of American workers, Roosevelt's New Deal was turning into a raw, old deal.

Two years' experience with the NIRA and Section 7a taught even the A.F. of L.'s old guard the reasons for organized labor's ineffectiveness. "Only where labor was well organized," wrote John Frey, the custodian of the A.F. of L.'s craft union tradition and its voluntaristic political policy, "was there anything like adequate enforcement. . . . Labor did have a voice in N.R.A., but business had a greater voice and much more control of the situation."

Beyond coal and the needle trades, organized labor had won little of positive value during the New Deal's first two years. Slightly more than three milion workers, or about 12 percent of the nonagricultural labor force, belonged to trade unions in 1934—a smaller proportion than in 1922. By midsummer 1934 labor's upheaval had produced more company unions than independent unions and more aborted strikes or defeats than victories. John Frey appeared right: Employers were better organized, more class conscious, more determined to prevent union growth, and, consequently, more influential in Washington.

Labor leaders seemed to face an insoluble dilemma. Without mass organization, labor lacked effective political influence; without the guardianship of a benevolent government, unions could not defeat recalcitrant employers. During the New Deal years, more so than ever before, the federal government acted as society's arbiter; it determined the outcome of conflicts between private disputants. While government action was publicly defended as promoting justice and equality, in reality its influence was customarily shifted to favor the better-organized, and hence the stronger, party in the conflict.

Even while he recuperated from illness in Charleston and enjoyed Europe as a tourist, John L. Lewis doubtless pondered labor's dilemma.

His own experience with the coal strikes and code negotiations of 1933 and 1934 had convinced him that federal officials would henceforth exert a decisive influence in labor relations and that only a militant, organized group of workers could compel public officials to assist unions against management. Lewis realized that labor's economic and political futures were inextricably linked and that union leaders had to lobby intensively for support among Washington politicians and then use legislative or executive sanction to organize workers who would vote for their "benefactors." Politicians, like businessmen and union leaders, Lewis sensed, operated in a utilitarian universe; how much you invested depended on your estimation of the potential payoff. Such utilitarian values prompted Lewis to cast aside all hoary labor traditions. Where William Green, John Frey, and Matthew Woll viewed the issues of the 1930s as colored by the past, Lewis counted votes, estimated power, and seized opportunities.

New times called for new methods, and Lewis, the perfect union politician, was always ready to change to suit a new environment. Life was a contest to Lewis in which success went not to the best sportsman or the man who followed established rules but to the man who made his own rules and played the game according to present needs, not past rituals. As he explained to William Green in June 1936: "I am not concerned with history. . . I am concerned with the problems of today and tomorrow." While other labor leaders of his generation turned to the past to guide them in the present, Lewis never allowed what had been to limit what might yet be, and he turned to a younger generation— the restless, rebellious, and even "red"—to point him toward the future.

Lewis returned home from Europe in the summer of 1934 with one aim in mind: to organize the nation's mass-production workers and build a labor movement of twenty-five to thirty-five million members. The political implications of such an achievement needed no exegesis, nor did one have to be a prophet to realize that such an accomplishment would establish Lewis as the nation's most influential labor leader.

From June 1933 through July 1934, the A. F. of L.'s leaders had squandered an opportunity, letting power slip through their grasp as their hesitancy, fear of militancy, and respect for outdated jurisdictional boundaries caused them to dismay or betray millions of mass-production workers. In the summer of 1934, however, labor's future remained open; latent power still existed in the factories, streets, and neighborhoods of working-class America. And Lewis proposed to offer his fellow barons of trade unionism another chance to build a powerful mass working-class movement.

By 1935 Lewis was ready to gamble all the resources at his command

and his place and prestige in the labor movment on the chance that millions of mass-production workers could be organized. Nothing would deflect Lewis from that objective—neither past union failures in that sector of the economy, nor a generalized suspicion that semiskilled factory operatives were unorganizable, nor fear of jurisdictional battles among craft unions, nor knowledge that such an organizing campaign would cost huge sums of money. Lewis could, when the occasion demanded, be as profligate a gambler as he was a cautious, cunning opportunist. What became perhaps the greatest gamble in Lewis's entire life paid off, but not before it split the A.F. of L. and led to the creation of the Committee for Industrial organization (CIO).

The story of Lewis's crusade to organize mass-production workers into industrial unions and convert the A.F. of L. executive council to the cause is a tale of thrusts and counterthrusts, of quick advances and rapid retreats, of rhetorical triumphs and substantive defeats. In this saga of parry and thrust, Lewis's decision to create the CIO flowed as much from the actions of his critics in the A.F. of L. as from the logic of a preconceived plan.

By late summer of 1934 the New Deal seemed at a dead end. With full recovery from depression no nearer than it had been during the Hoover days, left-wingers and right-wingers freely criticized the Roosevelt administration. Trade unionists, especially, accused Roosevelt of subservience to big business and denigrated NRA as the "national runaround."

But if Roosevelt had fooled the nation, so, too, had the majority of American labor leaders. The attitudes and practices of the A.F. of L. hierarchy made American industrialists by comparison seem innovative, adventurous, and almost radical. More concerned with defending than expanding their existing fiefdoms, most craft union leaders raised barriers to the organizaton of the less skilled, mass-production workers. Rather than squander money or risk a diminution of their own power, the craft unionists preferred to cite union traditions and jurisdictional claims as reasons not to build mass industrial unions.

Successful organizaton of the mass-production workers in no way threatened Lewis's union power. Indeed, he might well ride organization of the masses to increased power inside the labor movement. The potential expense of organizing millions of workers also did not trouble Lewis. In the summer of 1933 he had gambled the remainder of the UMW's treasury in an organizing campaign among coal miners—and won. In late 1934 he was willing to take the same risk in a bid to unionize much larger numbers of workers. Lewis, who could cite jurisdictional claims with the most legalistic of craft unionists, implored that labor leaders submerge their particular union's jurisdictions to the greater necessity of organizing workers. Organization first, jurisdiction later, became Lewis's battle cry. In a Labor Day 1934 statement, Lewis asserted that the A.F. of L. *must* authorize a policy of industrial unionism for employees in the mass-production industries.

If Lewis played a radical and militant inside the labor movement, he acted as a reformer and moderate outside. Nowhere was this aspect of Lewis's character better revealed than in a speech he delivered on October 10, 1934, before the Commonwealth Club in San Francisco. Delivering ideas formulated by Jett Lauck (who referred to the speech as "simply made up of our old lines of thought in a rearranged form"), Lewis defended the New Deal and NRA as the "Middle Way," an American democratic response to depression preferable to fascist or communist dictatorship. He forcefully reminded his listeners of what had recently happened in Germany (Hitler) and Italy (Mussolini) and what might occur in the United States if "those reactionary industrial groups who have 'eyes but see not' and 'ears but hear not'" thwart sound public policy and the labor movement. Placing the responsibility first for depression and then for violations of Section 7a squarely on a Wall Street financial elite (the Morgan-Dupont-Rockefeller triumvirate central to the Lauck-Lewis demonology), Lewis warned that their indefensible tactics would inevitably cause "an industrial revolt ... attended by the menace of Communism or Fascism. ... If I may speak as a prophet," he told his audience. "I ... say that full organization on the part of free labor, with the free right to enter into collective agreements with employers, is bound to come sooner or later, if the economic system, as we now know it, is to endure. ... Labor cannot, and will not, and should not ever be content until its partnership becomes a real one and not merely one in theory. To oppose such a movement is, to paraphrase an old saying, not only a crime against labor—it is a social blunder which may lead to the toppling over of our whole economic edifice."

While Lewis invited the Bay Area's elite to support the New Deal in seeking a middle way for the United States, he told the A.F. of L.'s resolutions committee and its 1934 convention delegates that there was only one way to organize the nation's mass-production workers, and it was not the middle way preferred by craft unionists. Mass-production workers could not be parceled out by trade to competing craft unions, nor could the less skilled among them be offered an inferior status.

But Lewis in 1934 spoke for and to an A.F. of L. minority. The majority, weighted with the votes of Arthur Wharton, Bill Hutcheson, and Dan Tobin (of the machinists', carpenters', and teamsters' unions, respectively) and the parliamentary leadership of John Frey and Matthew Woll—lawyers and legalists more than labor leaders or organizers—preferred craft to industrial unions and determined to guard the jurisdictional claims of the former.

Nevertheless, in an attempt to preserve harmony, Woll and Charles P. Howard of the Typographical Union engineered a compromise acceptable to Lewis. It recognized the principle that the mass-production industries must be organized on "a different basis" and that charters, implicitly industrial in character, be issued to unions in the automotive, cement, aluminum, and other mass-production industries as deemed necessary by the executive council. The executive council, moreover, was charged with inaugurating promptly an organizing campaign in the iron and steel industry. Having moved that far in satisfying Lewis and the industrial unionists, the A.F. of L. majority recommended that "the jurisdictional claims of existing unions be protected by authorizing the executive council, for a provisional period, [to] direct the policies, administer the business, and designate the administrative and financial officers of . . . newly organized unions."

The 1934 A.F. of L. convention had thus recommended a middle way in the dispute between craft and industrial unionists. Lewis accepted this singular compromise, of which Howard Brubaker wrote in the *New Yorker:* "The A.F. of L. has adopted the industrial form of organization without abandoning the craft-union plan. If it can be horizontal and vertical at the same time, prizefighters would be pleased to know the details."

Brubaker's sarcasm notwithstanding, the 1934 convention seemed a triumph for Lewis. He thought so. Not only had the convention endorsed the principle of industrial unionism, however equivocably, but it had also expanded the executive council from eight to fifteen members, elected Lewis to one of the new seats, and welcomed the Amalgamated Clothing Workers of America and its president, Sidney Hillman, an outspoken advocate of industrial unionism, into the A.F. of L.

Although the convention left the issue of industrial unionism and the campaign to organize mass-production workers to the discretion of the executive council on which Lewis represented a minority (among the other newly elected council members were Hutcheson and Tobin, the most bitter opponents of industrial unionism), the UMW president obviously expected to influence the council's decisions. Lewis's ego surpassed that of any other council member, and his intellect, wit, and command of the English language far exceeded that of his fellow labor leaders. Accustomed to absolute dominance in the inner councils of the miners' union, Lewis hoped to replicate his power on the A.F. of L. executive council, where his arrogance, self-assurance, rhetorical prowess, and adamance would overwhelm less verbal and more epicene colleagues. One might also assume that Lewis expected sympathy and support from the A.F. of L. president, William Green, who had served in Lewis's shadow within the UMW and been elevated to his position in the federation partly through Lewis's influence.

In late 1934, Lewis had no intention yet of splitting the labor movement or forming his own industrial union federation. Quite the contrary. But from January through August 1935, Lewis occupied a position on the A. F. of L. executive council as a persistent critic of the trade union movement. The first meeting Lewis attended as a member of the A. F. of L. executive council from January 29 to February 14, 1935, brought into sharp focus the clash between craft unionists and industrial unionists. The related questions of issuing an industrial union charter to the auto workers and organizing the steelworkers occupied much of the council's time and occasioned the most heated discussion, in which Lewis participated prominently.

Whereas the council's majority appeared most concerned with guarding the jurisdictional claims of the craft unions, Lewis addressed the realities of economic and political power. The failure of the A.F. of L. to organize the auto workers and its alacrity at accepting presidential awards for the industry that subverted trade unionism, warned Lewis, "is an exhibition of public weakness that reflects itself in the White House and makes it possible for the Recovery Administration and the White House to make decisions with impunity or without fear of any successful challenge from the American Federation of Labor. Our weakness is fundamental." We are weak, he added, because the public believes, and rightly, that we have no organization among auto workers. Our enemies, as well as our potential allies in Washington, measure labor's strength, analyze its possibility as an adversary. "Our weakness to get anything is the absence of effective competent organization." Remember, advised Lewis" "It is axiomatic . . . that you can get just about what you are ready to take."

Lewis asserted that the time had come to *take* the auto workers, to use the energy and talent of the young men in the industry, and to "give them an international union and money enough to carry on a campaign." It must be done, he proceeded, for "we are all on trial. . . . There is a distinct anti-Federation sentiment abroad. The White House is tainted with that anti-Federation sentiment. So many stories have been given to the White House about our weakness that they have become contemptuous." We must throw money and men into the auto industry and postpone jurisdictional disputes until the men are actually organized. Lewis formulated a seven-point program for organization of the auto workers that, in effect, temporarily placed the auto union under executive council guardianship and hence conformed to the 1934 convention resolution on industrial unionism. Lewis pleaded with the craft unionists to subordinate their jurisdictional claims "for the greater consideration of safeguarding American labor in mass production industries and regenerating and again restoring to normal the lowered prestige of the American Federation of Labor before the American people."

Ignoring Lewis's impassioned plea that "contention over the fruits of victory [jurisdictional claims] be deferred until we have some of the fruits in our possession," the council's craft union majority defeated Lewis's motion to postpone the settlement of jurisdictional claims in the auto industry until after the workers were organized by a margin of twelve to two (only David Dubinsky of the ladies' garment workers voted with Lewis).

Lewis was also frustrated in his effort to institute industrial unionism in the iron and steel industry. Again Lewis addressed the realities of power, reminding his colleagues that the A.F. of L. was threatened by its own ineffectiveness and that the Amalgamated Association of Iron, Steel, and Tin Workers, the old craft union that claimed absolute jurisdiction in the steel industry, had been bypassed by history and relegated to the dustheap. The past, the present, and common sense all teach, advised Lewis, that the steel industry can only be organized by placing the workers in one union.

But the executive council again preferred equivocation to decisiveness and, instead of granting an industrial union charter to a new organization in steel, it authorized Lewis, Tobin, and Wharton as a three-man committee to negotiate with the officers of the Amalgamated Association—Michael "Grandmother" Tighe and Louis "Shorty" Leonard—concerning Lewis's proposal for industrial unionism. Naturally, Tighe and Leonard refused to relinquish their union's jurisdiction in the steel industry or to allow a special A.F. of L. committee to organize steel for them. Rebuffed by the Amalgamated Association, the executive council refused to act in steel. A twice-defeated Lewis persisted in claiming that labor's "fundamental obligation is to organize people."

Before the next A. F. of L. executive council meeting scheduled for the first week of May 1935, Lewis decided to force the issues of industrial unionism and organization of mass-production workers to a resolution. Hints began to emanate from UMW headquarters that Lewis needed the assistance of the young, the rebellious, and the "red" to organize the nation's workers. On April 23, Germer, again on the UMW payroll, learned that a bitter feud was on between Lewis and William Green, no doubt because the A.F. of L. president had failed to endorse Lewis's demand for unionization of the auto, steel, and other mass-production industries. Even as the executive council met from April 30 to May 7, Louis Stark reported in the May 3 *New York Times* that the formation of a bloc of unions into a separate national labor federation led by the

UMW appeared an eventual possibility because, according to the miners, the executive council had repudiated the San Francisco convention's resolution on industrial unionism. Earlier in April, Lewis welcomed union insurgents from the steel industry to meet with him in his office at UMW headquarters. The same local leaders expelled from the Amalgamated Association for their alleged communist connections were embraced by the president of the mine workers.

Lewis's tactics upset the A.F. of L.'s old guard. On March 21, John Frey, craft unionism's most pedantic defender, worried that William Green had joined the "industrial unionists." Certain, however, of support for his position by fellow craft unionists on the executive council, Frey prophesied a showdown between industrial and craft unionists at the 1935 convention. "There must be a show down," he informed an English acquaintance, "for it is becoming intolerable to have some International Unions determined that other International Unions must change their form of organization against their desire."

Frey's prophesy concerning the 1935 A.F. of L. convention proved accurate, but his fears about Green's loyalty were unwarranted. When the executive council convened on April 30, again to consider the issue of industrial unionism and organization of the mass-production workers, Green offered Lewis neither solace nor support.

Focusing his case for industrial unionism this time on the rubber industry, Lewis insisted that its workers demanded solidarity—a union structure that encompassed all employees of the industry regardless of job classification or skill. Let craft unions serve their members and even flourish, Lewis said, but do not allow theories about union structure to obstruct the organizaton of mass-production workers never before unionized and employed in industries traditionally resistant to craft unionism.

To Lewis's consternation but not surprise, the overwhelming majority of executive council members (fourteen to two) evinced more concern about jurisdictional rights than about organizing the unorganized. Not even the prospect of imminent passage of the Wagner Labor Relations Act, the most pro-union legislation ever to emerge from Congress, motivated the A.F. of L. old guard to heed Lewis's advice.

Not long after the executive council adjourned on May 7, rumors again circulated predicting a split in the labor movement. "It has grown increasingly clear," commented an editorial writer in the *Nation* of May 22, "that secession of industrial unions from the A.F. of L. may be inevitable if the young industrial unions are to grow. Leadership will naturally fall to John L. Lewis of the United Mine Workers and Sidney Hillman of the needle trades." Earlier in the month, when Louis Stark had published information leaked by Lewis or his associates in the pages of the *New York Times,* the purpose had obviously been to pressure the executive council majority into granting industrial union charters to auto, steel, and rubber workers. That bluff having failed, the *Nation*'s story suggested quite plainly that Lewis finally had decided to act independently concerning industrial unionism unless the old guard in the A.F. of L. changed its collective mind between May 1935 and the convention in October.

Lewis's actions threatened a rift in the trade union establishment. He attended neither the August 1935 nor the October 1935 session of the executive council. Not one to accept minority status equably, the lord of the UMW refused to play vassal in the councils of the A.F. of L. In July Lewis embraced the American Left more firmly. Writing to his wife on July 24, Powers Hapgood observed: "It's surprising how many radicals think I ought to see Lewis, saying it's much less of a compromise to make peace with him and stay in the labor movement than it is to get a government job and cease to be active in the class struggle."

Lewis also occupied himself in the spring and summer of 1935 by lobbying Congress and by cementing political alliances that would prove essential to his campaign to organize mass-production workers. First Lewis had to protect the UMW from economic competition and antiunion operators. He did this by joining with northern coal operators in pressuring Congress to enact legislation that would transform the soft-coal industry into a federally regulated utility. Lewis and his operator allies obtained passage of the Guffey-Snyder Coal Stabilization Act, which established a little NRA for bituminous coal, guaranteed miners the right to organize and bargain collectively, mandated minimum wages and maximum hours, and created a federal commission to fix prices and allocate production (and thus markets).

May and June 1935, however, brought Lewis frustration as well as triumph. A series of Supreme Court decisions in May paralyzed the New Deal. On May 27 the Court, in a unanimous decision, declared the National Industrial Recovery Act unconstitutional—a ruling that threatened labor's rights under Section 7a and presidential employment codes setting minimum wages and maximum hours; it also presaged a similar legal fate for the Guffey-Snyder Act.

But in June Congress passed the Wagner Act, granting organized labor far greater protection than it had been ceded under Section 7a. Signed by President Roosevelt in early July, the new labor law effectively outlawed company unions, declared illegal the most widely used employer antiunion weapons, placed no restraints on trade unions, and created a National Labor Relations Board to administer the new law. Never before had the federal government, or for that matter any American political jurisdiction, offered the union such substantial protection against employers. The Wagner Act indeed provided organized labor with Lewis's often cited once-in-a-lifetime opportunity to unionize the nation's mass-production workers.

By early September Lewis acted as one of the nation's most ardent Roosevelt admirers. Speaking to a September 2 Labor Day rally in Fairmont, West Virginia, the largest outdoor meeting ever held in the area and attended by forty thousand coal miners and their families, Lewis demanded the reelection of Franklin D. Roosevelt. Lewis told an enthusiastic audience that "the era of privilege and predatory individuals is over." He called on American workers to join Roosevelt in a struggle against the Liberty League and the reactionary elite that for too long had dominated the United States.

Its 1935 convention in Atlantic City was like no other in the A.F. of L.'s fifty-year existence. The brisk October sea breezes and salt air scarcely cooled the passions about organizing the unorganized that Lewis had inflamed during the year that had passed since the San Francisco convention; nor did they chill the ardor of the young and rebellious who came to New Jersey's resort determined to participate in the building of a mass labor movement.

The hotel chosen as convention headquarters personified the character of the A.F. of L. old guard. In its garish elegance, the Chelsea Hotel seemed an antiquarian relic in depression America. Lewis consciously and calculatingly set himself and his union apart from the ambience of the Chelsea; he established UMW convention headquarters in the more modest President Hotel, where he held court and advised the militant young delegates from the steel, auto, and rubber industries. Welcomed by a labor leader with power, the delegates, in Len DeCaux's words, "came away glowing." As Powers Hapgood had discovered in July, a new Lewis was in the making, one who seemed not to care whether his associates in the labor movement were left or right, red or pink.

But Lewis was too experienced a labor politician to believe that he could stampede the convention delegates. The craft unionists who opposed Lewis on the council (usually by twelve to two) controlled the votes of their convention delegates as tightly as Lewis dominated his UMW group. What support Lewis had, aside from the needle trades unions and several old A.F. of L. affiliates with industrial union traditions, came largely from state federations and city centrals, which each cast only a single vote, and from federal labor unions, whose voting rights bore no relation to actual membership. Even if the vast majority of organized workers favored Lewis's bid to organize the unorganized— and later evidence would suggest they did—they had no means to express their sentiments in Atlantic City. Hutcheson spoke for the carpenters, Wharton for the machinists, and Tobin for the teamsters, and their voices would strike the same chords at the convention that they had hit at every session of the executive council. What, then, was Lewis's strategy? What motivated his desire to associate himself with younger insurgent delegates in a losing cause?

Several likely answers come to mind. First, the possibility of long-term gains for Lewis far outweighed the short-run risks. If he read reality correctly and gauged political power accurately, the moment was propitious for organizing mass-production workers. Even if defeated on the convention floor, Lewis would leave Atlantic City as the heroic advocate of industrial unionism, the brave spokesman for the aspirations of millions of unorganized workers. Second, defeat in October 1935 did not foreclose an ultimate victory. If Lewis was right, most rank-and-file trade unionists sympathized with his policy, as did millions of unorganized mass-production workers. He not only sought to organize the unorganized; Lewis also called on craft union members to rebel against an unresponsive and unrepresentative leadership. Third, a mystical quality underlay Lewis's decision to fight for industrial unionism in 1935, a quality captured in Heber Blankenhorn's later remembrance of a chance meeting on the Boardwalk with Lewis the night before the convention's climactic debate on industrial unionism.

Late that evening [October 15] I went for a walk on the Board-walk . . . when a sudden shower came up and I took refuge under a tin shelter over some benches. Before long a big man with his coat collar turned up and his hat brim pulled down, sat down at the other end of the bench. . . . When he struck a match . . . I said, "Hello, John."

Lewis waved the match in my direction . . . and said, "Hello, Blank," without cordiality. . . . I mentioned his industrial union resolution at the 1934 convention . . . and asked if he had been thinking about organizing the new units in the basic industries on an industrial union basis.

Lewis' big hand fell on my forearm with an iron grip. He said, "I have been thinking of nothing else for a year. Day and night. Night and day. Last night I could not sleep. I sat in my bathrobe, at the window, facing east, looking over the sea, where I could see nothing but dark night, not even the ocean or the sky. Mrs. Lewis called, asking why I did not go to bed, what was I waiting up for? I said, 'I am waiting for the sun to rise!' After a little while the first ray appeared and I could see the line of sky and sea, and gradually the rays slowly spread and dawn was breaking. Then with startling speed, the sun's rim glinted and I said, 'Behold, at last the sun arises, the day is here, day has come.' And I went to bed and slept soundly."

I was awed by this mystic. When he took his big hand off my forearm it was numb. We sat there silently, while he tried again to light his cigar. The rain stopped, and Lewis stood up. He said, "I shall go back to my hotel now and tonight I shall sleep for the day is here and I am ready."

The climactic day indeed arrived on October 16, as delegates to the 1935 A.F. of L. convention debated from 2:30 to 11:45 p.m. a report by a minority of the Resolutions Committee that the A.F. of L. issue industrial union charters to workers in the mass-production industries. The minority report stressed the failure historically of the A.F. of L. to organize workers in the basic industries along jurisdictional lines outmoded by technological change. Of almost forty million wage workers, the A.F. of L. at most represented three and a half million. No one, including the most militant of industrial unionists, desired to strip craft unions of their members. The real issue was not craft versus industrial unionism; it was whether or not the A.F. of L. would authorize a large-scale organizing campaign among the mass-production workers on the only foundation that promised success—industrial unionism.

After Matthew Woll delivered a lengthy rebuttal to the minority's position—studded with misread history lessons, arid legalisms, and an exegesis of the A.F. of L. constitution worthy of a Medieval divine—Lewis arose and made the debate's most dramatic speech.

A year ago at San Francisco [he declaimed] I was a year younger and naturally I had more faith in the Executive Council. I was beguiled into believing that an enlarged Executive Council would honestly interpret and administer this policy—the policy we talked about for six days in committee, the policy of issuing charters for industrial unions in the mass production industries. But surely Delegate Woll would not hold it against me that I was so trusting at that time. I know better now. At San Francisco they seduced me with fair words. Now, of course, having learned that I was seduced, I am enraged and I am ready to rend my seducers limb from limb.

The labor movement, Lewis proclaimed, "is organized upon a principle that the strong shall help the weak." Calling upon the strong craft unions to assist their weaker brothers in the mass-production industries, Lewis now asked A.F. of L. delegates to "heed this cry from Macedonia that comes from the hearts of men." If you reject the minority report, he warned the delegates, "despair will prevail where hope now exists. . . . High wassail will prevail at the banquet tables of the mighty."

The debate raged on for several more hours, ever more heated, ever more ad hominem and scurrilous, but it changed few votes. In the event all the large international craft unions, the dominant sector of the federation, voted against the minority report. The UMW, the brewery workers, the mine, mill, and smelter workers, the needle trades unions, the state federations, city centrals, and federal labor unions voted in favor of the report. Thus by a margin of 18,024 to 10,933 the minority report went down to defeat, rapidly followed by the adoption by voice vote of the majority report.

On the succeeding three days the advocates of industrial unionism suffered further setbacks, all by virtually the same voting margin. The triumphant old guard even sought to silence the industrial unionists through parliamentary rulings. When a delegate from the rubber workers raised the question of jurisdiction for his union, Hutcheson of the carpenters interjected a point of order. It was a moment that Lewis had waited for, an event he would have manufactured if necessary. "This thing of raising points of order all the time on minor delegates," Lewis challenged the burly, oversized carpenters' leader, "is rather small po-tatoes." More heated words passed between the two labor barons, with Hutcheson finally calling Lewis a "bastard." At that, Lewis jumped to his feet, leaped over a row of chairs toward Hutcheson, jabbed out his right fist, and sent the carpenters' president sprawling against a table. Moments later the fight was over, as a blood-streaked Hutcheson left the convention floor guided by friends. "Lewis," wrote the labor jour-nalist Edward Levinson, "casually adjusted his tie and collar, relit his cigar, and sauntered slowly through the crowded aisles to the rostrum."

Cool calculation, not passion; purposeful tactics, not anger, explained Lewis's resort to physical force. Hutcheson, unlike Tobin, was neither an old enemy nor personally obnoxious to Lewis. Instead, they were old Indianapolis poker cronies, a relationship that would be resumed in the 1940s. Lewis's blow to Hutcheson's jaw was intended to symbolize publicly the UMW president's irrevocable rupture with labor's old guard. It also dramatized, as no number of words or convention resolutions would, the split between Lewis and his critics. No one could now doubt that Lewis was serious about his plans to organize the unorganized. Lewis's punch resonated through the working class. One of Hutcheson's own constituents, a Kansas City union carpenter, wired Lewis: "Con-gratulations, sock him again."

11

Founding the CIO, October 1935–October 1936

Lewis quickly took the offensive against the A.F. of L. old guard. On Sunday morning, October 20, the day after the 1935 convention adjourned, Lewis had a breakfast meeting at the President Hotel with Phil Murray, Tom Kennedy, John Brophy, Sidney Hillman, and David Dubinsky, as well as Charles Howard of the printer's union, Thomas McMahon of the textile workers' union, and Max Zaritsky representing the capmakers. Lewis told his eight companions that only they could answer the pleas of the unorganized, that they must not let their defeat obstruct efforts to unionize mass-production workers. But the breakfast ended with the advocates of industrial unionism as far from achievement of their primary objective as they had been when the A.F. of L. convention opened the previous week.

Less than three weeks later, on November 9, 1935, Lewis invited his Atlantic City breakfast associates as well as Thomas Brown of the mine, mill, and smelter workers, and Harvey Fremming of the oil workers to a meeting at UMW headquarters. There the eleven labor leaders created the Committee for Industrial Organization as an organized bloc inside the A.F. of L. dedicated to unionizing mass-production workers along industrial lines. Beyond appointing Lewis as chairman, Howard as secretary, and Brophy as director and obtaining $5,000 pledges from the UMW, ACWA, and ILGWU, the labor leaders at the November 9 conference made no plans, adopted no policies, and simply reiterated their commitment to promote the organization of mass-production workers inside the A.F. of L. They also invited other trade unionists sympathetic to industrial unionism to join the CIO.

Nine days later, on November 18, John Brophy opened the CIO's first office, in the Rust Building, at Fifteenth and K Streets, N.W., in Washington, across the street from UMW headquarters. Aided by two secretaries—Katherine Pollack and Bernice Welsh—Brophy planned, in the words of a "Proposed Outline of Activities for the CIO" prepared by Pollack, "to foster recognition and acceptance of collective bargaining in [mass production] industries; to council and advise unorganized and newly organized groups of workers; to bring them under the banner and in affiliation with the American Federation of Labor." Brophy and his assistants prepared pamphlets explaining the history and principles of industrial unionism, circulated them among workers and union groups, and planned to publish a regular newsletter (the *CIO News*). Shortly afterward, with Lewis's consent, Brophy hired Len DeCaux—a talented journalist of British origin, a communist, and a former critic of Lewis— as editor of the newsletter and CIO publicist. DeCaux's appointment was yet another indication of the transformation in Lewis's values and his apparent willingness to collaborate with leftists.

In a real sense the CIO at birth was Lewis. Brophy was an extension of the UMW president, a man who served at Lewis's pleasure and who was paid by the mine workers' union. Lewis's fellow committee members David Dubinsky and Max Zaritsky lacked national influence and seemed as eager to maintain the respectability that the A.F. of L. conferred on them as to please Lewis. Fremming, Brown, and McMahon represented weak unions, negligible political influence, and no power in the A.F. of L. Howard, perhaps the most principled and unselfish of all the CIO founders, spoke only for himself, not his union, which never affiliated with the CIO. Only Sidney Hillman approached Lewis in stature and influence. Much admired by labor journalists, academics, and social reformers, Hillman, however, led a union—the Amalgamated Clothing Workers—that operated in a peripheral industry and represented a narrow strata of the American working class: largely Jewish and Italian immigrants. Among the CIO's founders then, only Lewis had in the past bargained as an equal with the men who ran the A.F. of L., and only Lewis led a union situated at the heart of the American industrial economy.

With the founding of the CIO, the struggle to organize the unorganized turned into a personal conflict between William Green and John L. Lewis—a clash that had dark, unconscious Freudian undertones. In the past, whether as a UMW official or as president of the A.F. of L., Green had customarily deferred to Lewis's more arrogant and commanding personality. Now, suddenly, in November 1935, Green sought to establish his personal prowess, to prove to the more "manly" members of his executive council that he was their equal and that he would discipline Lewis as a rebellious child.

In late November, before the CIO had done anything that could be construed as a violation of A.F. of L. policies, Green sent a letter to each member of the committee warning him to desist from his current course of action. Green made a special point of having the letter hand-delivered to Lewis so that the CIO chairman received it late on the evening of the twenty-second or early on the morning of the twenty-third, before any other CIO member had had a chance to read it. Green filled his missive with dire warnings and exaggerated allegations, even accusing the CIO's founders of dual unionism. From your actions, he prophesied, "bitterness and strife would inevitably follow." In a particularly pointed warning, Green stressed that the minority inside the A.F. of L. must abide absolutely by the decisions of the majority.

Lewis responded immediately and dramatically. "Effective this date (November 23)," he wrote to Green and for release in the newspapers, "I resign as vice president of the American Federation of Labor." Those fourteen words captured the headlines in the Sunday newspapers, producing more publicity for the CIO than any event since its founding on November 9. As Lewis subsequently informed first Hillman and then other CIO members, his resignation from a "worthless post" where his future membership "would avail nothing" had electrified the nation and stimulated interest in the CIO.

Lewis intended to make the most of the publicity attendant on his resignation. On Monday, November 25, he held a well-attended press conference in his office during which he expounded freely on the necessity for industrial unionism as a means to organize the mass-production workers. And on Thursday, November 28, he delivered a radio address that explained why economic evolution and technological innovation dictated the establishment of industrial unionism in the mass-production industries. Seeking to appeal to white-collar workers, Lewis linked American antiunionism to fascism in Italy and Nazism in Germany and asserted that only the emergence of effective industrial unions would guarantee "real recovery and reform" from depression.

Lewis's response to Green's letter won the CIO "four days of continuous publicity," newpaper coverage that Hillman and others found exceedingly favorable to their point of view. It also reinforced Lewis's conviction that he had acted wisely.

Green's letter, however, required an official response from the CIO. More concerned about publicity than questions of union legitimacy, Lewis preferred that members of the CIO planning board respond individually and that subsequently the committee print a pamphlet containing Green's original letter and the CIO replies. Harvey Fremming replied first to Green, and his letter captured the essence of the dispute. "Whether industrial unionism is right or wrong is not the issue," wrote Fremming. "The whole question is one of *tactics, not of principle*" (emphases added). Additional responses from Thomas McMahon, David

Dubinsky, John Sherwood of the mine, mill and smelter workers, and Sidney Hillman emphasized that the founders of the CIO intended to strengthen, not weaken, the A.F. of L. "We all feel," wrote Hillman on December 12, "that the activities of this Committee will help the American Federation of Labor in extending organization to the unorganized mass production industries."

But the most dramatic response, as might be expected, came from Lewis. As usual, he acted without consulting his CIO colleagues and with care to obtain maximum publicity. On Saturday, December 7, he released to the press a letter addressed to William Green that would dominate the next morning's news. "Your official burdens are great," Lewis commiserated with Green.

> I would not increase them. I do not covet your office. . . . It is bruited about . . . that your private sympathies . . . lie with the group espousing the industrial type of organizaton, while your official actions and public utterances will be in support of their adversaries. Such a policy is vulnerable to criticism and will hardly suffice to protect you against attacks that may ensue from advocates of the craft philosophy. . . . Why not return to your father's house? You will be welcome. If you care to dissociate yourself from your present position, the Committee for Industrial Organization will be happy to make you its Chairman in my stead. The honorarium will be equal to that you now receive. The position will be as permanent as the one you now occupy. You would have the satisfaction of supporting a cause in which you believe inherently and of contributing your fine abilities to the achievement of an enlarged opportunity for the nation's workers.

Lewis's offer to Green was a typical calculated gamble, one that he was certain would cost the CIO nothing. He addressed himself directly to Green's weakness of character. Lewis presented the A.F. of L. president a choice: Green could occupy his present position and serve as a supine agent for the most powerful craft unionists, with whose philosophy he did not sympathize, or he could serve Lewis in a cause in which he believed. Two days after he had released his letter of December 7 and received Green's rejection, Lewis observed at a meeting of the CIO executive board: "If Green had accepted my invitation, it would have revolutionized the American Labor movement."

By early December 1935 Lewis had formulated a strategy to organize the mass-production workers, and his letter to Green formed part of a larger plan. Reports from his fieldworkers indicated to Lewis that considerable union sympathy remained alive among mass-production workers, but that employees in autos, rubber, and steel associated the A.F. of L. with craft exclusiveness and labor failure. Such workers rejected organizing ventures promoted by the A.F. of L. To gain their loyalty, Lewis learned, CIO organizers would have to differentiate themselves from A.F. of L. agents. Thus Lewis consciously declared war on the craft unionists, derided the possibility of neutrality in the conflict, and compelled Green to choose sides. As CIO organizers proselytized for industrial unionism in the mass-production industries, the A.F. of L. would either tacitly recognize the success of Lewis's committee and impotently watch the formation of a new power bloc inside the federation, or Green and his associates would reject Lewis's union army. In no event, however, would Lewis secede voluntarily from the A.F. of L.; instead, he preferred to make his craft union enemies their own executioners. Tobin, Hutcheson, Wharton, et al. would be forced to accept minority status inside the A.F. of L. or maintain their hegemony only by expelling the CIO. In either case, Lewis would become the dominant power in the national labor movement, a leader whose massive union army would guarantee him unprecedented economic and political influence.

The December 9 CIO executive board meeting adopted policies in accord with Lewis's grand strategy. The board agreed unanimously to organize along industrial union lines in autos and rubber, a campaign to be initiated by Lewis speeches in Akron and Cleveland. It sanctioned Lewis's observation that "We ought to show results. . . . If we don't do anything, we lose our prestige. Now everyone is talking about us—even politicians, bankers, the Pennsylvania Railroad, and one of the Wall Street magazines." Expect reprisals from the craft unions, warned Lewis, for "we are likely to be made the object of an attack by the A.F. of L.," but give them no cause for conflict. That is precisely what the CIO resolved to do, delaying action in the steel industry until the A.F. of L. executive council acted first and refusing to accept donations from individuals and organizations outside the A.F. of L. In an official press release issued the next day, the CIO cited its determination to organize auto and rubber workers and "to encourage them in building strong unions, *within the A.F. of L.*" (emphasis added).

In the days and weeks that followed the December 9 CIO executive board session, Lewis's agents were busy among the auto and rubber workers. Even the more conservative and reactionary of trade unionists in the Detroit area, according to one report, responded to the CIO with "progressive sentiment" and "warm friendliness." Although CIO representatives encouraged organization among auto and rubber workers without regard to craft union jurisdictional claims, they also advised against precipitous action or divisive steps before the A.F. of L. executive council session scheduled for January 15, 1936.

In strategy formulated by Lewis and implemented by John Brophy at Washington headquarters, Adolph Germer among auto workers, and Powers Hapgood among rubber workers, the CIO acted to incorporate the auto workers' and rubber workers' unions within the A.F. of L. as industrial organizations amd sought an accommodation with the craft unionists—yet prepared for the worst. By January 6, 1936, Lewis had decided that unless the A.F. of L. recognized the claims of the industrial unionists, industrial unionism would have to be implemented outside the federation. And he bluntly warned Green of the likely result if the executive council again repudiated industrial unionism. "Opportunity to organize may knock more than once at labor's door," John Brophy wrote to Green on January 10, delivering Lewis's message. "But seldom has it knocked with such insistence . . . and never perhaps has disregard of its call been fraught with such peril not only for labor but for our country as a whole."

Lewis's warning had no discernible impact on the craft unionists who dominated the A.F. of L. and manipulated Green. No differences of opinion divided the "Council of Patriarchs" on the issue of industrial unionism: They refused to consider any compromise with the CIO.

Lewis was too busy with the real business of the labor movement to worry about his foes on the executive council. Instead he traveled to Akron and Cleveland to deliver speeches to auto and rubber workers. On the afternoon and evening of January 19, despite one of the worst blizzards in Ohio history, thousands of workers packed meeting halls in Cleveland and Akron; indeed, in both cities the halls were too small to contain the crowds, and thousands stood in the streets outside in driving snow and numbing temperatures to listen to Lewis over a loud-speaker system. The speech, written as was customary by Jett Lauck, stressed the traditional theme of industrial democracy versus industrial autocracy, of the need for mass-production workers to organize eco-nomically and politically to save the nation from fascism or commu-nism, and of the role of the labor movement in liberating the United States from thralldom to a reactionary financial elite. Lewis also sounded one new, clear note: the CIO's commitment to rescue mass-production workers from the A.F. of L. and its craft union majority.

As Ruth McKenney wrote in *Industrial Valley,* her historical novel about the organization of Akron's rubber workers, Lewis's speech made a profound impression. "His audience went out of that chilly hall to make John L. the most talked of man in town. A hero to his listeners, he was next morning a hero to every second man in the rubber shops." His impact was similar in Cleveland, and it spread from there to auto workers in Toledo, Detroit, Milwaukee, and Kansas City. Every CIO fieldworker and industrial union organizer began to demand a personal appearance by Lewis. Workers responded enthusiastically to Lewis's

oratorical style—his purple passages and hyperbolic flourishes notwithstanding—because as McKenney noted, workers "liked hearing
their dreams, their problems, their suffering cloaked in Biblical phrases."
Lewis's sonorous voice transformed cliches into battle cries, malaprop-
isms into epic prose, solecisms into revelations. He did not enlighten
his audiences; he hypnotized them. When he sneered at the advocates
of partnership between labor and capital, Lewis caught the gut feelings
of auto and rubber workers, who left the hall determined to battle their
employers. Whatever the A.F. of L. decided in Miami, Lewis assured
his listeners, they could count on him, the UMW, and the CIO; there
would be no repeat of the betrayal that mass-production workers had
experienced in 1933–34.

Miami's winter sun may have warmed the bodies of A.F. of L. leaders,
but it failed to soothe their tempers. When Charles Howard appeared
before the council to defend the CIO, his inquisitors, led by Green,
castigated the industrial unionists for instigating dualism, divisiveness,
and bitterness within the labor movement. Howard's reply failed to
assuage anti-CIO council members, who proceeded, with Green's bless-
ing, to ram through a resolution that accused the CIO of dual unionism,
ordered the CIO to dissolve forthwith, commanded CIO members to
abide by the majority decisions of the 1935 convention, and appointed
a committee of three (George Harrison, G. M. Bugniazet, and Joseph
N. Weber) to confer with CIO representatives and hand them the executive council's ultimatum. In rapid order thereafter, the council rejected industrial union charters for auto, rubber, aluminum, and radio
workers.

The executive council's action stunned many trade unionists. Lewis,
however, took the news from Miami in stride. He eagerly awaited the
UMW's 1936 convention, scheduled to open on January 28 in Washington, where he would set the stage for a dramatic confrontation
between himself and Green, the CIO as labor's wave of the future and
the A.F. of L. as heir to an ebbing nineteenth-century union tide.

The 1936 UMW convention opened in a triumphant mood. "We are
meeting," the miners' president informed more than eighteen hundred
delegates, "at a time when our industry is more completely organized
than ever before, when collective bargaining is more universally accepted
in the coal industry than at any time in the lives of any of us, when
the membership of our Union is greater than ever before, when the
financial resources of our Union are greater than ever before, and when
the potential strength of our organization . . . transcends the imagination
of the organized labor movement." Whenever he addressed the delegates,
Lewis, in the words of a *Nation* editorial, "drew forth roaring cheers,

rising votes, and hostile boos as he desired." "John certainly has a hold over the crowd," Sidney Hillman later reflected.

One issue more than any other stirred emotions and stimulated debate at the miners' convention: the A.F. of L. executive council's demand that the CIO dissolve. Referring to that order, Lewis observed that the executive council "seems to have buried its head in the golden sands of Florida and is issuing pronunciamentos that cause the worker to despair." Phil Murray threatened that "the sooner we get the hell away from them [the A.F. of L.] the better it will be for us." And in his most powerful speech, midway through the convention Lewis declared that "all the members of the Executive Council of the American Federation of Labor will be wearing asbestos suits in hell before the committee [CIO] is dissolved.... I don't work [for the American Federation of Labor].... I work for the United Mine Workers of America . . . and . . . I do not . . . intend . . . to see a policy ratified and followed that is designed to disrupt, emasculate, and destroy the union that I have the honor to represent." The nation needed a labor movement, Lewis stressed, that would represent the millions of unorganized workers whose exploited condition makes them a drain upon the well-being of every American citizen whether a hand or brain worker. Lewis promised to devote all his strength to the organization of the unorganized. At the conclusion of Lewis's speech, the delegates, by a unanimous rising vote, empowered their officers to withhold per capita dues payments from the A.F. of L. "The feeling of the crowd toward the A.F. of L.," Hillman noted, "is very bitter."

That bitterness was exemplified on the convention's last day, when William Green returned to his "father's house" to plead with the delegates to remain loyal to the family of American labor. In his plea to the miners to respect labor unity, Green resorted to the same domestic metaphor that Lewis had used when he invited the A. F. of L. president back into his "father's house." "A child and some associate children of the organized labor family of the nation are in open rebellion against the action of a convention," warned Green. "I plead with you to show loyalty and devotion to your father, your parent, the great organization that chartered you and that has fathered you and protected you. Remain at home, for the American Federation of Labor will remain supreme."

Green's emotional one-and-a-half-hour speech failed to save the parents of the American labor movement from a rebellion by their metaphorical children in the miners' union. Miners instead saw their decision more in terms of a divorce between freely consenting adults whose longtime union had been strained by the emergence of irreconcilable differences.

When Lewis asked all the delegates who had changed their minds as a result of Green's speech to rise, he observed two delegates. Lewis then asked those delegates who believed that the CIO should be dissolved to rise. "The Chair," recorded the official convention proceedings, "sees one delegate arise." And when Lewis requested that all rise who believed that the convention's policies should be executed by the UMW president, the delegates rose en masse and applauded. "President Green," responded Lewis, "you have received the answer of the United Mine Workers to your ultimatum." Jett Lauck recorded in his diary for February 3, 1936: "Very dramatic scene. Green ruthlessly obliterated."

Not all Lewis's allies were pleased by his behavior at the UMW convention. David Dubinsky, Max Zaritsky, and other Social Democrats among the New York garment workers seemed troubled by Lewis's threat to desert the A.F. of L. To them, Lewis had not displayed good judgment and diplomacy, because by "striking a belligerent note [he] will tend to drive friends away who want to preserve the unity of the trade union movement." Even Charles Howard and Sidney Hillman were vexed by the militancy displayed at the convention. They agreed "that the way to fight the industrial question is on the inside and that sooner or later we are bound to get on top."

Lewis, however, kept his ultimate aims a closely guarded secret. He did nothing publicly or overtly to indicate any intention of splitting the labor movement. His CIO director, John Brophy, asserted that fears about a split in the labor movement were much exaggerted. Brophy, like Howard and Hillman, expected to give the CIO a majority inside the A.F. of L. "After long years of apathy and apparent stagnation," Brophy noted, "the stir within the ranks of labor is welcome and the upsurge of interest is the promise of a stronger labor movement."

Events after the 1936 UMW convention proved that some members of the A.F. of L. executive council "would rather retain control of the organization with a small membership than to lose control through doubling or tripling the present membership." While the CIO sought to organize workers under the auspices of the A.F. of L., Green treated the CIO as a schismatic organization. On February 5 the A.F. of L. president directed his staff not to recognize any requests or communications from John Brophy. Two days later, Green wrote to Lewis and other members of the CIO executive board informing them of the executive council's January 15th ruling that the CIO must dissolve and asking Lewis and his representatives to confer with the A.F. of L.'s three-man committee to discuss preservation of labor unity.

Lewis and his associates promptly accepted Green's invitation to a conference. But A.F. of L. leaders evinced little desire to compromise the issues in dispute with the CIO, as demonstrated by George Harrison's decision to attend an overseas labor conference precisely when Lewis agreed to confer with the Harrison committee.

Unable to confer with the A.F. of L. committee, the CIO held its own executive board session on February 19 at the UMW headquarters. Board members decided to respond bluntly to the A.F. of L.'s order to disband. On February 21, in a letter signed by Lewis and his associates and addressed to Green, the CIO spokesmen emphasized that they "were trying to remove the roots of dualism by making it possible for the millions of mass-production workers now outside the A.F. of L. to enter on the only basis they will accept—industrial unions." Denying vigorously that they intended to usurp the federation's functions, CIO leaders implied "that many of those who are trying to brand us falsely as dualists are themselves none too eager to see the unions in the mass-production industries grow in influence." Once more offering to meet with the Harrison committee, Lewis warned that any attempt by the executive council to interfere with the CIO's organizing activities "would be completely undemocratic and contrary to the policies of the labor movement."

Not until mid–May 1936 did the Harrison committee confer with CIO representatives. By then, however, prospects for accommodation between the advocates of industrial unionism and the A.F. of L. old guard had evaporated. Nevertheless, the A.F. of L. and CIO committees met for about two hours on May 19, with John L. Lewis and George Harrison dominating the discussion. Aware that Harrison not only refused to negotiate but also lacked the authority to do so, Lewis bluntly informed the A.F. of L. committee: "I am not going to advocate dissolution. Proceed with your judgment of execution. . . . We're part of the AFL and like to remain. We hold AFL responsible because of eternal policy of doing nothing. You can talk about convention mandate but you have no policy except frittering away time and shutting the door to those clamoring. No longer believe in your promises. I have mandate."

Lewis knew that the A.F. of L. executive council had decided overwhelmingly to submit another ultimatum to CIO members. On May 20, the executive council authorized Green to summon all international unions affiliated with the CIO to appear before the council beginning on July 9 to answer charges that the CIO was a dual organization in violation of the A.F. of L. constitution and its rules.

As expected, CIO members refused to comply with the A.F. of L. ultimatum. Those who responded formally, such as David Dubinsky and Charles Howard, denied emphatically that the CIO was dual in character or that its activities threatened the A.F. of L. Lewis refused even to reply and instructed Thomas Kennedy to write directly to William Green. Our international executive board directed me by unanimous vote, Kennedy informed Green on May 29, to "question the right and authority, or the propriety, of the Executive Council . . . to make such demands upon . . . the Committee for Industrial Organization; or upon any International organization to cease constructive work . . . in bringing about effective organization . . . in the mass production industries . . . I am instructed to say further to you . . . that the United Mine Workers of America emphatically refuses to accede to either the call or the request of the American Federation of Labor to discontinue its constructive and logical course of action."

Throughout the protracted war of words, letters, and ultimatums between the A.F. of L. and CIO, Lewis attended to his main objective: organization of the unorganized. Germer labored around the clock in Detroit, Toledo, Cleveland, and other auto production centers to spread industrial unionism among auto workers and to encourage hitherto independent unions in the industry to merge into a large, all-inclusive international union. Powers Hapgood and other CIO organizers in Akron acted as midwives at the birth of industrial unionism among rubber workers.

From late 1935 through the first half of 1936, Lewis personally devoted his energy to organizing steelworkers. Before the rupture between the CIO and A.F. of L. became irrevocable, Lewis pursued a variety of tactics aimed at pressuring Green to initiate an aggressive organizing campaign along industrial union lines among steelworkers. Because Mike Tighe, the ancient and ailing president of the Amalgamated Association of Iron, Steel and Tin Workers, showed little interest in organizing the mass of semiskilled steelworkers, Lewis dispatched his own agents among the rank and file. By the end of 1935, then, Lewis had decided to unionize steel, yet he still preferred to function under A.F. of L. auspices and within the jurisdictional authority of the Amalgamated Association.

On February 21 Lewis sent a letter to Green that also bore Howard's signature and that suggested the inauguration of an organizing effort in the steel industry. Lewis offered the services of trained organizers and $500,000 of a suggested $1,500,000 organizing fund. He demanded that organization must be along industrial lines and "that all steel workers organized will be granted the permanent right to remain united in one industrial union." Finally, Lewis declared that a responsible, energetic person (meaning an organizer outside the Amalgamated Association) who understood the industry must direct the campaign. Time being of the essence, Lewis promised to confer with Green at the earliest convenient opportunity, because "we are sincerely anxious for immediate action to organize the steel industry."

As usual, the A.F. of L. equivocated for nearly two months. By mid-

April Lewis could wait no longer. On April 15, he wrote to Mike Tighe directly, repeating the offer he had originally made to the A.F. of L. Lewis assured Tighe that the rights of the Amalgamated would be honored and that the CIO, unlike the A.F. of L., would respect the steel union's right to an unrestricted industrial union charter. He then presented the following terms to the Amalgamated Association "regardless of the stand taken by other organizations": (1) assurance that all steelworkers would remain united in one industrial union and be protected against future division among craft unions; (2) the establishment of a joint committee on which the Amalgamated Association would be represented as well as the CIO and other unions willing to contribute to a joint campaign. The committee would select a "responsible and energetic person" to direct the organizing drive. Lewis again promised to provide $500,000, and he asked that Tighe bring this proposal before the delegates to the Amalgamated Association convention scheduled for April 28.

Tighe proved as leery of Lewis's plans as Green. The Amalgamated Association president feared opposing the A.F. of L. and aligning himself with the CIO against Green's wishes. He was even more fearful of Lewis's proposal to create an organizing committee separate from the Amalgamated Association under an outside director. "Under no circumstances, while I am President," Tighe told fellow executive board members, "will I surrender to any other organization the right to direct the affairs of our organization."

Events, however, soon forced Tighe into Lewis's grasp. Delegate sentiment at the Amalgamated Association convention clearly favored an aggressive organizing campaign along industrial union lines, a type of campaign the A.F. of L. proved unwilling to sponsor. Heber Blankenhorn, an adviser to rank-and-file militants in the steel industry, informed Lewis on May 6, from Canonsburg, Pennsylvania, the convention city, that "my guess is you can have steel right now if you want it." Two days later, May 8, Lewis wired the Amalgamated Association convention disparaging the A.F. of L.'s proposal to organize steel through a committee of craft unions that would later parcel out union members among a variety of crafts, and reaffirming his original offer of funds, organizers, and the creation of a special organizing committee.

Still fearful of losing his authority and influence in the steel industry to Lewis, Tighe desperately negotiated with Green to arrange an A.F. of L. alternative. But Green refused to promise unlimited jurisdiction to the steelworkers; nor did he seem eager to organize steelworkers. Consequently, on May 30, Louis Leonard, secretary of the Amalgamated Association (AA), wired Lewis to arrange a meeting between AA and CIO representatives.

On June 3, 1936, Leonard and his associates conferred with Lewis at UMW headquarters. Lewis minced no words in explaining what he desired. He promised immediate action, large sums of money, industrial unionism, and no red tape provided that the AA accepted CIO leadership. An executive committee appointed by Lewis would be established in Pittsburgh, where it would direct the organizing drive. The committee would rely on the AA's technical knowledge of the steel industry, but the CIO would dominate the organizing drive. In a small concession, Lewis promised to appoint to the steel organizing committee any two men the AA chose, but, in return, the AA had to join the CIO, which, as Lewis observed, "I'm so goddamned proud of." He gave the AA committee twenty-four hours to make up its mind. "If you don't want it," warned Lewis, "we want to find out as soon as we can. We're tired—want action. I think we're going to help steelworkers with or without you. If you spurn it, we'll announce to country and you can do your own explaining. If accept, you stand to have great power, encomiums, etc." As Leonard subsequently reported to his own union's executive board: "Lewis . . . made it very plain that the Committee for Industrial Organization had practically decided to begin a campaign of organization . . . whether they had the cooperation of the Amalgamated Association or not."

Presented with Lewis's ultimatum, the AA officials made their choice on June 4. As Lewis expected, they accepted his terms and signed a written agreement to affiliate with the CIO and serve as part of the Steel Workers Organizing Committee (SWOC), consisting of persons appointed by Lewis. In every essential respect the June 4 agreement bound the AA to the terms Lewis had enunciated at the previous day's meeting. He not only secured a new affiliate for the CIO—one whose charter conferred legitimacy on the CIO's organizing drive in steel—but his triumph also publicly ridiculed Green and the A.F. of L. old guard. The AA, moreover, had surrendered all vestiges of its authority to Lewis, who selected his longtime right-hand man, Phil Murray, as chairman of SWOC; staffed the committee with fieldworkers from the UMW; and funded it from the mine workers' treasury.

Lewis's seizure of the Amalgamated Association infuriated Green. The A.F. of L. president blasted the CIO publicly and derided its plan to unionize steelworkers. Green's angry outburst occasioned a notable Lewis riposte. "I overlook the inane ineptitude of your statement published today," Lewis wrote to Green on June 6. "Perchance you were agitated and distraught. . . . It is inconceivable that you intend doing what your statement implies, i.e. to sit with the women, under an awning on the hilltop, while the steel workers in the valley struggle in the dust and agony of industrial warfare." Reminding Green of his honor and obligations to the UMW, Lewis observed that members of the A.F. of L. executive council intended to suspend the ten unions associated with CIO. "I cannot yet believe," wrote Lewis, "that you would be a party to such a Brutus blow." If Green joined the anti-CIO majority, Lewis warned, "you [Green] would destroy yourself. . . . It is known to you that your shipmates on the Executive Council are even now planning to slit your political throat and scuttle your official ship. They are caviling among themselves over the naming of your successor when the perfidious act of separation is accomplished. Why not forego such company and return home to the union that suckled you, rather than court obloquy by dwelling among its adversaries and lending them your strength? An honored seat at the Council table awaits you, if you elect to return."

The same day Green replied to Lewis in a letter in which he stressed his own personal honor, integrity, and organizational loyalty. "I am the President of the American Federation of Labor," wrote Green. "I took a solemn obligation to uphold its laws, to be governed by its decisions and to be loyal to its principles and policies. . . . Nothing can be offered as a justification for the sacrifice of honor and a solemn obligation. The mandate of the American Federation of Labor Convention becomes law to me. There will be no resort to subterfuge or expedience in order to evade the discharge of this solemn obligation." Compelled to choose between subservience to Lewis in a cause in which he believed or alliance with a majority of his executive council whose policies he rejected, Green elected the latter course, for while Lewis challenged his manhood, the craft union leaders extolled Green's dignity and courage.

Again Lewis publicized his disagreement with Green and his commitment to action in steel. Ridiculing the A.F. of L.'s failure to organize a single worker in the steel industry as contrasted to its intention of expelling CIO unions, Lewis acidly rebuked Green. "Your lament is that I will not join you in a policy of anxious inertia. . . . Candidly, I am temperamentally incapable of sitting with you in sackcloth and ashes, endlessly intoning, '*O tempora! O Mores!*'" Let us discuss personal honor no more, concluded Lewis. "For myself, I prefer to err on the side of America's underprivileged and exploited millions, if erring it be."

The bitter public exchange between Lewis and Green worsened the rupture between the A.F. of L. and the CIO and intensified the executive council majority's desire to punish the insurgents. As Lewis had suggested in his letters to Green, the executive council planned to suspend from federation membership all affiliates of the CIO at its July session. So much did men such as Tobin, Hutcheson, and Wharton despise

Lewis, so bitterly did Green resent Lewis's insults, that they intended to expel unions representing more than one-third of the federation's total membership. The federations's attorney, Charlton Ogburn, had already advised Green that the council could suspend autonomous unions after they had been presented with a bill of particulars, provided a formal hearing, and found guilty as charged.

Lewis and his CIO associates refused to believe that the executive council would suspend them — at least not in July 1936. Lewis informed members of the CIO executive board on July 2 that Green seemed confused: "Saw Green on a train — the more I talked with him, the woozier." Lewis thus advised his associates to ignore the A.F. of L. threats and edicts. "Doubt if we can spare time to go one after another like boys — and be lectured — unless Ex Ccl completely insane, will not suspend at this meeting. . . . I think members of organized labor will straighten [them] out. Am tired of conversation and letters," concluded Lewis. Hillman agreed that CIO members should disregard the A.F. of L. executive council. "Let them go ahead and discuss — we work." Aware as always of reality and public relations, Lewis concluded that it was "inconceivable that AFL Ex Ccl could split labor" and that if the CIO leaders ignored the council's fulminations, it would "make them [A.F. of L. leaders] ridiculous."

With CIO officials absent and David Dubinsky, the lone member of the executive council sympathetic to the CIO, away on other business, Green and the craft unionists followed Ogburn's script at their July meeting. John Frey presented a bill of particulars against the CIO affiliates that accused them of "dual unionism," infringements on established jurisdictions, violations of the A.F. of L. constitution, and even communism. The council adopted Frey's specifications, and on July 16, Green sent a letter to all CIO leaders that presented them with Frey's charges and ordered them to appear at an A.F. of L. hearing on the afternoon of August 3.

Within a week Lewis called a meeting of the CIO executive board to discuss an official response to Green's order and Frey's charges. In his comments to CIO associates, Lewis remarked that he had tried to compromise the dispute through private conferences with Green, who preferred accommodation to conflict. Under pressure from the carpenters and other arrogant craft unions, however, Green had violated the confidence of his private negotiations with Lewis and thus killed the prospects for a peaceful accommodation. A.F. of L. leaders, Lewis reported, lacked the will to negotiate or compromise on the issue of industrial unionism, and their executive council members planned to arrogate to themselves "powers not in the constitution." Lewis consequently advised that for CIO members to appear before the executive council on August 3 "would weaken the position of the associated organizations, prolong the agony, and add to newspaper notoriety, which detracts attention from the organizing campaign."

In their reply to Green's letter, of July 16, the CIO officials pointedly criticized the unconstitutional and undemocratic nature of the council's action. They also derided the "heads of certain craft unions" who feared the inclusion of industrial workers in the A.F. of L. "as a jeopardy to their own dead-hand control of the Federation. Satisfied now, as they have been for years, they regard the labor movement in America as having culminated. They are mistaken; it has just begun, and if it cannot continue within the Federation it will be because of the desperate course of the Council itself." The fundamental issue in dispute, argued the CIO, was neither dual unionism, labor traditions, legalisms, nor craft versus industrial unionism; it was primarily one of organizing the unorganized in the mass-production industries.

By August 1936, then, the A.F. of L. executive council compelled CIO leaders to choose between organizing the unorganized or remaining inside the federation. "It appears," Sidney Hillman wrote to Charles Howard on July 22, "that the Council would rather break up the organization than lose its face. The feeling at the last CIO meeting was very strongly against submitting to the Council's arrogance."

"Arrogance" was the proper word to characterize the executive council's attitude toward the CIO. As scheduled, the council met in Washington on August 3 to consider Frey's allegations against the CIO. As expected, the executive council sustained all Frey's charges against the CIO and instructed Green to transmit its finding to all CIO members, who were given until September 5, 1936, either to abandon the CIO or to stand suspended from the A.F. of L.

Four days after Green informed CIO members of the executive council's ruling, Lewis called a meeting of the CIO executive board. Lewis evinced more concern with the impact of the CIO's response on the media, the "man-in-the-street," and workers' morale than with the legalities or ethics of the A.F. of L.'s decision. More fatalistic than legalistic, more concerned with economic reality than trade union tradition, Lewis now relished the impending split in the labor movement and planned to obtain the most from it. He rejected as futile any legal action against the executive council or an appeal against the ruling.

Responding to their leader's advice, members of the CIO executive board unamimously reaffirmed their position as stated in the letter of July 21, declined to undertake legal action against the A.F. of L. executive council, and agreed to boycott the November 1936 Federation convention in Tampa. The CIO leaders shared Lewis's belief that they should all ignore their suspension and forcefully pursue union organizing and political activity.

The November 1936 session of the CIO executive board sealed the split in the American labor movement. Max Zaritsky and David Dubinsky came to Pittsburgh eager to urge a compromise with the A.F. of L., but their voices found no echo among CIO associates. Lewis, Hillman, and Murray exemplified the prevailing sentiment. "The question of peace is secondary to organizing the unorganized," remarked Lewis. "This is the premise on which the fight was made in the convention, and on which the C.I.O. was formed. Why," he asked, "continue on a course of action that means only embarrassment to the C.I.O?" Mass-production workers, he observed, "have lost confidence in the A.F. of L. Affiliation with it means nothing to them." Hillman echoed Lewis. "Can we afford to do anything that may make it impossible to take advantage of what may be the last opportunity to organize," he asked? "We know that the C.I.O. is an absolutely necessary instrumentality. I am for peace," Hillman continued, "but I do not believe that the Executive Council have the intention of allowing any peace that will make organization possible." Peace conferences, thought Hillman, had already demoralized CIO people. Clearly committed by now to go their own way independently of the A.F. of L., the CIO majority ritualistically pledged its loyalty to a united labor movement.

Yet CIO executive board members made one last effort at peace negotiations. At Lewis's suggestion, they voted unanimously to sanction their leader to engage in direct peace negotiations with William Green. The peace proposal was merely intended to assuage Zaritsky and Dubinsky; Lewis openly told the executive board: "I am conscious that a conference with Green will lead nowhere. I suggested so that some of you will be satisfied." Lewis, moreover, practically declared the rift in the labor movement permanent. From the beginning, he informed his associates, he knew that the A.F. of L. would never organize steel, auto, or rubber workers. "When we met on the Sunday morning after the Atlantic City convention, I knew what we were doing, what obligations we were putting on our organizations." Some of you, Lewis continued, may not have thought the question out clearly, but we in the UMW have our minds made up. "We have thrown the cream of our staff into the fight [organizing steel]. We knew we had crossed the Rubicon." Think about it, he advised, take time (but not too much) for I want you to join me in this "great enterprise for the weal or woe of the nation. . . . My patience," Lewis observed, "is a bit worn by this [AFL] cowardly undermining of a great movement." Be proud of this organization, he concluded, for "people everywhere are looking to us for leadership, and it is time to give it to them."

The executive board also made decisions that rendered an accommodation with the A.F. of L. impossible. Two new industrial unions—the United Electrical Workers and the Marine and Ship Building Workers—involved in jurisdictional disputes with A.F. of L. affiliates were admitted to membership in the CIO.

The proposed Lewis-Green negotiations never occurred. On November 8 Green agreed to meet with Lewis but advised the CIO executive board that the suspension of CIO unions would not be lifted and that peace negotiations would better be conducted with the Harrison subcommittee. Lewis wired back the same day declaring that discussions with Green would now be futile. "When the American Federation of Labor decides to reverse and rectify its outrageous act of suspension and is ready to concede the right of complete industrial organizations to live and grow in the unorganized industries," Lewis told Green, "it will be time to discuss and arrange the details of a reestablished relationship."

Ambition, even egomania, may have fired Lewis's refusal to negotiate on Green's terms in November 1936. But had he negotiated in good faith and had he accepted the peace agreement offered, Lewis would have surrendered only personal power, if that. The true losers would have been the mass production workers in steel, autos, rubber, and elsewhere, struggling desperately to build stable, independent trade unions. As Lewis knew and stressed repeatedly, an accommdation between the A.F. of L. and CIO could only come at the expense of the mass-production workers.

Lewis's decision to discontinue negotiations with the A.F. of L. and to concentrate the CIO's energies on organizing the unorganized created the modern mass American labor movement. From 1937 through 1940 Lewis and the CIO would transform the American labor movement from an association of select craft unions on the fringes of the economy with limited political influence into a significant power situated in the economy's core with real influence in the national Democratic political coalition. This, then, was clearly a case where Lewis's personal interests coincided with the welfare of the American working class.

Only at the deepest, perhaps most unconscious, level of human behavior did Lewis act irrationally and arrogantly in November 1936. The split between the CIO and A.F. of L. flowed from substantive issues on which Lewis argued the stronger case. The clash between Lewis and Green derived from more personal and psychological roots. Lewis had cast aspersions on Green's manhood, no small insult to an ex-coal miner who shared the exaggerated sense of masculinity associated with that occupation. Thus Green's intransigence about the CIO perhaps derived more from a need to assert his manhood and equality with Lewis than from the substantive issues in dispute.

Lewis, in turn, intended to diminish further Green's self-esteem. Acting vindictively, Lewis had his union bring formal charges against Green on November 11, 1936. Walter Smethurst, clerk to the international executive board, informed Green that on November 18, two days after the A.F. of L. convention began in Tampa, the board would consider allegations that Green had conspired illegally to suspend the UMW from the A.F. of L.; failed to conform to the established policies of the UMW; associated and fraternized with avowed enemies of the UMW; and distorted and misrepresented the aims of the UMW.

Green, of course, refused to appear before the international executive board and denied all the charges out of hand. The IEB hearing went ahead as planned and found Green guilty on all charges. "Life in the mines is naked and elemental," Smethurst informed Green on November 18 in words likely written by Lewis. "Relationships are not cushioned with sophistry. This union yields to none the right to appraise the act of a servant or the perfidy of a member. William Green wears the insignia of this Union. Let him abide by the decision of its Convention." Lewis, in effect, ordered Green to cease and desist from criticizing the CIO—that is, to resign as president of the A.F. of L. or lose his membership in the UMW. In the abstract that may have seemed an easy, painless decision for Green. But in reality, Green's emotional ties to the mine workers, as a charter member and longtime official, were deep and binding. In compelling Green to snap those emotional bonds, Lewis achieved precisely the psychological blow he desired.

12

CIO! CIO! CIO!
Labor on the March,
June 1936–June 1937

Although the CIO functioned as an independent national labor center by mid-1936, Lewis temporarily subordinated its trade union function to its political role. The politics of the New Deal were not only central to the rift within the A.F. of L., they were also the most salient factor in Lewis's thoughts and activities during 1936. He had concluded that the future of the CIO depended on a sympathetic federal government. His estimation of economic and political reality impelled Lewis to forge a political marriage of convenience with Franklin D. Roosevelt based on common necessity, not shared values.

Politics was indeed so central to Lewis's plans in 1936 that during the summer he neglected the CIO's campaign to unionize steelworkers and convinced Philip Murray, who headed SWOC and directed the actual organizing drive, that the effort to unionize steelworkers must be linked to the political situation. In the spring and summer of 1936, this meant that Lewis concentrated on securing the reelection of Franklin D. Roosevelt.

In 1936 Lewis transformed labor's political traditions. Together with George L. Berry of the printing pressmen's union and Sidney Hillman, Lewis, in April 1936, formed Labor's Non-Partisan League as organized labor's own political instrument, dedicated to the election of Roosevelt but independent of the Democratic party. Although the Non-Partisan League ostensibly united A.F. of L. and CIO spokesmen — craft unionists and industrial unionists — its finances and personnel came largely from the CIO and mostly from the United Mine Workers. Berry, the league's director, may have been a craft unionist and an A.F. of L. member, but Lewis and Hillman represented the organization's political brains, and appointees from the mine workers and the men's clothing workers dominated the leadership of the league at the state and local levels.

Lewis supported Roosevelt's reelection through an independent labor agency rather than as an integral part of the Democratic party for good reasons. In 1936 Lewis lacked a principled commitment to Roosevelt. Lewis's loyalty to Roosevelt hinged on the president's ability to satisfy the needs of the labor movement as defined by Lewis. Indeed, less than a month after the founding of the Non-Partisan League, Lewis and Jett Lauck discussed the possibility of forming a labor party after November 1936. But Lewis, ever the realist as distinguished from the more adventurous Lauck, desperately needed Roosevelt's assistance in 1936. Not until the CIO had organized the great mass of industrial workers— a development dependent, in Lewis's estimation, on federal assistance— could labor exert its political influence independently.

President Roosevelt, for his part, wanted organized labor's political aid in 1936. In the spring and summer the president could scarcely imagine the landslide victory that would be his in November. Instead, he feared a close election, one that might leave him without a clear mandate for further reform. Roosevelt thus sought a commitment from organized labor to deliver the vote, and to achieve that goal he looked more to the CIO and "its" Non-Partisan League than to the A.F. of L. and Dan Tobin, head of the Democratic party's labor committee.

The political relationship between Lewis and Roosevelt, however, faced a crisis in mid-June 1936. The single piece of congressional legislation most dear to Lewis, the Guffey-Snyder Coal Stabilization Act, had been defeated in the Senate partly as a result of the opposition of the Senate Majority Leader, Democrat Joseph Robinson of Arkansas. But the crisis instead reinforced the Roosevelt-Lewis alliance. The Guffey-Snyder Act failed on Saturday night June 20. On Monday morning, June 22, Roosevelt invited Lewis to the White House for a conference that lasted an hour and a half. The president promised Lewis that he would protect the United Mine Workers in every way possible until Congress reconvened in January and enacted new coal legislation. Roosevelt also pledged to cooperate in the unionization of the steel industry. Finally, the president read to Lewis sections of the 1936 Democratic party platform then being drafted that contained strong pro-labor clauses and recommendations for an amendment to strip the Supreme Court of the power to declare reform legislation unconstitutional. Lewis emerged from the conference to inform the press that he was entirely in accord with Roosevelt's proposed party platform, legislative recommendations, and labor program.

Even then, however, Lewis refused to link his political fortunes totally to Roosevelt and the Democratic party. On June 29, only a week after his conference with the president, Lewis attended a meeting at the office of Wisconsin Senator Robert LaFollette, Jr. The conferees on this occasion discussed the creation of an effective farm-labor political coalition, one that would campaign for Roosevelt in 1936 but that would lay the basis in the future for an independent farm-labor party. Alternatives to Roosevelt, the New Deal, and the Democratic party always remained a salient element in Lewis's political thought and strategy.

Yet in the summer of 1936 Lewis lacked political options. The immediate future of the CIO and the steel campaign hinged on Roosevelt's reelection. Consequently, Lewis inaugurated the drive to unionize steel with a national radio address that reiterated the message of Roosevelt's acceptance speech at the 1936 Democratic convention in Chicago. "I salute the hosts of labor who listen," Lewis began. "My voice tonight will be the voice of millions of men and women unemployed in America's industries, heretofore unorganized, economically exploited and inarticulate." Lewis then ripped into the Morgan financial dictatorship that selfishly sought to recreate the degenerate system of finance capitalism that had caused the Great Depression. Lewis warned of an impending struggle in which the primary question would be "whether the working population of this country shall have a voice in determining their destiny or whether they shall serve as indentured servants for a financial and economic dictatorship which would shamelessly exploit our natural resources and debase the soul . . . and . . . pride of a free people. On such an issue there can be no compromise." Freedom can only be won, Lewis told steelworkers, and also textile, lumber, rubber, and auto workers, by breaking the shackles that bound them to industrial servitude, joining an industrial union, and voting for Roosevelt.

Roosevelt invited Lewis to the White House three days after the speech. Lewis, who feared that the president had extended the invitation in order to compel a compromise between the CIO and A.F. of L., found instead that Roosevelt only desired assurance of labor's political solidarity. Lewis took the occasion of his July 9 visit to stress the link between national politics and the steel organizing campaign. Lewis commented that the steel operators, whose hostility to labor was unsurpassed in American industry and who supported the Republican party, motivated workers to unite for the reelection of Roosevelt.

In September Lewis devoted most of his time to politics. On Monday, September 7, he delivered a Labor Day address over the CBS network that again vilified the nation's "corporate dictatorship." And in keeping with an old theme, he called on workers to organize as "the best guarantee . . . and best insurance against the spread of alien and subversive doctrines." Four days later, September 11, he arrived in Chicago to attend a conference of "progressives" who organized the National Progressive Conference with Senator LaFollette as chairman. Attended by more than one hundred delegates, including eighteen congressmen and governors and twenty-seven labor leaders, the conference endorsed Roosevelt but not the Democratic party and promised an inevitable future realignment of party politics.

A week later, on September 17, Lewis traveled to Pottsville, Pennsylvania, in the heart of the anthracite district, to deliver his first major campaign address. Speaking to an audience of more than thirty thousand, Lewis as usual, castigated J. P. Morgan and the financial dictatorship that the New York banker personified—a dictatorship whose stranglehold on the nation could only be broken by the reelection of Roosevelt. But Lewis also introduced a theme that foreshadowed his subsequent political break with Roosevelt. Not only did Lewis charge the finance capitalists with causing the Great Depression and exploiting labor, but he also suggested that J. P. Morgan was responsible for United States' entry into World War I and that the interests of investment bankers and munitions makers threatened to involve the United States in another bloody world war. "I am convinced," he announced, "that the freedom of our country from war—the assurance that it will not be drawn into another world war—are dependent upon the reelection of President Roosevelt."

October proved a busier political month for Lewis. Early in the month, he promised Roosevelt: "Command me any time I can be of service." Lewis campaigned for the Democrats in Ohio, Kentucky, and Indiana coal mining centers, as well as in the nation's two most populous industrial states: New York and Pennsylvania. On October 27, at a meeting sponsored by the American Labor party in Madison Square Garden, Lewis spoke to an estimated twenty thousand packed inside the sports arena and more than eight thousand crowded into the street outside, where they listened to the speech over amplifiers. The audience responded ecstatically to Lewis's customary theme: Labor must organize politically as well as economically to free workers from the clutches of an unscrupulous economic dictatorship. Two days later Lewis closed his campaign schedule with a joint appearance with Roosevelt in Wilkes-Barre, Pennsylvania.

Lewis provided Roosevelt with more than oratory. The UMW spent almost $600,000 to reelect the president—an unprecedented expenditure of labor funds. Of that amount $148,378 went to Labor's Non-Partisan League; $206,250 went directly to the Democratic Committee; and $94,250 was spent on Non-Partisan League political broadcasts in September and October. Lewis expected a substantial return for the investment.

Roosevelt won a landslide victory, losing only Maine and Vermont and carrying by huge majorities industrial precincts heretofore customarily Republican. Lewis exulted at the extent of Roosevelt's victory, particularly the size of his margin in the steel towns of Pennsylvania's Monongahela Valley. At the CIO executive board meeting held just after election day, Lewis challenged: "We . . . must capitalize on the election. The CIO was out fighting for Roosevelt, and every steel town showed a smashing victory for him. . . . We wanted a President who would hold the light for us while we went out and organized."

Lewis pressed his political influence with the president. He suggested soon after the election that the federal government guarantee economic freedom and democracy to all wage and salary workers and introduce extensive national economic planning. On November 20, in a public statement, his union's international executive board demanded that Congress exercise its popular mandate to limit the power of the Supreme Court. And Lewis, together with Berry and Hillman, urged Roosevelt to heed their advice before making decisions affecting the office of secretary of labor or other matters concerning the labor movement.

Events quickly tested the Roosevelt-Lewis alliance. On December 30, 1936, workers at two General Motors Fisher Body plants in Flint, Michigan, occupied the factories, stopped the assembly line, and sparked the great General Motors sit-down strike of 1937. The subsequent conflict between the United Auto Workers–CIO and the largest industrial corporation in the world involved Roosevelt and Lewis and tested the strength of labor's alliance with the Democratic party.

Lewis immediately demanded that Roosevelt deliver on his campaign pledges to labor. On New Year's Eve of 1937, Lewis addressed a nationwide radio audience over the NBC network. The speech stressed the significance of the 1936 presidential election. "The people of our nation," said Lewis, "have just participated in a national referendum. By an overwhelming majority they voted for industrial democracy, and reelected its champion, Franklin Delano Roosevelt." Now, he suggested, it was time for the agents of the federal government to enter the plants of General Motors and gut them of the deadly weapons that federal investigators had discovered there in order that workers might exercise their rights as free men. "Labor," proclaimed its leader, "demands a new deal in America's great industries. . . . Labor demands legislative enactments making realistic the principles of industrial democracy." Lewis's peroration challenged President Roosevelt. "The time has passed in America," asserted Lewis, "when the workers can be either clubbed, gassed, or shot down with impunity. . . . Labor will . . . expect the protection of the Federal Government in the pursuit of its lawful objectives"

The General Motors strike thus promised to determine the future direction of the CIO, to establish the sagacity of Lewis's politics, and to evaluate his relationship with Roosevelt. It would also make 1937 a decisive year in United States labor history.

The year 1937 was without parallel in the history of the American labor movement. In 1937 as in 1919, militant union organizers and angry workers carried industrial warfare to the core of the nation's economy. In 1937 as in 1919 and also 1934, industrial violence rocked the nation as workers and their adversaries fought pitched battles in the streets of Flint, Youngstown, Johnstown, and Chicago.

But 1937 differed from previous turbulent years in United States working-class history. The conflict, violence, and even deaths that punctuated events in 1937 brought workers impressive and lasting gains. Before spring, CIO organizers had unionized workers in the two most powerful, oligopolistic, and antiunion basic industries: autos and steel. By mid–March 1937, CIO affiliates had wrested union contracts from the General Motors Corporation, the world's largest and wealthiest industrial firm, and United States Steel, for more than three decades a bastion of the open shop.

As a consequence of such major victories and subsequent lesser triumphs, organized labor gained more than three million members in 1937, a membership increase of nearly 100 percent. By December, the labor movement claimed almost 23 percent of the nation's nonagricultural workers among its members, the greatest proportion as yet unionized in American history. More significantly, the vast majority of newly organized workers belonged to CIO affiliates which, by the end of 1937, boasted a larger membership than the A.F. of L.

Just as 1937 was an unparalleled year for American workers, it was unequaled in the life and career of John L. Lewis. The triumphs that blessed the labor movement inflated Lewis's own power and prestige. Newspaper headlines and editorials, magazine feature stories, leftist and liberal journalists, and prominent politicians credited Lewis — not the workers who struck, suffered, and sometimes died — for labor's victories in the auto and steel industries. Officials of established labor unions and newly born ones implored Lewis to address their conventions; magazine and newspaper publishers beseeched him for articles on the future of American society; newspaper reporters clustered around mine workers' headquarters in Washington waiting for leaks from the UMW president's office or for Lewis's frequent and dramatic press conferences; millions of citizens gathered around their radios on the evenings Lewis spoke over national networks to listen to his mellifluous voice; and governors, congressmen, and the president himself sought Lewis's political support. Once again Lewis achieved the status of "labor statesman," but this time, unlike the years 1922–24, he claimed to speak for the entire American working class.

Lewis set the scene well for his 1937 triumphs. Committed to organizing mass-production workers in the nation's steel and auto industries, he knew that success or failure would hinge on the outcome of industrial battles in the crucial states of Pennsylvania, Ohio, Michigan, Indiana, and Illinois; he also realized that support from President Roosevelt, whatever its precise form, would be essential. That was why he had poured so much of his own energy and his union's money into the 1936 election and why the results delighted him. Not only had Roosevelt won an unprecedented national landslide, but pro-labor Democratic governors had also been swept into office in Michigan, Ohio, Indiana, and Pennsylvania, where the new lieutenant governor was not only a Democrat but also the secretary-treasurer of the UMW: Tom Kennedy. More remarkable, in scores of mill towns across the industrial heartland working-class voters, hitherto loyal to Republicanism and deferential to their employers, rebelled, electing Democrats and union members to local offices.

In 1937 the economy also favored the CIO. New Deal reforms, especially the pump-priming that preceded the 1936 election, brought results. For the first time since the depression's onset, manufacturers expanded production and recalled workers. By spring 1937 gross national production approached predepression levels, the auto industry forecast record profits, and steel companies relit long-banked blast furnaces.

When a militant minority of rebellious auto workers occupied Fisher Body Plant No. 1 in Flint on December 30, 1936, they acted propitiously. Although the Flint strikers moved without direct authorization from John L. Lewis (Lewis in fact planned to attack the steel industry before the auto industry), the CIO leader had no choice but endorse the struggle against General Motors. By unexpectedly stopping the assembly line and sitting down inside the plant instead of picketing outside, as was customary in labor disputes, a militant minority of auto workers catalyzed pro-union sentiment among the vast majority of apathetic workers in Flint and forced the hand of General Motors.

The scene had been set, the struggle joined. Auto workers, through their militancy, courage, and solidarity, and Lewis, through bluff, bluster, shrewd bargaining, and political manipulation, engineered the triumph of mass-production unionism.

The General Motors sit-down strike of 1936–37 pitted the infant United Auto Workers–CIO against the nation's wealthiest industrial corporation and brought John L. Lewis into direct confrontation with the financial oligarchy that he had repeatedly criticized. General Motors had sixty-nine plants in thirty-five cities, fourteen states, and two foreign countries (Germany and England), with total assets in excess of $1.5 billion. It also produced buses, trucks, and home appliances.

More than enormous capital resources and rising profits contributed to General Motors' ability to thwart organized labor. Between January 1, 1934, and July 1, 1936, the company spent about $1 million on private detectives who spied on union activists and ferreted out dissident workers. General Motors was the largest corporate client of the Pinkerton Detective Agency. In the words of the LaFollette Committee on Civil Liberties, General Motors "stands as a monument to the most colossal super-system of spies yet devised in any American corporation." Throughout the protracted struggle centered in Flint, the disparity in power between General Motors and the UAW-CIO clouded the prospects for a labor victory. CIO organizers like Adolph Germer counseled caution in November and December 1936. Sensing that strike sentiment was gaining momentum among UAW leaders and rank-and-file militants, Germer warned Lewis on November 30 that the time was not propitious for action.

Lewis acted on Germer's advice. Meeting in Washington on December 18 with John Brophy and UAW president Homer Martin, vice-president Ed Hall, and Wyndham Mortimer, the director of the Flint campaign and a left-wing communist militant, Lewis formulated the CIO's strategy for an impending confrontation with General Motors. Lewis's approach called for the UAW to communicate formally with the president and executive vice-president of General Motors enumerating the auto workers' primary grievances and suggesting a joint conference to negotiate all questions in dispute between the union and the company. Lewis, to be sure, expected General Motors to reject the UAW's suggestion. "The whole policy," Brophy informed Germer the next day, "is to move towards a climax in January in the event that General Motors refuses to confer and negotiate on a broad scale."

Lewis was particularly anxious that no walkout occur before January 1, 1937, when Democratic governors would come to power in Michigan and Ohio. After January 1, if a strike occurred in the auto industry as Lewis anticipated, strikers would more likely win political support not only from President Roosevelt but also from Governor Davey of Ohio and, more particularly, Governor Murphy of Michigan. Two other federal agencies also promised to assist Lewis in a struggle against General Motors: the National Labor Relations Board and the LaFollette Committee on Civil Liberties. Clearly Lewis saw the role of the state as vital to CIO success in the auto industry.

Power and force proved central to Lewis's strategy in the General Motors conflict. That was why Germer's advice fed Lewis's natural caution, leading him to counsel UAW leaders to avoid acting as the aggressors and to delay a strike. And that was why when the sit-down came to Flint ahead of schedule and without Lewis's authorization, he nevertheless supported the strikers wholeheartedly. By their surprising and decisive action, the Flint militants had established an unescapable reality: their power to paralyze two essential General Motors plants and, apparently, to win the support of a substantial majority of the hitherto nonunion workers. During the forty-four days between the workers' seizure of the Fisher Body No. 1 and 2 plants on December 30, 1936, and their victorious march out on February 11, 1937, Lewis never ordered the strikers to surrender the power they wielded through the seizure and occupation of company property by withdrawing from the plants before victory was theirs.

Had Lewis himself planned the Flint organizing campaign, he could not have devised a more ingenius strategy. The sit-down tactic enabled the union to magnify its own limited power and to compound General Motors' problems. By timing the factory occupation to occur when shifts changed, union strategists immediately doubled the number of activists available to stop the assembly line. And by actually stopping the line and successfully occupying the plant, the militant minority forcefully impressed the majority with the power of the union and attracted thousands of new recruits to the cause. By occupying company property on the inside instead of picketing it on the outside, strikers escaped the worst vicissitudes of a midwinter walkout. Finally, instead of strikebreakers marching into a picketed factory under armed guard in order to restart idle machinery, strikers themselves remained inside to ensure that the machinery stayed idle.

Other advantages blessed workers as a result of the sit-down strategy. Forced to exist together around the clock and away from the influence of family and other external forces, the strikers developed a sense of solidarity. With the factory silent as the assembly line lay still, strikers talked to each other conversationally, became more sociable with one another, and developed a "consciousness of kind." So impressive was this community and solidarity that journalist Paul Gallico wrote: "They had made a palace out of what had been their prison."

Labor solidarity extended beyond the occupied factories' gates. Auto workers from other cities came to Flint to assist their union brothers whenever events took a turn for the worse. And outsiders, both UAW members and sympathizers, provided the steady flow of food and messages that maintained the strikers' health and morale. Wives and children, too, played a crucial role. An unhappy wife or a forlorn child could do more to weaken the spirit of a sit-downer than company intransigence. Thus those strikers' wives and daughters most committed to the struggle organized an emergency brigade to enlist the energies of women in Flint.

The solidarity established by the strikers on the inside and their families and supporters on the outside provided Lewis with the power that enabled him to play the role of negotiator-extraordinary. Personally, Lewis had little to do with day-to-day events in Flint or the national General Motors strike. Even Germer and Brophy generally deferred to the wishes of such UAW leaders as Mortimer and Travis. Uninvolved in the more conventional activities of the strike, Lewis concentrated on eliciting federal and state support for the sit-downers and forcing General Motors to the bargaining table.

General Motors had no intention of negotiating seriously with the union or conceding to the strikers. Instead, the corporation's top executives, especially Alfred P. Sloan, fully expected to smash the strike. And they had good reason for their optimism. Flint was a company town: Its public officials, civic organizations, and newspapers served General Motors. Substantial numbers of local workers declared loyalty to the company, not the union, and some among them belonged to the Black Legion, a fascist-style organization that opposed unions, the foreign-born, and nonwhites. The law, too, seemed to favor the company. The sit-downers had seized company property—a seizure in violation of statutory and common law. General Motors could anticipate that the judiciary would order the strikers to return company property to its rightful owners and that public authorities would enforce such an injunction. And once the sit-downers had been evicted from the plants, the strike would collapse.

On January 2, 1937, the General Motors Corporation obtained from the Genesee County Circuit Court a "temporary restraining injunction" ordering the union to cease and desist from obstructing entrance to and exit from the plants, to halt mass picketing, and to evacuate the factories. The next evening at a union strategy meeting, Adolph Germer suggested that the judge who issued the injunction, Edward D. Black, an elderly local resident, probably owned General Motors stock. Lee Pressman, whom John L. Lewis had appointed as CIO's legal adviser, immediately contacted friends in New York, who informed him that Judge Black indeed owned more than $200,000 in General Motors stock. Pressman promptly released news of Black's material interest in the General Motors Corporation to the press and demanded that the temporary injunction be lifted. An embarrassed Black let his order lapse, and an equally embarrassed General Motors turned to another judge for relief.

During the first weeks of January the real battle was fought by auto workers in Flint, the strike's nerve center, and in GM plants elsewhere in the nation. What negotiations occurred during that time were a charade. If General Motors edged closer to the union's demands, it still resolutely refused to countenance the UAW's central demand: exclusive representation. The company's primary objective remained first to compel the sit-downers to evacuate the plants and only then to bargain with the union. The strike leaders still desired to gain exclusive representation for the union before marching the sit-downers out. In short, the company and the union as yet had nothing to compromise.

Even force failed to break the resistance of the stubborn sit-down strikers. On January 11, 1937, the Flint police, perhaps in collusion with General Motors, attacked the strikers at their weakest point, Fisher Body Plant No. 2, a factory occupied by at most one hundred strikers whose spirits had been sagging. In response to pleas for help from company guards, sometime after 9:00 p.m. the Flint police arrived armed with tear gas. About fifteen officers approached the plant, ordered the strikers to open the gates, and, receiving no response, fired gas canisters into the factory. The strikers retaliated. Using fire hoses, steel auto door hinges, bottles, stones, and other handy weapons, the sit-downers drove the police back.

The tide of battle ebbed and flowed. Pelted by the strikers' missiles and with the wind whipping the tear gas back into their own faces, the police retreated. Suddenly they halted, turned, drew their pistols and riot guns, and fired directly at their pursuers.

When the shooting stopped, fourteen strikers and sympathizers as well as two spectators lay wounded—thirteen by gunshot. Eleven law officers also had been injured. The "Battle of the Running Bulls" ended "with the strikers and their allies in command of the battlefield."

The "Battle of the Running Bulls" ushered the strike into a new phase, one that demanded a more active role by John L. Lewis. As was usually the case in labor disputes, the eruption of violence brought the intervention of the state. As soon as he learned of the violence in Flint, Governor Frank Murphy ordered elements of the Michigan National Guard to duty in the embattled city. Perhaps that was precisely what General Motors wanted. The appearance of troops during a strike customarily spelled disaster for strikers. Military men dispersed pickets, spread fear among them, and returned property to its rightful owners. But this was not to happen in January 1937, because Governor Murphy entered the Flint dispute with a deserved reputation as a friend to labor, a reputation that he meant to maintain.

After the arrival of the state troops in Flint on January 12, peace returned to the troubled city. Although Murphy believed that the sit-down strike created an illegal trespass on private property, he never intended to evict the strikers by force. Rather, Murphy used his considerable influence to compel UAW representatives and corporation officials to negotiate.

Beginning on January 15, General Motors met face to face with union officials in the governor's presence. Corporation spokesmen demanded that the strikers evacuate the plants; that accomplished, the company promised to bargain freely with the UAW concerning its demands of January 4. Speaking for the union, Brophy, Mortimer, and Martin (who were in telephone contact with Lewis) insisted that the strikers would evacuate the plants only if General Motors agreed to bargain exclusively with the UAW and made no attempt to open the struck plants during the subsequent negotiations. Finally, in an agreement in which the corporation surrendered more than it liked and the union accepted less than it wanted, Murphy arranged for a temporary truce in the sit-down strike.

Under the terms of the agreement, the unions agreed to evacuate all the occupied plants and the company promised not to resume production or to move dies and other machinery from Flint to other domestic plants and to bargain exclusively with the UAW over its January 4 demands. Murphy acted as the guarantor of the truce, which was to last for fifteen days from the start of the evacuation in Flint on January 17.

General Motors, not the union, broke the truce. William Knudsen, the chief operating executive of the company and the man least hostile to trade unionism among General Motors executives, gave the sit-downers cause to delay evacuation. Knudsen, acting either for himself or at the direction of his company superiors, invited George E. Boysen, leader of the Flint Alliance, a General Motors–sponsored organization of loyal employees, to join the negotiations as spokesman for the majority of nonunion workers. The reporter, William Lawrence, leaked word to the union of Knudsen's invitation to the Flint Alliance. Union representatives immediately informed Governor Murphy that General Motors had violated its promise to bargain exclusively with the UAW and that the sit-downers would now remain inside the occupied plants.

Frank Murphy's truce having collapsed, the federal government intervened through Secretary of Labor Frances Perkins. On January 19, Perkins met all day and into the early evening with Murphy and John L. Lewis. The Michigan governor remained committed to evacuation by the sit-downers and offered to surround the Flint plants with militia, keeping them idle while negotiations ensued. But Lewis refused to recommend evacuation before the strikers won substantial concessions from General Motors.

Unable to crack Lewis, Perkins pursued Alfred Sloan, president of General Motors. For four hours the secretary of labor pleaded over the telephone with the corporation executive to bargain with the union. Finally, Sloan consented to go to Washington to confer with Perkins and Frank Murphy—but not John L. Lewis. Not only did Sloan refuse to meet with the CIO leader, but he also insisted that his visit to the capital be kept in absolute secrecy; he wanted no sign that General Motors could be influenced by public officials to bargain with organized labor. Despite Secretary Perkins's best efforts to cloak Sloan's visit, reporters uncovered his presence in Washington, publicized it, and thus ruptured the new round of negotiations.

Federal intervention in the conflict offered Lewis the opportunity to apply his singular skills. During a news conference at UMW headquarters on the afternoon of January 21, the CIO leader delivered a direct message to President Roosevelt. "We have advised the administration that for six months the economic royalists represented by General Motors contributed their money and used their energy to drive this administration out of power. The administration asked labor for help to repel this attack, and labor gave its help. The same economic royalists now have their fangs in labor. The workers of this country expect this administration to help the workers in *every legal way,* and to support the auto workers in the General Motors plants" (emphasis added).

Lewis's public statement of January 21 simply reiterated the central message of his radio address of December 30, delivered the night Flint workers had occupied the factories. He merely asked the Roosevelt administration to assist the auto workers "in every legal way," meaning the enforcement of the Wagner Act and federal pressure on employers to bargain collectively with labor.

Why, then, did Lewis publically criticize Roosevelt? He apparently did so for two reasons. First, he perhaps intended to let Sloan and other General Motors executives know that in January 1937 they could not expect federal authorities to assist them in thwarting organized labor, as had happened in 1934 when workers were poorly organized and politically impotent. Sloan apparently received this message; immediately after Lewis's January 21 press conference, he informed Perkins that he was terminating all negotiations and leaving Washington. Second, Lewis addressed the strikers, reminding them that the CIO, unlike the A. F. of L., would not surrender their vital interests in negotiations with the federal administration. As long as they held firm in their occupation of Flint's auto plants, the sit-downers could rely on Lewis.

With Sloan's departure from Washington, Perkins's efforts to bring the disputants together collapsed. Evacuation of the General Motors plants in Flint remained the central issue. Sloan resolutely refused to bargain with the union until the plants were evacuated, a condition that neither Perkins nor Governor Murphy could satisfy. Not that federal and state officials failed to try. On January 26, Murphy offered to keep the plants closed with troops for two weeks if the sit-downers evacuated, and two weeks longer if negotiations failed to produce a settlement during the initial fortnight. But Lewis rejected the governor's proposal.

Lewis's political influence and his refusal to consider evacuation before a settlement brought positive results for the strikers. Federal officials fell silent about the intransigence of their friends in the labor movement but criticized publicly their enemies among the "economic royalists." At a press conference on January 26, President Roosevelt rebuked Sloan in much sharper language than he had directed at Lewis, and the same day Perkins criticized Sloan more emotionally and acidly.

As January ended, the General Motors strike seemed as far from settlement as ever. A month of fruitless negotiations, unsuccessful state and federal intervention, and continued occupation of the Fisher Body plants had rubbed nerves in Flint raw.

Then on January 31, 1937, General Motors worsened matters when it again resorted to the courts for relief. General Motors petitioned Circuit Judge Paul V. Gadola to issue an injunction ordering the sit-downers to vacate company property. The judge scheduled a formal hearing for February 1.

Before Gadola could act, the leaders of the Flint strike engineered a remarkable tactical coup. In one unexpected but devastating step, the auto workers intensified the economic pressure against General Motors. Of the many General Motors factories in Flint, none was more vital to the company's economic empire than Chevrolet No. 4, where the bulk of the top-selling car's engines were produced. Because it had remained open and in production throughout the strike, it became the logical target for strike strategists. On the afternoon of February 1, fighting erupted in front of Chevrolet No. 9. Immediately, company guards and city police raced toward No. 9, as did elements of the National Guard. Simultaneously another group of union members entered the gates of Chevrolet No. 4, walked inside the plant, and gave the signal to begin a sit-down. After a brief battle with supervisory personnel and antiunion workers during which the nonunion majority fled, the UAW's militant minority occupied the most vital General Motors plant in the city.

Just as the auto workers occupied Chevrolet No. 4, Judge Gadola heard arguments in the injunction case. The next day, February 2, the judge ordered the strikers in Fisher Plants Nos. 1 and 2 to depart by 3:00 p.m., February 3; forbade picketing and other union activities around the plants; and threatened to fine the UAW $15 million if its members failed to heed the injunction.

The conflict was once again in Governor Murphy's hands. Only he possessed power adequate to enforce the injunction if the strikers refused to obey Gadola's order. Only he had the resources to avert the civil war that impended in Flint as city and company officials organized a volunteer force to implement the court order, and union men prepared to resist.

But Murphy still declined to use state power to break the strike. When advocates of law and order insisted that the governor enforce Judge Gadola's order, Murphy allegedly said: "I'm not going down in history as 'Bloody Murphy!' If I sent those soldiers right in on the men there'd be no telling how many would be killed. It would be inconsistent with everything I have ever stood for in my whole political life." Instead, the governor sought to reopen negotiations between the company and the union and to bring Lewis to Detroit.

President Roosevelt endorsed Murphy's strategy. As long as negotiations occurred in Detroit, not Washington, and Murphy, not Roosevelt, was the central public figure involved, the president could separate himself from a sensitive, explosive political situation. If Murphy, however, could manage to settle the conflict amicably with behind-the-scenes presidential assistance, political credit would flow to all New Deal Democrats.

Lewis arrived in Detroit late on February 3 and immediately entered conferences with General Motors representatives and Murphy that lasted until February 11. As pressure built up on the governor to enforce Gadola's injunction, Murphy labored to bring the union and management closer together. Lewis refused to relinquish the union's primary demand: exclusive representation, nor would he consider evacuation by the sit-downers until General Motors agreed to negotiate exclusively with the UAW. Lewis realized that Murphy wanted the sit-downers out, but he knew that Murphy would not use force to evict the strikers.

Initial bargaining between Lewis and General Motors' representatives on February 4 and 5 slightly narrowed the differences between the union and the company. Lewis demanded exclusive bargaining rights only for workers in plants still on strike—some twenty in all. General Motors offered to bargain with the union for those workers it represented, promised not to discriminate against union members, pledged not to undermine the union, and stated that it would not sign a better contract with any other labor organization. The company, however, still refused to concede exclusive representation to the UAW, which remained Lewis's primary aim.

With the strike differences narrowing, President Roosevelt again intervened. Acting on the advice of Secretary of Labor Perkins, Roosevelt spoke by telephone to Lewis, Knudsen, and Donaldson Brown. He asked Lewis either to postpone exclusive representation for four months or to accept it for only two months; he requested Knudsen and Brown to implement the terms that General Motors had already offered the union, especially the pledge not to make more favorable agreements with other organizations during the life of the contract with the UAW or to encourage the emergence of any other union, and, most important, to "agree to give any guarantees required by the Government for the faithful performance of no discrimination, interference, restraint, or coercion."

But neither Lewis nor General Motors would defer to the president's wishes. Lewis would not relinquish possession of the occupied factories unless he could be more certain of winning union security. The company had little inclination to grant exclusive representation as long as the law validated its claim to possession of the occupied plants and the A. F. of L. endorsed the corporation's position on collective bargaining.

Throughout the tortuous and tense negotiations, Lewis acted typically. As always, he believed in the prevalence of power, not principle; might, not right. As Lewis told Heber Blankenhorn only two weeks after the strike had been settled: "We held those key dies in Flint and we were not going to let go of them. They crippled General Motors." (General Motors' car production had fallen from a rate of fifty thousand for the month of December to only 125 for the first week of February.) Moreover, added Lewis, "those were splendid boys in those plants. Nothing would have gotten them out except troops."

The strikers' occupation of the three General Motors' plants in Flint remained the key to union success. None of Lewis's rhetoric or sarcasm carried as much weight in the balance of the bargaining as the sit-downers' determination to risk their own lives. As long as the sit-downers remained inside, General Motors could not produce cars and faced the possibility of losing a permanent share of the market to its competitors. One way or another, the corporation had to regain possession of its plants. Neither the Flint police nor judicial orders, however, seemed sufficient to remove the strikers. Only the state and federal governments had the power in February 1937 to break the strike by enforcing the law—that is, Judge Gadola's injunction of February 2.

But no matter how often Murphy raised his obligation to enforce the law, Lewis realized that the governor would never order the State Guard to attack the strikers. The labor leader was also aware that Roosevelt, whose principal desire was a peaceful settlement in which the union won recognition, put no pressure on Murphy to restore General Motors to its occupied property. Publicly and privately, however, the governor and the labor leader acted out a strange charade, one in which Murphy threatened to uphold the law and Lewis challenged the governor to spill human blood.

Lewis's refusal to retreat showed his sagacity as a bargainer for labor's rights. When Lewis became ill and took to his bed on the eve of the settlement, the governor and the corporation executives came to the labor leader's room to seal an agreement. Unable to regain its property in any other way and with its auto sales plummeting, on point after point General Motors conceded to Lewis's demands, causing the militant Robert Travis to advise his boss, "We've got 'em by the 'balls,' squeeze a little." General Motors insisted that strikers convicted of acts of violence not be rehired; Lewis asserted that the corporation must rehire all strikers and union members without discrimination; the labor leader prevailed. The company offered the union a three-month period during which it would not bargain with any union other than the UAW unless it received permission from Governor Murphy to do so; Lewis demanded a six-month exclusive bargaining arrangement; he received it. And so it went. Finally, on February 11, a gratified Murphy could carry a completed agreement to Lewis's bedside. "We have left a place for you to sign at the top," the governor informed the labor leader. Lewis insisted on signing at the bottom, as befit the man without whose consent there would have been no settlement.

If the strikers had not won a total victory, they had nevertheless wrenched a good deal from the world's largest industrial corporation. General Motors formally recognized the UAW as the collective bargaining agent for employees who belonged to the union. It promised not to interfere with the workers' right to join the union or to discriminate on the basis of union membership. The company also pledged to start bargaining with the UAW on February 16 concerning the union's January 4 demands. For its part, the union agreed to evacuate the occupied plants and not to interfere with production pending negotiation of a final agreement. Most important, in a letter to Governor Murphy, William Knudsen promised that the company would not inspire activities among other worker groups that might weaken the UAW; and Knudsen pledged that General Motors would not deal with any other union or representative of its employees in the twenty plants covered by the agreement without Murphy's permission for six months after production resumed.

Lewis's own evaluation of the strike settlement a month later at a meeting of the CIO executive board was to the point. "GM strike," Lewis exulted, "CIO faced a united financial front—GM settlement broke it."

Rank-and-file auto workers felt the same way. The day the strike settlement was announced, a committee of eight Ford workers came to visit Lewis in his hotel room. One of the eight, the son of a UMW member, leaned over Lewis's sickbed with his hand on his heart and said to Lewis, in broken English, "Mr. Lewis, my heart is glad today. The hearts of 100,000 are glad for the union. Now we got the sons of bitches." Flint workers felt even more elated, one stating that recognition "was the most wonderful thing that we could think of that could possibly happen to people." And a hitherto antiunion man added, "We now . . . are treated as human beings, and not as part of the machinery. . . . It proves clearly that united we stand, divided or alone we fall."

The UAW victory over General Motors legitimized the CIO as a national trade union center competitive with the A.F. of L. and magnified Lewis's role and influence as a labor leader. In the aftermath of Flint, the auto workers' union surged ahead to build a mass membership. Claiming eighty-eight thousand members in February 1937, within a month the UAW practically doubled its membership to one hundred sixty-six thousand nearly another one hundred thousand joined in April, and by mid-October the union claimed four hundred thousand dues-paying members.

However decisive the auto workers' victory over General Motors, many have interpreted the Flint strike as a fortuitous or accidental incident in the CIO's basic strategy to organize mass-production workers. To them, activity among the auto workers appeared as a diversionary or flanking tactic to the main battle that Lewis intended to wage in steel.

Various facts lend credence to the belief that Lewis, in 1936 and early 1937, planned to attack steel. Rumors abounded that Lewis had never forgotten the defeats he had suffered as an A.F. of L. organizer from 1911 to 1917 in the Pittsburgh area and that he thirsted for revenge against the city's dominant industry, steel. Substantial evidence revealed also that he considered organizaton of the steel industry vital to the long-term security of the UMW in the coalfields and the best means to conquer the captive coal mines. The steel industry, moreover, symbolized the Wall Street financial oligarchy's dominance in the United States. Finally, Jett Lauck repeatedly urged a frontal assault against the steel industry's resistance to trade unionism.

Just as dramatic stories of the confrontation between Lewis and Murphy during the Flint strike make better reading than sober analyses of the economic and political realities of the dispute, so, too, do the secret negotiations between Lewis and U.S. Steel executive Myron C. Taylor appear more intriguing than the counterplay of the same economic and political forces that brought labor victory in autos.

On Saturday, January 9, 1937, Lewis was having lunch in the dining room of the Mayflower Hotel with his good friend, Senator Joseph F. Guffey, when Mr. and Mrs. Taylor entered. On the way to their own table, the Taylors passed Lewis's table, whereupon the business executive bowed. After seating his wife, Taylor returned to Lewis's table, where the three men chatted for about a minute. Several minutes later Lewis, having completed his own meal, walked over to the Taylor's table, where he conversed animatedly for almost half an hour.

The following day, Sunday, January 10, a day Lewis ordinarily devoted to his family, found him in Taylor's Mayflower Hotel suite. For the next several days the two men continued to meet secretly in this conspicuous Washington hotel. Events in Michigan, however, interrupted the negotiations when Lewis traveled to Detroit to bargain for the auto workers in the General Motors dispute. Not until February 17, when Lewis arrived in New York to participate in collective bargaining between the UMW and the coal operators, did he resume negotiations with Taylor. Then, for the next two weeks Lewis and Taylor again met secretly at the executive's gracious Upper East Side townhouse, where they put the finishing touches to what became the final agreement between U.S. Steel and SWOC. On Sunday, March 1, Lewis assembled Lee Pressman, Sidney Hillman, and Philip Murray in his suite at the Essex House. He told his associates that he had just returned from Myron Taylor's house; that he had secured an agreement with the steel corporation, the terms of which he quickly rattled off; and that if Murray and Pressman went down to Pittsburgh on Monday morning and met Benjamin Fairless, president of U.S. Steel, in his office, he would sign an agreement with SWOC. A stunned Murray, the director of the steel organizing campaign, had been presented with a fait accompli, the securing of a labor agreement in which he had played no role. As Lee Pressman later reflected, "That's his [Lewis's] function, to meet the Myron Taylors and knock down the doors of the might[y] citadels of the U.S.A., and then say, 'Now, go down to Pittsburgh and get your contract.'"

The contract that Murray and Fairless signed on March 2, 1937, for SWOC and U.S. Steel offered less than the February 11 UAW-GM contract. The steel corporation agreed to recognize SWOC and to bargain with it solely for the workers it represented; U.S. Steel, like GM, refused to relinquish the principle of the open shop. The corporation also accepted rudimentary grievance and seniority procedures; granted its workers an across-the-board wage increase; and conceded the basic eight-hour day, five-day week with time and a half for overtime.

But why had U.S. Steel conceded before to a strike? Why would a corporation that alone produced almost as much steel in 1934 as Germany; that controlled 38.4 percent of all American capacity, with assets of more than $2 billion; and that possessed its own iron and coal mines, ships, railroads, basic steel and fabricating plants as well as marketing agencies, surrender to trade unionism without a struggle? *Fortune* magazine provided one answer: the far-sighted leadership and vision of Myron C. Taylor. Lee Pressman offered another: the character of John L. Lewis. Let us examine both.

In the summer of 1936, according to *Fortune,* Myron Taylor was in a particularly philosophical mood when he left the United States for his customary vacation in Italy's Florentine hills. The emergence of the CIO had convinced Taylor that "a great change had come over the face of U.S. industry. The blood and brimstone labor philosophy of his predecessor, Judge Elbert H. Gary, was out of tune with the times. So was . . . the idea of the big steel 'family, for instance, and good will toward the worker, and social welfare. Labor was in arms'." A summer's reflection led the executive to formulate what *Fortune* characterized as "the Myron Taylor formula for industrial peace." Simply stated, U.S. Steel's new labor policy would be as follows:

> The company recognizes the right of its employees to bargain collectively through representatives freely chosen by them without dictation, coercion or intimidation in any form or from any source. It will negotiate and contract with the representatives of any group of its employees so chosen and with any organizaton as the representative of its members, subject to the recognition of the principle that the right to work is not dependent on membership or non-membership in any organizaton and subject to the right of every employee freely to bargain in such manner and through such representatives, if any, as he chooses.

Fortune, then, and many scholars, subsequently, viewed the Taylor formula of industrial relations as a substantial shift in company policy, an innovation that made possible the peaceful agreement between SWOC and U.S. Steel. A close reading of the above statement and supporting evidence suggests, however, that Taylor never altered company labor policy in principle. U.S. Steel, even in the days of Judge Elbert H. Gary, had never denied its workers the theoretical right to join unions, provided the rights of nonunion workers received equal consideration and protection. In Gary's era, company executives believed, as Taylor tried to convince himself from 1935 through 1941, that most workers preferred *not* to join unions. And Taylor, quite contrary to *Fortune*'s assertion, still preferred "the idea of the big steel family." In a private memorandum of September 11, 1935, to President Roosevelt, Taylor expressed his deepest personal feelings on labor policy. Referring to the emergence of company unions in the steel industry after the passage of Section 7a and the Wagner Act, Taylor asserted that his company's employees "have shown a decided preference in managing their own affairs and the tendency, therefore, has been toward the formation of company unions." The overwhelming percentage of employees, he asserted, lack class consciousness and "do not want to become members of outside labor organizatons, to which workingmen who become members are required to pay dues and assessments." Taylor never deviated from the principles he enunciated to the president in September 1935. But in 1937, the events in Flint forced him to dilute his principles when faced with the reality of labor's power.

Taylor and U.S. Steel shifted labor policy between July 1936 and March 2, 1937, not because a summer's reflection transformed Taylor's beliefs, but because workers and their labor movement had refashioned American economic and political reality. The results of the 1936 elections displeased steel executives. Not only had Roosevelt been returned to office by a landslide, but in states and local communities that the companies had long dominated, their candidates fell before labor's. In a new political milieu, many more steelworkers signed up with SWOC, and scores of company unions declared their independence. For the first time since 1919, a national strike in the steel industry seemed a real possibility, and if it came, executives could not rely on the power of the state to smash it.

Taylor and his steel associates thus watched events in the auto industry carefully. They saw what a militant minority achieved in Flint. More important, they noticed with trepidation that neither President Roosevelt nor Governor Murphy had enforced the law against the sit-downers. Labor's victory in Flint presaged a bitter conflict in steel, one that might cause untold damage to property and life. Rather than risk such a conflict and sacrifice the profits his company made as a consequence of the New Deal–stimulated economic recovery, Taylor chose to beat a strategic retreat in labor policy. He voluntarily agreed to recognize SWOC and committed U.S. Steel to collective bargaining with the labor organization, yet he steadfastly refused to surrender the open-shop principle or to believe that most workers voluntarily preferred to join unions.

Clearly, the success of the auto workers in Flint was the single most important reason that the CIO triumphed over U.S. Steel. Lewis freely admitted as much on March 9, 1937, when he informed old fellow CIO executive board members, "a GM strike—sweeping effect on steel. CIO faced united financial front—GM settlement broke it."

What remains to be explained is why Lewis settled for less in the U.S. Steel agreement than he had wrested from General Motors. The steel company, like the auto company, consented to bargain with the CIO union, SWOC, for the workers it represented; but it refused to rule out negotiations with other labor groups for any time period, and it reiterated its commitment to the open-shop principle. Only one explanation seems plausible: Lewis believed that he was bargaining from a weaker position in steel. But why?

No easy answer emerges to this question. Comparing the situation in steel to that in autos, *Fortune* asked in the spring of 1937 if the sitdown strike could "tie up the auto industry, which had been hastily organized, what would prevent it from tying up steel, where the CIO was firmly and forethoughtedly entrenched?" Yet the strengths of the CIO's position in steel paradoxically produced significant weaknesses. So completely was SWOC administered from the top down, so firm was its oligarchic leadership, that officials could not be sure how the rank and file would act in a crisis. The steel union lacked the militant cadres who could force the hands of both corporation executives and labor leaders. And in steel as in autos only a minority—and a small minority at that—of workers belonged to the union on the eve of victory. Steel also differed from the auto industry in structure. Not dependent on assembly line methods of manufacture, although continuous flow characterized some aspects of steelmaking, the steel industry was not as vulnerable to economic damage inflicted by worker occupation of a single strategic plant. Furthermore, the CIO's strategists in steel were convinced that the Iron and Steel Institute (the industry's major trade association) had established an agreement among its members that, in the event of a strike against one company, profits on orders then filed by other companies would be shared with the struck company. Finally, the state had strengthened labor's position during the auto strike. Could state and federal officials be relied on again to disregard judicial injunctions or blink at labor violence in the event of a steel strike? Lewis wasn't sure. In the event, then, rather than risk a protracted industry-wide general strike, possible repudiation by public officials, and an irremediable defeat for labor, Lewis chose to accept Taylor's terms.

Lewis, moreover, realized the importance of symbols and images, that what people believed to be true was often more significant than what in fact happened. When Myron Taylor accorded recognition to organized labor in March 1937, newspaper columnists, public officials, scholars, and many labor leaders did not examine the terms of the settlement microscopically. They were awestruck by news that the fortress of the open shop had surrendered without a struggle to the CIO. The U.S. Steel–SWOC agreement coming just three weeks after the General Motors–UAW settlement proved the potency of the CIO. If the outcome of the auto strike had certified the legitimacy of the CIO, the U.S. Steel contract apparently made Lewis's organization the dominant national labor center. What the A.F. of L. had failed to accomplish in half a century, the CIO had achieved in three weeks. In March 1937, the CIO's future seemed unlimited.

The CIO signified a new epoch in the history of American labor. Lewis observed to fellow CIO leaders at the March 9, 1937, executive board meeting, "As years go by, this period will be marked as epoch in life of labor organizations—and economic, social, political history of America. Gigantic implications."

The CIO meant to capitalize on those implications. Its director, John Brophy, told the same March 9 meeting that the organization must centralize its operation in order to lessen the danger of unmanageable local situations. Brophy urged that the board appoint additional national representatives, authorize the formation of central bodies (counterparts to the A. F. of L.'s city centrals and state federations) where the situation warranted, and move the CIO into more commodious office facilities in Washington. Less than two weeks later, Charles Howard advised Brophy that the CIO should consider seriously the affiliation of a large number of new unions, including such substantial A. F. of L. affiliates as the meat cutters, bakery and confectionary workers, government employees, hotel and restaurant workers, and retail clerks. Howard proposed a strategy that avoided conflict with the most stable and powerful A. F. of L. affiliates yet allowed the CIO to charter local unions in certain cases where jurisdiction remained disputed.

Acting on the advice of Brophy and Howard, the CIO embarked on an aggressive organizing campaign that competed directly with the A. F. of L. for members. William Green soon complained to his executive council that "the country seems to be filled with CIO organizers. Every town and every city, small and great, seems to be filled with organizers employed, appointed and assigned to work for and by the CIO."

By the end of August 1937 the CIO laid claim to 3,419,600 members (more than the A.F. of L. claimed at that time) organized in thirty-two national unions and 510 local industrial unions directly affiliated to the CIO. Among the national unions were some of giants of the American labor movement: the mine workers, with 600,000 members; the UAW, with 375,000; SWOC, with 500,000 (463,000 actually held union cards, but 510,000 were employed by companies under SWOC contract); the Textile Workers' Organizing Committee (TWOC), with 400,000; the Amalgamated Clothing Workers, with 200,000; and ladies' garment workers, with 250,000.

In October, the CIO prepared to celebrate its successes. And it could find no more suitable location for a festival than Atlantic City, where

John L. Lewis had fired the first shot in American labor's civil war in November 1935. In mid-October the new hosts of labor gathered along the Boardwalk for their first national conference. They came from the steel towns of the Monongahela Valley, Akron's rubber factories, Detroit's auto plants, the West Coast waterfront, New York's subways, and the rain forests of the Pacific Northwest. The delegates included gnarled old class warriors from the coalfields and young militants from the mass-production industries, pure and simple unionists, and flaming reds. Practically every shade of labor and radical opinion found a voice in Atlantic City, and the old joined the more numerous young in toasting the labor movement's bright future.

But the man whose imagination, drive, and daring had breathed life into the CIO could not fully share in the celebration. As now seemed to happen more frequently when the sun shone less strongly and the temperature fell, John L. Lewis took to his bed, a victim of the flu. The man who exuded enormous vitality in his formal speeches suddenly seemed inordinately susceptible to physical ailments. Lewis was now fifty-seven years old and his life-style had taken its toll; he had paid a price for labor in the coal mines and years of ceaseless train and auto trips broken only by strange hotels and best-forgotten restaurants.

Yet there can be no doubt that Lewis created the CIO. From June 1936 to September 1937, the CIO was not a self-sustaining organization. In that period the CIO spent $1,745,968 and earned only $308,388, leaving a deficit of $1,437,580. Of the total funds the CIO received to support its operations, the UMW alone provided $1,245,000 (SWOC received $960,000 from the mine workers); without Lewis's generosity, then, there would have been no CIO.

In 1937, Lewis's gamble, his decision to use UMW funds to build a new labor movement, seemed a wise investment. "In a little over a year," Benjamin Stolberg wrote in the *Nation* of February 20, 1937, "the CIO has changed significantly the relation of social forces in American industry. It is changing both the structure and orientation of American labor. . . . It is gradually killing off the A.F. of L. in all but the most craft-ridden industries. It is profoundly affecting our two major political parties. It is transforming the relationship of government to industry." Lewis's extraordinarily shrewd leadership, Stolberg concluded, had made the CIO "the most progressive and vital force in American life today." In 1937, to the public and to millions of workers, Lewis was the CIO, and the CIO was Lewis.

13

The Man Behind the Mask:
Lewis in Legend and Reality

The year 1937 was undoubtedly the zenith of John L. Lewis's career. It began with *Nation* magazine placing the labor leader on its 1936 honor roll "for continuing to give strength and backbone to the American labor movement." The columnist Heywood Broun compared John L. Lewis to Joe Louis, the black heavyweight champion (the "Brown Bomber") and idol of the black masses. Arguing that Lewis the labor leader had done more for black people by organizing the mass-production workers than Louis the fighter had done by annihilating white boxers, Broun quipped, "I think that Lewis is the greatest heavyweight of our day."

Wherever Lewis went in 1937, masses of people seemed to share Broun's opinion. Invited to address an anti-Nazi rally in New York's Madison Square Garden sponsored by the American Jewish Committee and the Jewish Labor Committee, Lewis found himself wildly, ecstatically cheered minute after minute by a crowd estimated at twenty thousand. In May 1937, when Lewis addressed the convention of the International Ladies' Garment Workers, delegates rose to their feet for several minutes and chanted in unison: "CIO! CIO! CIO!" And in August, at the United Auto Workers convention in Milwaukee, delegates preceded Lewis's featured speech with twelve minutes of wild applause, punctuated the address itself with more applause, and followed it with five minutes of raucous snake dancing through the aisles. This scene was repeated as Lewis became the labor movement's most sought after public speaker, a man who commanded the rapt attention of hundreds of convention delegates and millions of radio listeners.

Public esteem and mass popularity seemed to alter Lewis's character and mode of behavior as a labor leader. Some of Lewis's closest associates sensed the change. John Brophy later reflected "there's no question in my mind that Lewis's aims in those early years of the CIO were definitely tied to the good of the general labor movement, and the workers as a whole. . . . I think that he too was stirred by the drama. I think he was moved by the sense of opportunity and fulfillment that lay in the situation." Gardner Jackson, who went to work for the CIO late in 1936 and came to know Lewis personally as well as officially, believed that the CIO transported Lewis out of his narrow trade union power role and into leadership of a mass popular uprising. The masses of workers and small people who appealed to Lewis for leadership in 1937 fired the labor leader's imagination recalled Lee Pressman, the CIO's chief counsel and one of Lewis's most trusted advisers in the early CIO period. Lewis, Pressman suggested, discovered a new career in 1937, during which the labor leader would embark on a long campaign to carry the common people to the pinnacle of national power.

How did Lewis's personality and character in 1937 compare to what it had been in the past? What were his essential beliefs and goals? What manner of man was he? And how did he relate to others in official and personal capacities? How did his private life and values contrast to his public persona and behavior? Was Lewis a Churchillean enigma wrapped in a riddle cloaked in mystery? Or was there a consistency and logic to his public career and private existence?

From the summer of 1936 through the summer of 1937 many Americans and also foreigners asked themselves the same questions. Newspapers and magazines hastened to provide their readers with answers by featuring articles exploring Lewis's origins, life, and career. Ben Stolberg dissected the labor leader's tactics and beliefs in the *Nation;* Louis Adamic probed Lewis in *Forum;* and a French journalist examined the United States labor leader from a European perspective in the *Atlantic Monthly.*

From these prose portraits and scores of similar brief biographies, there emerged an image of John L. Lewis as labor leader and public figure—one that he cultivated assiduously. For those journalists eager to gloss Lewis's image, the labor leader appeared, in the words of Heywood Broun, the most visible sight in the nation's capital next to the Washington Monument. For C. L. Sulzberger, who as a young reporter for United Press made his journalistic reputation by publishing the first popular biography of Lewis in 1938 (*Sit-Down with John L. Lewis*), Lewis seemed always to have a spare moment, time to prepare a written statement of his beliefs and goals. For Louis Stark of the *New York Times,* a CIO sympathizer, there were always timely and significant news leaks. For Louis Adamic and other free-lancers preparing sketches for mass circulation weeklies and monthlies, there was time for a gracious luncheon in Lewis's favorite dining place, the Carlton Hotel. And for the mass of working journalists, there were dramatic press conferences that Lewis staged as successfully as his chief competitor for news space, President Roosevelt.

First and foremost, Lewis cultivated an image of size, strength, and anger. "Big" is one of the first words that tumble into the description of John L. Lewis, reported Adamic. "He weighs in the vicinity of 230 pounds . . . but has little excess flesh anywhere about him. . . . Lewis," added Adamic, although in his late fifties, "seems to have just reached his prime. His great body is a marvelously fit and efficient organism, all its parts, working, clicking, integrated . . . he does not know from experience what illness is. . . . Lewis' head is the most impressive affair I have ever seen on top of a man's neck. . . . Alongside it, the average male head is something faint and inane." The whole impressive face dominated by aggressive features could register every important human emotion, according to Adamic, "but seems most effective in wrath, scorn, contempt and bulldog tenacity. . . . The face holds just a hint of incongruity. Above the nose is the face of a philosopher, a brooder; below, that of a fighter, a man of action. The two are not fused or integrated. The fighter dominates the brooder."

Lewis refused to alter that image when friends suggested that he cultivate public favor. Asked by Gardner Jackson not always to frown publicly, Lewis rejected the suggestion outright. "Why, Gardner," he responded, "my stock in trade is being the ogre. That's how I make my way." To Frances Perkins, the labor leader observed: "Madame Secretary, that scowl is worth a million dollars." And to a business acquaintance who suggested that the labor leader hire public relations men to improve his image, Lewis replied that if he were going to fight for the coal miners, he was simply going to have to be disliked and disrespected by the majority of American people.

Alongside the image of size and strength went the notion of Lewis as the center of all attention. When the UMW finally moved into its luxurious new Washington headquarters in the former University Club building, no visitor could escape Lewis's eyes. Every passageway, corridor, wall, and office bore a photograph of Lewis, usually full-face. Marquis Childs, the newspaper columnist, described a visit to Lewis's office in this way. "You go to see him and he receives you almost like— I once went to Mussolini's office in the Palazzo Venezia and he gave somewhat the same impression. A great office and you waded through the rug a couple of miles and got over to the great man."

Len DeCaux tells a revealing story of Lewis's grip on public attention. After the victory over GM at Flint, Lewis arrived for a rally at a large local stadium. As the crowd surged around the labor leader, he headed away from the platform and in another direction. DeCaux, together with hundreds of others, decided to remain close to Lewis, who forged slowly ahead. As the procession halted, DeCaux pushed forward to see where Lewis had disappeared. Finally, at the head of the large crowd stationed at a respectful distance from the labor leader, DeCaux witnessed a strange sight. "They were watching solemnly," DeCaux wrote, "while the great man relieved himself at a urinal. No one cracked a smile or a jest. Least of all Lewis. He zipped up his pants and washed his hands. Then he headed into the ranks of his admirers."

Such public behavior by the labor leader led the newspaper reporter Kenneth Crawford to quip: "Lewis had come to believe that his own birthday should be celebrated instead of Christmas." "To ask Lewis to exercise magnanimity, to ask him to be humble," wrote John Chamberlain, "is just about as futile as trying to get gold from pyrites or blood from a turnip."

The final element in the public image that Lewis cultivated was the picture of himself as the prototypical coal miner. "Think of me as a coal miner," he told Saul Alinsky, who spread the word in his life of Lewis, "and you won't make any mistakes." Trying to capture the essence of Lewis's personality, John Chamberlain concluded: "The man is still a miner in his psychology, still a 'man from the pits.'"

Lewis's private behavior among those he preferred to be with scarcely fit his public image. For one thing, Lewis was not an accessible person. Marquis Childs, for example, described Lewis as "a pretty aloof figure. . . . He lives in a kind of Olympian way. I don't know any newspaperman, except maybe one or two, who ever got very close to him." Ed Levinson, another newspaperman more familiar with Lewis because he went to work for the UAW in 1937, asserted that Lewis understood the psychology of making himself inaccessible, "thus making himself more effective for public assemblages and gatherings." John Brophy and Lee Pressman, who, as close associates and advisers in the CIO knew Lewis well, agreed. "Friends?" John Brophy responded to an interviewer's question. "I don't think he [Lewis] had any real friends. I think he lives—I was going to say in lonely grandeur, using grandeur facetiously. I think he likes to appear in the grand manner. . . . Grandeur for him is a material and formalized thing." Pressman remembered Lewis as close personally to only one associate in the labor movement, Phil Murray. Although other close associates might refer to him as "John," only Murray could call Lewis "Jack."

Rather than being a perfect physical specimen of prodigious strength and undiluted health, Lewis was especially susceptible to respiratory ailments—and at the most inopportune moments. During the final days of the 1925 anthracite coal strike negotiations, Lewis lay ill in a

Philadelphia hotel bed, as he did during the climactic moments of the 1937 General Motors negotiations in Detroit. And flu restricted Lewis's personal appearances at the October 1937 CIO national conference in Atlantic City. Flu was the least of Lewis's health problems. In 1941, he suffered a heart attack that kept him on the critical list in a Washington hospital. He had future heart problems, and perhaps past ones, that he labored to keep out of the press and secret.

The ogre's image that he presented to the public, the abruptness with which he treated associates in the labor movement, and his unrestrained egotism quickly dissolved when Lewis was among corporation executives, high government officials, diplomats, military men, and socialites. Cyrus Ching remembered Lewis in private meetings as a "shy, bashful man, the soul of courtesy." Rather than acting flamboyantly in private conversation, Lewis, according to Ching, spoke softly, with a dry, keen sense of humor; he was "a brilliant conversationalist," a wonderful man to sit down and talk with. James M. Landis, too, recalled the Sunday afternoon tea parties at the Lewis's Alexandria home, where prominent public officials came and good talk flowed as Lewis acted like a perfect gentleman. The image of Lewis as a gentleman, frequently as a "southern gentleman," crops up often in the remembrances of socially prominent individuals who knew him.

The portrait of Lewis as a prototypical coal miner also suffers by comparison with private reality. He did not descend from a long line of Welsh coal miners. Moreover, no one can be certain how much time John Lewis himself actually spent in the mines, a vocation that he had fled successfully and permanently by 1909. The further Lewis removed himself from the mines by career, income, and life-style, the less he resembled the typical coal miner in behavior, character, and values. Unlike the ordinary coal miners, among whom comradery and brotherhood were two of the strongest values, Lewis, according to Brophy, "had the arrogance of the boss, the superior."

The discrepancy between Lewis's public image and private behavior led Pressman to conclude that "he's just one of those strange creatures that God throws up every now and then." Marquis Childs reached almost the same conclusion: "This is a very curious man, this man Lewis."

Perhaps Lewis's role as trade union official and his leadership of the United Mine Workers and the CIO can illuminate his character and personality. In his 1938 history of the CIO, Edward Levinson presents a Lewis who appears every bit the counterpart of the stereotypical corporate executive whose work never ends and who must exert total control of his enterprise. "Hours after the sun has set and marked the end of a working-day for the rest of Washington," wrote Levinson, "the lights burn in Lewis' oak-paneled office at the United Mine Workers office. During the crises of the General Motors strike, of the U.S. Steel negotiations . . . he kept telephone wires open nightly, determined that no important detail should escape his attention."

Precisely what Lewis did during those long days and evenings in the office, aside from speaking on the telephone, remains uncertain. One can search the extant files of the UMW and the CIO in vain for any policy statements, administrative reports, or detailed proposals of union objectives bearing Lewis's signature. Reports and policy statements proliferated—but they were the products of John Brophy, Jett Lauck, Lee Pressman, Ralph Hetzel (a young academic economist whom Lewis hired as a CIO consultant), and scores of other little-known or undistinguished individuals who worked for Lewis. David Dubinsky remembers how surprised he was whenever he visited Lewis at the latter's Washington office to find the leader of the largest single international trade union and the dominant labor federation of the late 1930s sitting behind an immense desk absolutely devoid of the smallest scrap of paper.

Although reporters might compare Lewis to a corporation executive, and the labor leader himself preferred the appellation *executive* to that of *union official,* Lewis operated more in the style of big-city political boss than modern business executive. He dealt in power, not policy; patronage, not principles. Many of the deals he negotiated and methods he used were best left unrecorded. The telephone was preferable to the letter (or written memorandum); the private face-to-face conversation was preferred to the impersonal communication. And after he was convinced that the FBI, at the behest of President Roosevelt, was tapping his phones and eavesdropping on office and hotel room conversations, Lewis preferred to do business over lunch or dinner in crowded restaurants.

There are hints, however, of Lewis's mode of union operation. As in the universe of the political boss, in Lewis's labor world loyalty to the organization (the extended shadow of its leader) was the element essential to success. Nearly any error, sin, or crime could be forgiven except disloyalty. Lewis easily countenanced alliances with communists, anticommunists, Democrats, Republicans, trustbusters, and business tycoons—provided the union benefited. Like the political boss, Lewis also used the trade union as an institution to reward family members, whose loyalty to the chief could never be doubted, with lucrative positions. Finally, Lewis approached the development of young trade union leaders much as the boss chose his political heirs. When John Brophy asked him in 1938 how he would educate workers for union leadership, Lewis replied, "whenever I see a bright young fellow I pick him out and place him on the payroll of the union." "This," observed Brophy, "was his conception of how leadership was developed."

An element of brutality also marked Lewis's character. When Lewis felt betrayed, Brophy said, "he strikes with all the venom of which he is capable." Gardner Jackson sensed the same streak of violence in Lewis's character. When Jackson complained to his boss about the tactics of Donald Henderson, the leader of the CIO cannery workers, Lewis responded, "There is only one way to handle that, Gardner. You ought to have chosen your opportunity, found Don Henderson alone, and slugged him until he never forgot it. That was the only recourse you had." Subsequent relations with Lewis convinced Jackson that Lewis "has actually relied a considerable number of times on the use of direct violence in achieving his end." Asked by an interviewer if Lewis had a capacity for ruthlessness, Lee Pressman replied: "Oh, completely so. He was the kind of guy would commit murder."

In one way, and an important one, Lewis differed from the political boss. If he preferred to exert power behind the scenes and perhaps use force to achieve his ends, Lewis nevertheless desired to be esteemed publicly as a man of influence. Not satisfied with the knowledge that he exerted power, his inordinate pride commanded him to seek public manifestations of his potency. Thus none who saw or read a Lewis letter could mistake the fact that here was a puissant individual. The signature proved it—carefully practiced large, flowing letters that flooded the page and shrank every other word or phrase in the document. President Roosevelt, especially, experienced Lewis's thirst for power. To compete with the president of the United States, whose stationery bore the simple imprint "Office of the President" and the presidential seal at the top of each sheet, Lewis's unofficial UMW stationery also featured "Office of the President" at the top of each sheet and just below it (and barely visible to the human eye) was the union seal.

If Lewis's public behavior serves more to cloak his character than reveal it, perhaps the values he espoused during the late 1930s offer glimpses into his personality. Here, too, however, the student of Lewis meets insuperable problems. Almost all Lewis's major addresses and publications were written by Jett Lauck. Only rarely during sessions of the CIO and UMW executive boards or the mine workers' conventions did Lewis voice thoughts that expressed his values rather than tactics. If one relies on Lewis's statements before congressional committees, on the air, and on the speaker's platform (the same could be said of newspaper, magazine, and opinion journal contributions) to fathom the labor leader's beliefs, one may, in fact, be learning more about the ideology of Jett Lauck, Lee Pressman, Ralph Hetzel, or even K. C. Adams.

At times Lewis sounded radical, at other times conservative, and sometimes downright reactionary. Before union groups, he sounded the tocsin of militancy; the more militant the union he addressed, the more radical Lewis seemed. Before congressional committees and audiences of prominent individuals, he extolled organized labor as the primary bulwark against communism and the defender of Americanism. To businessmen he promised to behave as one practical entrepreneur to another.

No single issue caused Lewis more problems in the late 1930s than his association with communists. Two of his closest and most trusted advisers in the CIO were one-time Party members or sympathizers: Len DeCaux and Lee Pressman. Some of the most prominent new generation of labor leaders who emerged within the CIO—Joe Curran of the merchant seamen, "Red Mike" Quill of the transit workers, Harry Bridges of the West Coast longshoremen, James Matles and Julius Emspak of the electrical workers, and Wyndham Mortimer of the auto workers, to name just a few—were linked either to communism generally or the Party specifically. To such staunch A.F. of L. members as John Frey and Matthew Woll, to southern Democratic and Republican congressmen, to most of the nation's press, and to many antiunion businessmen, the CIO, in its halcyon days, seemed bolshevism's American vanguard, and John L. Lewis seemed the head of a subversive Trojan Horse. Yet this was the same labor leader who had routed all varieties of "reds" from the UMW during the 1920s and exceeded any other trade unionist in his red-baiting.

What, indeed, was Lewis's relationship to communism in the late 1930s? Without doubt, he had no sympathy with or even understanding of communism's principles and objectives. Determined by late 1936 to build a new national labor center, Lewis needed all the help he could find, and he found no more dedicated and selfless union organizers than the young communists who rallied to the CIO cause. Lewis, moreover, never contemplated for a moment that communists or socialists or any other group—Catholics included—could develop independent influence or strength in the CIO. Lewis could never, Pressman asserted, have developed Phil Murray's subsequent fear about Communist party influence in the CIO. "To contemplate him [Lewis] being aware of somebody else's power or influence over the organization that he had given birth to—that's something you just couldn't contemplate. I mean, it would be like talking to him about the atmosphere on Mars."

Yet many trade union communists considered Lewis their advocate in the internecine struggles between Left and Right that roiled many new CIO unions, especially the UAW. So well did Lewis disguise his own goals that John Frey castigated Lewis publicly for abetting communist penetration in the United States, trade union communists looked to him as their protector, and influential businessmen such as Walter Chrysler valued him as a bulwark against bolshevism.

Appearing to be all things to all people, did Lewis have any consistent or central values? Was there a solid, unshakable core to the man, or was he simply an ideological chameleon who discarded principles as easily as the lizard changed colors?

Despite his own adamant refusal to be drawn out during interviews and discussions on matters of philosophy, a consistent core of beliefs motivated Lewis's public behavior. He believed that cycles governed history, that the present invariably repeated the past, that bad times inevitably followed boom times, and, hence, that men must seize the main chance during prosperity and act defensively during adversity. But his belief in cyclical history was more intuitive than intellectual, more acted out in practice than expressed in words or theory.

The same might be said of his relationship to religion. Raised by a Mormon mother and a nonbelieving or nonpracticing father, Lewis evinced no interest whatsoever in formal religion as an adult. To the best knowledge of his closest associates in the labor movement, he attended no church, never referred to religion openly, and, if he subscribed to Christianity at all, he did so as part of a broader civic religion subsumed under the rubric *Americanism*. Like politics, he treated religious controversies opportunistically.

Americanism characterized Lewis's fondest beliefs. It was a word he had used frequently in *The Miner's Fight for American Standards* and continued to use repeatedly during the 1930s. To Lewis, Americanism had many connotations: It meant a society in which prosperity and well-being were widely diffused. And prosperity, in turn, was founded on technolgoical innovations and high wages. Technological innovation increased per capita industrial productivity and, hence, provided the source of wage increases. Unless wages rose in direct proportion to increases in productivity, consumers would be unable to purchase the products of American industry, and depression would follow as logically as day passes into night. Experience, moreover, had taught Lewis that employers refused to raise wages voluntarily. Only the power of organization, the trade union, enabled workers to reap the material rewards of technological innovation, to win for themselves the higher wages that kept the American economy prosperous. When Louis Adamic asked Lewis if he did not sometimes worry about excessive labor power, the CIO leader replied, "Recently a businessman of my acquaintance asked me a similar question. . . . I answered him, 'No one can guarantee the future; but I am certain that if labor does develop great power it cannot possibly make a worse mess of things than did big business in the last two decades, to go back no further in our history.'"

Linked to his belief in the necessity of trade union power to maintain economic prosperity was Lewis's distrust of a conspiratorial financial elite that he associated with Wall Street and the House of Morgan. Two sources contributed to his antipathy to eastern bankers and monopoly capitalists. One was the geographical and cultural environment of the first three decades of his life—Iowa, Illinois, and the Mountain West, a region in which hostility to Wall Street flourished along with corn, wheat, pork, beef, coal, and precious metals. The other was the advice of his friend and longtime economic consultant Jett Lauck, an intellectual critic of the House of Morgan and unregulated oligopolistic enterprises.

Paradoxically, Lewis's distrust of Wall Street and finance capitalism scarcely influenced his more general attitude toward businessmen and capitalism as a system. Some of his best friends were businessmen, and capitalism was for Lewis the source of the American success story. As Brophy later recalled, Lewis never sought a fundamental change in the national economy; instead, he appeared perfectly satisfied to work with the business community. More specifically, Brophy suggested, "I think Lewis accepts the basic relationships set up by the business community. I think he accepts completely their dominance."

Businessmen saw the same characteristics in Lewis. Alfred Staehle, publisher from 1942 to 1955 of *Coal Age,* the industry trade journal, perceived no difference whatever between Lewis and the operator's position on mechanization in the mines; they simply quarreled about the proper division of the proceeds of technological improvement. Staehle, moreover, had never met anybody "with a more penetrating and precise knowledge of what makes industry work, what produces profits than that possessed by John Lewis." To businessmen even more than to fellow labor leaders, Lewis personified integrity. "I could trust John L. Lewis," said Cyrus Ching, "and if he ever gave his word on anything, you could rest assured that's the way it was going to be. John L. Lewis is a man of very high integrity."

At a time when Lewis appeared to the public most radical and dangerous to the established order, the year 1937, Louis Adamic grasped the labor leader's essence as few others have: possessive individualism. Lewis, thought Adamic, believed that every individual desired to improve himself, that selfishness—the intensive human desire for material possessions, social mobility, and status—was the root of human progress as well as misery. "Though an exceptional man," Adamic wrote in 1937,

Lewis is also a deeply ordinary one . . . he has a chauffeur in whipcords to drive him about in the twelve-cylinder automobile his union bought for him; which is what every ordinary American would like to have . . . there ride in that shiny car . . . vicariously—the four hundred thousand United Mine Workers of America, most of them ordinary men . . . full of the instinct and impulse to improve themselves, to get on, to acquire the material symbols of well-being, power, and progress that are the chief contemporary elements of the American "Dream." That fine machine and the snappy cap on the chauffeur's head are ordinary symbols, generally craved in America, though rarely attained, and which, incidentally are apt to be an important source of Lewis's power in this country.

Occasionally Lewis himself openly revealed his possessive individualism and status striving before union audiences. The same man who excoriated the financial and corporate dictators of Wall Street told delegates at the 1938 UMW convention that their union "stands for the proposition that the heads of families shall have a sufficient income to educate [their children who] . . . go forth when given that opportunity. . . . They become scientists, great clergymen in the church, great lawyers, great statesmen. . . . Many of our former members are successful in great business enterprises." No dream or visions of contented craftsmen or self-respecting laborers—not even a great labor leader in the bargain. In 1938, after almost ten years of depression—in fact in the first year of the new Roosevelt depression—Lewis still beguiled coal miners with the gospel of individual success. Two years later, at his union's 1940 convention, Lewis stated his belief in possessive individualism more bluntly. "You know," he said, "after all there are two great material tasks in life that affect the individual and affect great bodies of men. The first is to achieve or acquire something of value or something that is desirable, and then the second task is to prevent some scoundrel from taking it away from you."

One may well wonder, given Lewis's belief in individualism, the gospel of success, and status striving, why he was content to act in the role of labor leader. A position in big business might have offered Lewis greater material remuneration than a union presidency and certainly conferred heightened status. But union leadership offered Lewis one compensation that business could not provide: overt power and the public esteem that flowed from it. Like other labor leaders who deserted the union for corporate careers, Lewis would likely have disappeared from public view had he chosen to be lured by the salary and status of an executive position. Lewis's colossal ego, however, required more; it demanded attention, esteem, and, most of all, social, economic, and political power.

In the labor movement, Lewis could have his cake and eat it. The UMW provided him a substantial salary, unlimited expenses, and assorted fringe benefits; it also enabled him to become a financier through the National Bank of Washington and through the union's subsequent role as trustee for its members' pension and welfare funds; and it brought him into contact and business relationships with such latter-day lordly entrepreneurs as Cyrus Eaton. As a labor leader—moreover, one who commanded a large and militant union situated in a strategic industry— he could command public attention whenever he chose, exert economic and political power, and directly challenge presidents of the United States.

Lewis's private life appears still more unfathomable. He guarded his and his family's privacy zealously. Journalists and associates in the labor movement (he had no friends among trade unionists) were scarcely if ever invited to the Lewis home either in Springfield, where the family lived from 1917 to 1933, or Washington, where they rented an apartment at the Wardman Park Hotel in 1933–34, or in Alexandria, where they first rented a notable old American colonial home and later purchased one of the Washington suburb's more famous colonial houses. Lewis also seldom referred to his family life in conversations and interviews with inquisitive reporters or prospective biographers, which is why so many of the sketches and biographies of the labor leader contain inaccurate personal data or, more often, neglect his private life.

Still, from scraps of information that appear in the unlikeliest places, observations by prominent individuals who knew Lewis, and inference, certain conclusions may be drawn about the character of the Lewis family. No hint of social deviance touched any member of the Lewis clan, an extended family that included sons, daughters, brothers, sisters, nephews, nieces, and in-laws. Husbands and wives remained outwardly loyal and faithful to each other, children were obedient, and all family members were temperate in their private behavior. Neither John, Myrta, Kathryn, nor John Jr. drank alcohol. At the Lewises' Sunday afternoon parties for Washington influentials, tea, not liquor, was served. Sunday, moreover, held a special place for Lewis as a sort of secular sabbath, the one day of the week on which he abandoned union affairs and devoted himself to family matters.

Lewis's intense family loyalty protected and rewarded materially all members of the extended clan. His younger brothers served as union functionaries either on the UMW or CIO payrolls, and his sister Hattie ran the UMW's district headquarters in Springfield, where she could live in one of the three homes Lewis owned in that city and care for her elderly mother. Floyd Bell, his brother-in-law whom Lewis had earlier made treasurer of the United Labor Bank and Trust Company of Indianapolis, in 1936 became comptroller of the CIO. And Kathryn served as her father's private secretary and later sought office as secretary-treasurer of the CIO—a desire that caused conflict between Lewis and Sidney Hillman, among others.

Blood, not ability, motivated Lewis's selection of relatives for important official positions in the labor movement. When Lewis decided that the CIO should compete directly with the A.F. of L. for membership among building trade workers and established the Construction Workers' Organizing Committee, he selected Dennie Lewis as director. A Chicago labor reporter succinctly characterized Dennie Lewis's talent. "I mean," said Edwin A. Lahey "Denny's [*sic*] a meathead. . . . I can't imagine Denny [*sic*] doing anything more responsible than going for coffee. He's a likeable guy, a saloon fighter, a crap-shooter, living on his brother's eminence." Kathryn may have been more intelligent and talented, but as a female in an overwhelmingly male trade union universe she suffered irremediable handicaps. Yet Lewis selected his daughter as secretary-treasurer of UMW District 50, the union's catchall subdivision for all noncoal miners and, after Lewis's departure from CIO in 1942, his own organization's competitor to the CIO and A.F. of L. Athough District 50 recruited few women, and the male trade unionists associated with it believed that women belonged in the home, Kathryn remained, as long as her father desired it, the district's secretary-treasurer.

The outward manifestations of closeness among members of the Lewis family and the intense loyalty that characterized their behavior hid a variety of tensions and peculiarities. Just as John L. Lewis tended to shrink all those he came into contact with officially, and indeed desired to do so, he undoubtedly had the same impact on family members. Myrta Lewis seemed to disappear physically and affectively in the presence of her husband. Individuals who dined with the Lewises recall Myrta as a dim figure who seemed to vanish into obscure corners of the home. Small, sensitive, reserved, unexpressive, without John L.'s command of the English language—those were the words and phrases that Gardner Jackson used to describe Mrs. Lewis. Every sketch and biography of Lewis stresses Myrta's role as cultural tutor to her husband. Yet Lee Pressman, who worked closely with Lewis for five years and tried to talk with his boss about intellectual and philosophical matters, concluded that John L. Lewis had no interest in books, literature, history, or culture. Lewis's reading, according to Pressman, ended with the newspapers and news magazines.

Many factors undoubtedly strained the relationship between Myrta and John. Myrta Lewis had extravagant social pretensions, a desire to be accorded status as an upper-class Virginian who traced her lineage back to the colonial era. But her husband's role as a public figure threatened Myrta's striving for status. John L. Lewis's image in the

1930s as radical labor leader, ardent New Dealer, and tribune for American plebeians caused the grand dames of Alexandria to remove the Lewis home from their annual tour of notable colonial residences—likely a blow to Myrta's self-esteem, as she had devoted considerable time, energy, and money to decorating it.

The relationships between the Lewises and their children were fraught with unconscious conflicts and personal tragedy. Kathryn, the eldest child after the death of her sister, Mary Margaret, worshipped her father, who, in turn, showered affection and attention on her. No acquaintance of the Lewises ever remarked about the mother-daughter relationship or thought to compare Kathryn to Myrta. A bright, precocious girl, Kathryn excelled in the public primary and secondary schools of Springfield. Upon her graduation from high school, she entered Bryn Mawr College in suburban Philadelphia—a labor leader's child in a universe of women raised in the American upper classes. Unhappiness marked her college days, a time when her weight problem—she weighed upwards of three hundred pounds—caused grave psychological problems. At another time in her life she isolated herself for two years in a little cottage in Croton-on-Hudson, New York and practiced Yoga. And finally, Kathryn fell under the spell of Nicholas Roerich, a mystic and guru whose paintings decorated her bedroom walls.

John L. Lewis tried hard to compensate Kathryn for her physical handicap. He made her his secretary, later offered her an official position in the labor movement, pressured the Roosevelt administration to appoint Kathryn as one of the U.S. delegates to a Pan-American labor conference in Lima, Peru, and took her wherever he went. He also protected his daughter from photographers, whose lenses threatened to embarrass the obese young woman already so traumatized by her weight.

Kathryn was the complete subject of her father—"Daddy's girl"—and she in turn sought to shield her protector from any criticism or snub. Kathryn, in fact, came to hate Franklin D. Roosevelt because the president did not obediently bend to her father's will; and, in her own way, Kathryn played a part in the political rupture in 1940 between John L. Lewis and Franklin D. Roosevelt. However, as intense and loyal as was the surface relationship between daughter and father, Kathryn was in a continuous state of rebellion against her dependency, as revealed by her adventures with psychoanalysis, Yoga, and Roerich.

Father and son developed an entirely different, almost impersonal, relationship. For most of the 1930s, John L. Jr. seemed to be the missing member of the family. When the Lewises dined out as a family, he was absent. When the Lewises entertained others at home, John Jr. was not to be seen. To be sure, he was away from home during most of the decade as a student at a private secondary boarding school and at

Princeton University; still, friends and acquaintances of the Lewis family came to believe that Myrta wanted her son completely shielded from the influence and controversy that surrounded his father. Rather small physically, shy and retiring, John Jr. turned his life into a flight from his father's reputation, a desire inculcated in him by his mother. The son evinced no interest in his father's career or the labor movement. Upon graduation from Princeton in 1941, John Jr., like his maternal grandfather, chose a career in medicine. He matriculated at the Johns Hopkins University Medical School and eventually specialized in psychiatry. Closeness to his mother compensated John Jr. for distance from his father. When John L. Lewis and Kathryn occupied themselves during the summer of 1936 on trade union business, Myrta and John Jr. traveled together in Europe. If later in life at various stages of his own career John Jr. remained dependent on his father for financial assistance, he remained personally and emotionally distant from his father's world. Indeed, after John L. Lewis's death in 1969, John L. Lewis Jr., the only surviving heir, actually sought to destroy all remaining traces of his father's career. One can only wonder at what John Jr.'s life reveals about Myrta Lewis's deepest feelings toward the man to whom she was married for thirty-five years.

Social climbing occupied as significant a place in the Lewises' family life as did respectability. Permanent residence in Alexandria afforded Myrta and John the chance for social advancement that they had lacked in Springfield. A part of their social ascent derived directly from John L. Lewis's role as labor leader. Regular invitations to White House dinners, receptions, and presidential inaugurations were the respect the nation's leading politician paid to the dominant figure in the labor movement. The same might be said of invitations to address the National Press Club and to appear as a featured guest at the annual Gridiron Club Dinner — the prestigious event sponsored by newspaper publishers.

Much of the social climbing, however, was carefully and consciously planned. Kathryn was not sent to a well-known women's college by chance; nor was John Jr. enrolled at Virginia's Woodbury Forest Academy and Princeton University by accident. The Lewises, moreover, did not first rent and then purchase seventeenth- and eighteenth-century houses in Alexandria because of an abstract love for the architecture of the era. An original colonial-style home provided the ideal setting in which Myrta Lewis could display the expensive antiques that she had been purchasing in American and European shops for more than ten years. The choice of social acquaintances and dinner companions, a choice that excluded all trade unionists, was also not accidental. Lewis made clear to Jett Lauck his eagerness to gain entry among the elite of the nation's capital. For weeks and months, precisely at the moment he was forming the CIO, Lewis pestered Lauck with requests that the economic consultant use his influence to have Lewis accepted as a member of the Cosmos Club, Washington's most prestigious private men's social institution. And that was why the guest list to the Lewis home, whether for dinner or Sunday afternoon tea parties, featured senators, cabinet members, diplomats, Supreme Court justices, military leaders, and men and women of inherited wealth.

The Washington elite reciprocated. Lewis became the first labor leader invited regularly to dine at the Cosmos Club. Drew Pearson invited the trade unionist to attend his regular stag dinners, a meeting place for many influential Washingtonians. Kingman Brewster invited Lewis to spend a weekend at the former's Catoctin Lodge in Thurmont, Maryland. And Evelyn McLean Walsh, the dowager queen of Washington society, showered dinner and cocktail party invitations on the Lewises.

By 1937 the social activities of the Lewis family made the newspapers. In a story that appeared in July 1937 on the society page of the New York *Telegram,* Helen Worden reported that "The phrase 'Rich as John L. Lewis' was born in the antique shops of Alexandria, Va., during the past year." According to Worden, Mrs. Lewis—who refused to shop on Sunday because, as she told a local antique dealer, "I'm an old-fashioned Presbyterian. I don't like to do anything on the Sabbath that can be done on a week-day"—claimed to be descended from old Virginia aristocracy. Everyone among Alexandria's best society, to which the Lewises belonged according to the society columnist, spoke well of Myrta, a small, quiet, gray-haired woman of conservative inclinations. "It isn't as if the Lewises were strangers," remarked Mrs. R. R. Sayers, the wife of a local doctor and occupant of the Robert E. Lee house. "In coming to Alexandria they are really coming home. You know, her people were Virginians. He's very well connected in Wales."

The Lewis family lived as sumptuously as the wealthy individuals whose behavior they emulated. Mrs. Lewis shopped at the Shoreham Market, the capital's most exclusive butcher and grocery store. Helen Worden asserted that Mrs. Lewis never questioned price. Bills and receipts for the antiques, furniture, tapestries, rugs, and paintings that Mrs. Lewis purchased on two continents proved as much. When Myrta attended church on Sunday mornings as she did regularly, her husband's chauffeur-valet, James Lewis, drove her. Not only did John L. Lewis, Sr. possess a twelve-cylinder Lincoln limousine upholstered in plush velvet and leather and fitted with the most expensive accessories (all paid for by the UMW), John Jr. had his own late-model sedan garaged together with his father's vehicle at a monthly cost of $40.

No luxury was spared the Lewis family in the 1930s. Besides employing a chauffeur-valet, the Lewises hired a black cook-maid and a second maid. In 1937, it was estimated that the chauffeur earned $40 weekly; the cook-maid, $30 weekly; and the second maid, $80 monthly — for a total annual wage bill of approximately $4,600, or 37 percent of Lewis's annual UMW salary of $12,500 until it was doubled to $25,000 in 1938. (Even then, servant expenses consumed 18 percent of his annual salary.)

Lewis himself enjoyed the good life, not only the limousine and snappy chauffeur in whipcords that so impressed Louis Adamic, but also fine clothes, good cigars, superb food, and costly vacations. Lewis had his well-tailored suits, vests, and trousers custom-made by a clothier. As always, wherever he traveled Lewis stayed in the best hotels and occupied their finest suites. He lunched regularly in the Carlton Hotel's plush dining room, and on days when he remained late at the office, he also dined there. Lewis regularly stopped at the florist shop next door to UMW headquarters to buy flowers for the women who served as union secretaries or the society hostesses who constantly entertained the Lewis family. The Gulf Coast of Florida and a group of islands just off the Tampa–Saint Petersburg peninsula became his favorite vacation place. There, first in a rented cottage and later one he purchased himself on Pine Island, Lewis took the sun, relaxed, and enjoyed his favorite sport, deep-sea fishing on a charter boat.

A labor leader, in the case of John L. Lewis, could indeed live the good life. His was a true American success story, striking proof that in the United States ambition combined with talent brought material rewards, individual success was more than myth, and possessive individualism had proved itself a valid system of belief.

Much as Lewis's life-style may have impressed coal miners and inflated their self-images as Adamic suggested, it was nevertheless an existence that Lewis could scarcely defend before his union rank and file. When delegates at the 1936 coal miners' convention rebelled at a recommendation that they double their officers' salaries (in Lewis's case from $12,500 to $25,000), Lewis beat a hasty retreat, reporting to delegates on the convention's final day that he and his fellow officers would not accept salary increases. Lewis asserted that union officials sought office only to serve mankind, not to enrich themselves; "their hand," he swore, "is always giving, giving, what they have to give." Aside from the clothes that they wear and the food they eat, Lewis assured the delegates, the UMW's executive officers "are just as poor in this world's goods as any delegate to this convention." No man, asserted the UMW president, "holds a lesser quantity of this world's goods than the executive officers of your International organization."

14

Denouement,
June 1937–December 1939

For much of 1937 and 1938 John L. Lewis symbolized the emergence of organized labor as a significant force in economics, politics, and society. The accomplishments of the CIO and Lewis seemed indistinguishable to most Americans and many Europeans. It was Lewis, not auto and steel workers, who had stormed the ramparts of monopoly capitalism and battered General Motors, Chrysler, and United States Steel into defeat. It was Lewis alone among labor leaders who publicly criticized trade unionism's protector and the common man's idol: Franklin D. Roosevelt. It was Lewis who, in numerous network radio talks and even more frequent public speeches, asserted his prerogative to articulate the aspirations of forty million American workers hitherto mute in national affairs. And it was Lewis, according to two early biographers, who dreamed of becoming the United States' first labor president. "He would like to be President of the United States," wrote Cecil Carnes in 1936, and "the prospect of leading perhaps 30,000,000 voters does not frighten him." And in 1938, C. L. Sulzberger glowingly portrayed the mine workers' chieftain as a prospective presidential candidate.

Yet the same historical moment that brought Lewis acclaim and power also produced a series of setbacks to the man and his movement. By the end of 1938 Lewis's claim to articulate the aspirations of *all* the nation's workers had been vitiated by events scarcely visible to the public. Less than two years after its unprecedented triumphs over General Motors and United States Steel, the CIO had lost momentum, members, and direction. Simultaneously, the A.F. of L. and its affiliates recovered from the initial shock of schism, regrouped, and surged ahead of the CIO in membership, income, and political influence. Lewis, like the organization that he personified, lost momentum and floundered about in a search for new directions, a fruitless endeavor in which he never recaptured the esteem, labor power, and political influence that had been his from the summer of 1936 through the summer of 1937.

The single most substantial obstacle to John L. Lewis's claim to be the unrivaled leader of the American labor movement was the split between the A.F. of L. and CIO. As long as the A.F. of L. survived, Lewis necessarily shared influence with William Green. The rift in the labor movement also limited organized labor's political influence, as politicians played one faction off against the other. In theory, then, for Lewis to achieve maximum power required a united labor movement.

For almost five years, from 1937 to 1941, presidential emissaries, several A.F. of L. officials, and some CIO leaders maneuvered to reunite the labor movement. All their efforts, however, failed, and as their dreams dissolved, the quondam peacemakers most often blamed John L. Lewis. Certain factors must be borne in mind in analyzing Lewis's behavior during the unity negotiations. First, Lewis had much to gain and little to lose from an agreement that recognized the principle of industrial unionism for mass-production workers. Second, one must distinguish carefully between those in the A.F. of L. who served as peacemakers and those who wielded organizational power. One must also differentiate between the positions of the Federation's publicists and its power barons. If that is done, the A.F. of L. may well appear the more intransigent party in the negotiations. Third, one must separate President Roosevelt's public pleas for labor unity from his real political motives. A united labor movement might, in theory, strengthen working-class support for the New Deal, but Roosevelt could wield power more comfortably by playing one labor faction off against the other.

Despite the enmity between Green and Lewis, several factors impelled the CIO to launch new peace feelers in the fall of 1937. Having lost the momentum it achieved during the Flint sit-down strike and the subsequent settlement with United States Steel, the CIO could not afford to fight enemies inside the labor movement. Losing influence with Roosevelt, Lewis desired to confront the president with a united labor movement. Finally, prominent leaders of the CIO found themselves uncomfortable tenants in labor's divided house. Lewis thus initiated peace negotiations with the A.F. of L., however unpromising the actual prospects for achieving labor unity.

Unity negotiations resumed in the second week of October 1937. On October 12 Harvey Fremming wired A.F. of L. Secretary Frank Morrison suggesting that each union federation select a committee of 100 to meet jointly in order to discuss labor unity. Fremming's wire also stipulated that the A.F. of L. must accept the principle of industrial unionism in the mass-production industries, maritime trades, public utilities, service, and basic fabricating industries.

Lewis expected little from negotiations, yet he wanted to ensure that Green and the A.F. of L. bore the responsibility for sabotaging labor unity. Thus, after a series of snide and sarcastic telegrams among Fremming, Morrison, and Murray, the CIO and A.F. of L. agreed to meet jointly on October 25 in Washington. The Federation chose to send its three-man peace committee as originally appointed by the executive council in the summer of 1936, and the CIO selected a ten-man negotiating committee that included such prominent industrial unionists as Hillman, Murray, Dubinsky, Howard, Joseph Curran, and Mike Quill but excluded John L. Lewis.

On October 18, only a day after the two groups agreed to meet, Lewis confided to Jett Lauck that no hope then existed for peace with the A.F. of L. and that independence would better assure the CIO's size and prestige. The A.F. of L. hierarchy harbored equally little enthusiasm about the conference's prospects. The most powerful craft union leaders in the Federation stressed that its negotiating committee lacked the authority to arrange a settlement with the CIO delegation and that only the full executive council could make peace. Hutcheson even threatened to withdraw the carpenters from the A.F. of L. if the CIO was invited back on terms he deemed unacceptable. Green, of course, assured his testy labor barons that their interests would not be sacrificed.

Yet the negotiations opened as scheduled. On the second day, October 26, Philip Murray presented a breathtaking proposal for unity. He called for the A.F. of L. to "declare as one of its basic policies that the organization of the workers in the mass production, marine, public utilities, service and basic fabricating industries be effectuated only on an industrial basis."

Murray's proposal left the A.F. of L. negotiators speechless. Its audacity, the suggestion that the Federation simply violate the principles that had precipitated the original schism, apparently stunned them. On the morning of October 27, the A.F. of L. presented its counterproposal. As Phil Murray promptly observed, the Federation proposal reaffirmed the policies that had caused the initial split in the labor movement, rejected the principle of unrestricted industrial unionism for the mass-production industries, and suggested that the A.F. of L. remained determined to stifle organization of the unorganized.

Despite the width of the chasm that separated the two labor centers, peacemakers sought to build bridges. Neither party wanted to appear responsible for breaking off negotiations, and each sought to blame the other for failure. Lewis and his principal advisers, Lee Pressman, Len

DeCaux, and Jett Lauck, maneuvered to portray the A.F. of L. as unyielding and regressive and its leader, Green, as ridiculous.

The A.F. of L. did indeed make concessions to industrial unionism. It agreed to recognize industrial unionism in certain industries then being organized by the CIO and to convene a special A.F. of L. convention in the event of a peace agreement.

Having achieved that much, Lewis sought more. After a delay of almost three weeks, the peace conference resumed on November 29 and met intermittently and without success until mid-December. Notes of the discussion between the A.F. of L. and CIO committees on November 29 partly explain the reasons for failure. Two men dominated the negotiations: Murray for the CIO and George Harrison for the A.F. of L. The A.F. of L. still declined to specify which industries organized by unions not originally in the Federation were susceptible to industrial unionism or to put such an agreement in writing. Harrison agreed only to the readmission of the nine unions originally suspended. Disband the CIO, Harrison told Murray, and the remaining differences can be solved. Define the rights and extent of industrial unions, challenged Murray, and then we can consider the CIO's place inside the Federation. "Do you agree to abandon the CIO?" responded Harrison. Let's have a written understanding, demanded Murray. Whereupon Harrison agreed that twelve unions could return to the A.F. of L., including autos, steel, and rubber, yet still refused to put such an understanding in writing or to waive the rights of machinists, carpenters, and teamsters in those three industries.

Further discussions between the two committees continued during the first week in December in Murray's absence, and the labor leaders in attendance allegedly produced a satisfactory peace settlement. Only the self-serving statements of the Harrison committee in reports and documents to the full A.F. of L. executive council, however, and the comments of such needle trades unionists as David Dubinsky and Max Zaritsky, whose desire for labor unity blinded them to power realities, suggest that agreement was reached. Murray, it was alleged, accepted the peace accord but refused to commit the CIO until he spoke to John L. Lewis, who then sabotaged the peace agreement. In Dubinsky's own dramatic account, Murray took the proposed unity agreement to his chief's hotel room. Picking up the piece of paper with the peace terms on it, Lewis glanced quickly at its contents, sauntered toward the window, tore the paper into little pieces, and tossed the shreds to the street below. There, said Lewis, you have my answer.

What really happened? The answer, to be sure, is scarcely as dramatic as Dubinsky's version of events. Throughout the protracted peace negotiations, the A.F. of L. committee equivocated and also never retreated

from its demand that the CIO disband before a final peace settlement—
a demand that most CIO unions could not accept, especially the twenty-
three affiliates that had not originally been A.F. of L. members. This
was made clear at a CIO policy conference attended by all thirty-two
affiliates held at UMW headquarters on December 21, 1937. Lewis
informed the assembled delegates that peace negotiations had reached
an impasse, that the A.F. of L. refused to negotiate except on its own
terms, and that he would recommend termination of negotiations until
such date as the Federation became more reasonable. After a prolonged
discussion during which delegates from the clothing trades unions offered several alternative peace formulas, the conference unanimously
sanctioned Lewis's policy and adopted his motion to terminate peace
negotiations.

A few blind advocates of labor unity within the CIO such as Dubinsky
might misconstrue Lewis's behavior and leak items to the press suggesting that the CIO leader had rendered labor peace impossible. But
most CIO members, especially those closest to Lewis, shared Adolph
Germer's belief that "I am . . . firmly of the opinion that the controlling
men on the A.F. of L. Executive Council do not want to see the mass
production workers organize and that they do not want peace between
the CIO and the A.F. of L."

The year 1938, then, was a time for war, not peace, in the labor
movement. As Germer had suggested, the A.F. of L. attacked the CIO
directly on a broad front. State and city centrals purged all CIO affiliates
and sympathizers. A.F. of L. unions recruited new members as aggressively as the CIO, disregarded hallowed craft and jurisdictional lines,
and competed in the same industries as CIO affiliates. Federation officials, most notably John Frey, appeared regularly before congressional
committees, especially the House Committee on Un-American Activities, to allege communist influence in CIO and to seek amendments
to the Wagner Act that would restrict mass-production unionism.

Lewis readily accepted the A.F. of L.'s challenge. By the fall of 1938
the CIO could no longer continue in an anomalous institutional position. Its nine original affiliates and three later ones having been expelled
from the A.F. of L. and its twenty other international unions never
having been a part of the Federation, the CIO could no longer claim
to exist as a legitimate A.F. of L. committee that had been unconstitutionally ejected. By November 1938, the CIO functioned in all but
name as an autonomous, independent, effective national labor center.
It was time to end the charade, call a constitutional convention, and
announce the formation of a permanent new trade union federation to
the nation.

Lewis thus instructed all CIO affiliates to select delegates to attend a constitutional convention on November 15 in Pittsburgh. Because such a convention would doom labor unity, David Dubinsky refused to allow his union, the ILGWU, to attend the Pittsburgh convention.

In Dubinsky's absence, newspaper reports to the contrary notwithstanding, harmony and enthusiasm prevailed among the CIO delegates present. Hillman, Murray, and Lewis intended to run the CIO convention as they would their own unions. Asked to vote on constitutional clauses that they had scarcely seen, delegates representing the newer unions—many of whom were indeed red and rebellious—balked. Such minor convention splits—and they were minor—appeared in the press greatly magnified as a "red revolt." In fact, the alleged "red" delegates, led by Harry Bridges, Joe Curran, and Mike Quill, met privately with Lewis to pledge their loyalty and publicly tumbled over themselves to prove the CIO's solidarity. "What struck me most forcibly at Pittsburgh," reported Robert Bendiner in the *Nation,* "was not a trend toward factionalism but rather the advance notice served by John L. Lewis . . . that no such tendency would be tolerated—and the complete humility with which the left-wing . . . accepted the rap on the knuckles. . . . Not division but excessive unanimity was the order of the day."

As expected, delegates unanimously elected Lewis as CIO's first president and Philip Murray and Sidney Hillman as vice-presidents. The only surprise, if it could be called that, saw young James Carey of the United Electrical Workers elected as secretary-treasurer—the one salaried executive position. Many stories spread concerning Carey's election. John Brophy alleged that Lewis intended to make his daughter Kathryn CIO secretary but was discouraged by objections from Murray and Hillman. Lewis certainly felt no embarrassment in practicing nepotism, but logic suggests that he was unlikely to have considered Kathryn a candidate for office in the CIO. Kathryn could serve him better as a UMW official, as the president's personal secretary. Second, Lewis knew that a convention of predominantly male delegates would rebel at electing a woman to high union office, even their esteemed leader's daughter and hand-picked choice. Third, too many individuals from the UMW and Lewis's own personal circle already held influential positions in the CIO. More diversity was needed.

Carey's selection was natural and logical. He represented the "new unionists," coming from the second largest union outside the original CIO nine. He was young, personable, a good man to meet the press and circulate on the Washington cocktail party circuit, but not hardworking or capable enough to threaten Lewis. Finally, among the leading "new unionists," Carey was the one clearly not linked to the Left or communism.

The creation of the CIO as an independent national labor center with its own constitution, bylaws, and elected officers should have logically ended for a time talk and action aimed at labor unity, as Dubinsky believed it would. Yet the CIO convention called for unity negotiations.

Peace negotiations resumed between the CIO and A.F. of L. in March 1939, primarily in response to the president's public demand for labor peace, a request labor leaders could not refuse. Yet however much Roosevelt apparently desired labor unity, he may not have been displeased when negotiations collapsed. A united labor movement theoretically offered Roosevelt political benefits; it also involved potential dangers. Just as a united labor movement could pressure Congress and produce Democratic voters on Election Day, it could also undermine presidential policies that it opposed. By diluting the authority of John L. Lewis, a reunited labor movement would have rendered him less able to threaten the president's domestic and foreign policies. But what of the other possibility? What if Lewis emerged as the dominant figure in a reunited labor movement and if he allied with Bill Hutcheson, labor's leading Republican and an arch-isolationist in foreign affairs? Such a prospect could only frighten Roosevelt, and it was as likely to occur as any other result of a peace agreement between the A.F. of L. and CIO.

The evidence suggests inferentially that the CIO approached negotiations more seriously than the A.F. of L. Green's three-man negotiating committee boded ill for success. He selected Matthew Woll, Harry Bates, and Dan Tobin, who soon withdrew to be replaced by Tom Rickert. The A.F. of L. could not have chosen more poorly. None represented a major union; Woll was a self-aggrandizing bureaucrat; Bates was scarcely known outside his own union, the bricklayers; and Rickert was an aged functionary best known for splitting his own union in 1914 and engaging in numerous corrupt practices. Such a committee could not negotiate seriously, nor could it have been granted much authority by the executive council. The CIO's negotiators were a different matter. Lewis himself, Hillman, and Murray represented the industrial unionists.

Formal negotiations between the A.F. of L. and CIO committees began on March 7 in the White House, with President Roosevelt in attendance. Lewis called on representatives of the A.F. of L., CIO, and the four railroad brotherhoods to convene not later than June 1, 1939, to form the American Congress of Labor. This entirely new national federation would elect its own officers for one-year terms, excluding Lewis and Green. Green and A. F. of L. Secretary Frank Morrison, Lewis recommended, should be pensioned at their current salaries. The ACL's executive board would consist of an equal number of representatives from the Federation and the CIO, with proportional representation from the railroad unions, from whose ranks would come the Congress's president. During the first year after the formation of the new organizaton, Labor Department agents would assist affiliated unions in settling all jurisdictional questions. Finally, Lewis proposed that President Roosevelt serve as presiding officer during the founding convention.

Not only did the A.F. of L. promptly reject Lewis's peace proposal and Roosevelt refuse to endorse such an outrageous plan, but Sidney Hillman also opposed it. By mutual agreement between Woll and Lewis, on April 5 all meetings were indefinitely postponed, never to be resumed. Lewis announced the termination of negotiations to reporters, whose stories portrayed an angry, militant Lewis glad to be done with peacemaking. Matthew Woll's confidential memorandum to Green revealed a different Lewis, a labor leader who had terminated negotiations because bargaining between the miner's union and the coal operators had reached a crisis that would occupy all Lewis's time for the foreseeable future.

The negotiations, however, were indeed dead, not to be resumed, and for the same reasons that had doomed the 1937 peace proposals. As Lewis reported to the CIO executive board on March 25, the A.F. of L. still demanded that CIO unions make the most concessions. The A.F. of L. demanded that the UMW confer with the Progressive Miners, surrender members organized in UMW District 50 to A.F. of L. federal unions with jurisdiction in related fields, and that all CIO unions transfer members recruited by expansion to the A.F. of L. unions that may have legitimate jurisdictional claims to them. Finally, the A.F. of L. insisted that no settlement could be arranged until a mutually approved firm of certified public accountants examined and audited the books of the A.F. of L. and CIO in order to determine true paid-up membership as a basis for allocating real jurisdictions and voting rights at a joint convention. Such a procedure posed a threat to the CIO, which followed the UMW practice of exonerating unemployed union members from dues payment, a policy that produced a paper membership far in excess of the paid-up membership as calculated by A.F. of L. unions. In short, the A.F. of L. asked the CIO to respect all Federation affiliates' jurisdictional claims and to reenter the federation as a numerical minority, a peace proposal that was as unacceptable to Lewis in March 1939 as it had been in December 1937.

Instead, conflict between the A.F. of L. and CIO intensified. On July 31, 1939, Lewis announced the creation of the Construction Workers Organizing Committee (CWOC), led by his younger brother Dennie and intended to carry labor's civil war directly to the most influential bloc of unions in the Federation: the building trades. Early in January

1940 Dennie Lewis informed Jett Lauck that the CWOC would bring peace to the labor movement by breaking the building trades power in the Federation.

Peace within the labor movement now depended on a clear victory either for the CIO or the A.F. of L. or on the disappearance of William Green or John L. Lewis from the scene. The latter being an unlikely alternative, both labor federations fought for ascendancy among workers—before the NLRB, in Congress, and with President Roosevelt. In the course of this struggle, a frustrated Lewis watched his adversaries grow more numerous and influential as his own relationship with President Roosevelt soured.

The first sign that the CIO had lost its momentum came in the spring and summer of 1937, when SWOC waged a bloody and unsuccessful strike against the so-called Little Steel companies, small only in the sense that they operated independently of the industry's giant, United States Steel. SWOC's unexpected and easy triumph over U.S. Steel made its officers and organizers eager to unionize the remainder of the industry's major concerns. It also may have upset Phil Murray emotionally. Finally the commander of his own labor organizaton, SWOC, Murray had been thrust into the background during negotiations with U.S. Steel by John L. Lewis. Saul Alinsky, David McDonald, SWOC's secretary in 1937, and Lee Pressman alleged that Murray's emotional needs and insecurities compelled him to authorize a strike against Little Steel in order to prove his manhood.

In reality, however, Murray's decision flowed as much from pressure on him by SWOC organizers and subalterns as from any emotional desires to prove his masculinity. At a conference of SWOC officials, nearly everyone present, especially the local leaders from the mills, favored a strike. Never at this prestrike stage of affairs did Lewis counsel Murray against a walkout. And never during the course of the battle did Lewis ever lend less than his total support to the strikers.

The steel companies, led by Republic's Tom Girdler, as resolute and intransigent an antiunion entrepreneur as existed in the nation, fought SWOC with a full arsenal of antilabor weapons. Company spies honeycombed SWOC locals; firms hired strikebreakers and stocked their plants with weapons and tear gas; local police and county sheriffs broke picket lines and terrorized strikers; clergymen, local professionals, and newspaper publishers red-baited SWOC and CIO mercilessly; and a core of loyal antiunion workers led "back-to-work" movements conceived by the struck companies.

Strikers waged the struggle with equal intensity. In the streets of Youngstown, Massillon, Bethlehem, Johnstown, and Gary, they fought strikebreakers, police, and deputies. The violence climaxed with a bloody incident in Chicago.

On Memorial Day, 1937, Republic Steel strikers and their wives, children, friends, and sympathizers—between fifteen hundred and two thousand people in a holiday mood —gathered on a broad vacant lot near the company's South Chicago mill to protest police interference with legal picketing. As the crowd marched peacefully toward the mill gate, an altercation erupted with the Chicago city police. Suddenly the front ranks of the police fired guns and tear gas point-blank into the crowd, which fled hastily across the field. When the shooting stopped, ten marchers lay dead—seven killed by bullets in the back and three in the side; thirty others had been wounded by gunshot; and an almost equal number had been the victims of lacerations and contusions.

This, then, should have been the occasion for Lewis to use the CIO's vaunted political influence to obtain relief for the Little Steel strikers. The governors of Pennsylvania, Ohio, Illinois, and Indiana had all been elected with CIO support, and Roosevelt was reputed to be labor's president. Lewis, in fact, urged the governors in whose states the strike was centered and also Roosevelt to assist the strikers by using state power to thwart corporate terror. But to no avail. The governors of Indiana and Ohio dispatched militia to strife-torn industrial cities— only, however, to disperse pickets, protect property, and guard strikebreakers. And in Pennsylvania where the lieutenant governor was the UMW's own Tom Kennedy, the state implemented a neutral policy that in practice aided the steel companies to break the strike.

President Roosevelt's role in the conflict exposed graphically the limitations of Lewis's and the CIO's political influence. Shortly after the Memorial Day massacre, Lewis indicated that "labor will await the position of the authorities on whether our people will be protected or butchered." A week later, on June 29 at his regular press conference, Roosevelt observed about the Little Steel strike that "the majority of the people are saying just one thing, 'A plague on both your houses'." Newspaper headlines the following day stressed that the president had cast a plague equally on Little Steel and CIO—Tom Girdler and John L. Lewis. When reporters read Roosevelt's statement to the CIO leader at his own subsequent press conference, one journalist noted afterwards that Lewis "said nothing, but his heels drummed against the desk's lower panels with a violence that just missed reducing them to splinters."

Roosevelt acted as he did for good political reasons. His advisers warned against his becoming involved in a dangerous situation from which he had little to gain. The new unionization movement in the mass-production industries, reported Harry Hopkins, "is a complicated situation, and full of all kinds of dynamite, political as well as social."

Advising Roosevelt that the Little Steel strike was then (July 2) coming to a natural end, Hopkins counseled the president against offering public encouragement to Lewis. By summer 1937, presidential support for the CIO and mass-production unionism carried as many, if not more, political liabilities as benefits. Ever the politician, Roosevelt maneuvered to avoid the labor-capital quagmire, in the process diluting the CIO's political influence and straining the relationship between charismatic labor leader and popular president.

The CIO defeat in Little Steel was merely one example of its loss of momentum during the summer of 1937. A similar tale repeated itself in the textile industry. On March 9, 1937, the CIO had established the Textile Workers' Organizing Committee (TWOC), which simply swallowed whole the long-dormant United Textile Workers' Union. Two CIO officials, Sidney Hillman and Tom Kennedy, acted as TWOC's leaders, and the Amalgamated Clothing Workers and other CIO affiliates provided the bulk of the committee's finances and organizers. After winning several contracts rather easily from northern textile mills, TWOC's organizing drive fizzled in the South—the center of cotton textile production. Unable to organize more than 5 percent of the region's mill workers, by the late autumn of 1937, as the economy again declined, TWOC acceded to wage reductions and experienced a loss of membership in northern mills. TWOC suffered further setbacks, none more unsettling than the emergence of a competing textile union in the A.F. of L.—the United Textile Workers—which by 1939 successfully seized contracts and members from TWOC.

Other Lewis-CIO organizing gambits endured similar fates. On June 21, 1937, Lewis announced the creation of a new union—the United Federal Workers—to organize an estimated eight hundred thousand federal employees. Opposed by federal officials, including most New Dealers, who doubted that public employees had the right to unionize or to strike, the new organization made little headway.

An even more ambitious Lewis scheme to organize more than three million workers laboring on WPA and other federal emergency employment projects suffered a ruder administration rebuff. Lewis presented his idea directly to New Dealers Harry Hopkins and Aubrey Williams, saying bluntly, "it's the least that the Administration can do for the C.I.O." Lewis's proposal shocked Hopkins and Williams; they simply refused to consider the notion that the government should actively recruit members for CIO.

All across the labor organizing front, by the end of 1937, Lewis surveyed an uninviting terrain for CIO. In the Pacific Northwest, Bill Hutcheson's carpenters and Dave Beck's teamsters united to thwart the organizing forays of the CIO International Woodworkers of America.

Up and down the entire Pacific Coast conflict between Harry Bridges and Harry Lundeberg wrecked the Lewis-CIO vision of a united industrial union of all maritime workers.

Before 1937 ended worse news awaited the CIO. In August, just as the industrial union drive faltered, the American economy cracked. During the next four months all the economic gains made since 1935 evaporated. Industrial productivity plummeted, stock prices fell precipitously, and between Labor Day and the end of the year two million workers lost their jobs. By early 1938 starvation again threatened millions of Americans. The economic collapse that occurred between August and October 1937 struck more rapidly and deeper than even the Great Depression of 1929–33.

Lewis and the CIO paid an enormous price for Roosevelt's economic miscalculations. The CIO's membership strength was concentrated in those industries most sensitive to the economic cycle. Steel, autos, rubber, electrical goods, and other mass-production workers experienced a second wave of mass unemployment that made it impossible for many CIO members to pay union dues and for other workers to consider joining a labor organization. The impact of the depression on the CIO makes all estimates of the organization's membership for 1938–39 totally unreliable. How many of the members claimed by the CIO in steel, autos, and rubber actually paid dues in 1938 and 1939 may never be known. Most A.F. of L. leaders, however were convinced that by the end of 1938 their organization far surpassed CIO in paid-up membership.

The downturn in the CIO's fortunes left Lewis temporarily rudderless. Aside from retrenchment and conservation of resources, Lewis, in 1938, appeared unsure of his economic and political strategy. His uncertainty, moreover, was compounded by personal, political, and ideological disputes that threatened to demoralize industrial unionism and the CIO. Economic prosperity and union success had stimulated organizational solidarity; depression and failure induced recrimination and factionalism.

Factionalism practically paralyzed the United Automobile Workers and entangled Lewis in a sordid trade union power struggle. Only six months after the great General Motors victory and a month after the UAW national convention celebrating that victory, the UAW seemed a shambles. Wyndham Mortimer, among others, complained to Lewis about UAW president Homer Martin's reliance on Jay Lovestone, the excommunist turned antiradical factionalist and current associate of David Dubinsky. Lewis, too, worried about developments in the UAW. Yet, from late 1937 through June 1938, he separated himself from UAW factionalism and took no overt action to control affairs among auto workers. But conditions in the UAW continued to deteriorate. Auto manufacturers raged at the union's inability to prevent wildcat strikes and threatened not to renew contracts. Dues-paying membership declined, and the UAW's officials spent more time quarreling among themselves than recruiting members. The factional politics of the UAW proved too much even for Lewis. Homer Martin had completely accepted Lovestone's policy of driving the red and rebellious from the union. At Lovestone's urging, Martin removed alleged Stalinists from appointive union office, replaced them with Lovestone's sympathizers, and even sought to purge his critics from the UAW executive board.

In June 1938 Lewis complained to Germer about the influence of Lovestone's faction in the UAW, and by August the CIO leader seemed to be cooperating with UAW communists preparatory to making the union a ward of the CIO. In early September Lewis dispatched Hillman and Murray to Detroit, where they delivered an ultimatum to Martin. Lewis's lieutenants ordered Martin to reappoint forthwith the members that he had purged from the union's executive board, eliminate the influence of the Lovestone group in the UAW, and rely on advice from the CIO.

Lewis's intervention in UAW affairs through the Hillman-Murray mission neither ended factionalism nor restored union stability. Martin and Lovestone accused Lewis of serving Communist objectives. The Martin faction and those who disagreed with them continued to fight each other throughout 1938; the battle raged with great intensity until January 25, 1939, when a frustrated Homer Martin officially resigned from the CIO executive board. Soon afterward, Martin marched "his UAW" into the A.F. of L., and in April 1939 dual unionism entered the auto industry as it already plagued other industries in which the CIO and A.F. of L. competed for members.

Lewis, however, seemed satisfied with the outcome of the UAW's factional struggle. "The Opposition, with crystallized resistance, made the victory all the greater," Lewis wrote to Germer on May 16, 1939. "I feel sure the settlement will be of value to our entire movement."

Despite Lewis's optimism, at the end of 1939 the UAW was weaker in many respects than at any time since its March 1937 victory at Flint. The same was true of the CIO. The personal and political quarrels that produced factionalism and red-baiting among auto workers repeated themselves in the CIO during 1938 and 1939. There, too, depression replaced harmony and euphoria with cacophony and anxiety.

The solidarity that characterized the first constitutional convention of the CIO at Pittsburgh in November 1938 cloaked quite real differences that divided the organization's hierarchs. Dubinsky and Zaritsky, to be sure, left the CIO even before the 1938 Pittsburgh convention. But the relationship among Lewis, Murray, and Hillman appeared cordial and secure.

Beneath the surface, however, real differences divided Lewisites and Hillmanites. The Hillman wing of the CIO, and also Phil Murray, linked their political fortunes to Roosevelt and acted deferentially toward the president. Lewis and his loyalists preferred to exercise some independence from the Democratic party and expected the president to respect labor, not patronize it. On foreign policy, Hillman's followers shared Roosevelt's internationalist-interventionist sympathies and had few reservations concerning an activist United States foreign policy overseas, especially in Europe. Lewis, on the contrary, persistently opposed active United States intervention in European affairs and recurrently warned the nation against drifting into war. Differences regarding domestic and foreign policies were complicated by the anomalous role of communists within the CIO. Members of the organization's far-left wing preferred Lewis's domestic policies to Hillman's but supported the latter's foreign policies—that is, until the signing of the Nazi-Soviet Non-Aggression Pact in August 1939. Hillman and his associates, moreover, grew increasingly sensitive about communist influence in the CIO, whereas Lewis refused to consider communists a threat to his power.

The opponents of the CIO in labor, business, and politics tried to aggravate factionalism among the industrial unionists. Led by John Frey, the A.F. of L. assiduously red-baited the CIO. Journalists once sympathetic to the CIO became critical. Beginning with the 1938 CIO convention, Louis Stark began to write stories about the role of communists in the CIO for the *New York Times.* Benjamin Stolberg in 1938 published *The Story of CIO,* a critical analysis of the organization. Stolberg's book, widely publicized by the A.F. of L., conservative politicians, and business associations, told the story of a great idea turned sour, of a decent labor organization subverted by Stalinist agents.

The rising chorus of red-baiting had its intended effect on the CIO. As the organization's 1939 convention approached, divisions between Lewisites and Hillmanites widened. Hillman had been drawn ever deeper into the web of Roosevelt–New Deal politics while Lewis increasingly asserted his independence from the president. Conflicts over foreign policy also intensified as the situation in Europe worsened.

CIO factionalism, as well as his relationship with trade union communists, obviously troubled Lewis. Certainly he was not one to feel comfortable in a role such as that of the labor movement's spokesman for the far Left. Equally vexing was the fact that a majority of the CIO ardently supported Franklin Roosevelt and desired the president to run for a third term. These factors as well as the CIO's loss of momentum caused Lewis to consider resignation as CIO president. On October 8, shortly before the 1939 convention opened in San Francisco, Lewis prepared a statement for release to the press and also to the CIO's executive board. Referring to President Roosevelt's plea that labor leaders cast aside self-interest in this time of national crisis, Lewis responded, "I readily conform to his wishes. My personal pride and self-interest is of pitiful inconsequence as compared to the requirements of national interest. I will not be a candidate for reelection and at the close of the convention will retire as President of the Congress of Industrial Organizations." The statement, of course, was never released; nor did Lewis resign as CIO president. Most analysts prefer to think that Lewis's threat to resign was tactical and intended to compel delegates to sanction Lewis's domestic and foreign policy positions.

Yet it can be argued that Lewis meant what he said. He knew that Hillman and his followers and, perhaps, Phil Murray and other UMW delegates simply would not endorse Lewis's politics. To compel the delegates to vote for an anti-interventionist foreign policy and to reject Roosevelt meant on the one hand to split CIO irrevocably, which Lewis had no intention of doing. To achieve his aims completely meant on the other hand to appear publicly as a captive of the communists; that, too, Lewis would not consider.

The resolutions adopted by the 1939 convention also belie the notion that Lewis's resignation was a tactical ploy. First, delegates voted to endorse Roosevelt's proposal to amend neutrality legislation in order to lift the embargo against the shipment of materials to belligerents, meaning Britain and France. Lewis personally endorsed the revision of the neutrality laws, doing so in response to a direct plea from the president, a plea drafted by none other than Sidney Hillman. Second, although the convention declined to endorse Roosevelt for a third term, it did not directly oppose his reelection, Lewis's preferred policy. Third, Lewis's original report to the convention, a document that criticized Roosevelt's domestic and foreign policies, was never read to the delegates. Fourth, Lewis reserved his harshest criticism at executive board sessions and in private meetings for communists, not Hillman's supporters. Lewis, indeed, warned that no known communist was to be employed in any capacity; and to prove that he intended to limit communist influence in the CIO, he restricted Harry Bridges's role as West Coast regional director to California, placing two men who were not left-wingers in charge of Oregon and Washington. He also replaced John Brophy—who was then a left-wing sympathizer—as national director of the CIO with Allan Haywood, a UMW loyalist.

Other factors also suggest that Lewis's threat to resign was more than tactical. By late 1939 the presidency of the CIO brought Lewis as many headaches as compensations. At public and private meetings during the 1939 convention, Lewis had to warn CIO affiliates to pay full per capital dues on claimed membership or suffer the consequences. Lewis did not even deign to offer the convention delegates a written report on the organization's finances or organizational status, so anarchic were the CIO's administrative operations. Such considerations may well have led Lewis to ponder resignation—an act, moreover, that would not have left him bereft of influence in the CIO. With minimal opposition he could have selected Phil Murray as his heir apparent (he indeed discussed that prospect with Murray before the convention), and ex-UMW officials still dominated the leadership positions in numerous CIO affiliates. "The impression is," reported an A.F. of L. observer at San Francisco, "that the CIO remains in the main a sort of large holding company, in which the miners hold the controlling shares." Lewis's resignation from the presidency would not have altered the distribution of shares in the CIO.

What needs to be analyzed, then, is why Lewis chose not to resign at the 1939 convention. The threat may have led Hillman, as some contemporary observers believe, to cancel an open attack on Lewis's leadership and preserve instead the CIO's facade of solidarity. But it brought Lewis no further gains. As late as November 1, two weeks after the convention adjourned, Jett Lauck considered Lewis's talk of res-ignation sincere. Why, then, did Lewis change his mind? Only one possibility suggests itself. By the fall of 1939 Lewis may have realized that an open break with Franklin Roosevelt was inevitable and that when the rupture came, as it must, Lewis would need every ally he could possibly attract. With that thought in mind, October 1939 was no time to resign as president of the CIO.

Much of the nation's political history between 1936 and 1940 and the most salient features of its labor history oscillated around the shifting relationship between John L. Lewis and Franklin D. Roosevelt. Saul Alinsky wrote that "the break between them ruptured an incipient new American revolution. . . . The break between them broke the militant surge of the labor movement and broke much of the New Deal. His-torians will describe it as the great American tragedy of the labor move-ment."

Alinsky, however, could not explain why two leaders split who, in his version of history, shared a commitment to political reform and economic egalitarianism. Unwilling to comprehend the rupture as the result of Lewis's and Roosevelt's respective roles as spokesmen for opposed political tendencies, Alinsky interpreted the quarrel in terms of personality, abnormal psychology, and hatred.

Irving Bernstein, in his history of labor during the New Deal, endorses

Alinsky's interpretation. Dismissing policy differences as the cause of conflict between Lewis and Roosevelt, Bernstein suggests that "more fundamental was the clash of personalities and of roles. The styles of the two men were completely different. Lewis was dour, angry, direct, and demanding. Roosevelt was cheerful, chatty, effusively vague, a master of indirection." In this irrational clash for individual power between the chief executive of the CIO and the chief executive of the American nation, the American presidency naturally carried all the advantages. Bernstein, like Alinsky, believes that when Roosevelt chose to run for a third term, Lewis vainly sought the vice-presidential nomination. Thwarted in his political ambitions, Lewis turned bitter, and a relationship with Roosevelt "that had earlier been merely strained . . . degenerated into hatred."

Such history makes good reading and drama, but it also mystifies the past. Both Lewis and Roosevelt were too experienced and adept at politics to allow personal idiosyncracies or irrational hatred to thwart the achievement of their goals. Lewis, to be sure, often seemed dour, angry, and demanding; yet when it suited his purposes he could be sweet, charming, and amenable to compromise, just as Roosevelt, in private, could be harsh, sullen, and recalcitrant. Lewis, moreover, certainly knew that the president of the CIO could not share power equally with the president of the United States. True, in 1936 and early 1937 when Lewis appeared most popular and influential, talk abounded about Lewis as the labor movement's first presidential candidate. But by late 1937 and 1938 when conflict between Lewis and Roosevelt gathered momentum, the labor leader had lost much of his popularity and influence. A Gallup poll released in October 1938 that asked its sample, "Which labor leader do you like better: Green or Lewis?" reported that 78 percent preferred Green and 22 percent favored Lewis, an 11 percent loss for Lewis since the previous July. Those closest to Lewis during the 1930s—Jett Lauck, Lee Pressman, and Len DeCaux—saw little overt evidence of the labor leader's ambition to be president.

[If neither personality differences nor Lewis's desire to succeed Roosevelt as president explain the clash between the two men, social and class factors do.] However much Roosevelt conceived of himself as an idealistic social reformer dedicated to the interests of the American people, in practice he acted largely as the defender of the existing order. His aim was to preserve the existing structure of society, not to transform it; to save a social and economic system that offered more to capitalists than to workers. By the mid-1930s only two approaches promised to preserve the economic system that had caused the Great Depression: repression or extensive social reform. Roosevelt exemplified those who preferred reform to repression. To this end, Franklin Delano Roosevelt found revolutionary class rhetoric indispensable; it frightened the powerful into concessions and won working-class voters for the Democratic party.

Lewis, however much he preferred to think of himself as an executive rather than a labor leader, however little he associated with the working class personally, functioned as the leader of a militant working-class movement. Where Roosevelt sought to contain working-class militancy through reform, militant workers pressured Lewis to demand more than the president was willing to concede. The labor militants demanded a fundamental reordering of the American economy and society—demands that Lewis as leader of the CIO came to express more forcefully than any other trade unionist. "No matter how much Roosevelt did for the workers," wrote Len DeCaux, "Lewis demanded more. He showed no gratitude, nor did he bid his followers be grateful—just put on the squeeze all the harder." DeCaux captured a part of the Roosevelt-Lewis relationship in these words: "Roosevelt may not have thought of himself as the liberally inclined head of a capitalist government; nor Lewis of himself as a momentary leader of an insurgent working class. But that is how they behaved to each other in the early years of CIO."

Despite the material forces that made a break between Lewis and Roosevelt inevitable, for most of the years 1936–39 they required each other's support and strove to remain political allies. "For the time being," wrote Louis Adamic, "they are using one another. Roosevelt is holding the fences for Lewis, who is momentarily helping him to be reelected so that he can hold the fences." During the General Motors sit-down strike and during the early stages of the organizing campaign in steel, Roosevelt acted precisely as Lewis desired and expected. And in the late winter of 1937 and into the spring as the president struggled unsuccessfully to reform the Supreme Court by increasing the number of sitting justices, Lewis and the CIO provided Roosevelt with one of his few unswerving sources of support. "The future of labor in America," Lewis declared on May 14, 1937, "is intimately connected with the future of the President's proposal to reform the Supreme Court."

The fight over the Supreme Court, the rise of the CIO, and Roosevelt's daring proposals for reform produced, in Congress and elsewhere, an anti-New Deal conservative coalition that united northern Republicans, southern Democrats, antilabor businessmen, and A.F. of L. hierarchs. Roosevelt required CIO assistance against these political enemies, and Lewis gave it unstintingly.

Yet ill feelings between Roosevelt and Lewis festered beneath the surface of an apparently cordial political alliance. Lewis, for example, as early as March 1937 voiced dissatisfaction with the administration's

mine safety program, although he kept his complaints private in order
not to undermine Roosevelt. Lewis also felt disappointed that the president paid scant attention to his recommendations for federal appointments. As late as June 23, 1937, however, the *New York Times* reported
in a front-page story that John L. Lewis had initiated a movement in
Pennsylvania to make Roosevelt the Democratic presidential nominee
in 1940.

Thus many journalists and observers were stunned when only a week
later the rift between Roosevelt and Lewis surfaced as a consequence
of the president's refusal to support the steelworkers during the Little
Steel strike. When Roosevelt, on June 29, declared a plague on both
houses—labor and capital—Lewis quipped, "Which house: Hearst or
Dupont?" A week later, at a presidential press conference on July 6,
and at another two days later, reporters queried Roosevelt about his
relationship with Lewis. "Will you comment on reports that you and
Mr. John Lewis are going to break off friendly relations?" asked reporters
on July 6. "I don't think that a report like that needs comment," replied
the president. Asked again two days later about stories alleging a break
between the administration and Lewis, Roosevelt commented, "that is
the same old story, press reports," which he would neither deny nor
confirm. Such interchanges led Irving Bernstein to conclude pungently
that "a brief and not very beautiful relationship had come to an end."

Still both men played an opportunistic, sometimes duplicitous, political game. At various times in July and August, Lewis threatened to
build a new third party that would unite the nation's majority of dis-
possessed workers and farmers. At other times, he denied that he planned
to found a third party and asserted that he expected both Republicans
and Democrats to offer organized labor its just demands. Lewis did,
however, tighten his personal control over the Labor Non-Partisan
League, force George Berry to resign as league director, and focus his
political efforts in the most populous coal mining states, especially
Pennsylvania, Ohio, and Illinois. Throughout July and August Lewis
persistently criticized the Democratic party for allowing a clique of
conservatives on the House Rules Committee to thwart reform legislation. Such criticism prompted conservative Democrats to charge on
August 23 that a Lewis-Roosevelt alliance planned to seize total control
of the Democratic party by 1940. Lewis still asserted publicly that labor
had the most to gain by working with Roosevelt and would only consider
a third party in 1940 if the Democrats failed to implement their own
reform program. Interviewed on August 27, 1937, Lewis again raised
the prospect of a third party in 1940. Millions of Americans, he asserted,
now desired a third party, and if the two old parties failed to act decisively

to reorder national priorities, farmers and workers would know what to do. *Lewis's response to FDR's "plague on both your houses" statement of June 29, 1937*

Precisely one week later, on September 3, Lewis amazed millions of American workers. Speaking over the CBS network to an audience estimated at twenty to thirty million, Lewis delivered what the press described the next day as a bitter, angry, graceless personal attack on President Roosevelt. Listeners and reporters remembered best the labor leader's rhetorical flourishes—purple passages in which Lewis accused Roosevelt of stabbing his trade union friends in the back. Referring specifically to the events of the Little Steel strike, Lewis grieved, "Labor, like Israel, has many sorrows. Its women weep for their fallen, and they lament for the future of the children of the race. It ill behooves one who has supped at labor's table and who has been sheltered in labor's house to curse with equal fervor and fine impartiality both labor and its adversaries when they become locked in deadly embrace."

Such hyperbole led many reporters and listeners to miss Lewis's real message to the president, which was clear, direct, simple, and unexceptional. The CIO leader calmly explained that the labor movement was the true ally of the New Deal and the last defender of the American system. "Workers," he declared, "have kept faith in American institutions," and their unions have unreservedly recognized the "institution of private property and the right to investment profit." Workers, Lewis answered those who charged labor with promoting communism, "free in their industrial life, conscious partners in production, secure in their homes and enjoying a decent standard of living, will prove the finest bulwark against the intrusion of alien doctrines of government." To the president, Lewis promised the prospect of a farm-labor alliance that would defend the achievements and aims of the New Deal against those who fought it. Roosevelt, Lewis implied, could demonstrate his commitment to the New Deal by assisting the mass-production workers and their agrarian allies whose votes alone could save reform from congressional and corporate Tories.

The president apparently understood the political message implicit in the speech, because the next day at his press conference Roosevelt refused to satisfy reporters eager for a story blasting Lewis. Asked his reaction to Lewis's radio address, Roosevelt said, "There wasn't any."

Ironically, as Turner Catledge suggested in a story in the *New York Times,* Lewis's September 3 speech benefited Roosevelt politically. Because of popular reaction against the sit-down strikes and the labor turbulence associated with the CIO's rise, Lewis, Catledge implied, had become "a great political inconvenience, if not a downright liability, to the President." The future of the Roosevelt-Lewis relationship, concluded the reporter, would hinge on whether the president stood to gain or lose politically by a break with Lewis.

It soon became apparent that the Lewis-Roosevelt quarrel was more a late summer squall than a winter storm. On September 14, the two men met at the White House for a pleasant forty-minute chat, which reporters observed reestablished the "entente cordiale" between the CIO and the Roosevelt administration. As the 1937 elections approached, Lewis needed Roosevelt, and the president required CIO assistance, motivating them to patch up their alliance and cooperate during the campaign. As the year ended, some presidential advisers, Rex Tugwell among them, counseled Roosevelt to be more gracious to Lewis. Hold Lewis's hand once every three weeks regularly, Tugwell recommended. "Life for all of us will be so much easier if you will!"

Throughout 1938 Roosevelt apparently stroked Lewis often enough to maintain their political relationship in good order. CIO and Non-Partisan League lobbyists proved the most ardent and effective pressure group for administration reform legislation. Lewis promised to support Roosevelt's efforts to purge anti–New Deal Democrats during the 1938 primaries, providing the president with money, campaigners, and publicity among trade unionists—especially in such mining states as Kentucky, Alabama, Maryland, and Tennessee. On the eve of the CIO's first constitutional convention in Pittsburgh and only a week after the 1938 election, Lewis informed Louis Stark and other reporters that although conservative Democrats such as Governor Martin Davey of Ohio and Mayor Frank Hague of Jersey City must be defeated, the great majority of American people overwhelmingly supported Roosevelt. The Republican party, he charged, "for years past has done nothing but betray the interests of the common people. . . . it offers no program . . . except their . . . reiterated wail that the clock of time be turned back to yesterday."

In 1939 Lewis continued to defend what remained of the New Deal's domestic reform program against its critics. The nation had no greater advocate of public employment programs, public housing projects, and Social Security improvements than John L. Lewis. When the A.F. of L. and numerous employer groups sought to amend the Wagner Act and other basic New Deal labor legislation, Lewis testified before congressional committees. In 1939, when Vice-President John Nance Garner influenced congressional conservatives to thwart his own administration's wages and hours law, Lewis ridiculed the Texas politician publicly as a "labor-baiting, whiskey-drinking, evil old man." The bill passed as Roosevelt and the CIO desired.

Yet the apparent political reconciliation between Lewis and Roosevelt failed to eliminate fundamental sources of conflict between the two men. Throughout 1938 and 1939 the president continued to disregard Lewis's nominees for federal office. Rather than offer Lewis what he requested, Roosevelt acted on the advice of Frances Perkins that he chat with the labor leader by phone in order to "sweeten his [Lewis's] disposition a bit."

But it was hard to sweeten Lewis's disposition when he had substantial policy disagreements with the administration. Most of Lewis's dissatisfaction with Roosevelt in 1938 and 1939 flowed from two sources separate in their origins but related in their impact. The onset of the "Roosevelt depression" in the fall of 1937 and the decline of the CIO left Lewis frustrated and confused. Roosevelt simultaneously lost not only his claim to have restored the nation's economy; his political influence also slipped, as congressional conservatives defeated the president's court reform plan, diluted New Deal legislation, and triumphed generally in the 1938 primary and general elections. Roosevelt also became more interested in foreign than domestic affairs. And as the president sought to expand congressional and popular support for his foreign policy, especially among political conservatives and business groups, he perceived fewer political benefits in Lewis's recommendation that a farm-labor coalition become the core of the Democratic party. Rather than ally with Lewis in a militant domestic reform crusade, Roosevelt sought to undercut his labor rival in several ways. The president cultivated the friendship of such Lewis associates as Sidney Hillman and Philip Murray, consciously seeking to separate them from the "Big Boy." His new appointees to the National Labor Relations Board proved more sympathetic to the A.F. of L.'s jurisdictional claims than their predecessors. And by late 1939 the president ceased scolding "economic royalists" and "congressional Tories."

As early as December 1937 Lewis began to rail against the New Deal's economic failures. On December 12, Jett Lauck finished writing a long speech for Lewis's delivery at a SWOC meeting; the speech indicted federal economic policies for aiding business, not labor. In the spring of 1938 Lewis demanded that the federal government find jobs, on the public payroll if necessary, for thirteen million unemployed workers; that it spend billions, not millions, on public housing; and that it cure the Roosevelt depression by guaranteeing that one-third of the nation no longer remained ill-fed, ill-clothed, and ill-housed. Throughout the remainder of the year and all through 1939, Lewis refused to soften his demands for increased federal expenditures—jobs for public workers, billions for subsidized housing, and a Social Security system sufficiently generous to allow the elderly to retire in dignity and comfort. To achieve his goals, the labor leader persistently threatened to build a left-wing, farm-labor alliance that would incorporate student radicals and racial minorities either in an independent third party or as the dominant element in the Democratic party.

Yet the most bitter and the deepest source of the rift between Lewis and Roosevelt originated in a fundamental disagreement about the nation's foreign policy. The seeds of conflict flowered in Lewis's and Roosevelt's quite different conceptions of the United States' role in the world arena. The labor leader exemplified a tradition that dated back to Grover Cleveland, William Jennings Bryan, William Borah, George Norris, the LaFollettes, and Herbert Hoover—a tradition that perceived the American world role as largely symbolic. The United States would serve the world best by domestic example, not foreign adventure. Roosevelt exemplified the world view of William Henry Seward, John Hay, his own cousin Theodore, and Woodrow Wilson—a perspective that promoted a vigorous, sometimes adventurous, foreign policy. The president could not deliver what Lewis expected from him in foreign policy.

As Roosevelt increasingly devoted himself to the situation overseas, he and Lewis ineluctably split apart politically. At an anti-Nazi rally in Madison Square Graden in March 1937, Lewis warned an emotional audience of Jewish-American trade unionists that "Europe is on the brink of disaster and it must be our care that she does not drag us into the abyss after her." He never deviated from this position, insisting consistently that the United States' security lay in domestic economic reform, not overseas entanglements. Lewis even refused publicly and privately to lobby in favor of the president's preparedness program, which promised to reduce unemployment considerably.

Marginal disputes over foreign policy also separated labor leader and president. Proud of his reputation as "Good Neighbor" to Latin American nations, Roosevelt was disturbed by Lewis's own Pan-American diplomacy. At a time when the United States was involved in delicate negotiations with the Cardenas government in Mexico over the property claims of foreign oil companies, Lewis conducted his own discussions with the Mexican president. In September 1938, at a conference in Mexico City to discuss the founding of a new left-wing Latin American labor federation to replace the A.F. of L's defunct Pan-American Federation of Labor, Lewis attended a mass meeting of the International Congress against War and Fascism. Appearing before fifty thousand Mexican workers gathered in a bullring decked with red flags, Lewis warned the audience that fascism also threatened the United States. Two days previously Lewis had conferred privately with President Cardenas, who asked the labor leader to deliver diplomatic messages directly to Roosevelt.

If Lewis's adventures in Mexico City upset Roosevelt, as they undoubtedly did, the president was even more perturbed by Lewis's oil diplomacy. Working closely with William Rhodes Davis—a Texas entrepreneur, oil wildcatter, and sometime Democratic party financial backer—Lewis used his own Mexican contacts to enable the Texan to purchase oil from the recently nationalized properties for sale to Hitler's Germany.

Precisely what motivated Lewis to engage in this enterprise remains obscure. Davis's motives to be sure are lucid: profit made by buying oil cheaply from Mexico and selling it dearly to Germany. Cardenas's reasons for supplying oil to Nazi Germany are also obvious: It provided an opportunity to break the blockade imposed on the shipment and sale of nationalized Mexican oil by the dominant Anglo-American petroleum companies. But what did Lewis seek? It is unlikely that the labor leader was involved, unwittingly or not, in Nazi espionage schemes as Ladislas Farrago implied in *The Game of Foxes*. Only one explanation seems likely for Lewis's behavior. By enabling Mexico to evade the oil blockade, he hoped to earn the friendship of Cardenas and the left-wing Mexican Federation of Labor (CTM), link the CIO to Latin American labor, and establish his own influence as an anti-imperialist throughout the Western Hemisphere.

Events in Europe, however, remained at the heart of the Lewis-Roosevelt conflict. In his traditional Labor Day radio address in 1939, shortly before the outbreak of World War II, Lewis warned interventionist American politicians about their irrationality. "War has always been the device of the politically despairing and intellectually sterile statesmen," Lewis observed in referring to Democratic leaders unable to cope with the domestic economy.

> It provides employment in the gun factories and begets enormous profits for those already rich. It kills off the vigorous males who, if permitted to live, might question the financial and political exploitation of the race. Above all, war perpetuates in imperishable letters on the scroll of fame and history, the names of its political creators and managers.
>
> Labor in America wants no war nor any part of war. Labor wants the right to work and live—not the privilege of dying by gunshot or poison gas to sustain the mental errors of current statesmen.
>
> During the last fortnight our country has been subjected to an overdose of war propaganda. Patently an attempt is being made to create the illusion that when war breaks in Europe, the United States in some mysterious fashion will forthwith be involved. Such a concept is of course a monumental deception and amounts to a betrayal of national interest.

Lewis had good reason for his anxiety about possible United States involvement in European conflict. He knew that contingency plans were being prepared in Washington for possible American involvement and that an emergency war production proposal was then under consideration. Equally disturbing, Lewis had been informed by his friends and sources inside the Roosevelt administration that the president had been selecting prominent businessmen as the principal administrators of the war production planning program. Once again, as had happened during World War I, it seemed that labor would be treated as less than an equal partner during a national crisis—a thought never far from Lewis's mind. Much as Lewis opposed United States' intervention in the European war, he nevertheless intended to insure that labor won its full and equal share of all appointed positions on war planning agencies. Every hint that Roosevelt seemed more eager to involve corporation executives than trade unionists in emergency planning further angered the CIO leader.

Although Lewis supported Roosevelt's revision of the neutrality laws in 1939, he did not change either his attitude toward foreign affairs or his growing disenchantment with Roosevelt. During the same CIO convention speech in which he endorsed Roosevelt's neutrality legislation, Lewis reaffirmed his conviction "that our nation is not called upon to participate in any manner on one side or the other of a European conflict. Safety and security for Americans," he added, "lie in nonparticipation in this conflict and the addressing of ourselves to the major problem now confronting us in our internal economy and domestic establishment."

The year 1940 promised a unique presidential election. Lewis thought so. In his Labor Day 1939 speech, the CIO leader prophesied: "In the march of years 1940 will be one of the crossroads of destiny for the people of the United States. . . . Let those who will seek the votes of the workers of America be prepared to guarantee jobs for all Americans and freedom from foreign wars."

15

Naked to Thine Enemies: The Politics of 1940

The year 1940 proved fateful for Western civilization, the American political system, Franklin D. Roosevelt, and John L. Lewis. Seldom had an American presidential election occurred at a more crucial historical moment, and never had a labor leader sought so decisively to tip the political balance in the favor of one candidate. By the time the Republican party convention met in Philadelphia in mid-June, France had fallen, the remnants of Britain's European army had fled the Continent at Dunkirk, and only the English Channel and Winston Churchill's eloquence stood between Hitler's Germany and total domination of Western Europe. When the Democrats convened in July, Great Britain stood alone in Europe, a nation apparently doomed to invasion and defeat.

The year 1940 scarcely seemed a good one for tradition. It was a year in which the adversaries of Western liberal capitalism—from Berlin and Rome to Moscow and Tokyo—were in the ascendancy. Thus, not surprisingly, both major American political parties shattered precedent. First the Republicans selected a dark-horse candidate for president, a man who only a few years previously had been a registered Democrat and whose experience was administrative and managerial, not political. The nomination of Wendell Willkie shocked old-line Republicans, causing the crusty Indiana politico James Watson to quip: "I don't mind the church converting a whore, but I don't like her to lead the choir on the first night!" A month later the Democrats broke an older tradition by nominating Franklin Roosevelt for a third term.

John L. Lewis observed these events with great interest, and they prompted him to intervene dramatically in the politics of 1940. Lewis believed that the future of the United States hinged on the election results and that freedom and democracy depended on American insulation from Europe's debacle. A victory for Roosevelt, Lewis felt, would inevitably drag the United States into a European conflict, create the preconditions for the establishment of an imperial presidency, transform the United States into an imperialist power, subvert the nation's democratic liberties, and enable a corporate-financial elite to control economic policy. To avert such dire results, Lewis, in October 1940, staked his leadership of the CIO and his personal prestige on the result of the election. He implored America's workers to choose between Lewis and Roosevelt.

The most sensational and often-repeated story that purports to explain Lewis's behavior in 1940 was published initially in Frances Perkins's *The Roosevelt I Knew.* According to that tale, allegedly told to Perkins and Dan Tobin by President Roosevelt personally, Lewis came to the White House one evening in January 1940. "Lewis was in a most amiable mood," the president told Tobin and Perkins, "and he talked about the third term too, Dan, just the way you have, only much smoother. . . . When I told him what I told you, that the people wouldn't like a third term and that it would be very hard going politically, what do you think he said, Dan? He said, 'Mr. President, I have thought of all of that and I have a suggestion to make for you to consider. If the vice-presidential candidate on your ticket should happen to be John L. Lewis, those objections would disappear. A strong labor man would insure full support, not only of all the labor people but of all the liberals who worry about such things as third terms.'"

Asked by Tobin and Perkins how he responded, Roosevelt replied, "Why, he didn't press, he didn't press me. He just asked me to think it over and give it consideration."

Rejected as a vice-presidential candidate, Lewis, the Perkins story continues, engaged in the politics of vengeance. New evidence and logical analysis, however, cast grave doubt on the truth of Perkins's story and her role as its source. For one thing, the Lewis-Roosevelt conference she allegedly cited occurred shortly before the 1940 UMW convention. Yet the only recorded meeting between the two men in that period took place at the White House on January 10, when Lewis visited with his John Jr., in whose presence a delicate and tense political discussion was unlikely. For another, Edwin A. Lahey, a labor reporter for the Chicago *Daily News,* has asserted that he leaked the original story of Lewis's vice-presidential ambition based on a tip from Lee Pressman and that Perkins picked up the story later. In his own oral history interview, Pressman has further compounded the mystery of the story and conflated Perkins's version of it. According to Pressman, Roosevelt first reported the essence of his conversation with Lewis to Phil Murray from whom Pressman heard it. Moreover, in Pressman's version, Lewis specifically warned the president: "Mr. President, I think if you run for a third term, you may be defeated, unless you have a representative of labor on the ticket, and unless that representative is myself." To which Roosevelt supposedly replied, "That's very interesting, John, but which place on the ticket are you reserving for me?"

Yet in the same oral history interview, Pressman refers to the story as possibly apocryphal and suggests logical reasons why the conversation differed from Perkins's version. No doubt Lewis and Roosevelt discussed the political situation and organized labor's role in the forthcoming presidential election, perhaps on January 19 at an unrecorded White House conference. No doubt Lewis informed Roosevelt that labor deserved greater influence in national affairs and warned the president that he needed labor's political support. But for Lewis to have asked Roosevelt to be selected as his vice-presidential running mate was unlikely asserts Pressman. "Lewis is not the kind to put himself so completely at the mercy of another man, who would have the power and be in the position to say 'No.' That's why for Lewis to have made that specific request that he is alleged to have made would have been entirely out of character."

The entire history of the Lewis-Roosevelt relationship between 1936 and 1940 also casts suspicion on Perkins's story. By January 1940 whatever ardor that Lewis once had for Roosevelt as president had cooled. Shortly after the 1939 San Francisco CIO convention Lewis had quashed an effort by western political "progressives" to initiate a Roosevelt third-term boom and simultaneously promoted the presidential aspirations of Montana Senator Burton K. Wheeler. Also by January 1940 the differences in foreign policy between Lewis and Roosevelt were so great that only a marked switch in United States policy could have reconciled the two men.

Whatever the actual substance of the Lewis-Roosevelt conversations in January 1940, the labor leader faced grave political problems. What alternative to Roosevelt did Lewis have? Where any Democratic candidates, other than Wheeler—a dark, dark horse—more favorably disposed to organized labor? Would the Democrats dare to offer the second spot on the ticket to a labor leader, especially one from the CIO, or adopt a blatantly pro-labor platform? Could Lewis reasonably expect a better bargain from the Republicans, whose leading prospects seemed to be such anti-CIO spokesmen as Robert A. Taft? Would Lewis consider the creation of a third party, an alliance of farmers and workers that would also attract the then antiwar American communists? What real alternatives did Lewis have in 1940, and when would he indicate his choice among them? The first indication of Lewis's new politics came at the 1940 Golden Anniversary convention of the United Mine Workers.

To the more than two thousand convention delegates who had gathered to toast their union's fiftieth anniversary, Lewis, on Wednesday, January 24, recommended that they endorse no presidential candidate in 1940—a rebuke to many in the audience who had swamped the Resolutions Committee with Roosevelt reelection endorsements. Lewis minced no words in criticizing the president's desire for a third term. If Roosevelt unwisely and egotistically sought another term in office and the Democratic party acceded to his ambition, Lewis warned that "with the conditions now confronting the nation and the dissatisfaction now permeating the minds of the people, his candidacy would result in ignominious defeat."

Lewis addressed his speech as much to Democrats as to miners' delegates. For organization Democrats, Lewis provided a lesson in practical politics. The Democratic party, he taught, was a minority organization in twentieth century America. Limited by their southern sectional prejudices and commitment to the fallacious policy of free trade, Democrats achieved power only "under abnormal circumstances when [they] receive the support of the national independent vote. . . . Psychologically and politically," he thundered, "organized labor created the atmosphere of success that returned the Democratic party to power with an ample margin of safety." Yet 1939, three years after the great victory of 1936, organized labor lacked any substantial points of contact with the administration in power. No labor leader occupied the office of secretary of labor; nor did representatives of trade unionism hold any policymaking positions in federal agencies; nor did the president consult labor's spokesmen in handling unemployment, national economic planning, and foreign affairs. Such ingratitude by the Roosevelt administration to organized labor could have but one result: Democratic defeat in 1940. The Republicans could be prevented from winning in 1940, Lewis lectured, "only by an accord between the Democratic party and organized labor."

A day after his initial attack on Roosevelt, Lewis proved that his dissatisfaction was with the president personally and politically, not with the Democratic party. He introduced Senator Burton K. Wheeler as a featured convention speaker, thus offering the Montana Democrat an opportunity to launch a bid for the presidency before a sympathetic audience. Lewis and Wheeler shared many beliefs concerning foreign affairs and domestic policies. Both Lewis and Wheeler remembered World War I with regret. To them it had been a time when a reform president, Woodrow Wilson, had misled the nation into an unnecessary foreign war and then allowed reactionary businessmen and politicians to repress labor and persecute radicals in the guise of national security. In 1940 Franklin D. Roosevelt seemed likely to repeat Wilson's mistakes of 1917–18. Unfortunately for Lewis, the Montana senator failed to stir the audience of union delegates.

Lewis reiterated the themes of his opening speech repeatedly during the remaining week of the convention. He indicted Roosevelt for failing to end unemployment and called on the president to confess, "I am not equal to my job." In his closing address to the convention on February 1, Lewis again served notice on the nation's leaders "that labor in the United States wants no war or any part of war, and that it will hold to strict accountability any statesmen who depart from that declared policy."

Lewis's position in 1940 came from two decades' reflection concerning World War I's impact on the labor movement and domestic reform. With every day and week that passed after the outbreak of European war in September 1939, Lewis saw Roosevelt repeat what the labor leader considered to be Woodrow Wilson's mistakes. With "Dr. Win-the-War" about to replace "Dr. New Deal" in the White House and corporation executives becoming more prominent than labor leaders and academics in the administration, organized labor's future looked dim. Lewis worried, and quite rightly, as antilabor corporations that refused to heed the Wagner Act's mandate to bargain with unions of their workers' own choosing received lucrative defense contracts.

Domestic affairs influenced part of Lewis's behavior in January 1940. But one should not underestimate his passionate beliefs concerning foreign affairs and his commitment to American neutrality. Lewis honestly believed, as did Herbert Hoover, Robert A. Taft, and his U.S. Steel executive friend Tom Moses, that the European struggle did not directly threaten United States security and that the Atlantic and Pacific oceans provided the nation with unbreachable defenses. To go to war unnecessarily, thought Lewis, Moses, and Hoover, would transform the United States into a garrison society, expand dangerously the power of the presidency, make America an imperialist nation, and turn its citizens into servants, not masters, of the state.

By February 1940 little common ground remained available for Lewis and Roosevelt to occupy. Yet those most intrigued by Lewis's politics, including Roosevelt's closest advisers, still had great difficulty fathoming the labor leader's position. His anti-interventionism combined with criticism of the Democratic party as too conservative led some to consider Lewis as a communist ally.

Lewis, however, had a consistent record as a red-baiter and enthusiast of American values. Those who remembered Lewis's policies as president of the UMW during the 1920s and his politics during that decade wondered if he might not again opt for Republicanism. Most Republicans, especially the party's apparent front-runner for the nomination, Taft, and its elder statesman, Hoover, shared Lewis's foreign policy sentiments.

For most of the late winter, spring, and summer of 1940, however, Lewis seemed entirely liberated from his Republican, conservative political past. He repeatedly appeared on public platforms as the angriest man on the American Left, the most outspoken and effective critic of the New Deal's domestic failures. Confining his public appearances largely to trade union, youth, blacks, and radical meetings, he uttered words that stirred receptive, often ecstatic, audiences. Isolationists, youthful radicals, staunch communists, militant trade unionists, and gentle pacifists saw Lewis as a man whose policies could end unemployment while keeping the United States at peace, and many among them ached to enlist with the labor leader in a popular left-wing, third-party movement that would sound twentieth-century American populism's "first hurrah."

Roosevelt, despite refusing to comment publicly or even off the record about Lewis's political threats, worried and schemed to undercut Lewis's influence in the labor movement. Roosevelt cultivated his association with Phil Murray and Sidney Hillman, men much more susceptible than Lewis to White House influence and more deferential in the presence of power. On May 28, 1940, with France on the verge of military collapse, the president announced the appointment of a National Defense Advisory Council (NDAC), with Sidney Hillman as labor's representative on the council. At a press conference the same day, Roosevelt explained his choice of Hillman in these words: "for heaven's sake do not attribute it to me because somebody will call me names—he [Hillman] is just half way between John Lewis and Green."

In fact, Hillman was not a compromise choice; the ACWA president was as unacceptable, if not more so, to the A.F. of L. than to Lewis. Roosevelt selected him because Hillman would neither challenge nor deviate from the president's domestic and foreign policies, and the appointment was sure to enrage Lewis, create dissension in the CIO, and, hence, insure that the industrial union federation would not present a united front against Roosevelt's reelection.

The president calculated correctly. Lewis was indeed enraged by the Hillman appointment. The president neither approached the CIO leader before making his selection, nor did Hillman speak to Lewis before accepting appointment. Clearly, Roosevelt intended to subvert Lewis's authority as president of the CIO, and Hillman had cooperated in that plan.

As Lewis expected, Hillman proved more committed to defending the administration's labor policies than to pushing the CIO's demands. To Lewis's demand that Roosevelt issue an executive order that required recipients of defense contracts to bargain collectively with organized labor, Hillman pleaded the exigencies of practical politics and the overriding importance of national security. Supplying Britain with war materials to defend itself against the Nazi onslaught, argued Hillman, was more important for the moment than pleading the CIO's case.

Hillman would not even accede to direct requests from Lewis. In late July Lewis wrote to Hillman concerning the latter's refusal to appoint James J. Matles, a left-wing leader of the United Electrical Workers, to a role in defense planning. I hope, wrote Lewis, that charges concerning Matles's political nonconformity will not influence policy. The UE, added Lewis, "has a record of which I am officially and personally proud. . . . I do hope," he concluded, "that you will undertake to review this situation from the viewpoint of according a fair treatment to this great organization." Early in August, Hillman dismissed Lewis's request curtly: "I find it . . . impossible to accept the notion that non-inclusion of an individual on the committee is tantamount to unfairness to an organization of which he is a member."

Another door in Washington had shut in Lewis's face. His influence at the White House minimal, Lewis now discovered that labor leaders close to him (or to his policies) stood little chance of serving in defense planning agencies.

All during the time that Lewis parried and thrusted with Hillman concerning organized labor's role in defense planning, the CIO leader's political plans solidified. By the time the Republicans convened in Philadelphia in mid–June 1940, Lewis knew what he wanted and what he must do. Speaking to the national convention of the NAACP on June 18, the eve of the Republican convention, Lewis delivered a typical speech. He referred, as was by then quite customary, to the CIO's commitment to win for American blacks their full civil and political rights and criticized those statesmen who had no solution to domestic problems other than involvement in a European war, a policy "repugnant to every healthy-minded American." Toward the close of his speech, Lewis, however, delivered an analysis of the Great Depression that presaged a new politics. As if drafted by Herbert Hoover, Lewis's analysis of the depression asserted that it had been caused by European economic problems originating in World War I, that the United States and every other democratic nation had been rising from the economic trough in the spring of 1932, and that the United States alone in the Western world slid backward economically after the election of Franklin D. Roosevelt, whose policies made depression and unemployment "a chronic fact in American life." Not content to make his point, Lewis drove Hoover's lesson home. As a matter of simple justice, contended Lewis, Hoover had nothing whatever to do with the depression. "It was laid at his doorstep when he came to the White House. It is only the self-seeking politicians that blame Mr. Hoover. The policies he pursued . . . had a powerful effect in the start at recovery in 1932."

The next day Lewis appeared personally before the Republican party resolutions committee to denounce Roosevelt's policies, especially the president's compulsory universal military service bill, characterized as "a fantastic suggestion from a mind in full intellectual retreat." Speaking before the committee for a full two hours, Lewis demanded no alterations in the Wagner Act, no favoritism to the A. F. of L., the abolition of hunger and unemployment, and full civil rights for blacks and other American minorities. In response to a question from Alf Landon, he threatened to lead a third-party movement unless Republicans met labor's demands.

More interesting than Lewis's speech to the NAACP or his personal appearance before a convention committee was his behind-the-scenes activity. In conjunction with Herbert Hoover, the labor leader plotted to promote a convention boom for the former president. According to Lee Pressman, Lewis believed that Hoover had a chance to stampede the Republican delegates. And Lewis enlisted Pressman as a messenger in the plot to promote Hoover's candidacy. In the event, however, Hoover laid as big an egg among Republicans as Burton Wheeler had among Democrats.

That Lewis, by June 1940, detested Roosevelt was common knowledge; that he considered the New Deal a domestic failure was equally true; that the CIO's influence in Washington had declined since 1936 none denied. But why Hoover as an alternative to Roosevelt? Only one answer comes to mind. Lewis, in 1940, considered foreign policy more crucial than domestic affairs. He believed that however much United States involvement in Europe's conflict might do to solve unemployment temporarily, it would come only at the greatest long-range expense to American society. War, Lewis prophesied, would create a puissant presidency and an imperial nation; peace, moreover, would bring prosperity only if the United States remained a garrison state whose armed forces stalked the globe in the name of citizens who had surrendered their customary rights and freedoms. Hoover shared Lewis's fears of an imperial presidency, harbored no imperial dreams, and believed that national security lay in noninvolvement in foreign wars. In foreign affairs, Hoover, then, was the perfect candidate — perhaps the only major party choice likely to share Lewis's conception of the United States' proper role in world affairs.

What the Republicans offered Lewis, however, was worse than he expected. Not only did the resolutions committee recommend a platform antipathetic to organized labor's demands, the delegates also nominated Wendell Willkie, whose foreign policy barely differed from Roosevelt's and who was to become famous as an advocate of an interventionist American policy under the rubric "One World."

A month later the Democratic convention met, renominated Roosevelt, and left Lewis in a quandary. Both major parties had chosen candidates unacceptable to the labor leader. What choice did he now have but to form a third party, a political organization dedicated to noninvolvement in foreign affairs and radical reform at home, a party dependent on communist and other left-wing supporters?

As Lewis weighed his political options and perplexed his associates in the labor movement, several factors made his choice of a presidential candidate inevitable. By the late summer of 1940, few of those closest to Lewis criticized his politics. The left-wing and communist unions and their leaders in the CIO applauded Lewis's criticism of the president, especially in foreign affairs, where the party line demanded American neutrality. The two men on the CIO central office staff closest to Lewis—Len DeCaux and Lee Pressman—opposed Roosevelt's domestic and foreign policies. Jett Lauck declared the New Deal a failure and urged Lewis to lead a radical reform crusade. And K. C. Adams, the Republican, isolationist, and peddler of anti-Semitic canards, returned to the UMW at Lewis's invitation to be editor of the union *Journal.* No close associates urged Lewis to reconsider his criticism of the president or to alter his position on foreign affairs.

This became clearer as Lewis continued to speak out publicly on politics, war, and peace. In his annual Labor Day radio address, Lewis issued grave political warnings. "Labor Day in 1940," he observed, "finds labor and the things in which labor believes more in jeopardy than at any time during the history of the modern labor movement." War hysteria had been manufactured and merchandised wholesale in order to turn the nation's attention away from the New Deal's domestic failures, and peacetime conscription as urged by the president, asserted Lewis, "would be the beginning of the end of our democratic way of life." All Americans must, Lewis pleaded, "become articulate and . . . demand consideration of American problems, if America as we know it is to be preserved."

Roosevelt's advocates inside and outside the labor movement desperately tried to patch up the Lewis-Roosevelt relationship and effect a political reconciliation between the two men. Unfortunately they lacked direct influence with Lewis, who, as the election approached, withdrew even more tightly into the confines of his family.

Yet Roosevelt still sought a political reconciliation with Lewis. In mid-October Roosevelt's prospects for reelection seemed uncertain: the two-term tradition presented one obstacle; foreign policy and the threat of war made the votes of many ethnic blocs, especially the Irish, questionable; and the persistence of mass unemployment threatened to cost the Democrats votes. When Louis Stark reported on October 16 in the *New York Times* that Lewis was leaning toward Willkie and would endorse the Republican candidate unless Roosevelt quickly assuaged the labor leader's grievances, the president and his advisers took notice. They probably shared Lewis's reading of the forthcoming election, as noted by Stark: that support for Republicans and Democrats was closely balanced, that a small vote margin in several key industrial and agricultural states would decide the outcome, and that a few thousand CIO votes might swing New York state. Not unexpectedly, the day after the Stark story appeared, Roosevelt invited Lewis to the White House. Neither participant commented to reporters afterward, and both referred to their discussion as secret.

One can only imagine what transpired in the White House on October 17. Undoubtedly the president turned all his redoubtable personal charm on the labor leader. The president probably said little, if anything, about foreign policy. Lewis, it is clear, went to the White House determined not to be charmed by Roosevelt—in fact, determined to reject a reconciliation. Lewis later told Saul Alinsky that instead of discussing substantive political issues, he immediately accused the president of ordering the FBI to eavesdrop on him and demanded that Roosevelt end all such infringements on his personal privacy and civil liberties.

Lewis had thus placed the president in a position in which he could not mollify the labor leader. If Roosevelt now ordered the FBI to cease eavesdropping on Lewis, the president would have admitted publicly that he had originally issued such orders. If Roosevelt denied having issued such orders, Lewis would have further proof of the president's duplicity. Nothing Roosevelt might do or say could satisfy Lewis; by the evening of October 17 their political rift was complete.

There can be no doubt that Lewis actually accused the president of tapping his phones and invading his privacy. On October 30 the New York *Herald-Tribune* reported that such a confrontation had occurred and that Lewis cited three men in the Justice Department as the source of his information. For more than a year, Lewis had alleged that the Roosevelt administration used a domestic secret police force to spy on the private lives of alleged "fifth columnists." And finally, a Lewis associate informed the authors of this biography that the CIO president literally observed FBI agents trailing him wherever he went. For these reasons, Lewis believed that Roosevelt had ordered wiretapping and personal surveillance. But in the end, the wiretapping charge simply provided Lewis with an excuse to feign anger and outrage, stalk out of the president's bedroom, and break off all further discussions aimed at rapprochement. Lewis had made a firm decision about the presidential election three weeks before the October 17 conference.

On October 22 the press reported that Lewis would speak to the nation at 9:00 p.m. on Friday, October 25 on all three national radio networks. By then, most knowledgeable political observers including Roosevelt knew that Lewis would endorse Willkie, although at his press conference of October 22 the president denied any advance knowledge of what Lewis would say.

In the week before his October 25 speech, Lewis retreated into almost total isolation, soliciting ideas from none of his close associates or advisers and, according to Lee Pressman, even writing his own speech. Leaders in the CIO, the Republican party, and the Democratic party expected no surprises in Lewis's speech. The estimated twenty-five to thirty million Americans who listened to Lewis on the evening of October 25, however, had no idea what the labor leader would say. They listened expectantly.

Almost before his radio audience settled down, Lewis disclaimed any intention of speaking for labor or of controlling the vote of any man or woman. Instead, he promised to speak only for himself. Lewis then repeated the essence of every public political speech he had made since the January 1940 UMW convention. Roosevelt's motivation and objective, he stressed, was war. "The President has said that he hates war and will work for peace, but his acts do not match his words." Lewis charged that Roosevelt created an unprecedentedly powerful presidency—made more so by "the spectacle of a President who is disinclined to surrender that power, in keeping with traditions of the Republic. . . . Personal craving for power, the overweening abnormal and selfish craving for increased power, is a thing to alarm and dismay. . . . America needs no superman," thundered Lewis. "It denies the philosophy that runs to deification of the state. America wants no royal family." The United States, Lewis quipped nastily, has had enough of the "economic and political experiments of an amateur, ill-equipped practitioner in the realm of political science."

More than halfway into his speech Lewis finally struck its most dramatic, new note when he recommend Wendell Willkie. "He is not an aristocrat. He has the common touch. He was born in the briar and not to the purple. He has worked with his hands, and has known the pangs of hunger." To reject Willkie and elect Roosevelt, Lewis warned, "would be a national evil of the first magnitude."

Roosevelt, Lewis concluded, could win only with labor's support, and he implored CIO members not to give it. If CIO members spurned his advice, if they voted for Roosevelt, Lewis pledged to resign as CIO president. Then came what should have been the speech's peroration. "Through the years of struggle, you have been content that I should be in the forefront of your battles. I am still the same man. Sustain me now, or repudiate me." But instead of closing his address on that dramatic challenge to his union constituents, Lewis restated the issue that really separated him from Roosevelt. "You," he asked the youths among his audience, "who may be about to die in a foreign war, created at the whim of an international meddler, should you salute your Caesar?" And to their mothers, he pleaded in his best Victorian tone, "May I hope that on election day [you] . . . with the sacred ballot, lead the revolt against the candidate who plays at a game that may make cannon fodder of your sons."

After the speech, an obviously satisfied Lewis remained at UMW headquarters for several hours posing for cameramen, taking telephone calls, and opening telegrams. Among the wires was one from Herbert Hoover assuring Lewis "that speech will resound over years to come," and another from the Republican presidential candidate, who complimented the labor leader for making "the most eloquent address I ever heard."

Lewis's family and his closest associates in the labor movement either rallied round their leader or kept silent. On October 28, CIO publicity director Len DeCaux announced that 90 percent of the post-speech telegrams, many from trade union rank-and-filers, favored Lewis's endorsement of Willkie. DeCaux assured newsmen that Lewis thought that his radio speech had elected Willkie and that he would probably not have to speak on the air again.

Those expected to rally around Lewis but who failed to do so immediately became targets for pressure. The left-wing and communist union leaders Lewis had welcomed into the CIO received telephone call after call from Dennie Lewis demanding that they endorse Willkie. Left-wingers such as Harry Bridges, Joe Curran, and Ben Gold applauded Lewis's repudiation of Roosevelt, but they could scarcely countenance promoting the candidacy of a Republican "barefoot boy from Wall Street." Consequently they strained to avoid Lewis after October 25, and in the words of Lee Pressman, "were running so fast you couldn't see their coat-tails from then on."

Lewis's endorsement of Willkie caused consternation inside the CIO and among the entire American political Left. Resentment against Lewis's new politics had been mounting ever since the 1940 UMW convention, and it reached a climax after the October 25 speech. Many city and state industrial union councils repudiated Lewis's endorsement of Willkie, although they generally expressed their confidence in the CIO president as a labor leader. Hillman and the Amalgamated Clothing Workers (ACW) directly challenged Lewis's politics. Over the radio and also at an American Labor party rally at New York's Madison Square Garden on October 31, Jacob S. Potofsky, vice-president of the ACW, asserted that "neither John L. Lewis nor any other man can dictate labor's vote. . . . They will vote to continue the New Deal; they will vote for President Roosevelt. Labor will not scrap its newly won rights because of one man's personal grudge."

More vexing to Lewis was the emergence of dissent and division within the UMW. Even before his October 25 speech, Lewis's criticism of Roosevelt had led more UMW locals to submit nominations of Phil Murray for the union presidency than Lewis (five hundred to two hundred). After the radio address, observed Powers Hapgood, "The miners are all disturbed about Lewis's speech." Hapgood noted that most coalminers probably shared Van Bittner's observation that, "I am 100 percent for John L. Lewis as head of the CIO and also 100 percent for the reelection of Roosevelt." A presidential informant noted that he had never seen the coal miners worked up to such a pitch of excitement. Except for officials appointed directly by Lewis, all the miners and their locals had rallied behind the president. The informant observed that dummies of Lewis were hanged in effigy in the Ohio coalfields with cards proclaiming, "Judas, Traitor, Dictator."

When the votes were counted, they convicted Lewis of a glaring political miscalculation. Roosevelt won reelection by a substantial, if reduced, margin of five million votes (down from eleven million in 1936); the president's support remained firmest among working-class voters, especially those in regions of union strength, including coal miners. Lewis's troops had deserted him en masse.

Yet the day following the election Lewis seemed not the least depressed. Refusing to be drawn into a discussion of the campaign during a press conference, he nevertheless impressed reporters as cheerful and good-natured. Lewis, moreover, seemed as willing to abide by his pledge to resign the CIO presidency as to accept the election results.

What really prompted Lewis to endorse Willkie? Why did he stake his future as CIO president on Roosevelt's defeat? Why, moreover, did he risk splitting the UMW as well as the CIO in what many considered a vain political gamble?

Len DeCaux, who was at the radio studio with Lewis the night of his election-eve endorsement of Willkie, asserts that during a long chat later that evening, Lewis assumed that Roosevelt would win. Why, then, did he back Willkie? DeCaux's only answer is that Lewis resented the divisions Roosevelt had created inside the CIO and that if the president was reelected, Lewis then had an excuse to retire as CIO president. If, unexpectedly, Willkie won, Lewis would have the right to stay on as president of the CIO and demand absolute loyalty from his followers.

Saul Alinsky supports DeCaux's answer. Lewis allegedly told his biographer, "I carefully examined that election [1940], and there never was a momentary doubt in my mind but that Mr. Roosevelt was going to be re-elected. That was the very reason I deliberately publicly committed myself and my organization to the camp of Wendell Willkie. You see, I wanted to, I had to get out of the presidency of the CIO if I were to be effective in uniting the divided forces of labor." And TRB, in the *New Republic* of November 4, 1940, observed that Lewis's primary motivation was "to preserve the labor movement as a separate, independent entity under its own leaders. If Mr. Willkie were President, there would be no confusion about whether he or John L. Lewis spoke for organized labor. There would be no difficulty in rallying labor against Mr. Willkie."

In October and November 1940, Roosevelt intimates suggested that personal peeves and ambitions explained Lewis's behavior. Other rumors from the White House alleged that Lewis was especially piqued by Sidney Hillman's role as presidential labor adviser; and Senator Robert Wagner asserted publicly that Lewis's great desire was to become secretary of labor, a position Willkie had promised the labor leader.

The White House rumors can be dismissed easily. First, Lewis never allowed personal pique to influence, let alone control, crucial political decisions. Second, Lewis never consciously backed a sure loser. His whole career in the labor movement had reflected virtuosic opportunism—the ability to change policies, positions, and parties hastily as attitudes inside and outside the labor movement shifted. In the past he had evolved from a Wilsonian reformer to a 1920s-style Republican to an ardent New Dealer. That, however, does not mean that Lewis rejected risk-taking. Far from it. He was, as the history of the CIO proved, a consummate gambler, a man able to bluff industrialists and politicians as well as poker cronies.

Lewis, by 1940, believed that labor had received all it would from the New Deal, that continued support of Roosevelt would only vitiate labor's political influence and, worse yet, lead the nation into war. Willkie as president promised labor clear advantages. Lewis and Willkie had had a secret meeting on September 28 at which the Republican candidate assured the CIO leader that organized labor would be recognized as a real factor in national affairs and its leaders would receive key positions in the administration if the Republicans won. Although Willkie's interventionist foreign policy displeased Lewis, Republicans as a party were less likely to involve the nation in war and their protectionist economic policies, compared to the Democrats' free trade propensities, promised greater job security for American workers.

Willkie's promises and Republican foreign policy would have meant nothing to Lewis in the absence of victory. But the labor leader had been reading the election returns since 1938 and was certain that a Republican trend was in the making. Knowing that Democrats depended on the labor vote in 1940 as never before, sure that the election would be close, and egotistical enough to believe that he could influence the votes of a substantial number of CIO members, Lewis endorsed Willkie. Alinsky is correct when he writes that Lewis used his threat to resign as CIO president as a trump card. "He took the whip and laid down the ultimatum. 'It's either Roosevelt or me. Take your choice. You cannot have both.'" In the event that Willkie won, the Republican candidate would know whom to thank for his success. What better, more calculated gamble could a poker player take?

Lewis had no alternative to Willkie. Roosevelt was out of the question. Much as the American communists and the pacifist Left approved Lewis's attacks on the president, Lewis still despised communists and only by accident shared their foreign policy in 1940. Lewis remained too much the opportunist, too much the personification of vulgar pragmatism and business values, to lead a third-party political crusade. A third party would cost too much and obviously offer too little in return. Committed fundamentally to the central values of a business civilization and to the myth of the indestructability of the two-party system, Lewis had nowhere to turn in 1940 but to Willkie.

His turn to Willkie, however, cost Lewis and the American labor movement dearly. Democrats and Roosevelt-worshippers in the labor movement called Lewis's political bluff, and they held the better cards. Roosevelt's triumph sealed Lewis's resignation as CIO president and precipitated his eventual departure from the organization. Lewis would never again exercise the influence inside the labor movement that he had wielded from 1936 through 1940.

Well before Lewis endorsed Willkie and threatened to resign as CIO president if Roosevelt were reelected, many CIO members looked forward to the November 1940 convention with foreboding. Beyond the long-standing dispute between Hillman and Lewis and the internal schism in the United Auto Workers, trouble between Murray and Lewis had developed by early October. On October 9, Powers Hapgood informed his wife, Mary, that although "Phil Murray will never oppose John L. publicly, they have severe differences owing mainly to Lewis's refusal to consult anyone before he makes an important move and he insults people with whom he disagrees." Later that month, a day after

Lewis's radio speech for Willkie, Hapgood grew more worried about the upcoming CIO convention. "The [Lewis-Hillman] fight is now bitter," he wrote Mary. "If FDR is elected, there will be no split as Lewis will retire and Murray will probably be president. If Willkie wins Lewis will make life so embarrassing for the A.C.W. and other unions that they will probably secede."

But even after Roosevelt won, Hapgood and other critics of Lewis feared what Lewis might say or do at the convention. "There is a strong sentiment growing," Harvey Fremming of the oil workers reported on November 9, "in an effort to draft President Lewis to succeed himself." Two days later, Hapgood informed his wife that Lewis might accept a draft movement being organized by Joe Curran, Harry Bridges, Mike Quill, and representatives of other Communist party–controlled unions. If Lewis acceded to a draft or Murray declined to accept CIO leadership, Hapgood concluded, "there is going to be a split. . . . There will be an awful fight unless the convention is fair and that depends on Lewis and Murray."

The last session of the CIO executive board shortly before the convention offered further cause for anxiety. At this meeting, Lewis clashed with representatives of the clothing workers, and he accused Hillman of relinquishing trade unionism's legitimate rights. Why, asked Lewis, did Hillman tolerate the awarding of defense contracts to nonunion firms? Why did Hillman refuse to demand that President Roosevelt issue an enforceable executive order requiring the recipients of federal contracts to bargain with organized labor? Such questions led Hillman's associates to believe that Lewis would not relinquish the CIO presidency gracefully.

On November 18, 1940 in the Chelsea Hotel in Atlantic City, the site where Lewis had slugged Hutcheson in October 1935, twenty-six hundred CIO delegates were in an expectant mood, and the stage seemed set for another dramatic John L. Lewis performance. Crucial convention committees were firmly in the hands of Lewis loyalists. A large majority of the delegates, excluding only those from the ACW and a few of their allies, could not conceive of a CIO without Lewis. Whatever their president wanted, they would grant. Lewis would also deliver the convention's first major address. What would he say? Would he tender the resignation, or encourage a draft?

As Lewis made his way to the lectern, delegates erupted in an enthusiastic demonstration. According to the biographer of Sidney Hillman, Matthew Josephson, suddenly many of the delegates arose wearing huge "We Want Lewis" buttons. Placards with the same motto sprang up everywhere. "There were visible," writes Josephson, "all those little signs and warnings of what political scientists . . . characterize as a 'stampede.'" For forty-three minutes, faithful mine workers, communists, and other delegates demonstrated. They "paraded, yelled, sang, wept, and embraced each other," Josephson continues. "For a long time the chanting and roaring went on—*'Lewis is our leader! Lewis is our leader!'*—while he smiled and waved and drank in the intoxicating sight. Only the Amalgamated delegates and their allies sat impassively, and if they could be suppressed or driven out," concluded Josephson, "the road would be open to the Lewis steam roller. As the convention proceeded it became apparent that this was Lewis's intention."

Josephson is perfectly right in his description of the pro-Lewis demonstration and the consternation that it caused among Amalgamated delegates. But he is wrong about Lewis's motivation. The CIO leader played no part in organizing the demonstration or initiating the draft-Lewis movement; nor did any of his lieutenants. Subsequently, Lewis indeed clashed with Hillman supporters, insulted them, and even humiliated them rhetorically; but his opening address must be taken at face value, and as such, it was a valedictory—some even said an example of a man reading his own eulogy.

The address was vintage Lewis. From his opening paraphrase of the Gettysburgh Address ("Three score months ago a new union was formed; conceived in liberty and the spirit of progress and forever dedicated to the proposition that the workers in our modern industries should be organized into industrial unions. Today we are engaged in a great struggle to determine whether a union so conceived and so dedicated can endure") to his closing lines, Lewis played his audience for all it was worth. He intended to depart the CIO's stage in a display of emotion, tears, and histrionics.

Lewis also left no doubt that he planned to resign. He informed the delegates that their worst enemy was internal dissension and a lack of confidence in labor's leaders. Divide among yourselves, he observed, and at night there is the sound of revelry and rejoicing in the camp of the adversary. The meaning of his words should have been obvious. Lewis could not remain as president of CIO without causing dissension. To his most ardent supporters at the convention, the left-wing and communist delegates, he uttered the most discomforting words. "I yield to no man the right to challenge my Americanism nor the Americanism of the organizations which at this moment I represent." For those in the press who misrepresented communist influence in the CIO, Lewis remarked, "they lie in their beard and they lie in their bowels. My remark goes for Old Lady Green down in New Orleans, too, and old as she is, she really should know better."

Next Lewis stated explicitly that, "I won't be with you long. In just a day or two I will be out of this office which at the moment I occupy."

Do not trouble yourself or grow heartsick over my departure, he begged, giving the delegates his own philosophy of existence. "That is the way of life. Some are able to carry through and some fall, but there is nothing to worry about. We should not dwell in the past. Yesterday is gone and tomorrow is another day. I am concerned with tomorrow and I care nothing what happened yesterday." And then, with tears streaking his cheeks and his voice quavering, Lewis observed, "Some great statesman once said that the heights are cold. I think that is true. The poet said, 'Who ascends to the mountain's top finds the loftiest peaks encased in mists and snow.' I think that is true." That being the way of man and life, "we can't stop to weep and wear sackcloth because something that happened yesterday did not meet with our approval or that we did not have a dream come true. Tomorrow is the day that always faces the men and women." To any delegates who still thought that Lewis desired to continue as president, he reiterated, "You know when you first hired me I was something of a man, and when I leave you in a day or two I will still in my own mind be something of a man." Lewis thanked the delegates for receiving him so warmly, recalling the words of the Jesuit Gratian three centuries ago, "He shortly turns from the well who drinks his fill and the squeezed orange falls from the golden salver to the dung."

Thus did Lewis bid farewell as president of the CIO. Never before had he confessed publicly the personal loneliness that had been his life as labor leader. Having lived, in his own words, "among men and sometimes in far places," Lewis lacked intimate friends and the stable family relationships he most cherished. His sacrifice freely made, Lewis, in November 1940, fell to the ground like Gratian's squeezed orange— the departed leader of an army whose troops no longer rallied undivided behind their general.

Despite Lewis's explicit pledge to resign, friends and critics of the CIO leader refused to believe he would voluntarily relinquish the presidency. Communist and left-wing delegates still hoped that Lewis might be drafted, and the Hillman-ACW coalition feared that Lewis might change his mind. Instead of taking Lewis at his word and letting him depart gracefully and quietly, the ACW delegation assaulted the CIO president. They submitted a resolution criticizing the *CIO News* for printing no news on the Roosevelt campaign, and, losing that battle, charged Lewis directly with disrupting A.F. of L.–CIO unity negotiations. The ACW delegation, joined by Phil Murray, also demanded the passage of a resolution repudiating communism. When left-wing delegates appeared at Lewis's hotel room well after midnight to complain about the anticommunist resolution, Lewis responded, "What can you expect when the old man leaves, everybody will set their dogs howling at his heels. What can I do?" he asked. "What can a man do, a general who is being harried from the scene of battle? Whipped as his cohorts."

The ACW assault prompted Lewis to one last rhetorical flourish. Angered especially by the charge that he had sabotaged negotiations with the A. F. of L., Lewis rose to defend himself. Promising to spare the delegates a speech, Lewis delivered one of the longest and most frequently cited addresses of his career. To those who demanded further discussions with the A.F. of L. in order to explore its position on unity, Lewis characterized the Federation's negotiators disdainfully.

I have been an explorer in the American Federation of Labor. Explore the mind of Bill Green? Why, Bill and I had offices next door to each other for ten years. . . . I have done of lot of exploring in Bill's mind, and I give you my word there is nothing there.

Explore Matthew Woll's mind? I did. It is the mind of an insurance agent who used his position . . . to promote his insurance business.

Explore Tom Rickert's mind? I did, and here is what was in his mind. . . . I said he was getting $20,000 a year graft . . . and I had a paper in my pocket to prove it. He knew . . . that as true. And I thought then I had explored his mind enough.

Lewis next laid into the leaders of the needles trades unions, raising the suspicion that he planned to stir the anti-Semitism latent among many convention delegates. Dubinsky, remarked Lewis, had sworn by bell, book, and candle to remain loyal to the CIO. And where is he today?

He has crept back in the American Federation of Labor.... He is crying out now, and his voice laments like that of Rachel in the Wilderness, against the racketeers and the panderers and the crooks in that organization.

And Zaritsky. . . . He said, "Me too." And now above all the clamor comes the piercing wail and the laments of the Amalgamated Clothing Workers. And they say, "Peace, it is wonderful." And there is no peace.

Then, staring at the Amalgamated delegates, Lewis sneered, "Dubinsky took the easy way. Zaritsky took the easy way. If there is anybody else in the CIO who wants to take the easy way, let them go on." At this juncture, according to Matthew Josephson, "a great roar of applause came from the crowd, which burst into a renewed 'draft parade. . . . The whole convention seemed on the verge of riot and bloodshed.'"

Other observers at the convention, including most reporters who were then hostile to Lewis, saw it differently. Lewis, indeed, had many advocates among the delegates; but they scarcely seemed on the verge of riot and bloodshed, nor was Lewis eager to encourage such behavior. But the anti-Lewis element, especially that part associated with the Amalgamated, probably saw events as Josephson describes them. Ridiculed and frightened by Lewis, they hastened to telephone Hillman, then in Washington on official defense business, asking him to come to Atlantic City in order to assume command of the anti-Lewis forces.

On November 20, the convention's third day, Hillman arrived at the Chelsea well before the session's opening benediction in order to avoid a later entry that might engender an angry reaction from the Lewis claque. Advised by his lieutenants that Lewis intended a draft, Hillman acted to prevent that likelihood. Hillman spoke softly and unemotionally. If Lewis could steal from Shakespeare, so, too, could Hillman, although less dramatically. Playing the role of Mark Antony at great Caesar's funeral, Hillman heaped praise on the departing CIO president. Pledging that his own union would never desert the CIO, Hillman regretted that in the future John L. Lewis would not lead the organization. "I know that there is nothing else that he can do and will do and will agree to do but what he believes to be the best for the organized labor movement. . . . It is my considered judgment that when John L. Lewis steps down there must be a demand for Phil Murray." Those words, according to Josephson, coldly, logically buried the draft-Lewis movement.

If Hillman believed that his premature nomination of Murray for the CIO presidency killed the impending Lewis draft, he was deceiving himself. For Murray was already Lewis's hand-picked candidate as successor. All that stood between Murray and the CIO presidency in November 1940 was Murray's own fear about following in his master's footsteps. Murray feared that Lewis expected him to act in a subservient capacity to the UMW president. Before accepting the presidency, Murray, according to Lee Pressman, "went through the pangs of hell, because he knew that Lewis was putting him there . . . expecting him to act as an agent for Lewis, and that Lewis would have the hold over him as vice-president of the United Mine Workers. And Murray was . . . trying to ask himself . . . was he going to be a man in his own right, or not?"

But even Murray lacked alternatives. He was the only candidate acceptable to Lewis, the UMW delegates, the Hillman crowd, and, to a lesser degree, the communists. Crudely put, the choice for the CIO on November 20, 1940, was Murray or chaos. A left-wing successor to Lewis would have driven the Amalgamated and its allies out of the CIO; a right-wing nominee would have prompted Lewis, the miners, and a large majority of the delegates to rebel. Thus Murray allowed Lewis to weaken his resistance and to place his name in nomination on November 22, as a man "splendidly equipped with every natural and inherent talent, a gentleman . . . a scholar . . . a natural leader, an administrator, a family man, and a God-fearing man."

Elected president of the CIO unanimously, Murray rose to deliver a peculiar acceptance speech, an address in which he sought to dispel the self-doubt that had plagued him from the moment Lewis annointed him as successor. "I think I am a man," Murray remarked, recalling his chief's opening day allusion to his own manhood. "I think I have convictions, I think I have a soul and a heart and a mind. . . . with the exception, of course, of my soul, they all belong to me, every one of them." With this assurance to the CIO delegates that he would act for himself and no longer play the role of Lewis's loyal, unquestioning servant, Murray took the crown offered him by the departing champion.

For Lewis the 1940 CIO convention closed the most brilliant chapter in a long, varied, and tumultuous career as a labor leader. All that remained was leadership of the organization that he had built into the nation's largest and most powerful trade union. Lewis, in Lee Pressman's classical allusion to the Greek mythical figure Antaeus, who lost all his strength if lifted from the ground, returned to solid ground, the source of his strength, the United Mine Workers. "When Lewis uttered the words 'United Mine Workers of America'," recalled Pressman, "you had a feeling there that that was something much more important than when he said 'United States of America'." Or as Len DeCaux wrote in 1970, "John L. Lewis and the miners alone together—John L. Lewis/ UMW—that for him may have been a closer identification of man with many than was John L. Lewis/CIO."

16

A Man and His Union: John L. Lewis, the UMW, and the Coal Industry, 1935–40

For four decades the headquarters of the United Mine Workers had been in Indianapolis, a location which reflected the dominance of the Central Competitive Field in the soft-coal industry and, despite some exceptions, the private, voluntary character of collective bargaining in the coal industry. Convenient to the union's largest districts (Illinois and Pennsylvania) and to the largest operators' home offices (Pittsburgh, Cleveland, and Chicago), Indianapolis had served the UMW well.

With the coming of the New Deal, however, Indianapolis lost its locational advantages. Changes in the structure of the coal industry during the 1920s also rendered the Indiana capital less desirable. The rise of the southern Appalachian coal producers weakened the hegemony of the Central Competitive Field, and bargains struck in Pittsburgh, Cleveland, and Chicago no longer guaranteed stability in the nation's coal mines. More significantly, after the passage of the National Industrial Recovery Act in June 1933, decisions reached in Washington became as important to the future of coal mining as contracts between the miners' union and the operators. The locus of economic power in the coal industry had shifted for both union representatives and operators' associations from the coalfield to the nation's capital.

John L. Lewis grasped the significance of this change for his union. In 1934 he transferred UMW headquarters to Washington, first in rented space and then two years later to the University Club at Fifteenth and K Streets, N.W., which the UMW purchased for a half million dollars and refurnished in a style befitting a labor baron. Perhaps this was Lewis's way of showing that America in the 1930s had been turned upside down, that those born to wealth and power now had to share it with those who had thrust themselves up from the bottom.

From his new union headquarters in the nation's capital, John L. Lewis pressured the Roosevelt administration about coal-mining legislation, urged federal officials to enforce the basic coal industry codes of fair competition, and appeared regularly before congressional committees to testify in support of legislation. Lewis now entertained cabinet officers, ambassadors, congressmen, Labor Department bureaucrats, and the cream of Washington society. Wheeling and dealing among the American power elite, Lewis, by 1940, fashioned his labor organizaton into the largest, most secure, and most powerful single trade union in the nation.

Lewis built the mine workers into the nation's strongest union despite a protracted depression in soft and hard coal. The economic factors that had undermined the UMW during the prosperous 1920s continued to beset coal mining in the depressed 1930s. During no year in the decade 1930–39 did bituminous coal production ever equal levels reached during the 1920s. Anthracite coal, too, steadily declined in output.

Coal miners suffered as the industry in which they were employed declined. Although by the late 1930s coal miners earned higher hourly wages than other blue-collar workers, irregularity of employment reduced their weekly earnings. Among workers employed in manufacturing industries, only females in 1939 had substantially lower average weekly earnings than coal miners; even unskilled male workers earned almost as much: $22.82 a week compared to $22.99.

The economic plight of the mining industry plus the strength and stability of the UMW combined to bring five years of relative labor peace to the coal industry. Between 1934 and 1940, according to a special labor department report, an average of only 16 percent of all labor idleness caused by strikes nationally occurred in the coal industry, as compared to 61 percent from 1927 through 1932 and 42 percent from 1942 through 1944. Twice, in 1935 and again in 1939, national strikes closed down the bituminous mines; but in each case the dispute was more bargaining ritual than class war.

Labor stability, however, only relieved one of the coal industry's chronic ailments. Too many small operators still produced on the fringes of the soft-coal industry and reentered the marketplace and intensified competition whenever spot prices rose. Substantial differentials in wages, the largest factor in the cost of mining coal, still existed between districts and even within districts, further compounding the competitive difficulties of mine owners, especially the higher-wage northern operators. Despite the code of fair competition adopted by the bituminous coal industry in September 1933 and amended the following year, many operators continued to cut prices and also wages.

By mid-December 1934 Lewis bemoaned the NRA's inability to compel observance of the code of fair competition. In January 1935, at a public hearing to consider amendments to the bituminous coal code, Lewis reminded coal operators and NRA officials that the UMW no longer intended to tolerate the NRA's neglect "to enforce the provisions of the code upon those who flagrantly or otherwise evade its provisions," a failure that threatened to involve the coal industry in "a species of gorilla [*sic*] economic warfare," in which the union becomes responsible for maintaining the wage and price structure through incessant industrial conflict.

Lewis and the northern operators preferred federal legislation to regulate the soft-coal industry over rules of competition set under the NRA. Their desire for such special legislation intensified in May 1935, when the Supreme Court declared the price-fixing provisions of the NIRA unconstitutional. From February through October 1935 the UMW and the northern operators lobbied Congress and the White House to obtain passage of the Guffey-Snyder Coal Stabilization Bill, which would mandate the creation of a federal administrative agency to set minimum sale prices for soft coal, allocate markets equitably among different producers, eliminate wage differentials that caused unfair competition, and rationalize the entire structure of the industry.

While Congress debated the Guffey-Snyder Bill, Lewis and the mine operators bargained about a new union-management contract. Between February and October 1935, the negotiations broke down repeatedly, causing Lewis, unwilling to risk a strike when unemployment remained high, to gladly accede to requests from the Roosevelt administration that the UMW extend its 1934 bituminous agreement until a new contract could be negotiated. Yet he used the strike threat as a weapon with which to pressure Roosevelt into supporting the miners' bargaining position. If only the president would compel the operators to sign a new contract, Lewis advised Roosevelt, no walkout would occur.

But coal operators were too divided among themselves to come to terms with the union. Northern operators sought the abolition of southern wage differentials; southerners demanded the retention of such differentials; and operators everywhere worried that existing inter- and intraunion wage differentials offered some producers "unfair" competitive advantages.

From March to September, Lewis, at President Roosevelt's behest, agreed to several extensions of the 1934 agreement. Lewis also cut his union's demands to minor revisions in the wage terms of the 1934 contract. The operators, however, remained intransigent and sat silently as the miners' representatives did all the talking. Finally, when further bargaining brought no concessions from operators, Lewis, on September 23, called the miners out. What collective bargaining had failed to achieve in eight months, economic power won in a single day. On September 24 the operators made their first offer to the UMW, and on the evening of September 29, an agreement was reached that extended the terms of the 1934 contract, retained the basic North-South wage differential and other customary district differentials, and granted a marginal upward revision in wages. By October 4 the various steel company-owned captive coal mines also signed new contracts incorporating the wage increases into their basic 1933 agreement with the union.

The 1935 negotiations revealed graphically what had become the standard pattern in coal industry-union bargaining as practiced by Lewis. The strike functioned more as a threat than a reality, more as a weapon to inveigle presidential intervention than as a club to beat employers. Rather than risk precipitous or protracted strikes, conflicts that threatened to harm an industry in perilous economic condition and weaken the finances of a union recently recovered from the ravages of the 1920s, Lewis preferred temporary contract extensions and short, although massive, strikes that illustrated the UMW's potential power. The Roosevelt administration's aversion to industrial conflicts that threatened recovery and its relative sympathy for organized labor made Lewis's tactics effective. In the event, Roosevelt usually put more pressure on operators than on union negotiators.

In 1937 collective bargaining produced a two-year renewal (until March 31, 1939) of the basic 1935 agreement. Again operators consented to a modest advance in day and tonnage rates and yet retained their traditional regional wage differentials. Under the renewal's terms $6 became the basic minimum daily wage in coalfields north of the Ohio River and $5.60 the rate in fields south of the Ohio.

By 1937 the miners' union and coal operators also seemed to have achieved their legislative goals. In 1935, Congress had enacted the original Guffey-Snyder Coal Stabilization Act. But the act was declared unconstitutional by the Supreme Court less than a year later, largely because of its wage and hours provisions. Eventually, after a legislative struggle of more than a year, in 1937 Congress passed the Guffey-Vinson Coal Act, an act that retained all the economic stabilization provisions (primarily price-fixing and market allocation under federal administration) of the 1935 act but eliminated the wage and hour clauses. This act survived review by Roosevelt's reconstructed Supreme Court and attempted the federal rationalization of the soft-coal industry that Lewis had sought fruitlessly for more than a decade.

Harmonious relations between the UMW and the mine operators failed to restore economic prosperity to the soft-coal industry. During the two-year life of the 1937 agreement, the period of the "Roosevelt Depression," bituminous production stagnated, coal companies operated at a loss, and machinery continued to displace miners. Thus, as the moment approached in 1939 to negotiate a new contract between the UMW and the Appalachian Operators' Association, the time seemed less than propitious for Lewis to advance the claims of his membership.

Collective bargaining in the soft-coal industry in 1939 manifested Lewis's character as union negotiator. As usual during collective bargaining sessions between the UMW and the coal operators, Lewis, although accompanied by an international policy committee that numbered more than 150 members and a smaller negotiating group that included all the union district presidents, thoroughly dominated his bargaining team. Indeed, Lewis's voice was the only one that counted.

From the first, Lewis sought no costly new benefits for coal miners. He focused primarily on achieving union security. He thought that operators might concede one of two union demands that cost no money: abolition of the penalty clause (a contract provision that fined miners and union for strikes allegedly in violation of the contract) or institution of a closed shop. Throughout eight weeks of collective bargaining, from March 14 to May 14, and a combination strike-lockout that lasted a month, Lewis struggled solely to achieve one of his two nonmonetary objectives.

Lewis also pursued what had become by 1939 his customary strategy for achieving union goals. Once again he sought to obtain federal endorsement for the miners' claims. Only when moderation failed to produce tangible results did Lewis play labor's angry man, promising a full-scale nationwide strike that, he hastened to advise Labor Secretary Frances Perkins and President Roosevelt, would threaten the economy with severe damage.

The Appalachian Joint Conference opened on March 14 in New York with both sides far apart. Asking for a six-hour day (and thirty-hour week) and an advance in wages, the UMW negotiating team responded caustically to the operators' suggestion that the 1937 agreement be extended two more years with a fifty-cent reduction in the daily wage rate. The next day Lewis softened the union's position, asking the operators to join with him in pledging that there would be no closure of the mines on April 1 if a new contract had not yet been negotiated. Yet for the next two weeks the operators would neither discuss the union's proposals nor join with Lewis in pledging to keep the mines open on April 1.

Thwarted by the operators, Lewis turned to the federal government, asking federal mediator James Dewey to enter the negotiations. Joining the bargaining at the last minute, March 31, Dewey found the situation a complete mess. The federal mediator characterized the operators as "bitter, nasty, and antagonistic," even eager to risk a strike. Lewis, on the contrary, acted respectfully toward Dewey and pleaded for federal intervention.

Lacking an agreement on April 1, the Appalachian mines fell silent. April 1 was a miners' holiday and April 2 was a Sunday, another nonworking day; but on April 3 all the union miners in the region laid down their tools. Yet Lewis preferred to consider the shutdown a lockout, because he had offered to recommend that union members remain at work in the absence of a new agreement if operators pledged to bargain seriously.

Industry and union negotiators continued to talk in New York. During the lockout-strike's first week, the conferees made no progress, even though Lewis dropped all of the union's original twenty-eight demands but one—abolition of the penalty clause. According to Dewey, who apparently had become an advocate of Lewis's beliefs, the coal operators saw themselves as surrogates for large industry fighting to save American capitalism from the closed shop and union tyranny. The great steel companies, railroads, and utilities, Dewey reported to his superiors in Washington, had interfered in the negotiations and pressured the coal operators to reject Lewis's proposal.

The first week in May brought no resolution to the dispute, and the situation deteriorated when Lewis called out the miners in the outlying districts on May 4 and 5, thereby denying the nation all supplies of coal. On May 7, Lewis made public a letter addressed to John R. Steelman, director of the Department of Labor's Conciliation Service, which placed total responsibility for the impasse on the operators and criticized the federal role in the dispute.

Lewis's May 7 letter had the intended effect. The next day the joint Appalachian conferees met in special session, joined by Dewey, Steelman, and Secretary Perkins. Perkins pleaded with the operators to grant the union shop and presented, without modificaton, the union's case for it. Her plea was unanswered by the mine owners, who preferred an invitation to meet with President Roosevelt in the White House the next day, May 9, in an attempt to resolve the dispute. The president proved noncommittal. Perhaps to the surprise of the participants, he repeated worn platitudes. Warning of the national damage that would result from a protracted strike, Roosevelt asked the conferees to reach an agreement within twenty-four hours.

The president's injunction had little effect. On May 10, Perkins informed Roosevelt that the operators and miners were further apart than ever—indeed were so angry with each other that federal mediators thought it best to keep them in separate rooms. "John Lewis is mad, rough and angry and everybody is mad," reported the secretary. "There is no more of that peaceful talk that the President heard yesterday. John Lewis is very ugly today—very.ugly," lamented Perkins, "and we don't know how to handle him. One of those moods are on him. I really believe it would be a wise thing," she suggested, "for the President to call John Lewis at the Hotel Biltmore . . . and pacify him—give him a little flattery. It will go a long way with John."

Secretary Perkins obviously did not know her man or his personality quirks. Lewis's anger was feigned, not real—a tactic he had found useful in the past during collective bargaining and would use persistently in the future. Throughout the coal controversy, Roosevelt had sweet-talked Lewis without explicitly endorsing the miners' claim to union security. This presidential approach only angered Lewis. Now, on May 11, as the coal conflict reached its climax, Lewis demanded federal support, a commitment from the president or his lieutenants sanctioning the union shop for coal miners.

Precisely what Roosevelt did in response to Perkins's suggestion and Lewis's demands remains unknown. Certain inferences, however, may be drawn. On May 13 Lewis informed Jett Lauck that he was delighted with the president's endorsement of the bituminous miners' position. On May 11, Lewis had ordered the miners in the outlying districts back to work under a contract that included the union shop. And the next day, May 12, the northern Appalachian operators consented to a new contract with the UMW that extended the 1937 agreement to March 31, 1941, and granted coal miners a union shop. The southern operators left the conference and declared their intention of fighting to preserve the open shop. Under pressure from the Roosevelt administration, recalcitrant operators and the southern Appalachian mine owners soon acceded to similar demands. And on May 19, a contract signed between the UMW and the captive mines of U.S. Steel in Harlan County, Kentucky, set the pattern for the captive mine industry. That agreement simply extended the terms of the existing contract without including a union shop provision, because it never included a penalty clause. Pleased with his work, federal mediator Steelman reported to Perkins on May 19 that everything looked better now, especially for the UMW.

If Steelman smiled, the UMW *Journal* gloated. In its May 15 issue, under the headline "United Mine Workers Win First Union Shop Contract," the *Journal* bragged about the greatest victory ever achieved by the UMW—a union-shop contract for the entire bituminous coal industry. "The new agreement," UMW members read, "makes it impossible for any rival organization to obtain a foothold in the bituminous mining industry... and makes certain the future integrity, security, and permanence of the United Mine Workers of America."

Lewis had finally conquered the commercial mines, placing his union in an ideal position to reap the material rewards that would flow its way in 1940 and 1941 as the nation armed for war. Only the captive mines, 95 percent of whose employees belonged to the UMW, still refused to concede the union-shop principle, primarily because of its implication for the steel industry. So complete did Lewis's triumph of May 1939 seem that editorialists and columnists interpreted the settlement as a personal victory for Lewis, "strengthening his position in labor ranks to a point approaching dictatorship."

The character of the mine workers' union in the late 1930s lent credence to press portraits of John L. Lewis as a labor dictator. *Autocratic, imperious, bureaucratic,* and *machinelike* seemed terms most expressive of the nature of the UMW. By 1940 the internecine union struggles of the predepression years and the recurrent challenges to union leadership by insurgent rank-and-filers seemed only a distant memory. Served in the UMW hierarchy by close family members, loyal lieutenants, and sycophantic followers, Lewis ran a frictionless machine.

The men who had challenged Lewis's domination of the UMW from 1919 to 1932 had either disappeared from the scene or allied with their former foe. Frank Farrington, Alex Howat, John Walker, and Duncan MacDonald no longer disrupted union conventions nor disturbed Lewis. John Brophy, Adolph Germer, and Powers Hapgood now served Lewis loyally, primarily in the CIO and secondarily in the United Mine Workers.

Lewis, in 1940, commanded union troops many of whom were unfamiliar with their organization's past history. Although a lack of concrete evidence makes it impossible to quantify what proportion of UMW membership was new to the union in the late 1930s, reasonable guesses can be made. The regions in which the post-1933 UMW grew most rapidly included southern Appalachia and southwestern Pennsylvania — districts traditionally resistant to trade unionism. Most West Virginia, Virginia, Kentucky, Tennessee, Alabama, and Pennsylvania miners who joined the UMW in the 1930s had not hitherto been union members. Even in the Central Competitive Field and the once well-organized northern outlying districts, the UMW membership had fallen so low by 1933 that the members recruited during the New Deal years, especially the younger ones, probably had joined the union for the first time. Union members such as these sang the praises of John L. Lewis for building up the union.

With the old union insurgents absent or tamed and the new members and their convention delegates ecstatic about Lewis, the UMW conventions in 1936, 1938, and 1940 proceeded placidly. Lewis handpicked the chairmen of the major convention committees, who diligently served the interests of the international officers. Barring one exception that proved the rule, debate never flared among delegates on the convention floor.

The one issue that ignited debate at the 1936, 1938, and 1940 conventions—the question of district autonomy, that is, the right of the UMW's separate districts to elect their own officers—exposed both Lewis's dictatorial power in the UMW and his singular interpretation of union democracy. In 1936 most union districts, instead of possessing the right to elect their own officers, were governed by officials chosen by Lewis and responsible directly to the UMW president, not the district membership. By the late 1930s, however, as the union's size and strength grew, some districts began to demand the right to elect their own officers. Yet to each demand from below for district autonomy, the UMW's officers responded identically. "We believe," the officers reported to the conventions of 1936, 1938, and 1940, "that the International Executive Board should continue to exercise its good judgment . . . and to act at such time with respect to autonomy in any particular district as in their judgment will best meet the needs of the situation."

Lewis and his fellow officers also spelled out precisely what factors in their judgment would "best meet the needs of the situation." Democracy, for one thing, the officers declared not pertinent to autonomy. "Some people," they implied, "confuse democracy with license." But not the UMW's officers, all of whom defined democracy as that which best "protects and advances the . . . interests of the membership." In their view, the primary responsibility of international officers was not to extend the voting rights of union members but rather to ensure that the UMW faithfully observed the terms of its contractual obligations.

Lewis proved blunter in castigating the advocates of autonomy. "Do you want an efficient organization or do you want merely a political instrumentality?" he asked delegates. "That is all that is involved in this matter—business administration, effective internal policies, and no denial of the fundamental principles of democracy . . . learn to walk before you run and learn to wait while you train some of these young men . . . to be the successor of Van Bittner and President Mark and the men from these other districts." And Lewis invariably reminded delegates that in the past autonomy had often elected district officials who absconded with union funds, squandered such funds foolishly, and in other ways weakened and bankrupted the organization. We are not discussing a fundamental principle, Lewis suggested, but rather a question of "business expediency," that is, "whether you prefer to sacrifice the efficiency of your organization in some respect for a little more academic freedom in the selection of some local representatives in a number of districts." For Lewis, the answer was clear, and the advice that he gave delegates never varied: business before democracy, efficiency above "academic freedom."

In 1936 the advocates of autonomy were sufficiently numerous to demand a roll call vote on which they won the support of 602 (37 percent) delegates compared to 1,014 (63 percent) who supported their officers. How many of the 602 defenders of autonomy would have voted for union democracy had the choice been clearly between the legitimation of district autonomy and Lewis's continuance in office remains questionable. What is noteworthy is that such a large majority of the delegates in 1936 voted against the democratic principle and in favor of presidential prerogatives. The autonomy advocates of 1938 could not even obtain a roll vote, having to be satisfied simply with recording their own votes for democracy. Only eighty delegates, moreover, compared to the previous convention's 602, recorded themselves in favor of autonomy. At the 1940 convention again no roll call vote occurred on the question, and even fewer delegates declared themselves opposed on the record to "guided democracy."

Such placid, even harmonious, miners' conventions disappointed labor journalists. By 1940 reporters assigned to the UMW convention struggled to dramatize the banal and, as a consequence, manufactured imaginary insurgencies. Two incidents in 1940 that journalists cited to prove rank-and-file dissatisfaction with Lewis instead revealed the UMW president's invincibility. First was the issue of President Roosevelt's third term bid. Daily newspapers reported rank-and-file pro-Roosevelt resolutions as a revolt against Lewis. But convention delegates made no protest when Lewis ridiculed the president, nor did they demur when Lewis buried all the third term resolutions in committee and demanded instead that the UMW endorse no candidate in 1940. Whatever discontent flared among the UMW rank and file as a result of the Lewis-Roosevelt rupture produced at best a silent revolt, one that in no way threatened Lewis's hegemony in the miners' union.

Second, near the close of the convention's third day, as Lewis delivered a national radio speech in commemoration of the union's golden anniversary, a red flag with the hammer and sickle of the USSR rose behind the rostrum. Obviously intending to embarrass Lewis, who characterized the appearance of the Soviet flag as "a cowardly, reprehensible, and dastardly trick," the perpetrators of the incident were never discovered. Communists and labor leftists certainly had no reason to embarrass Lewis in January 1940, as he was then their firmest ally in the labor movement. Insurgent UMW members would more likely have criticized Lewis for his class collaborationist tendencies than for his leftist sympathies.

The morning after the flag incident, Lewis cajoled delegates into a display of solidarity. Reacting directly to press reports suggesting rank-and-file discontent with his leadership, Lewis observed sarcastically that in 1940, for the first time in the history of the UMW, not a single grievance had been filed against its officers. Where, he asked, "are the complaints against the dictator of the United Mine Workers of America? Where is the man in the United Mine Workers of America whom John L. Lewis has injured?" Beseeching delegates to vote on a resolution of confidence in their leaders, Lewis snarled, "Every once in a while I get a good laugh at our enemies." After the vote, he proclaimed that twenty-four hundred delegates had unanimously "affirmed that peace and tranquility and confidence dwell in the ranks of the United Mine Workers." Not satisfied with a unanimous vote of confidence, Lewis turned to reporters at the press table and remarked: "I commend that report to the attention of the *Chicago Tribune,* the New York *Herald-Tribune,* the Scripps-Howard newspapers, and various other publications in the country... who have been utterly convinced that the ruthless and terrible John Lewis was totally inconsiderate of the rights of members of his organization. Think it over gentlemen!"

Words Lewis first trumpeted before a miners' convention in 1930 bore real meaning ten years later. To a desperate band of men gathered in Indianapolis in March 1930, striving solely to preserve their union's integrity, Lewis proudly proclaimed that he "pleaded their case from the pulpit and the public platform, in joint conference with the associated operators... before the bar of state legislatures, in the councils of the President's cabinet, and in the public press of this nation—not in the quavering tones of a feeble mendicant asking alms, but in the thundering voice of the captain of a mighty host." Those words were indeed a fitting description of Lewis's labors for coal miners and their union during the New Deal years. They would prove even more descriptive during World War II.

IV

From Resistance to Resignation, 1941–69

17

A Man Alone, 1941–42

John L. Lewis's dramatic retirement as CIO president symbolized his break with the New Deal phenomenon of which he had been an integral part. From the UMW organizing drive of 1933 to the presidential election of 1940, Lewis had relished the role of charismatic leader of the masses. Now, in the 1940s, he found himself isolated as a lone defiant labor defender of free enterprise and voluntary collective bargaining against government encroachment.

At the close of the 1940 CIO convention, Lewis still possessed considerable influence and numerous allies. His close associate Phil Murray was CIO president, and his outspoken support of a noninterventionist foreign policy led communist-oriented unionists, Midwestern Populists, and conservative, pro-business America Firsters all to seek him as an ally.

Yet these were weak alliances. Over the next two years the bonds of friendship between Lewis and Murray snapped. And joining Murray in his forced departure from the UMW would be some of the organization's most able field generals: Van Bittner, Pat Fagan, William Mitch, and others. The Nazi invasion of Russia would terminate the communists' comradeship with Lewis, and Pearl Harbor would silence the remaining antiwar coalition. Lewis's economic policies, moreover, would alienate many in the business community and general public who had not already condemned him for his isolationist views. All this was followed by the death of his wife, Myrta. By the fall of 1942, Lewis and his union faced a world of enemies—alone.

In the months immediately following the 1940 CIO convention, Lewis retreated from public view. He sincerely hoped that his withdrawal from the limelight would enable Phil Murray to establish his own leadership of the CIO. A low profile might also help dissipate dissension inside the UMW that stemmed from Lewis's personal opposition to Roosevelt.

In the union elections held in December 1940, approximately twenty thousand miners directly expressed their disapproval of Lewis by refusing to endorse his uncontested reelection while casting ballots for Murray and Kennedy, both of whom also ran unopposed.

In either late January or early February 1941, Lewis's withdrawal became mandatory when he suffered a heart attack. Now sixty-one and faced with the most serious threat to his health, he hid his condition from the press and his own union membership. Aside from his immediate family, he allowed only Phil Murray and Lee Pressman to see him incapacitated, and as soon as the doctor permitted, he escaped to Florida to convalesce. It was not until the convening of the Appalachian Joint Wage Conference in New York City on March 11 that Lewis made his first major public appearance since resigning as CIO president.

Lewis believed the 1941 bituminous coal negotiations to be critical. Naturally, a major bargaining success would assure him the continued support of the miners, and the revived prosperity of the coal industry, generated by war abroad and mobilization at home, created an environment in which such advances could be won. Equally important, Lewis feared that the United States would soon enter the global conflict, and he wanted to achieve maximum gains for his organization before the government imposed stringent wartime economic controls. In large measure Lewis's behavior in the spring of 1941, as throughout the mobilization and war period, stemmed from his memory of the negative impact World War I had had on his union's members. Viewing the coal miners in 1917–19 as the "innocent victims of an ill-advised wartime economy," he vowed that they would not suffer again.

Even though the old contract was to expire at midnight, March 31, the Appalachian Joint Wage Conference did not begin serious negotiations until March 25, when the operators felt confident that Congress would renew the Guffey Coal Act (due to expire in April), which permitted price adjustments in proportion to rises in labor cost. Soon thereafter, the operators granted a dollar-a-day increase to daymen and commensurate raises to other classes of workers in exchange for the union yielding on its proposal for a guarantee of two hundred working days a year.

With one issue settled, Lewis next introduced the union demand for removal of wage differentials. Lewis felt that reenactment of the Guffey Act removed any justification for regional wage differentials, and he viewed the defense mobilizaton drive as a propitious moment for the UMW to act. He also feared that if war came and the government froze prevailing wage differentials, competitive advantages would shift coal production to the southern fields, where hostility to the union remained greatest. Northern operators endorsed Lewis's proposal. Southerners emphatically answered: Never!

When the old contract expired on March 31, President Roosevelt issued his customary plea for the mines to remain in operation and sent John R. Steelman to New York to sit in on the negotiations. April 1 being Miners' Day, a traditional UMW holiday, the mines would have closed anyway. On April 2 the miners continued to stay away from the pits, honoring the union's policy of "No contract, No work." According to government estimates, the nation then possessed a thirty-day supply of soft coal.

Since removal of the differential was mutually advantageous, the northern operators and the union united in an alliance to compel the South to accept this provision. As a consequence, on April 11, the southerners abruptly withdrew from the Appalachian Conference and appealed to Roosevelt and Perkins to certify "the case of the south" to the National Defense Mediation Board (NDMB). To create the image of moderation, however, they invited the union to confer with them in Washington. Lewis promptly rebuffed their gesture, criticizing it as unreasonable because negotiations were still proceeding in New York with both the northern operators and representatives of the anthracite industry.

The president's signing of the renewed Guffey Act on April 12 removed one impediment to a settlement. With the coal stabilization program assured for another two years, the mine workers and northern operators arrived at a tentative agreement on April 16. Despite a personal request from the Secretary of Labor, however, both parties refused formally to sign the contract and reopen the northern pits. The northern operators and the union intended to pressure the southern operators by blaming them for the continued curtailment of coal production.

Apparently, both Roosevelt and Perkins viewed the South's efforts to send the dispute to the NDMB as an attempt to escape the consequences of free collective bargaining. And so, on the evening of April 21, President Roosevelt issued a two-part appeal to the nation's miners and operators. He asked that (1) miners and operators already in agreement resume coal production under the terms of that agreement, and (2) that the operators and miners who had not yet reached an agreement enter into wage negotiations and at the same time reopen the mines, the agreement ultimately reached to be made retroactive to the date of resuming work.

The next morning representatives of the southern operators hurried to the White House, where they talked to presidential secretary Major General E. M. Watson. After the meeting a spokesman for the group informed the press that they were returning to New York to meet with the union "at the request of President Roosevelt." At 9:00 that night the Appalachian Southern Coal Operators Wage Conference commenced bargaining with a delegation from the UMW. Negotiations resumed the following day as Lewis shuttled back and forth between the southern meeting in the Hotel Commodore and the northern conference in the Biltmore Hotel.

Then, at 7:00 that night, word reached the southerners that the UMW and northern operators had accepted the president's plan. In doing so, Lewis and the northern operators skillfully blended Roosevelt's two-part proposal into one: Northern mines would open on the basis of the unsigned contract *with* the resumption of mining in the southern fields and continuation of negotiations along the lines outlined by Roosevelt. The responsibility for accepting the president's plan now rested solely on the southerners. Realizing that they had been outflanked, southern operators walked out of the conference without saying a word. Later that night conciliation chief Steelman informed newsmen that the southerners had not answered Roosevelt's plea. "By leaving the negotiations and by failing to comply with the President's request to open the mines," he observed, "they have taken upon themselves a grave responsibility."

The next morning, April 24, Secretary of Labor Perkins certified the dispute to the NDMB, which immediately appointed a panel to hear the case headed by William H. Davis, a New York patent attorney and NDMB vice-chairman. On April 27 the panel recommended that the southern operators accept the president's April 21 proposal. Lacking any other recourse, the southern operators agreed to the plan on April 28. During the next two days the union negotiated temporary agreements with the northern and southern operators reopening the Appalachian fields. With coal production renewed, the UMW consented to a request by the southern group for a recess in talks until May 12.

Throughout May and June bargaining between the union and the southern operators brought no results. The NDMB, taking up the case a second time, recommended that the southern operators eliminate the differential for day men, and on June 9 they agreed to do so.

But Lewis sought more for his men. He demanded that the southerners sign a contract identical to the one the UMW had negotiated with northern operators on June 19. One of the clauses granted the union the right to call workers out of the pits for "memorial periods." Another provision, the protective wage clause, authorized the UMW to "call and maintain strikes throughout the entire Appalachian Area when necessary to preserve and maintain the integrity and competitive parity of this Agreement."

The southern operators, naturally, resisted the additional clauses, but after some compromises and more threats by Lewis, twelve of the thirteen southern associations at the conference consented to a contract almost identical to the one the North had signed. Harlan County, the lone holdout in 1939, still objected to the imposition of the union shop. Lewis refused to sign with the other operators until Harlan County joined the fold. Following more negotiations and the intervention of William Davis, a settlement was finally concluded on July 5.

The 1941 bituminous contract constituted a significant victory for Lewis and the union. The UMW had compelled the South to accept a contract almost identical to that of the North. Lewis attained the union's primary objectives of a dollar a day or its equivalent in pay increases, elimination of the forty-cent differential, vacations with pay, and the union shop. The protective wage clause and the memorial period provision, moreover, granted Lewis additional weapons with which to impose his influence on the industry.

The prolonged negotiations also heralded a shift in Lewis's style. Always a resourceful negotiator, he now began to display a love of strategy for its own sake. No doubt the war news competing for headlines with UMW activities partly stimulated his fascination with the subtleties of maneuvers. Yet his new tactics also reflected the miners' lack of labor allies: The smaller the army, the more skillful must be the general.

In a poststrike analysis of "the great coal drama of 1941," Lewis found little to praise in the conduct of the government. The administration's intervention in the coal dispute, he charged, displayed a lack of coordination, direction, and even wisdom. Twice during March, William S. Knudsen, director general of Office of Production Management, conferred with operators on ways to keep the mines open, yet failed to consult with Lewis on either occasion and ignored the union's concern with insuring retroactive pay. Similarly, the National Defense Mediation Board, in its initial recommendations, failed to solve the dispute, and Lewis easily subverted its subsequent award.

Indeed, nothing the Roosevelt administration did by the spring of 1941 would satisfy Lewis. Although the president pressured the operators to meet the UMW's demands, Lewis was not grateful. Rather than thank Roosevelt for his behind-the-scenes intervention, Lewis preferred to humiliate the president publicly.

Lewis - Hillman animosity

Nothing, including mobilization efforts, came between Lewis and his feud with the Roosevelt administration. Yet Lewis adroitly avoided assailing the president personally, focusing his criticism instead on Roosevelt's lieutenants, particularly Sidney Hillman. At a testimonial dinner for Phil Murray in April 1941, Lewis raged about Hillman's collaborationist policies. Again, at a CIO leadership conference in July, he castigated Hillman for endorsing Roosevelt's use of the army to break a strike at North American Aviation in Inglewood, California.

Throughout 1941, Lewis's influence in the labor movement deteriorated. As defense efforts intensified, numerous CIO officials turned deaf to Lewis's cry of labor independent and unregulated, and they joined Hillman in working with the administration. Hitler's invasion of Russia on June 22, 1941, further splintered the Lewis anti-Roosevelt coalition, as pro-communists switched their foreign policy. Lewis remained silent on the international situation until early August, when he joined Herbert Hoover, Alfred Landon, Charles Dawes, and other conservatives in an appeal to Congress to halt Roosevelt's step-by-step projection of the country into the conflict. Immediately, communists and fellow travelers allied with New Dealers to attack Lewis. Left-wingers such as Lee Pressman and Len DeCaux divorced themselves from the man they once esteemed. Albert Fitzgerald, the newly elected president of the CIO's United Electric, Radio and Machine Workers, fervently denounced Lewis, and delegates to the State, County and Municipal Workers' convention acted as if the former CIO president had never existed.

Respect for Lewis diminished throughout the labor movement. In a poll of the nation's leading labor editors, fifty-two participants supported the administration and its defense policies; only three endorsed Lewis's views. Another survey, conducted by *Fortune,* indicated that factory workers disapproved of Lewis's part in labor relations more than they did the roles of Bethlehem Steel, General Motors, Henry Ford, or Roosevelt. Even in his citadel, the United Mine Workers of America, discontent with his policies emerged. Irritated over the increased union assessments by checkoff collection, in September and October anthracite miners staged a wildcat strike against the union's leadership.

Lewis reacted to the loss of influence in his customary manner. First, he strengthened his own position by fortifying the mine workers' union. The assessment policy that provoked the September anthracite rebellion was part of a drive to strengthen the organization against economic adversity. He also reorganized catchall District 50, placing Ora Gasaway at its head and his daughter, Kathryn, as secretary-treasurer. Intending to breathe new life into his private labor movement, Lewis demoted or forced into premature retirement about thirty District 50 officers. Leaders in both the A.F. of L. and CIO took note of this as a threat to their domains.

Lewis also lashed out at his antagonists with a zeal reminiscent of his attacks on Farrington, Howat, Brophy and other opponents in the 1920s. Visions of conspiracies against himself and his union pervaded Lewis's speeches and writings. He depicted Sidney Hillman as the sinister force behind the scenes who convinced the administration to inject the NDMB into the bituminous dispute. Likewise, he charged John Brophy with leading "a poison squad in the headquarters of the C.I.O." "This group," he maintained, "systematically and quite maliciously have been disseminating misinformation and propaganda to favored newspaper correspondents, radio commentators and columnists, designed to besmirch the character and impair the standing" of the head of the UMW.

Such behavior suggested to many, including Roosevelt, that Lewis no longer had full control of his full mental facilities. Yet behind each of Lewis's accusations lay some factual basis. Hillman and Roosevelt did, indeed, actively interject themselves in the mediation board's handling of coal disputes. And someone at CIO headquarters was releasing malicious stories about Lewis to the press. Lewis, moreover, had learned early in his career that his paranoid style generated sympathy among both coal miners and ordinary citizens. To observers then, Lewis appeared as an extremely complex individual with one foot rooted in reality and the other in fantasy. Lewis-watchers continually debated which foot was more firmly planted.

Accounts of the captive mine controversy in the fall of 1941 ascribe a host of sinister motives to Lewis. No longer able to attack him as a defender of Moscow, a few critics shifted to castigating him as an agent of Berlin. More frequently, commentators asserted that Lewis opportunistically grasped any occasion to embarrass Roosevelt. A third hypothesis suggested that Lewis sought to reestablish his leadership of the labor movement by challenging the emergency mobilization program's restraints on unions.

Such explanations reflected the conventional notion during the defense crisis and war period that anyone who acted in a manner seemingly detrimental to the nation's security must be either power hungry, traitorous, or mentally disturbed. Yet Lewis demanded the union shop in the captive mines neither as a megalomaniac, or paranoid hater of the president, nor even a saboteur of national defense. Rather, he behaved primarily as an aggressive labor leader who failed to anticipate fully the impact of his actions.

After settling with the northern and southern Appalachian operators in early July, the officers of the UMW began negotiating contracts with the nation's other coal producers. All of the outlying districts accepted the miners' demands except the steel companies' captive mines. Willing to grant most of the provisions in the basic contract, the steel industry steadfastly rejected the union shop. In 1939 the union had acquiesced to steel's intransigence. But in the summer of 1941 Lewis feared that the nation would soon enter the war. Under such circumstances, he felt it imperative "to 'batten down the hatches' and see to it that when the mine workers union was frozen, it would be with a union shop prevailing every place a man dug coal."

An industry-wide union shop including the captive mines, moreover, represented a reasonable and natural growth of the UMW. By the fall of 1941, 99 percent of the workers in mines under contract were union members, including 95 percent of the miners employed in the captive pits. Because 90 percent of the total annual bituminous production was mined under union-shop agreements, Lewis thought it only logical for the UMW to demand a similar status in the captive mines, where all but 5 percent of the eligible employees had joined the union. In more normal times, with the union free to unleash its full arsenal of weapons, it seems probable that the steel companies would ultimately have yielded to the demand for a union shop.

Indeed, hints exist that the steel executives recognized the logic of the UMW's position. Throughout the controversy industry spokesmen seemed aware that the union possessed the ability to win its point. But they opposed the demand out of fear that if they granted the union shop in the collieries, they would be forced to do likewise in the steel mills and shipyards. Steel company executives preferred that the government impose the union shop on the captive mines so that the industry might argue that the union shop in the mines should be considered neither a precedent nor a change in the steel industry's basic policy. In a memorandum to Roosevelt marked "Personal and Confidential," Myron Taylor expressed his belief that the directors of U.S. Steel "would abandon the defense of the freedom of the workers to join or not to join a union only if you issued an executive order in the captive mine case, or if Congress enacted legislation which took from the shoulders of the Board the responsibility for that decision. In either of those instances, I am confident the corporation would promptly comply."

Throughout the summer of 1941 the union and captive mine operators haggled over the union-shop issue. With the talks going nowhere, Lewis ordered a walkout of the fifty-three thousand captive mine workers on Monday, September 15. Then on September 17, with his point made, Lewis consented to reopening the mines for a month while the NDMB considered the dispute.

For the next thirty days the miners worked, the steel industry profited, and the NDMB panel procrastinated. The union waited patiently, expecting the logic of the situation to compel the panel to recommend in its favor. Finally, on October 21, Lewis informed Davis that he wearied of delay and that the temporary agreement under which the mines operated would terminate at midnight October 25. Because October 26 fell on a Sunday when the mines normally closed, the NDMB still had five days to render a decision.

The pace of activity at the board promptly quickened. According to the UMW *Journal,* Sidney Hillman led "Chairman Davis up to the White House where the captive coal problem was tucked into the category of a political issue." On October 24 the NDMB subcommittee investigating the dispute released an opinion adroitly sidestepping the central question. "It became clear to the members of the Mediation Board," the report explained, "that there could be no meeting of minds in the conference before it with respect to the two conflicting rights asserted in the present dispute."

Although unwilling to rule on the union-shop issue, the members of the NDMB subcommittee proposed two new ways of resolving the controversy. First, they suggested submitting the question to the full mediation board, with both parties pledging beforehand to accept the final verdict. Second, they recommended renewed collective bargaining and, if that failed to produce agreement, binding arbitration. In either event, mining operations were to continue.

A memorandum presenting the president's views accompanied the panel's opinion. The memorandum expressed the president's hope that "if the parties to the dispute adopt the second alternative procedure recommended by the Mediation Board" that Myron Taylor of U.S. Steel and Lewis of the mine workers would assume the leading positions on a joint conference board. To make the second procedure more appealing to Lewis, Roosevelt magnified Myron Taylor's role. In previous dealings with Taylor, including the famous 1937 steel negotiations, Lewis had won great victories.

Whatever hope Roosevelt harbored of achieving a private, voluntary solution to the crisis collapsed the following day, October 25, when Taylor informed the president of his disappointment at being nominated "for a joint activity with Mr. John L. Lewis to settle a question which the Mediation Board seems not to be courageous enough to act upon themselves. It will be no surprise to you to know," he continued, "that I immediately wired Mr. Davis that I was not available for service." Taylor outlined for the president the two factors that shaped his decision. First, as a result of his previous dealings with Lewis, his credibility with Little Steel had suffered, and he doubted that he could provide the industrial leadership needed in this crisis. Second, he asserted that the board of U.S. Steel would withhold the union shop until the government ordered it. Taylor, in effect, handed the crisis back to the president.

Taylor also informed Roosevelt that he had telephoned Lewis that morning and urged the miners' leader to extend the temporary agreement for two more weeks. He also indicated that if a two-week truce was arranged, he and Lewis could meet in Washington. "This sort of conference, however, would not be a part of the Mediation Board activities but only a personal and private conference between Mr. Lewis and myself."

Lewis responded to Roosevelt's October 24 memorandum after his 8:00 a.m. telephone conversation with Taylor and was aware, therefore, that the plan outlined in the memorandum would never materialize. He politely accepted the president's invitation to meet with Taylor but then fumed at being given the runaround by the government. The NDMB's approach to the captive mine dispute, he lamented, appeared "casual and lackadaisical to the point of indifference. . . . The Board now emerges with a report devoid of conclusions as to merit, evasive as to the responsibilities of the Board, and dumps its own sorry mess into the already over-burdened lap of the Chief Executive."

Then came the crucial point of the letter. "Under these circumstances, I do not feel warranted in recommending an additional extension of the temporary agreement . . . in advance of an opportunity to negotiate with the qualified policy making executives of the corporations." Lewis, in effect, informed the president that it was unfair to demand that the miners continue work before the steel industry officially agreed to enter negotiations with the union.

The dispute now entered a new stage. The steel industry would not formally respond to the president's memorandum and the NDMB's report until at least Tuesday, October 28, when the directors of U.S. Steel were to meet. Lewis, however, had ordered the coal miners not to report to work after midnight, Saturday, October 25. For strategic and personal reasons, Lewis could not postpone the work stoppage without some concessions from the steel industry. Roosevelt, however, insisted that the international situation demanded the uninterrupted operation of all defense industries. Unwilling to impose the union shop, Roosevelt preferred to force Lewis to cancel the strike in order to suppress a practice that other unions might later emulate.

On Sunday, October 26, Roosevelt sent Lewis a letter, which he also released to the press. Acknowledging Lewis's communique of the previous day but ignoring its substance, Roosevelt, "as President of the United States," asked Lewis and his associate officers "as loyal citizens, to come to the aid of your country" by keeping the captive mines in operation. "That is essential to the preservation of our freedoms, yours and mine."

The notion that a miners' strike threatened mobilization served Roosevelt's purpose of turning public opinion against Lewis but did not conform to reality. The U.S. Steel Corporation's mines, Myron Taylor had informed the president, could be closed "for two or three weeks in the North and about five weeks in the South without affecting steel production." Likewise, the Bureau of Mines estimated that the steel companies possessed at least a thirty-day supply of coal.

Lewis raged at Roosevelt's transformation of a labor-management dispute into a confrontation between the union and the government. "There is yet no question of patriotism or national security involved in this dispute," he challenged Roosevelt. "Defense output is not impaired, and will not be impaired for an indefinite period. This fight is only between a labor union and a ruthless corporation." In a clever move designed to remind an incited public that the controversy was essentially a labor dispute, Lewis jibed: "If you would use the power of the State to restrain me, as an agent of labor, then, Sir, I submit that you should use the same power to restrain my adversary in this issue, who is an agent of capital. My adversary is a rich man named Morgan, who lives in New York." If Morgan will permit Myron Taylor to implement the Appalachian agreement in the captive mines, Lewis concluded, then the entire problem could be settled in ten minutes, and coal production could be quickly resumed.

Lewis's letter provoked Roosevelt to issue, on October 27, yet another public appeal to the UMW leadership from "your Government, through me" urging the immediate resumption of work in the captive mines. And in his Navy Day address broadcast later that night, in a clear reference to Lewis, he assailed "selfish leaders." More privately to Thomas Lamont of U.S. Steel, Roosevelt expressed anger "at Lewis' unwarranted, untrue, and demagogic statement about Jack [Morgan]." When you see Morgan, he instructed Lamont, "tell him for me not to concern himself any more about Lewis' attack, for after many years of observation, I have come reluctantly to the conclusion that Lewis' is a psychopathic condition."

The president's public pronouncements fed popular indignation against Lewis and the mine workers. As international developments entangled the nation in the global conflict, journals of liberal and conservative opinion alike accused Lewis of deliberately jeopardizing the country's security. Conservative legislators charged the coal union leader with treason and urged the president to act decisively.

Tuesday, October 28, dawned on fifty-three thousand miners remaining away from the captive collieries. In New York, directors of U.S. Steel learned that the firm's earnings for the first nine months of 1941 were almost one-third greater than they had been during the same period the previous year. They also decided to allow the federal government to resolve the captive mines dispute by asking the full mediation board to arbitrate the issue. Immediately following the directors' meeting, Myron Taylor journeyed to Washington, where he conferred with Roosevelt and William Davis.

The following morning Lewis and Taylor began bargaining. As a possible solution emerged, they summoned William Davis and informed him of their desire to have the full NDMB hear the case and issue a recommendation concerning the union shop. Neither party, however, would be bound by the board's decision. Lewis also demanded that the mines stay closed while the NDMB pondered the case; but the mediation board chairman refused to acquiesce. To break the impasse, Taylor led his fellow conferees to the White House, where, apparently after a personal plea by the president, Lewis agreed to order the miners back to work. In announcing the plan to newsmen, Lewis intentionally minimized Roosevelt's role.

At 11:30 a.m., Thursday, October 30, Lewis summoned the captive miners back to work. At 2:30 that afternoon—in an act designed to reaffirm labor's right to strike—he informed the press of a new strike deadline of November 15. At the time most commentators viewed this last move as a symbolic gesture rather than a serious threat. They generally believed that the NDMB would simply follow the precedent set in a decision made in June granting the closed shop to the A. F. of L. metal trades in Bethlehem Steel's shipyards on the West Coast. The captive mine controversy seemed settled.

Then, on November 10 the unexpected happened. By a nine-to-two vote the NDMB rejected the union shop in the captive mines. Only Philip Murray and Thomas Kennedy supported the union's case. All four employer representatives, all three public representatives, and both A.F. of L. alternatives voted in the negative. The unexplained absence of the two regular representatives from the A.F. of L. on a question of such critical importance to organized labor heightened some observers' suspicions that political intrigue lay behind the decision.

The day after the ruling, Lewis maintained an uncustomary silence while Murray and Kennedy resigned in protest from the NDMB. The board's opinion, they proclaimed, "discloses that regardless of the merits of any case, labor unions shall be denied the right of normal growth and legitimate aspiration, such as the union shop, and the traditional open-shop policy of the anti-labor employers shall prevail." Their departure from the board led to its collapse.

Roosevelt, realizing that Lewis would now enforce the November 15 strike threat, summoned Benjamin Fairless of U.S. Steel, Eugene Grace of Bethlehem Steel, and Frank Purnell of Youngstown Steel, along with the three top UMW leaders, to the White House on Friday, November 14. At the conference, the president forcefully threatened antistrike legislation and implied his right to seize mines if the pits failed to stay open. He urged both parties to resume negotiations and, if they were unable to reach agreement, to appoint "an arbiter, or arbiters, or anyone else with any other name, and that in the meantime coal production continue." The union shop, he insisted, could only be achieved by voluntary collective bargaining and not through government decree. "I tell you frankly that the Government of the United States will not order, nor will Congress pass legislation ordering, a so-called closed shop." To do so "would be too much like the Hitler methods toward labor." Jawboning completed, Roosevelt requested the gathered parties to continue coal production as they negotiated.

But on Monday, November 17, for the third time in as many months the captive coal miners refused to work. For the next few days, the president seemed stymied. He suggested that if the union would abandon the union-shop demand, he would personally encourage the remaining 5 percent of the captive miners who did not belong to the UMW to join the organization voluntarily. The implication that Roosevelt might do Lewis's job angered the labor leader.

Some members of the administration also toyed with the idea of having the president order the miners back to work. To explore this option, the administration had earlier sounded out captive miners' views. Ninety-two percent of those surveyed wanted the union shop. A majority, however, indicated that they had not favored the October walkout, and the group divided nearly evenly when queried about their willingness to strike if the NDMB ruled against them. "There is little doubt that the men would follow John Lewis if he called a strike," the report indicated. "But there is also little doubt that the men would *prefer* to follow the President." After a few days out picketing, informants advised the Federal Conciliation Service, the miners will be ready to go back to work.

But time worked against the administration. On November 20 news reached Washington of increased violence among pickets, law enforcement agencies, and some miners wishing to work. Confrontation polarized the situation and led the striking captive miners to close ranks. Simultaneously, thousands of miners from the commercial collieries walked out to demonstrate solidarity with their union brothers.

On November 19 Roosevelt again requested Lewis either to accept the status quo for the duration of the national emergency or to submit the union-shop issue to arbitration. Lewis promptly responded that he believed that the UMW policy committee, when it convened to consider the requests, would be ill-disposed toward them. "Your recent statements on this question, as the Chief Executive of the nation," Lewis noted, "have been so prejudicial to the claim of the Mine Workers as to make uncertain that an umpire could be found whose decision would not reflect your interpretation of government policy, congressional attitude and public opinion."

Whether intentional or not, Lewis's statement provided the key to ending the crisis, because it carried the implication that the mine workers would agree to arbitration if assured beforehand of a favorable decision. This was the route the union had thought it had traveled when it resubmitted the case to the NDMB. Its expectations then had been disappointed; now it demanded certainty.

As the UMW policy committee gathered at 10:00 a.m. on November 22 to respond formally to the president's request, Lewis received a telephone call from Secretary of Labor Perkins urging him to take no action until Roosevelt made a final appeal. With the committee waiting in the headquarter's basement, Lewis left the building, returned at 11:15 a.m., and then sat in his sixth-floor office until shortly after noon, when a messenger delivered the president's letter. In it, Roosevelt informed Lewis that the steel industry had agreed to arbitration, and therefore he was appointing Fairless for steel, Lewis for labor, and Steelman for the public as a board to settle the dispute. Steelman's appointment guaranteed Lewis his victory, because it was well known that the conciliation service director favored the union's position. The policy committee, following Lewis's recommendation, eagerly agreed to the plan.

This scheme met the steel industry's desire to have the union shop in the mines imposed through government action. And to satisfy Roosevelt's pledge that the government would not order the union shop, Steelman resigned from his post in the conciliation service, and the board's meetings were held in New York rather than Washington.

After two weeks of discussions, the board issued its decree granting the union shop to the mine workers. Lewis and Steelman composed the majority; Fairless defended the steel industry's commitment to the open shop. Lewis once again appeared triumphant. But no one paid much attention. The board announced its decision on December 7; the Japanese had just attacked Pearl Harbor.

After the United States entered the world conflict, Lewis pledged the UMW's full cooperation in defeating the nation's enemies. The national organization and its affiliates fully subscribed to every loan drive. The UMW *Journal* and the organization's leaders persistently urged the miners on to new production records. Throughout the war years, Lewis advocated policies that he, at least, felt did not seriously threaten the success of the GIs in battle. Yet the public image of Lewis as an enemy of the nation persisted.

Amidst the spirit of unity prevailing for the first weeks after Pearl Harbor, Lewis appeared on the verge of regaining some of his lost prestige within the labor movement. On January 17, 1942, Lewis, as chairman of the CIO's standing peace negotiating committee, publicly called upon Phil Murray of the CIO and William Green of the A.F. of L. to resume unity talks. The wartime crisis, the increasing pressures to curtail labor's rights, and the possible economic dislocations at the end of the conflict made it mandatory, in Lewis's opinion, for the two houses of labor to merge. "If labor is to be mobilized, transported here and there under terms and conditions set by employers and bureaucrats, with its forces divided," he pointed out, "there could be but one result— labor will be short-changed in the process."

Lewis's act elicited favorable responses from a number of prominent union officials and opinion makers. After consulting the A. F. of L. executive board, Green immediately accepted the peace overture. ILGWU President David Dubinsky expressed delight over the prospects of unity, as did Hillman's lieutenant Emil Rieve. To Eleanor Roosevelt the idea of unity was simply "grand." For a few brief days a labor merger seemed likely. Still to be heard from, however, were Murray, the president, and the *New York Times*.

On Monday, January 19, the *Times* carried a front page story by A. H. Raskin describing secret negotiations between Lewis and Daniel Tobin of the A. F. of L. teamsters. Together they reportedly had devised a scheme for merging the two organizations that called for Green's retirement, George Meany's promotion to the presidency of the new federation, and Murray's demotion to the position of secretary-treasurer. The A. F. of L. executive board, according to Raskin, had already informally accepted the plan. Press accounts the following day embellished Raskin's story by contending that Lewis, Norman Thomas, Burton K. Wheeler, and other opponents of the president had concocted the plot at a cocktail party.

Lewis's failure to consult with Murray before making the merger proposal wounded the CIO president deeply. Absent from Washington when Lewis made the announcement, Murray learned of the proposal the next day from the newspapers. "No one has the right to trade me for a job," he bellowed to reporters when finally contacted for a statement. "My manhood requires a little reciprocity—and, by God, despite this feeble frame of mine, I will fight any living man to maintain my manhood." In an official reply to Lewis, begun coldly with "Dear Sir and Brother," Murray curtly informed the miners' leader that all arrangements in behalf of unity "will necessarily have to be initiated through the office of the President of the Congress of Industrial Organizations."

To a large extent the unity proposal constituted an attempt by Lewis to end the CIO's subordination to the president. Seen from Lewis's perspective, a united labor movement would end the administration's strategy of divide and control, would strengthen the antiadministration forces by placing Lewis and Hutcheson in the same camp, and would weaken the influence of Murray and Hillman by compelling them to share power with individuals less deferential to Roosevelt. Evidently, Lewis calculated that a wave of favorable sentiment, both among the general public and within the labor movement, would compel Murray, and indeed Roosevelt, to go along with a merger despite their suspicions. Raskin's story in the *Times,* whatever its merits, enabled Murray and the president to resist.

Roosevelt, realizing that a merger would weaken his influence over labor, moved quickly to thwart unity. Within a week of Lewis's proposal, he created the Labor Victory Committee, composed of three representatives each from the A.F. of L. and the CIO to consult with him frequently on labor problems. Desiring to wield some influence with Lewis and also to have the three largest unions in the CIO represented, Roosevelt requested Murray to appoint the leader of the miners to the new committee. Enraged at Lewis's treatment of him, Murray refused. Disagreements between Lewis and Murray now erupted into full-scale war.

With the advantage of hindsight, the bitter estrangement between Lewis and Murray can be traced to fundamental differences in philosophy as well as personality. Throughout his career, Lewis envisioned the labor movement as a force able to exert its will independently, beholden to no one. In the New Deal period Lewis freely accepted Roosevelt's aid, but he did so not as one receiving a gift, but as one being given his rightful due. When, after 1937, Roosevelt failed to meet Lewis's expectations, the latter felt ill-disposed to perpetuate the relationship for the sake of securing a few more crumbs. Murray, to the contrary, acted much more deferentially to a president whose policies had rejuvenated the UMW.

For most of the 1930s Murray's loyalty to Lewis served to mute the differences between the two men. Omens of Murray's divorce from Lewis, however, had appeared much earlier than the contentious unity movement of January 1942. Lewis's secret and dramatic negotiations with U.S. Steel in 1937 perturbed Murray. Lewis's failure in 1940 to consult with him in advance of the Wendell Willkie endorsement further exasperated Murray, as did the assertions by reporters and convention delegates that Lewis would remain the power behind the throne after Murray's elevation to the CIO presidency.

Actually, Lewis made a sincere effort in early 1941 to allow Murray to establish his own claim to leadership. Lewis stayed away from CIO headquarters more than was his custom, and when union officials dropped into his office in the mine workers' building to chat about CIO business, he would drive them out and order them to consult Murray.

Temperament and fate combined, however, to prevent Lewis from sustaining this role for long. A few months after Murray's accession to the CIO presidency, for instance, the mine workers' leader accepted an invitation to attend a testimonial dinner for the new CIO chief. His absence, Lewis realized, would be interpreted as an affront to Murray. Yet when he arrived the delegates rose to their feet and cheered, and on the following morning the newspapers featured Lewis's remarks while giving only cursory treatment to the guest of honor.

Murray also seemed temperamently unable to adjust to his new station. Rather than operate out of the CIO headquarters, he did all his work from the miners' building. "It became almost like a Freudian symbol," observed Lee Pressman, "the act of leaving there to go over to the C.I.O. buiding." He became extremely sensitive, interpreting every act by Lewis as a rebuke. When Murray suffered a heart attack in the summer of 1941, his Pittsburgh partisans—David McDonald, Vin Sweeney, and others—went so far as to contend that Lewis consciously sought to drive Murray to his death so he could regain the CIO presidency.

According to some acquaintances, enmity between their kin further widened the rift between the two men. Shortly before the United States entered the war, Kathryn Lewis and Mercedes Daugherty, Murray's niece and ward, vacationed together. During their travels they engaged in a violent feud, and thereafter, David McDonald maintains, "they set out deliberately to poison the minds of Murray and Lewis against each other."

The struggle between the Lewis and Hillman wings of the CIO over defense policy further complicated Murray's position. Murray was a man split in two, with old loyalties linking him to one camp and personal convictions pushing him into the other. Into the summer of 1941 he tried to equivocate between the two groups hoping to preserve some semblance of unity within the CIO. With news of the Nazi invasion of Russia and reports of German and Japanese attacks on American vessels, this precarious stalemate collapsed as more and more unionists entered the Hillman camp. Murray, reacting both to international developments and the changing political situation in the CIO, began to shift toward the emerging anti-Lewis majority.

In an effort to reach an accord, Lewis and Murray conversed in Atlantic City in mid–October 1941. Afterward each party to the talks related a different story of what had happened, although both men agreed that the meeting terminated their long relationship. To Lee Pressman, Murray painted a scene of Lewis pleading with him not to endorse Roosevelt's foreign policy. In response, a composed Murray asserted that he was going to follow the dictates of his conscience even if it meant that the two men would part.

Lewis's version is presented in much more dramatic fashion by Saul Alinsky. Alinsky depicts Murray, still convalescing from his heart attack, as emotionally unstable. He refused to talk directly on the issues, speculated about his place in heaven, and broke into fits of tears. "Frankly," Lewis reportedly informed Alinsky, "I think he is a little bit out of his mind." At the end of the conversation with Murray, Lewis reportedly remarked: "It was nice to have known you, Phil."

Regardless of which account is nearer the truth, the fight between the two men did not degenerate into open hostilities until Lewis's ill-fated A.F. of L.–CIO unity proposal in January 1942. On November 11, 1941, Murray demonstrated his solidarity with the mine workers by resigning in protest from the NDMB. And although the CIO convention later that month reelected Carey and endorsed Roosevelt's foreign policy, it also approved Murray's motion of support for the striking captive miners. At a mid-December presidential labor-management conference, the CIO president still appeared to follow Lewis's lead. The aborted unity maneuver and Murray's decision not to appoint the miners' chief to the Victory Board ended the period of coexistence.

Administratively, Lewis had little choice but to expel Murray from the UMW and then to cut the miners' ties with the CIO. Otherwise an intolerable situation would have existed, in which UMW Vice-President Murray would be championing, as president of the CIO, policies that Lewis and the mine workers rejected. Such a situation would weaken the UMW internally as the rank and file took sides, and it would undercut the union's credibility with employers by exposing a divided organization.

The problem confronting Lewis was to devise a method to remove Murray that would least alienate the union's membership, long accustomed to supporting both men. Lewis decided to force a direct confrontation with his former colleague. His strategy would be to pit Murray's responsibilities as CIO chief against his obligations as a UMW officer.

First, Lewis engaged in a series of jurisdictional conflicts with other CIO affiliates, thereby skillfully cornering Murray into supporting either District 50's claims or those of other organizations. Next, Thomas Kennedy notified the CIO that the mine workers union would not pay its monthly assessments but, rather, wished the sum deducted from the Congress's $1,665,000 debt to the UMW. When the CIO executive board refused to recognize the mine workers' claim, Murray again had to choose between the UMW and the larger federation that he headed.

To side with neither, as he initially attempted to do, would enable Lewis to depict Murray as both indecisive and anti-UMW.

Lewis's conduct provoked numerous CIO officials to denounce him. Seizing the opportunity, Lewis and his agents magnified this criticism to demonstrate to the miners the hostility of the CIO and applied constant pressure on Murray to repudiate the assaults. Murray tried to avoid a touchy situation by praising Lewis's patriotism and devotion to the labor movement without acknowledging that unfair charges had been made against his person. The UMW chief had no intention of settling for such gestures.

In early May Murray ended his efforts at appeasement and initiated a Lewis-like attack on Lewis. Speaking to coal miners and steelworkers in western Pennsylvania, Murray rebuked his "traducers" in the UMW — "men who steal about in the silence of the night spreading poison and seeking to disorganize instead of organize." Charging Lewis and his henchmen with "back-stabbing" and "Tom Girdler" tactics, he declared that he would yield to "no dictator in or out of the labor movement." Despite his new aggressiveness, however, Murray recognized that Lewis's hold on the mine workers' union was too firm to be broken, and on Friday, May 22, he accepted the salaried presidency of the United Steelworkers of America.

The following Monday, May 25, Murray went to the basement of the UMW headquarters, where, in a room filled with Lewis's mementos, the policy committee and executive council gathered to transact pending business. Murray waited nervously throughout the day. When he finally spoke, he did not utter the pugnacious phrases of the past few weeks, but rather mellow statements of praise and loyalty to Lewis. After he finished, the two men shook hands.

At the next day's executive council session, Lewis commenced his attack. In a dramatic performance, he flared out at Murray for failing to act against the UMW's detractors, criticized his response to the January unity proposal, and lambasted him for repudiating the CIO's outstanding financial debt to the UMW. Several times the CIO chief attempted to correct the "nasty record" being presented, but he was cowed by Lewis and the hostile delegates. When the miners' chief finally yielded to his "former friend," Murray offered a meek rebuttal.

Murray's aggressiveness reemerged the following day, when the executive council began to consider formal charges against him. Murray based his defense on his authority as president of the Congress of Industrial Organizations. Lewis retorted that Murray's first obligation must be to the United Mine Workers of America, and then he raised the issue of Murray's new salaried position with the Steelworkers. When Murray asserted that Lewis had also held other positions in the labor movement, the leader of the miners replied that he had never done so for pay and always "in behalf of our union." Lewis had found the issue that the rank-and-file members would accept as grounds for Murray's dismissal. The heated debate ended when Murray departed for a meeting with Roosevelt. With the victim closeted with the president, the executive board expressed Lewis's will by voting seventeen to one to declare the office of vice-president vacant.

Throughout the summer Murray and his associates aimed a steady barrage of criticism at Lewis. Demonstrating a style he learned from over two decades of study with the master, Murray depicted himself as Christ, Lewis alternately as Peter or Judas, and the basement of UMW headquarters as the Garden of Gethsemane. Lewis devoted little time to replying, pausing only long enough to utter his characteristic blend of ridicule and pomposity. Life, he observed, "is too short for me to answer the yappings of every cur that follows at my heels. I hear the pack in my rear at times. I can turn my head and see the lap dogs and the kept dogs and the yellow dogs in pursuit. But I am serene in the knowledge that they won't come too close."

During the summer of 1942 Lewis delegated fighting the CIO to K. C. Adams, O'Leary, Edmundson, and other lieutenants, while he sought to cope with his wife's long illness. In February and again in March 1942, Myrta underwent major surgery for relief from a brain malignancy and spent most of eight months in the hospital before her death on September 9. She died at home in Alexandria with her husband and daughter by her bedside, and she was buried in the Lewis family plot at Springfield.

Myrta's death naturally saddened Lewis; they had been married for thirty-five years. Some biographers and commentators, however, have tended to dramatize unduly the impact of her passing on Lewis. "Those who saw the anguish and deathly pallor of Lewis marked up 'finished' to Lewis's career," Alinsky wrote. "Those who saw Lewis and knew what Myrta Lewis had meant to him not only marked up 'finished' but underscored it."

Lewis's career was not "finished," and it is doubtful that Alinsky or many others actually understood what Myrta had meant to him. The miners' leader worked hard at keeping his private life private. What public information he provided about his wife took the form of a Lincolnian myth with Myrta in the role of Mary Todd, carrying culture and sophistication to the folksy coal miner who had been born on February 12. Although there are doubtless parallels in the wifely roles of Myrta and Mary Todd—such as applying pressure on their husbands to attain success and material possessions—for the most part, the myth lacks credence.

Whatever grief Lewis felt at Myrta's death hardly showed when he presided over the UMW's 1942 convention one month later. He hinted at his bereavement only once during the seven-day proceedings. The 1942 convention testified to Lewis's power over the miners. Since the last gathering in January 1940, he had led his union into situations that would have disrupted most organizations: a confrontation with a popular president; two coal strikes that antagonized both government and public opinion; outspoken and unpopular criticism of the nation's foreign policy; the expulsion of Philip Murray; and, finally, the separation of the union from the CIO. Yet despite such potential sources of discontent, open disagreement with Lewis's views barely appeared. Lewis's machine, his agility as a union politico, and above all the fact that he "brought home the bacon" kept most miners in his camp and enabled him to sway the convention to his will.

The convention granted even more authority to its president. The delegates increased monthly assessments, thus adding a projected $2,400,000 annually to the UMW treasury of $6,346,852. They also amended the constitution of the Gas, By-Product Coke, and Chemical Workers, District 50, to give it jurisdiction "in such other industries as may be designated and approved by the International Executive Board." Another amendment permitted supervisory personnel to join the union.

The convention also provided Lewis with a forum from which to issue policy statements on the war and government economic regulations. He insisted that since December 7 the organization had supported the war effort to the utmost. The record "should commend this Union and its officers to the representatives of our government," he declared. "That record should entitle the United Mine Workers of America to be consulted with relation to the economic and industrial policies of this government necessary in pursuit of the war. That record . . . should cause the administrators of our government to lift that blacklist, figurative or real, which in the minds of many people has been imposed upon the United Mine Workers of America by officials in Washington." Lewis, in effect, challenged Roosevelt to readmit him to the circle of power. If the president refused, Lewis made clear, he would work to undermine what he perceived as unfair wartime regulations.

18

"Damn His Coal Black Soul": The Wartime Strikes, 1943

After the Japanese attack on Pearl Harbor, Lewis stilled his public opposition to Roosevelt's foreign policy and announced his support of the war effort. Soon afterwards he concurred with other labor leaders in a "No-Strike Pledge" to prevail for the duration of the struggle. Personally, Lewis remained skeptical but essentially cooperative. In a time of national crisis, he told the union's policy committee, "every individual owes an obligation to temper his utterances to a point where the rights of the whole and the interests of the many are not set aside, intellectually or otherwise, by the arbitrary intellectual conclusions of an individual." "Our nation is at war and coal production must not cease," he lectured wildcat strikers in July 1942. "Our every effort must be directed toward this end."

By late 1942, however, the spirit of national solidarity had begun to fade. Various wartime controls, which the nation initially greeted with enthusiasm, now came under criticism. Along with other segments of society, miners felt aggrieved by unfair rationing standards, victimized by administrative chaos, and abused by preferential treatment for the rich and powerful.

Such sentiments among the rank and file enabled Lewis to speak more freely on wartime policies. Past events had made it practically inevitable that Lewis would become a leading critic of Roosevelt's domestic policies. His disdain for the president and his disavowal of the New Deal removed any political reason for remaining silent.

Lewis recognized the need for some government regulation of the economy during the national emergency, but he wanted the government to limit its role to what was absolutely necessary. In particular, he desired minimal interference in labor-management relations. By and large he felt that the government should confine its activities to assuring fair play between contending parties and upholding basic labor standards. On all regulatory and policy boards—not just those dealing with labor matters—he wanted union spokesmen granted equal representation with delegates from capital. Reflecting his continued belief in the primacy of voluntary associations, Lewis also desired the formation of industry councils composed equally of labor and management representatives and charged with coordinating the policies of specific industries with the national defense effort.

The reality of wartime policy differed substantially from Lewis's concept. Conservative businessmen and bureaucrats came to dominate government councils while labor leaders enjoyed only limited participation in the affairs of state. "Indeed, there seems to be a blacklist against effective labor spokesmen," the UMW *Journal* complained, "and only those are admitted to the inner circle who can be trusted to nod acquiescence after decisions are made by others." Nothing came of Lewis's industry council idea, although other labor leaders endorsed it. Nor was Lewis successful in having a code of principles formulated that would serve as a guide for the government's labor policies. Finally, the federal government substantially restricted collective bargaining as the National War Labor Board (NWLB) evolved from an agency to adjust differences between labor and management to an institution to check inflation through wage controls.

For Lewis, the wartime measures threatened to reverse his life-long struggle to attain for labor an equal position with capital in the chambers of power. He saw Roosevelt's actions reducing the American worker to a position of second-class citizenship as the administration demanded an inordinately greater sacrifice from the men and women who toiled than it did from the owners of mines and mills. In Lewis's view the government implemented "a paradoxical policy that runs to the premise of rewarding and fattening industry and starving labor. . . ."

Lewis was acutely aware of the extreme sacrifice made by some coal miners. The longer hours and increased mechanization imposed by the wartime demand for coal made mining—already one of the most dangerous jobs in America—even more dangerous. The statistics of miners dead and injured offered Lewis an ultimate justification for wartime strikes. He understood as did neither Roosevelt, William Davis, nor most Americans, that for miners the battle for production on the homefront produced its own body count. A sensitivity to such suffering constituted one of the factors that impelled Lewis to challenge the government in 1943. He did not think the dangers of mining could be substantially eliminated, but felt that his miners should be awarded adequate compensation for risking their lives.

The government policies most vexing to Lewis were those implemented to combat inflation. He believed that an increase in the cost of living was unavoidable during a military conflict. "Inflation to some degree is a concomitant of any war," he lectured Senator Harry Truman's watchdog committee.

Of all government measures, the NWLB's Little Steel formula most upset Lewis. He contended that Roosevelt had created the National War Labor Board in January 1942 "to hand down in every wage controversy a decision based upon a *judicial determination of the issue,*" in exchange for labor's "No-Strike Pledge." This bargain ended in July 1942, he maintained, when the board promulgated the Little Steel formula and thereby transformed itself from a court of equity into an anti-inflation instrument. "The WLB violates the government agreement with labor each day that it operates," Lewis raged in February 1943. "Under its arbitrary and miserably stupid formula, it chains labor to the wheels of industry without compensation for increased costs, while other agencies of government reward and fatten industry by charging its increased costs to the public purse."

On July 16, 1942, the National War Labor Board first applied its Little Steel formula, which was intended to regulate the wage demands of all workers. In the Little Steel case, a fact-finding panel had informed the NWLB that the four steel companies involved in the dispute with the steel workers were able to afford a wage increase without raising prices. The board felt that this fact alone was not a sufficient safeguard against inflation. It therefore calculated that because the cost of living rose approximately 15 percent between January 1, 1941, and May 1, 1942, workers were entitled to a composite 15 percent wage increase above their base rate on New Year's Day 1941. The board further contended that the president's anti-inflation program, announced on April 27, 1942, would restrain any significant increase in living costs and thus eliminate the need for future wage advances above the 15 percent ceiling, except in cases of unusual inequities. The board used New Year's Day as the base date so that the wage gains made by the major unions in the spring of 1941 could be charged against the 15 percent formula.

John L. Lewis felt that the Little Steel formula imposed a great injustice on the members of the UMW. Because the miners had won a 16 percent wage advance in the spring of 1941, they were automatically ineligible for any further increases under the Little Steel formula. The union had interpreted the 16 percent gain as an adjustment to cover the pace of inflation and other factors for the period from April 1, 1939 to April 1, 1941.

According to Lewis, the War Labor Board "fouled its own nest" when it proclaimed its wage control policy. "When the mine workers' children cry for bread, they cannot be satisfied with a 'Little Steel Formula'," he taunted. "When illness strikes the mine workers' families, they cannot be cured with an anti-inflation dissertation. The facts of life in the mining homes of America cannot be pushed aside by the flamboyant theories of an idealistic economic philosophy."

The injustices of domestic wartime policy and the suffering of his miners influenced Lewis during the hectic months of 1943. Yet other important but less articulated forces were also at work. By 1943 many workers demanded the elimination of the "No-Strike Pledge," and unauthorized wildcat strikes infested American industry. Lewis definitely hoped that his actions would thrust him once more to the forefront of the labor movement. This ambition was rooted as much in his psychological need for power as it was in his desire to take labor down a different path. The same factors underlay his gestures at humiliating Roosevelt, William Davis, and the National War Labor Board.

Many commentators at the time perceived Lewis as a psychopathic personality and his ideological arguments simply as manifestations of psychosis. For those who began with this belief, Lewis's deviant behavior in 1943 confirmed the theory. Yet for those observers who recognized considerable merit in Lewis's criticism of wartime policy, his actions — although perhaps antisocial — were nonetheless rational. Not even Lewis understood his own motivation. "What makes me tick?" he once asked himself. "Is it power I'm after, or am I a Saint Francis in disguise, or what?"

As 1943 began, Lewis still remained uncertain on how to fulfill his threats against Washington's wartime policies. The nation's involvement in a conflict of unprecedented scale made it difficult for him to predict how the administration would respond to various moves on his part. More important, Lewis recognized that his rank and file confronted conflicting pressures that made their loyalty uncertain. With many of their own friends and relatives in military service, they naturally desired to do everything necessary to protect the men at the battle front. At the same time, they felt that the government's domestic program called upon them to make unnecessary and unreasonable sacrifices.

In January 1943, the anthracite miners helped Lewis to arrive at his course of action. During the first week of the new year various locals initiated wildcat strikes, apparently to Lewis's surprise. Each day the walkout gained momentum until by January 9, almost one-half of the forty thousand hard-coal miners remained away from work. Although initially in opposition to an increase in union dues, the protest quickly shifted to an attack on the Little Steel formula, with the wildcatters demanding that Lewis immediately negotiate a pay boost from the operators of $2 a day.

Lewis normally responded ferociously to such challenges to union discipline, but now he seemed intent on seeing how the situation would develop. Although he denounced the strikers for the public record, he proved less decisive in exercising his more effective powers for getting the miners back to work. Not until the morning of January 15—only hours before he testified before the National War Labor Board on the stoppage—did he send telegrams to the locals in the anthracite districts ordering their members to remain at work. Even at that, the telegram expressed more concern over the insurgent character of the committee formed to coordinate the wildcat than it did over the walkout.

In the end, the strikers demonstrated their determination to correct their grievances by first ignoring a NWLB back-to-work directive and then resisting an appeal from Roosevelt to resume production. The strike finally ended in late January after Lewis, having publicized his determination to win a pay increase for the miners, expelled the leaders of the walkout from the union.

Lewis found the unauthorized strike highly instructive. For one thing, it revealed to him the government's lack of decisiveness when confronted with a challenge to its authority by labor. Drastic, punitive action seemed ruled out. Equally important, the strike illustrated the commitment of the rank and file to action. Neither patriotism nor presidential pleas had deterred the wildcatters from their unpopular strike. Lewis, recognizing that the membership had decided the direction it would march, artfully maneuvered his way to the head of the parade.

He seized his January 15 appearance before the National War Labor Board as an opportunity to embrace the rebel's cause. In a masterful performance directed more at his membership than the board, he relegated complaints over increased union dues to a secondary issue "when as a matter of fact the basic trouble in the anthracite industry has been low wages and part-time employment."

Throughout the subsequent 1943 upheaval, Lewis would be doing his miners' bidding as well as executing his own assault on wartime regulations. The secret of the miners' support for Lewis during the unpopular wartime strikes rests simply in the fact that he was championing their cause. The figure of $2 a day that Lewis initially demanded at the beginning of negotiations was set by the January wildcatters, not by the union's economists after scrutiny of cost-of-living indexes. Indeed, Lewis called upon Jett Lauck, K. C. Adams, and Percy Tetlow to develop a statistical justification for this sum. Likewise, when Lewis, following Lauck's advice, decided to achieve the wage advance through the subterfuge of a portal-to-portal pay, he stumbled onto a genuine rank-and-file grievance. Throughout the coal controversy, tremors from his membership forced Lewis to act in particular ways.

On March 10, Lewis led the UMW delegation into New York's Roosevelt Hotel for contract talks with the Northern Appalachian Wage Conference. He had warned them in public statements since February of the miners' insistence on a wage increase of $2 a day. Other major demands now outlined by Lewis included the elimination of occupational charges, an increase in vacation pay, and compensation for travel time within the mine. Traditionally, American coal miners had been paid only for the time they spent digging at the mine face. Lewis now proposed that they be paid from the time they passed through the mine portal into the dark underground until they reemerged through the portal at the end of their day's work. Although portal-to-portal pay would become a central issue in the 1943 coal dispute, its inclusion among the original demands was apparently to provide the union negotiators with an item that they could trade away for a $2 wage increase.

Neither the northern nor southern operators believed that Lewis would defy the government in time of war. Consequently Charles O'Neill, leader of the northern producers, refused to consider any wage increases and calmly evaded meaningful bargaining. Edward Burke, representing the southerners, initially insisted that the miners take a pay cut and then proposed that all negotiations be suspended until the war ended. On March 15, after five days of aimless talk, Lewis emphatically informed the operators "that without a negotiated contract the miners will not trespass on your property on the first of April."

Unlike Edward Burke, whose blind hatred of Lewis and unionism led him to underestimate his adversary, Charles O'Neill paid Lewis heed. His interest in negotiating became further aroused when he learned that the U.S. Court of Appeals in Alabama had upheld portal-to-portal pay for iron ore miners. The court decision thrust the travel time issue to the center of negotiations, causing O'Neill to explore with Lewis a thirty-day extension of the 1941 contract so that the talks could continue after April 1. The southern operators, alarmed at the weakening of the North, appealed to Roosevelt to turn the dispute over to the National War Labor Board.

The president refused. Instead, on March 22 he sent identical telegrams to Lewis, O'Neill, and Burke requesting them to arrange a temporary settlement while negotiations continued. In a situation that required a decisive statement, Roosevelt proved equivocal. The operators took comfort in the president's assertion that any wage adjustment had to conform to the Stabilization Act of 1942 and Executive Order No. 9250. Lewis, however, interpreted Roosevelt's failure to send the dispute to the NWLB and his reference to the vague statute and executive order rather than the precise Little Steel formula as indications that the 15 percent wage ceiling could be broken. Supporting this view was the telegram's closing paragraph that indicated the administration's willingness to consider a price increase if the operators suffered "undue hardship" from a retroactive pay increase.

The UMW, northern operators, and various outlying fields consummated a thirty-day contract extension by March 24. The southern operators proved more reluctant and wavered for a week until, on March 29, John Steelman of the Conciliation Service arrived on the scene and prevailed upon the southerners to accept an extension. The nation was now guaranteed coal production until May 1.

In the ensuing negotiations, Steelman unsuccessfully sought a compromise that circumvented the Little Steel formula by increasing the miners' total earnings without altering their basic wage rate. During these talks, Lewis began to view portal-to-portal pay as his ultimate weapon if the government interpreted a straight pay increase as a violation of the Little Steel formula. Jett Lauck sent him a series of notes in early April outlining both the long-term and immediate benefits to the coal industry and the miners of portal-to-portal pay. The establishment of a seven-hour day on a portal-to-portal basis, Lauck predicted, would mean "a 'new heaven and a new earth' for mine workers."

Then, on April 8, President Roosevelt issued a "hold-the-line" order, one provision of which directed the NWLB to allow no further wage increases other than those necessary to correct substandard conditions. The order also instructed the Director of Stabilization to approve all National War Labor Board decisions, thus ending the board's independence. Naturally, Lewis was peeved; the operators interpreted the president's order as a vindication of their refusal to yield to union demands and stopped negotiating over portal-to-portal pay.

Lewis now faced three unpleasant options: surrender to the operators, send the case to the NWLB where the union's position would automatically be rejected as a violation of the Little Steel formula, or lead a direct confrontation against the government. He made one last effort to salvage both collective bargaining and something he could claim as a union victory. The mine workers would drop the demand for $2 a day, he promised, if the operators would guarantee six days of work a week. Lewis pointed out that the operators had already received a price hike to cover the additional cost for six days of operation and that part of the increase was designed to offset the higher wage bill. A guaranteed six-day week, moreover, would only result in the miners earning the amount that the operators publicly contended they were averaging under the old contract.

Edward Burke and the southern operators promptly rejected the proposal. O'Neill spent three days considering the offer and then joined Burke in petitioning the president to send the coal dispute to the NWLB.

With no compromise in sight and the contract extension running out, Secretary of Labor Perkins certified the dispute to the National War Labor Board on April 22.

With the National War Labor Board's formal entrance into the coal dispute, tension gripped the nation. According to one survey, 58 percent of the nation recognized some justice in the miners' demands. Yet this sympathy was far outweighed by the public's hostility toward Lewis, who was surely one of the most hated men in America. Most newspapers and journals reinforced this animosity by interpreting coal developments in light of Lewis's opposition to Roosevelt.

Franklin Roosevelt could not, as president, act overtly hostile to Lewis. Yet his animosity toward the miners' chief was well known. Under the president's orders the Justice Department sought grounds to indict Lewis, including tax evasion, conspiracy with the Illinois operators in fighting the Progressive Miners, and violation of the War Labor Disputes Act after its passage in July 1943. He kept informed of Lewis's dealings with the antiadministration camp through a series of reports from personal associates and the F. B. I. At one point during the 1943 coal dispute Roosevelt hinted at the depths of his rancor when he joked of his willingness to resign if only Lewis would commit suicide.

Lewis also loathed Roosevelt, but there were fundamental differences in the nature of the hostility that they displayed toward each other. To a large extent, Roosevelt's public personality was shaped by his political career. A master of the politics of compromise, he perceived himself as a broker seeking a just means. He displayed the political skill of giving something to everyone, and in exchange he expected everyone to behave. His commitment to a consensus society ill-prepared him to deal with those unwilling to play the game of compromise. Accustomed to persons who would arrive at a polite accord, he could not cope with Lewis, who preferred polarization. The wartime crisis further strengthened Roosevelt's desire for a harmonious, solidified nation. Believing that those who promoted division subverted the operations of civilized society, he reacted with an emotional vehemence held in check primarily by his appraisal of the American people's sense of fair play.

Lewis, on the contrary, was a master of the politics of confrontation. In more than two decades of dealings with the coal barons, he had found this the most effective approach. It also served as the modus operandi within the union, as Lewis's struggles with Howat, Farrington, Brophy, and others attest. To a large degree it was Lewis's skill at the politics of confrontation that enabled him to establish the CIO and lead it to several victories.

Whereas Roosevelt, the broker in the politics of compromise, emphasized the complexity of problems as he sought to blend differences and diminish controversy, Lewis as a combatant in confrontation politics worked to polarize issues so that the alternative became simplisticly self-evident. Lewis, moreover, tolerated opposition and rancor as part of conflict resolution. Animosity was a weapon he used; it was rational as well as emotional; he could turn it on or off almost at will. For public consumption he could punch William L. Hutcheson or vilify Green, but it is doubtful that he hated them personally. Of all his public enemies, he came closest to despising Roosevelt. Yet because he accepted the legitimacy of confrontation, he always restrained his feelings. In 1943, he set two goals: winning an advance for the miners and tearing down the wartime economic regulation structure in the process. Humiliating Roosevelt was less important.

From the start of the coal controversy, Lewis sought to achieve his ends by confrontation. Both the operators and the government, he believed, had absorbed the lesson of the 1941 captive mine dispute and would do everything necessary to avoid another crisis. Despite his early strike threats, Lewis seems not to have planned a walkout. Lauck's correspondence with him in February, March, and April contained no hints of strike plans; and as late as April 15, the UMW *Journal* predicted long negotiations and the possibility of several contract extensions, but no closing of the mines.

Lewis was, after all, posing as the champion of "free" collective bargaining against government wartime regulations, and apparently he felt he could win his objectives at the negotiating table. Before Roosevelt's hold-the-line order, he had moved the northern operators to an exploration of occupational charges and portal-to-portal pay. And Lewis believed that where the northern operators traveled, the southerners would grudgingly follow. But after the hold-the-line order, the operators reverted to their initial intransigence. Lewis had expected that the Roosevelt administration would deal with him through the politics of compromise. Instead, Roosevelt, motivated in part by principles but also by passion, stepped out of character and engaged in the politics of confrontation.

On April 22, Lewis learned that the coal dispute had been turned over to the NWLB. Immediately he dashed off a letter to Conciliation Director Steelman informing him that the union would consider the thirty-day contract extension terminated with any discontinuance of negotiations.

On April 24, representatives of the Mine Workers boycotted the board's preliminary hearings. Simultaneously, groups of miners across the nation failed to report to work, apparently on their own initiative. Ignoring these scattered walkouts, the board proceeded to outline the ground rules for the coal controversy, with Chairman Davis announcing that any wage settlement must be resolved within the limits of the Little Steel formula. The board also ordered uninterrupted production of coal and called upon the parties each to appoint a representative to a tripartite panel to hear the case. When Lewis ignored the board's communique, Davis appointed David B. Robinson of the Brotherhood of Locomotive Firemen and Engineers as surrogate representative of the miners.

As Lewis and the NWLB maneuvered for advantage, more miners refused to work. By April 26 sixteen thousand miners in Pennsylvania, Kentucky, and Alabama had left the pits; three days later the number had grown to seventy-five thousand and the area had expanded. On Wednesday, April 28, Davis followed traditional NWLB policy and suspended all hearings on the dispute until the miners resumed production. He then referred the matter to the president for appropriate action.

On the following day Roosevelt sent Lewis a telegram that he also released to the press because it was really intended for the rank-and-file miner and the general public. Roosevelt appealed for an end to the strike, "not as President—not as Commander-in-Chief—but as the friend of the men who work in the coal mines." He condemned the stoppages as "not mere strikes against employers of this industry to enforce collective bargaining demands. They are strikes against the United States government itself." Then the president issued an ultimatum: "if work at the mines is not resumed by ten o'clock Saturday morning [May 1], I shall use all the power vested in me as President and as Commander-in-Chief of the Army and Navy to protect the national interest and to prevent further interference with the successful prosecution of the war."

The first response to Roosevelt's telegram came that same day in Ohio where another 9,700 miners walked off the job. A more formal reply was sent the following morning—the last day in April—by the UMW policy committee meeting in New York. Under Lewis's guidance the committee specified its objections to the NWLB and "its fixed mathematical measuring device." Again the committee stressed the miners' patriotism and productivity, but it ignored Roosevelt's warning.

When Saturday, May 1, arrived, millions of Americans waited nervously as the moment of reckoning drew near. A calmer atmosphere prevailed in miners' homes, with some of the men still asleep as 10:00 approached. The thirty-day extension agreement had officially expired at midnight, and without a contract a union miner would not work. Lewis had not ordered the stoppage, although the miners knew he approved. Nor did they stay home out of spite for Roosevelt, although they also knew he disapproved. Pride, self-respect, and loyalty to the union motivated these patriotic citizens to strike during wartime.

Roosevelt now had to execute his ultimatum. Lacking statutory authority, he could not imprison Lewis and his lieutenants. Inducting the miners into military service would be too time-consuming and disruptive of production, and many of the miners were over draft age. If the miners still refused to work once drafted, it would be self-defeating to lock them up; as Harold Ickes reminded the president, "a jailed miner produces no more coal than a striking miner." Sending troops into the coalfields would not work either, because as a miners' saying went, "bayonets can't mine coal." In considering his options, Roosevelt believed that the public would not condone any extreme use of force or punishment against the men who actually dug the coal. In the end he had only one alternative. He could seize the mines and hope that Lewis would cooperate. Consequently, on May 1, Roosevelt directed Secretary of Interior Harold Ickes to take possession of the nation's bituminous mines and to manage them in the public interest until a threat of strike no longer prevailed.

Although Roosevelt dramatized his move, Lewis had won a significant victory. The miners lost nothing through seizure; the operators lost formal control of their businesses. Lewis felt that before long the coal barons would squirm under government control as their fears about eventual nationalization mounted. In the meantime Lewis could engage in his accomplished tactic of pitting one government official against another. Finally, the president's action allowed Lewis to call off the strike in the name of patriotism and therefore avoid a prolonged shutdown that would have undoubtedly produced a vicious attack on the union.

The president having made his move, it was now Lewis's turn to respond. To compel the labor leader to act promptly, Roosevelt scheduled a radio address to the nation for 10:00 p.m. Sunday, May 2. On Saturday Lewis arranged a meeting with Secretary of Interior Ickes for Sunday afternoon. After journeying from New York to Washington, Lewis and three associates conferred for three hours with the new custodian of the mines and his staff. Lewis saw Ickes as a man with whom he could do business. The secretary was not enamored of the Little Steel formula and wanted to insure coal production for the duration of the war. New to the job, he asked Lewis to send the miners back to work for at least two weeks so he could have time to evaluate the situation. Lewis responded that such action would need the approval of the UMW policy committee in New York. With the meeting ended, Lewis made the return trip.

The train bearing Lewis pulled into New York City at 9:10 p.m.

Sunday. He went straight to the Hotel Roosevelt, where the policy committee was awaiting his arrival. Lewis briefed the committee on his talk with Ickes and presented the secretary's request for a two-week resumption of work. Although the resumption would abridge the union's no contract–no work tradition, the policy committee concurred in the request. At 9:40 Lewis telephoned Ickes the good news. By 9:44 the president's advisers knew of the miners' decision to return to work for two weeks beginning on Tuesday, May 4.

At 10:00 Roosevelt delivered his scheduled radio talk to the nation "and in particular to those of our citizens who are coal miners." It is hard to believe that the president had no knowledge of the Ickes-Lewis talks that afternoon, or that his staff had not drafted an alternate speech to be presented if the strike was settled before airtime. Possibly overtaken by anger, Roosevelt delivered a hard-line talk that ignored the policy committee's decision. In a stern but fatherly style he asked the miners to end the strike and resume coal production. His tone toward Lewis was unmistakably hostile. "The responsibility for the crisis we now face," he told an already exasperated nation, "rests squarely on the national officers of the United Mine Workers, and not on the Government of the United States."

On Tuesday, May 4, the nation's bituminous miners returned to work. Technically they were now employees of the United States. Yet although the American flag flew over the tipples, the old managerial personnel greeted the miners as they passed through the portals.

In Washington, Harold Ickes announced that the president had decided that the government would not negotiate with the union. If the UMW wanted a contract, he stated, it would have to deal with the coal operators under the watchful eyes of the NWLB. Lewis responded to the secretary's pronouncement with cries of double cross and deceit. For the most part his outburst was for public consumption. Lewis viewed Ickes as one of the few reasonable men in Washington and sensed that pressures from the War Labor Board lay behind the secretary's announcement.

On May 6 the NWLB's fact-finding panel opened public hearings on the coal case. As before, the UMW refused to send representatives, causing the board to appoint one of its own legal counselors as union spokesman. On May 14 the full board ordered the miners and operators to resume collective bargaining under NWLB guidance. Coal production was to continue during negotiations and the parties were to report the results of the talks to the board in ten days. Any agreement arrived at would be subject to the NWLB's approval and by implication had to conform to the Little Steel formula.

Lewis would have nothing to do with the board's May 14 directive, claiming that only Ickes, as the government official in charge of the mines, could order contract talks. As if to underline his responsiveness only to Ickes, he granted the secretary's request to extend the back-to-work order to June 1. The members of the NWLB were outraged at Lewis's affront, with Chairman Davis accusing him of giving "aid and comfort to our enemies." To prevent Lewis from subverting their authority, they forbade any further negotiations involving Ickes, the operators, or anyone else until the union complied with its May 14 orders.

Throughout May public agitation over the coal situation mounted. Newspapers, taking up a theme from Roosevelt's May 2 speech, published column after column on the GIs' irritation with Lewis. The words from an editorial in *Stars and Stripes* became a national chant: "Speaking for the American soldier, John L. Lewis, damn your coal-black soul!"

Lewis responded to the widespread hostility with a bold move designed to unsettle his foes. On May 17 he sent William Green a letter requesting reaffiliation with the American Federation of Labor. To make the idea more palatable to the business unionists in the Federation, he enclosed a check for $60,000 to cover the first year's dues. The UMW's application, sponsored by William Hutcheson and greeted as "wonderful" by Green, created the intended consternation among the White House palace guard, CIO leaders, NWLB members, and others striving to isolate the miners' chief. Lewis knew full well that AFL action on his petition would not occur for months. In the meantime, the idea would haunt those charged with resolving the coal crisis.

With only days left before the expiration of the third contract extension on June 1, Secretary Ickes frantically tried to prevent another walkout, even summoning Lewis and O'Neill to his office at 5:00 p.m., May 31, where he proposed a temporary compromise to the portal-to-portal question. Lewis accepted Ickes's proposal; O'Neill simply agreed to meet with representatives of the miners and explore the plan. At 8:30 that night Lewis arrived at the Statler Hotel to negotiate with O'Neill. The latter refused to meet with him and insisted that their conference was not scheduled until 10:00 the next morning. Because midnight brought an end to the latest contract extension, half a million miners refused to report to work the next day.

The second bituminous coal strike caused the operators to reconsider temporarily their strategy of letting the government restrain the union. They now feared that they might become a casualty in the intensifying warfare among Lewis, Ickes, Roosevelt and the NWLB, and they began to think that Lewis might win. Thus, at 10:00 a.m., June 1, the operators started negotiating seriously with Lewis. By adjournment that evening, individual mine owners had begun to break ranks, and as the parties reconvened the following morning, the Washington *Post* reported that only fifty cents separated the contending parties.

Members of the National War Labor Board responded adversely to the prospect of an agreement. They feared that the NWLB would be placed in an embarrassing position if its own guidelines compelled it to reject a negotiated contract. Lewis would then publicly assail the board as the sole obstacle to a settlement. To avoid these prospects, the board ordered all negotiations to cease until the miners returned to work and again remanded the dispute to the president.

On the afternoon of June 2, Secretary Ickes, Stabilization Director James F. Byrnes, and members of the War Labor Board gathered at the White House to discuss the coal crisis with the president. At the end of the conference Roosevelt issued a public statement as "President and Commander in Chief" instead of his May plea as a friend of the miners. In forceful language he ordered "the miners who are not now at work in the mines to return to their work on Monday, June 7, 1943." Two days later, Ickes repeated the government's demand that Lewis order the miners back to work.

By Friday, June 4, Lewis was also eager for the miners to return to work. The strike had prodded the operators into serious negotiations. Yet the NWLB had suspended the talks just when a breakthrough seemed imminent. Lewis recognized that the only way to win was to discontinue the strike so negotiations could resume. Thus, the policy committee ended the strike but set June 20 as the termination date for this latest contract extension.

For the next two weeks, Lewis labored at the conference table to divide the operators and then to negotiate a contract with at least part of the industry. Meanwhile, legislators on Capitol Hill strove to end his defiance of the government. Each flurry of labor unrest produced renewed cries for Congressional action against labor. Senator Thomas Connally had an antistrike bill prepared, and when the miners struck in May he capitalized on the public uproar to push it through the Senate and send it on to the House. Interest in the measure declined when the miners returned to work, but with the second strike on June 1, Representative Howard Smith brought the bill to the floor. By June 15 the Smith-Connally bill, more formally known as the War Labor Disputes Act, had cleared Congress and awaited Roosevelt's signature.

The bill contained several provisions designed to enable the government to deal with Lewis. To terminate Lewis's boycott of the NWLB, for instance, the bill gave the board power to compel parties to appear before it. The board also received authority to make a final, binding determination in any dispute. The president's power to seize production facilities threatened by strikes was confirmed, and criminal penalties were established for anyone who would strike or otherwise disrupt property under government control. The provisions of the bill requiring an NLRB-supervised strike vote and a cooling-off period also had application in the coal situation.

Roosevelt recognized, however, that the bill would punish his labor friends as well as his enemies. He also realized that Congress had passed the bill in a fit of passion and that many of its provisions would not fulfill their intent and could possibly cause even greater havoc. Advised by both Ickes and Davis to veto the measure, Roosevelt chose for the time being to hold it as an ax over Lewis's head as the next deadline in the coal crisis drew near.

Members of the NWLB also hoped that the threat of the Smith-Connally Act would compel Lewis to capitulate. On June 18, two days before the next contract termination date, the board issued a directive order, that essentially rewrote the 1941 contract to include the board's recent rulings. It increased the miners' vacation pay, transferred occupational charges to the operators, and raised the "substandard" pay of inside unclassified labor and slate pickers. The board refused to guarantee the six day week, and in a move to weaken Lewis's power over the coal industry, it nullified the controversial Protective Wage Clause. Finally, the board made no provision for portal-to-portal pay. In closing, the board instructed both the UMW and the operators to accept these terms as the contract in force until March 31, 1945.

Accusing the board of attempting to "economically disembowel" the miners, Lewis characterized the directive order as an "infamous yellow-dog contract." The rank and file agreed and on June 19 they began to lay down their tools; fifty-eight thousand miners stopped work that day; a full five hundred thousand quit the next.

Officially the strike lasted only two days. On Sunday, June 20, Lewis prepared a policy board statement proclaiming that the UMW would not sanction a wartime strike and would urge miners to continue work under the direction of Ickes or anyone else chosen by the president. In a meeting with Ickes and his staff on June 21, Lewis forthrightly expressed his desire to end the walkout. All present agreed, however, that the problem was not only "of returning the miners to work, but also of retaining enough morale so that maximum production would be assured."

By the following morning Lewis had determined his new strategy. Unwilling to accept the NWLB's dictates but with nowhere else to turn, he planned to sit tight with the mines under government control. He spent most of his second meeting with Ickes discussing the widening of the secretary's management of the collieries. After the conference, he summoned the policy committee and attained its approval of a back-to-work order. The members of the UMW, Lewis informed the press, would willingly dig coal "for the Government itself under the direction of the custodian of mines. The mine workers have no favor to grant the coal operators nor the members of the War Labor Board, who have dishonored their trust, but will make any sacrifice for the Government, the well-being of its citizens, the upholding of our flag, and for the triumph of our war effort." Lewis's effusive patriotism, however, had definable limits. As long as the government kept possession of the mines, he announced, the contract extension would last until October 31.

Lewis's official call terminating the third soft-coal strike defused Roosevelt's counterattack. On June 23 the president issued a statement menacingly asserting: "It's a good thing that the miners are returning to their work." He still refused to acknowledge publicly the degree of rank-and-file militancy and concentrated his criticism on the UMW's leadership. Lewis's behavior, he informed newsmen, "has been intolerable—and has rightly stirred up the anger and disapproval of the overwhelming mass of the American people."

The president renewed his attack on Lewis two days later in a message accompanying his veto of the Smith-Connally Act. He requested that the Selective Service Act be amended so that men up to age sixty-five could be inducted into the service. Lewis was sixty-three. The Congress, eager for an immediate weapon to wield against Lewis, overrode Roosevelt's veto and made the Smith-Connally Act a law.

Clusters of miners across the coal fields, incensed over the NWLB's June 18 directive order, Roosevelt's hostile comments, and Congress's passage of the Smith-Connally Act, continued to remain away from the mines despite the union's back-to-work order. Production at the pits did not reach normal levels until July 5. Although such rank-and-file militancy served Lewis's immediate purposes, the continuation of local strikes represented a breakdown of union discipline. With the possibility of his membership taking events out of his control, Lewis was perhaps glad that the next contract termination date was four months away. By then, he hoped, the dispute would be over.

Throughout the 1943 coal dispute, Lewis publicly projected the image of a stern, inflexible individual determined to achieve all or nothing. In reality, however, he had made substantial concessions by the end of June. When negotiations began in March, he had demanded four primary items: a wage increase of $2 a day, portal-to-portal pay, an increase in vacation pay, and payment of occupational charges by the operators. In its May 25 directive, the NWLB granted the last two demands, but the first two, which the miners most desired, remained unsettled. Seeking compromise, Lewis first offered to yield on the $2 increase and travel-time pay in exchange for a guaranteed six-day work week, but the operators balked. In late May Lewis merged the $2 proposal and portal-to-portal pay into one demand: an increase of $2 a day granted as travel-time pay. Then, in his aborted early June negotiations, he conceded more ground by accepting a combination of portal-to-portal pay, vacation increases, and occupational charges that would average out to approximately $2 a day. As the crisis worsened during the summer and fall, Lewis dropped public advocacy of the $2 figure, and the UMW *Journal* no longer heralded it as the miners' battle cry.

Lewis's tactics had also changed between March and June 1943. He opened negotiations in March certain that he could secure a contract from the operators at the bargaining table and then force its acceptance by the NWLB. When the operators found sanctuary in the NWLB's temple, Lewis shifted tactics and created a confrontation between Ickes and the board. Ever mindful of Lewis's strategy, Roosevelt blocked the labor leader's machinations by denying Ickes the right to negotiate a settlement. Lewis hoped, however, that the prospect of long-term government control of the mines would motivate the operators to seek accord with the union.

Fortunately, Harold Ickes acted as a willing accomplice in Lewis's design. The Interior Secretary believed that only Lewis's voluntary concurrence in an agreement would assure full coal production for the remainder of the war. Thus, Ickes appointed a Coal Mine Administrator likely to satisfy Lewis. Ickes also advanced Lewis's objectives through his interpretation of the Smith-Connally Act. Under the law, plants or mines seized by the government had to be returned to their owners within sixty days of the resumption of normal production. Ickes realized that terminating government possession of the mines would likely generate a strike, and thus he sought to interpret the "normal production" provision narrowly. The secretary mandated stringent requirements that the owners had to fulfill before they could individually regain their property.

The enactment of the War Labor Disputes Act emboldened both the operators and the NWLB in their struggle with Lewis. They petitioned Roosevelt to return the mines to their private owners. On July 13 the president announced that the mines would revert back to the operators within sixty days. A month later the cause of the operators and the board received another assist when Roosevelt interpreted the punitive provisions of the Smith-Connally Act as authorizing the NWLB to sequester the dues of unions failing to comply with the board's order. He also threatened to cancel the draft deferments of strikers.

In a countermaneuver, Lewis attacked his opponents' flank. Illinois had enjoyed a rejuvenation of its coal industry as a result of booming wartime economy. In relations with the union, however, it was compelled to follow the decisions made by the Appalachian operators. Lewis sensed that the Illinois operators would gladly negotiate a contract favorable to the UMW in return for a more influential role in the coal industry. And the NWLB, when confronted with a labor agreement achieved through voluntary collective bargaining, would be under pressure to bend its Little Steel formula. The Illinois contract would then become the model for the whole industry.

On July 21, the Illinois Coal Operators Association presented to the NWLB for its approval a contract negotiated with the UMW. The agreement would run until April 1, 1945, with the UMW pledging no strikes during that time. It incorporated all the awards previously granted by the NWLB, provided for a forty-hour work week, and contained a settlement of the portal-to-portal pay issue. Two days later Lewis courteously wrote Davis to ask for approval of the agreement.

On August 3 Lewis appeared before the board members he had so recently vilified. The UMW chief wanted his new contract approved. For most of the hearing he sat by contemplatively, while an attorney presented the union's case. When he finally did speak, Lewis expressed none of the belligerence that he had formerly sounded towards Davis and the others. Now was the time to be ingratiating.

Neither the attorney's presentation nor Lewis's presence satisfied the board. In issuing the majority opinion on August 25, Davis pointed out that although most of the contract complied with previous NWLB directives, the portal-to-portal arrangement failed to constitute "a genuine settlement of alleged claims arising under the Fair Labor Standards Act." Davis proceeded to warn the union that the board would not approve a wage increase in the guise of travel-time pay.

In scattered mines in Ohio and Alabama miners reacted to the board's decision by staging brief wildcat strikes. Most UMW members, however, waited for Lewis to act. Having few options open, Lewis resumed negotiating with the Illinois operators and emerged on September 23 with a new contract for the NWLB's consideration.

Lewis felt confident that the board would uphold the new agreement. In line with NWLB criticism of the first contract, negotiators had changed the underground miners' work day from seven hours at the face to eight and one-half hours from portal to portal, thus putting the contract more in harmony with the provisions of the Fair Labor Standards Act. Lewis expressed his "considered personal judgement that for reasons of logic, the board cannot escape approving the pending contract and making it applicable throughout the industry."

The NWLB pondered the second Illinois contract for thirty-three days. During that time, the government returned the mines to their private owners, a move that incited a wave of wildcat strikes throughout

Alabama, Indiana, Kentucky, Ohio, and Pennsylvania and involved more than ninety thousand miners. On October 16, Lewis joined with the NWLB in ordering the striking miners back to work, but few obeyed. The UMW president now found himself in the awkard position of becoming a tail on the rank-and-file's kite. As his followers grew more militant, Lewis worried that firm action against wildcat strikes might alienate the UMW membership. Yet he feared another strike, because he realized that the NWLB was prepared to destroy the union.

On October 26, the NWLB issued its decision on the second Illinois contract. By a vote of seven to five the board rejected the agreement, contending that its portal-to-portal pay provisions still violated the government's anti-inflation program. Perhaps aware that their actions created a new crisis, the board's majority went on to spell out an acceptable settlement. They consented to payment on an eight and one-half hour day from portal to portal in place of the old seven-hour day excluding travel time. By their calculations, however, the miners would be entitled to $8.125 a day, and not the $8.50 figure embodied in the second Illinois contract.

Lewis kept his own counsel in the days immediately following the board's decision. Meanwhile, the number of miners engaged in wildcat strikes increased dramatically, leading Lewis to attempt what Davis graciously characterized as "a sincere endeavor to end local stoppages, but without success." As a result of the wildcat strikes, on October 28 the NWLB once again referred the coal crisis to Roosevelt for action. In doing so, Davis directed the president's attention to the board's proposed solution to the controversy and then reminded Roosevelt that "the issue is the same clear one which it has always been since the beginning of the coal controversy; namely, shall the wage stabilization policies of the Government be applied and enforced irrespective of the displeasure of any group toward these policies."

Roosevelt's public reply to Davis exposed a softening of the president's hitherto intransigent anti-Lewis position, because the urgency for coal constituted a stronger theme in Roosevelt's response than the need to preserve government authority. The president was generally firm but conciliatory toward the UMW and "the patriotic American miners." For the first time in the nine-month dispute, he extended to the union the courtesy of not instituting action until the policy committee met. He felt confident that when the committee gathered, it would see "the substantial increase in benefits the Board's proposal offers" and would consent to a contract along those lines. To make the NWLB proposal even more attractive to the miners, he asked Davis to consider the wisdom of announcing that the NWLB "has no objection to the insertion of a clause in the contract that in no case shall a miner receive for a day's work less than he would have received for his productive work at the straight time hourly rate under the old contract." "But if I am mistaken and the miners do not accept the Board's proposals," Roosevelt ended, "I shall take decisive action to see that coal is mined."

Roosevelt was mistaken. At dawn on Monday, November 1 — hours before the UMW policy committee would convene to consider the president's plea — five hundred thousand bituminous and anthracite miners again went on strike. They walked out voluntarily, Lewis would argue in a 1944 *Collier's* magazine article on the coal dispute. "It was the unanimous protest of men who were tired of serving as guinea pigs for Washington's campus theorists, and sick of sabotage and double-crossing. More than that, it was the answer of the rank and file to the repeated charge that they were not behind their elected leaders, and that our demands were 'purely political,' put forward by me to embarrass and harass the Roosevelt Administration."

Roosevelt probably rejected Lewis's self-serving interpretation of the walkout, but he did recognize that rank-and-file militancy could disrupt the war effort. He brooded over the situation all day and then at 8:00 p.m., November 1, again ordered Ickes to place the mines under government control. This time he directed the secretary to negotiate a contract with the UMW to prevail for the duration of the seizure. In order not to undermine the board totally, however, he insisted that the contract be in accord with the NWLB's ruling on the second Illinois agreement, and that the final document be presented to the board for its approval. Roosevelt probably recognized that the NWLB could scarcely afford to reject a contract to which a representative of the government was a party.

Lewis and Ickes wasted no time negotiating. After two days of talks, on November 3 they announced the signing of a memorandum of agreement and the return of the miners to work. On the following day the UMW policy committee approved the agreement by acclamation and joined Lewis in greeting Ickes warmly.

In essence the Lewis-Ickes agreement made the terms of the second Illinois contract approved by the War Labor Board applicable to the entire bituminous industry. On the critical issue of portal-to-portal pay, they used as a base the board's proposal of $8.125 for a day of 7.75 hours at the face and ¾ hours travel-time. Then they reduced the thirty-minute lunch period to fifteen minutes and applied the other fifteen minutes to production time. As compensation for this adjustment, they agreed to pay the miners another .375 cents, bringing the basic daily wage to the $8.50 figure Lewis had sought in the rejected second Illinois contract.

The Lewis-Ickes agreement settled the coal dispute. The controversy no longer competed with battle accounts as front page news, although until the spring of 1944 aspects of the controversy would occasionally make headline stories.

The reversion of the mines from government to private hands took several more months. While the northern operators dutifully negotiated a contract with the UMW paralleling the Lewis-Ickes agreement by December 17, the southerners refused until mid-1944 to come to terms with the union, and the National War Labor Board delayed approving the northern contract until May 29, 1944. The northern mines finally reverted to their private owners on May 31, 1944, whereas the southern pits were returned in piecemeal fashion as the year progressed.

Lewis showed signs of strain as the coal dispute came to its conclusion. Although the *New York Times* and other papers cursed him as the victor, he knew that he had fallen far short of his original goals. The Little Steel formula and the NWLB had not been smashed. A miner working eight hours a day, six days a week under the 1941 contract would have made $54.50 according to calculations by economist Colston E. Warne. The same miner working the same amount of time under the Lewis-Ickes agreement of 1943 would have earned $57.06.

After Lewis and Ickes signed the agreement the government contended that the country lost seventeen million tons of coal because of the work stoppages, scarcely threatening when compared to a total production of around six hundred million tons. In another sense the coal crisis did obstruct the conduct of the war. A response to discontent, it generated even more discontent. Most directly, the miners' example encouraged workers in other industries to resist wartime controls. Similarly, thousands of men and women began to wonder in an uninformed way about a government that seemed to let the miners bully it. Equally important, the coal crisis forced the country's leaders to turn some of their attention away from winning the war toward settling a domestic dispute.

Finally, the labor and liberal communities criticized Lewis and the miners for provoking a new wave of antiunionism. Clearly the 1943 coal strikes intensified the antiunion trend. Lewis's actions were partly a response to the government's antilabor drift. He chose to challenge the trend, and he lost. Murray, Hillman, Dubinsky, Green and others preferred to appease the conservative forces. The miners' militancy in 1943 makes it impossible to determine whether the labor moderates' strategy would have succeeded.

19

"Between Scylla and Charybdis": 1944-50

By the midpoint of World War II, hostility toward labor leaders and unionism had become an ever-increasing phenomenon on the American homefront. Although such animosity had long prevailed in the nation, it became particularly intense as a result of the 1943 coal strikes and other wartime labor disruptions. Each day of the war further eroded the public's sense of tolerance and fair play. And the conflict's end actually aggravated the already strained spirit of national unity as the tensions of reconversion—inflation, shortages, dislocations, and labor unrest—intensified public rancor toward assumed "enemies" within our borders.

John L. Lewis was a key target in the assault on organized labor. Throughout the war and the postwar years, numerous newsmagazine articles, often with loaded captions, fired the public's rage: "Lewis the Dictator" (*New Republic,* 1941), "John L. Lewis's Commandos" (*Nation,* 1942), "John's Vengeance" (*Time,* 1942), and "Cunning John" (*Time,* 1948). On May 29, 1946, *Newsweek* featured his face on its cover with the lead "Lewis: The Power to Paralyze." Most newspapers concurred in the Hudson, Massachusetts *Sun*'s characterization of him as a labor racketeer and Washington *Post*'s condemnation of his "holdup methods" and "rule-or-ruin technique."

Various influential persons perceived Lewis as a diabolic figure; a few, led by Special Assistant Attorney General O. John Rogge, maliciously branded him a Nazi collaborator. John Brophy believed him a participant in "a conspiracy on the part of American Firsters, composed of certain business, financial and political interests" intent on driving the New Dealers out of Washington. "John L. Lewis is an enemy," James G. Patton of the Farmers' Union warned Roosevelt. "Consciously or unconsciously, he is an ally of reactionaries and defeatists." The veteran labor reporter Louis Stark tagged him "The Warwick of the House of Labor" for his delight in "manipulating men, initiating maneuvers, and above all, engaging in the hurly-burly of the fight." Like others, Stark saw Lewis as "imperious and dominating" and as "craving power for its own sake and for what may be accomplished through it."

No matter how uncomplimentary the press and opinion makers were toward Lewis, however, their accounts also contained an underlying sense of awe. Professional journalists helped create a myth of the invincible Lewis by crediting him with victories in situations that were actually compromises or defeats. At times they let their imaginations run wild in fathoming his motives, and they forgot whatever sociology they knew when they claimed that the UMW president only needed to nod and subservient miners would execute his will.

Lewis consciously fostered this image. When cameras clicked he would wear a scowl that often vanished as soon as the photographing was over. He adroitly cultivated reporters, calling them by first names, occasionally joking with them over their stories, and staging exciting press conferences. Before them, he ranted against employers, other labor leaders, and politicians in an intentional effort to picture all men of prominence as his enemies.

The sparsity of news coverage on Lewis's private life further served to remove many of his human qualities from public view. In the 1940s Lewis was a major news figure, but not a national social celebrity. Consequently, the public came to know the Lewis who flaunted Shakespeare and not the man who read mystery novels and loved western movies. They knew the belligerent and accusative Lewis, but not the charming raconteur at cocktail parties occasioned by the very men he ridiculed publically. They were told of the pugnacious man engaged in an unceasing war on society, and not of the relaxed figure driving along wooded Virginia roads, fishing off the Gulf Coast of Florida, or journeying cross-country for extended vacations at a Wyoming dude ranch. The public Lewis radiated energy. The private Lewis progressively limited his socializing and took extended periods of rest in order to conserve his strength.

During the summer and fall of 1944, Lewis confronted a challenge to his authority within the Mine Workers' Union. Occurring at a time when rank-and-file militancy continued to disrupt the coal industry by wildcat strikes, the uprising blended membership protest against the internal operations of the union with a power play by one of Lewis's trusted lieutenants.

One of the talents promoted by Lewis under his policy of provisionalism was Ray Edmundson. In the war between the Progressive Mine Workers and the UMW, Edmundson obtained a reputation as a gunman, a bullet wound in the neck, and the attention of Lewis. Needing someone who could keep the rebellious Illinois miners in line, in 1935 the UMW president appointed Edmundson head of provisional District 12.

For the next nine years Edmundson proved a faithful Lewis lieutenant. Yet in 1942, Lewis bypassed him in selecting a successor to Philip Murray as UMW vice-president. Edmundson, however, claimed his troubles began during the 1943 coal crisis when he criticized Lewis's policy and turned to Secretary of the Interior Ickes and others in the administration for support. Apparently Lewis tolerated this defiance until the spring of 1944 when he moved to reduce the staff and income available to Edmundson. The latter recognized the scenario—having played a key role in undermining Murray—and resigned as head of District 12 and director of the Illinois division of District 50.

Rather than surrendering, Edmundson was simply selecting his own field of battle and enlisting his troops for a challenge to Lewis for the UMW presidency. After taking a job in a mine to demonstrate his links to the rank and file, he proceeded to broadcast across the coalfields his conversion to the cause of district autonomy and self-government. He cunningly focused on issues that dealt solely with Lewis's stewardship and the internal policy of the union. The UMW president would not be able to transform the dispute into an attack on Roosevelt, communists, or southern coal operators as he often did when challenged about his wage policies or political positions. Nor could Lewis obfuscate the issue, for he had trumpeted his defense of provisionalism throughout the union. And most important, Edmundson believed, a large number of miners otherwise sympathetic to Lewis disapproved of his "provisionalism."

Publicly, Lewis and his followers ignored the autonomy movement and Edmundson's candidacy, with the UMW *Journal* failing to inform its readers of the challenge. Behind the scenes, however, Lewis's agents scouted the two conferences held to explore the issue of self-government and applied pressure on other District 12 officers in order to prevent a mass resignation in support of Edmundson. Above all, they took the necessary steps to assure their boss of an unqualified triumph at the upcoming UMW convention.

The entire proceedings demonstrated Lewis's command over the structure of the union, if not all its members. The delegates mechanically approved committee recommendations on resolutions, referred to only by number, so fast that reporters were unable to look them up in the resolution booklet and record the action. So controlled was the gathering that although wartime regulations imposed an eight-day limit to the convention, it adjourned a day early.

Under such manipulated conditions Lewis easily eliminated Ed-

mundson and defeated the autonomy challenge. First, some Lewis supporters questioned Edmundson's right to serve as a delegate, a tactic
that allowed the Lewis-appointed credentials committee to delay hearing
the case until after the convention had disposed of the autonomy issue.
Lacking their leader, the self-government forces proved ineffective in
their opposition to the resolutions committee's antiautonomy report.
The entire debate on the issue lasted only two hours, and when the
standing vote was taken, a mere one hundred of the 2,728 delegates
made known their objections to provisionalism. The convention then
found Edmundson ineligible to be a delegate, which inspired Lewis to
decree a constitutional ruling barring his opponent from seeking union
office. No delegate appealed the decision of the chair.

Not satisfied with thrashing his opponents, Lewis proceeded to magnify his victory. Without advance notice, his functionaries proposed—
and the delegates dutifully approved—changes in the union's constitution. National union elections and constitutional conventions in the
future would be held only at four-year intervals, with smaller policy
conventions occurring in the biennial off-years. Indeed, the only area
in which Lewis did not achieve his will was in the field of political
action. Recognizing that many miners still esteemed Roosevelt, Lewis
settled for a "statement" critical of the administration's labor policies.

Lewis's reluctance to force his anti-Roosevelt politics on the convention suggests that he could not have thwarted the autonomy movement
so easily had a sizeable number of miners been deeply committed to
the cause. District self-government was essentially a pre-depression tradition in the UMW, but the majority of union members had affiliated
after 1932. As old timers died or left the union, the cause of autonomy
faded. For newer recruits, Lewis's accomplishments on wages, hours,
and working conditions offset the never-experienced right to vote for
district officers. Lewis knew this and paid close attention to his members'
complaints. Lewis, moreover, also knew when to forgive. Within a year
he invited Edmundson to rejoin the flock—and eventually appointed
him a regional director of District 50.

Far more troublesome for Lewis than minor challenges within the
UMW was his increased isolation from the controlling circles of power
in the country. Abandoned by most liberals and moderates, he increasingly cultivated the support of those who opposed Roosevelt, the New
Deal, and Washington's conduct of the war. Some of these ties extended
back to prewar days and were social as well as political. Alf Landon,
Alice Roosevelt Longworth, Walter A. Jones, David I. Walsh, and—as
Senator Joseph Guffey divulged to the president's staff—"a few other
reactionaries" all came to Lewis's home as guests. Beginning in 1941,
moreover, the miners' chief engaged in intimate meetings with Paul

Palmer, the political adviser to De Witt Wallace, right-wing owner of the *Reader's Digest.*

Now without strong liberal or radical influence as a ballast, Lewis became deeply entwined in conservative politics. In the spring of 1944 he corresponded with and met with Herbert Hoover. The parties purposely concealed "the subject" in their letters, but most likely Lewis was exploring the possibilities of Hoover or someone with similar views running for the presidency. When the Lewis-Hoover machinations produced no results, Lewis expended his political energies denouncing Roosevelt. Although he did not personally endorse Thomas Dewey in 1944, he did praise the Republican candidate as "a firm believer in equal justice, fearless and courageous action." Lewis, however, courted Republicans solely to improve his own hand.

Lewis also maneuvered to tighten his connections in a business community that was dividing over prospective postwar economic policies. His own desire to weaken the political influence of United States Steel and other offsprings of the House of Morgan coincided with that of Cleveland industrialist and financier, Cyrus Eaton. Similarly, his interest in protecting the domestic market for coal led to collaboration with H. L. Derby of the American Cyanide and Chemical Corporation and Joseph A. Brown of the Chemical Bank, both of whom feared that the newly created International Bank for Reconstruction and Development might enable England to invade American markets.

But Lewis and the UMW most needed allies within the labor movement. Yet Lewis would have nothing to do with the CIO, which he considered sycophantic to the Roosevelt administration. He viewed the A.F. of L. as less subservient and pressured it to act on the UMW's application for reaffiliation that had been pending since May 1943. By the spring of 1944, however, Lewis realized that the A.F. of L. would delay the UMW's readmission. Daniel Tobin and other council members close to the White House wanted to wait until after the presidential elections before strengthening antiadministration forces in the Federation. Other council members were concerned over Lewis's use of UMW District 50, which contested the jurisdictions of more than thirty A.F. of L. unions and had designs on the chemical industry—one of the fastest growing sectors of the wartime economy. In the end, the American Federation of Labor offered the UMW unacceptable terms for reaffiliation.

Spurned by the A.F. of L., Lewis found his domain in the labor movement confined for the next two years to the miners' union and its all-inclusive District 50. In 1941, Lewis had revitalized the district as part of his mounting challenge to the CIO. For a time labor commentators predicted that the catchall unit would become the core of a third mass labor organization. In March 1942, Kathryn Lewis, the district's secretary-treasurer, announced an organizing drive among the three million workers in the dairy industry. New York Governor Thomas Dewey feared that with the nation's dairy farmers behind him, the "frustrated" Lewis would control "the most staggering slush fund" as well as "the food supply of the nation." "By such a throttlehold on the lifeblood of the nation," portended Dewey, Lewis "would be in a position to dictate America's destiny."

Such alarm distorted the actual threat posed by the dairy industry drive and all District 50 activities. Although between December 1940 and June 1943, the UMW invested $3 million in the district and had several hundred organizers in the field, by the latter date the district paid per capita dues to the parent organization on only forty-eight thousand members. As a third force in the labor movement, District 50 flopped.

Ironically, District 50 actually gained its greatest strength after the dairy drive soured and the UMW leadership abandoned the concept of recreating a second CIO. Instructed by Lewis to disregard jurisdictional lines, District 50 organizers signed up workers in a variety of unrelated industries. By 1948, "50" had a membership estimated at more than two hundred thousand and included in its ranks clam diggers, taxi drivers, dairy farmers, pool parlor employees, and railroad ticket takers. It had locals in pulp and paper mills, gas plants, bus lines, construction projects, ladies and men's garment shops, as well as plants making or processing drugs, rubber, fish, and steel. Until the Taft-Hartley Act outlawed his efforts, Lewis attempted to enroll mine foremen in the district's United Clerical, Technical, and Supervisory Workers Union. The district also made inroads among chemical employees.

District 50 provided Lewis with an instrument to harrass his enemies. Its organizers concentrated their efforts at critical points from which he was able to negotiate concessions from employers or labor leaders whose unions had jurisdiction in that field. This strategy also enabled Lewis to magnify his national influence.

In 1945 Lewis's disaffection with government interference intensified as he found himself repeatedly restricted in his efforts to transfer a larger share of the coal industry's war-stimulated profits to the men who worked the mines. Employer and government firmness backed by an antagonized public forced Lewis to have to settle for modest gains in overtime pay during the spring bituminous negotiations. In anthracite, a strike was frustrated by government seizure of the mines, and he could only win for the hard-coal miners the portal-to-portal pay structure that the soft-coal men had obtained in 1943. In the fall, Lewis again challenged the bituminous operators, and this time suffered unmistakable defeat. His goal was to organize the managerial personnel around the mines, but the public's indignation against the union became so intense that he was forced to call off a strike in order to prevent adverse government action.

Such setbacks increased Lewis's apprehensions about the postwar reconversion period. He feared that the economic dislocations associated with demobilization would plunge the nation into a postwar recession, perhaps even a rerun of the Great Depression. The end of overtime work, he envisioned, would drastically reduce the wage earner's take-home pay, and the return of millions of GIs to civilian life would produce widespread unemployment. Impressed by technological advances made during the war, he also dreaded an increased maldistribution of wealth unless all sectors of society shared in the economic gains derived from greater productivity through science. To protect workers against a fore-boding future, Lewis believed it imperative that the government lift all restrictions on organized labor and collective bargaining.

Lewis's apprehension over labor's fate in the reconversion era, combined with his still crying needs for allies, led him once again to seek affiliation with the A.F. of L. In January 1946 he dashed off a message to Green announcing the UMW's renewed interest. After a week had passed without formal reply, he sent Green another letter, this time enclosing a check for $9,000 to cover the union's first month's dues.

The arguments previously employed against the UMW had lost much of their impact when the A.F. of L. executive council took up the subject at its winter meeting. The 1944 Federation convention had chartered a chemical workers' union that now had official jurisdiction in that field. With the death of Roosevelt and the succession of Truman to the presidency, Daniel Tobin and other A.F. of L. Democrats seemed to lose influence at the White House to men from the CIO, and most members of the council resented the administration's practice of basing its labor policies on developments in the CIO-dominated auto and steel industries. The council members thus concluded that Lewis's position on collective bargaining was now more important than the jurisdictional problems posed by District 50.

On January 24, the council readmitted the UMW to the American Federation of Labor and elected Lewis thirteenth vice-president. Delighted, the miners' leader joined his new colleagues in Miami, where he melodramatically handed Green back his UMW membership that he contended had been secretly maintained in good standing since the break in 1936. "These boys have been my friends and I didn't know it," a touched Green declared.

For all Lewis's preparations, he was still ill-prepared for the tensions that gripped America in the reconversion era. In late 1945 and 1946, a wave of strikes swept the nation as workers now sought to recoup the wartime sacrifices they had made. In November 1945, 200,000 General Motors employees walked out of their plants. Two months later, 300,000 meat packers and 180,000 electrical workers struck, and they were followed shortly thereafter by 750,000 steelworkers. In all, 4,630 work stoppages involving 5,000,000 strikers occurred in the twelve months after Japan's surrender. Although little physical violence characterized these stoppages, they generated violent emotions as middle- and upper-class Americans feared that unions would disrupt their economic security.

The postwar labor struggles involved far more than simple disputes over immediate union demands. Rather, they constituted the first peacetime test of the new alignment of social, economic, and political forces that had come into being during the Great Depression and World War II. At the heart of the labor unrest and the government's, employer's, and public's response lay the issue of the role of unions in the postwar era. Unfortunately for organized labor, the policies of the Truman administration accorded with industry's efforts to establish limits to trade-union power.

Within this context, on March 2, 1946, the nation prepared for another coal crisis as Lewis notified the bituminous operators that he desired to reopen negotiations. When the wage conference convened on March 12, Lewis surprised everyone by laying before the operators loosely defined "negotiable suggestions" instead of "demands." Included among his recommendations were the creation of a welfare fund, a wage increase of an unspecified amount, various improvements in the miners' working and living conditions, and recognition of the foremen's union. Journalists covering the session considered his two-hour opening speech "mild," noting the lack of attacks on the Truman administration and the absence of a strike threat. They paid too little attention to Lewis's dramatic recital of the record of miners killed and injured.

Throughout the subsequent controversy, Lewis proved unable to convince the public of his sincerity on the issues of health and safety. From the outset, most reporters interpreted his actions as a crusade to destroy federal wage-price policies, and, in the process, to show up Philip Murray who had just won a wage increase for his steelworkers. Lewis's lack of credibility was partly of his own making; his passion for maneuvers, plotting, and secret dealings over the years had created the image of an opportunistic, cunning, power-hungry man of few principles. Recalling past episodes, journalists came to suspect his altruistic demands as facades for baser goals.

In fact, Lewis's interest in promoting health care and mine safety went back at least a decade. He had first turned to these issues in the late 1930s and early 1940s, using them as a means to embarrass Roosevelt and the operators when he could not arouse public sympathy for the miners' economic plight. Yet the more he studied and developed his arguments, the more sincere became his commitment to alleviating these ills. His increased dedication to improving health and pension services for his members, moreover, coincided with demographic changes among the mining population. Whereas in 1940, 50 percent of the miners were thirty-two or younger, by 1944 the average age had risen to forty-five, with only 16 percent under thirty. Thus Lewis's drive for a health and pension fund blended with this new majority of older workers' own anxieties in life.

At the wage conference, Lewis dramatically related the dismal details of a UMW investigation into mining accidents, health care, insurance programs, state compensation laws, sanitary facilities in mining camps, and a variety of similar subjects. Bristling under these disclosures, the operators charged Lewis with "filibustering" and tried to focus the conference on more traditional subjects. To Lewis's demand for improved company housing, O'Neill snapped that he had come to negotiate a contract and not to act "as a sanitary expert." Throughout the haggling, Lewis refused to talk of wages or hours until the operators agreed "in principle" to a health and welfare fund.

The miners struck on April 1, and ten days later all negotiations stopped. For the next month, the nation burned away its coal reserves while little progress was made to resolve the crisis. By the second week in May the country's coal supply was dangerously low, causing the steel industry to cut production almost in half and Detroit auto plants to close. The Office of Defense Transportation clamped a tight embargo on rail freight and reduced passenger train service 25 percent. Harry Truman dimmed the lights in the White House, and the New York's Great White Way lost its glow.

Lewis knew that the railroad trainmen and engineers were planning a strike that would disrupt the delivery of coal. He thus calculated that a temporary halt to the miners' walkout might placate public and legislative opinion without sacrificing the union's strategic position. After leaving a conference with President Truman on May 10, he therefore announced that in order to protect the nation's health and safety, the miners would return to work until May 25. At the same time, a White House source indicated that the operators had finally agreed "in principle" to a health and welfare fund.

In the days that followed, the operators squirmed out of their commitment. Consequently, on May 16 Lewis and O'Neill informed the president that negotiations had collapsed and that further talks were futile. Faced with a deteriorating situation, on May 21 Truman ordered

Secretary of the Interior J. A. Krug to seize the mines and negotiate an agreement with the union on "the terms and conditions of employment for the period of the operation of the mines by the government." Once again, and perhaps not without design, Lewis found himself in a position similar to the one he had been in in 1943 when he had achieved portal-to-portal pay through an accord with Ickes.

Lewis maintained constant pressure on the government during the ensuing negotiations. Krug and his staff interviewed various experts on existing health and welfare funds, and apparently they grew sympathetic to the idea. Finally, on May 29 President Truman looked on as Krug and Lewis signed an accord that sent the miners back to work.

The Lewis-Krug agreement provided miners with a welfare and retirement fund jointly supervised by the union and the government. Initially, the government had planned to finance the fund out of a tax on the industry's payroll, but at the request of the operators this was changed to a five-cent royalty on every ton of coal mined. A second medical and health fund was also established, to be administered solely by the union and financed by the companies depositing moneys previously deducted from the miners' wages for company-run medical and health programs. The union also won a wage increase of 18.5 cents per hour, an increase in vacation pay, an agreement to accept the NLRB's pending ruling on the issue of the right of foremen to unionize, and a promise that a federal mine safety code would be formulated and enforced while the mines were under government control.

The strain of battle began to show on Lewis, who had aged considerably during the war years. At sixty-six he tired more easily and occasionally appeared to catnap or at least daydream. His world-famous eyebrows grew bushier than ever. His eyes had assumed a cavernous quality; his face became a study of lines and clefts. His hair—now almost white—was no longer kept trimmed and well groomed; and as it grew longer and became wavier and more unruly, it at times resembled a lion's mane.

For six weeks in the summer of 1946 Lewis escaped the tensions of Washington and drove west to a Wyoming dude ranch. Along the way he visited various UMW locals, patching up small differences and touching base with the rank and file.

Lewis was back in Washington performing his duties when in late September he suffered an acute attack of appendicitis and underwent an operation at the Johns Hopkins Hospital in Baltimore, at least according to reports in the newspapers. Actually, he may have suffered a coronary thrombosis. Whatever the case, he spent the next several weeks convalescing with little to do except, perhaps, ponder future victories.

On October 21, a still recuperating Lewis shocked the nation by demanding that Secretary of the Interior Krug negotiate a new contract with the union. He claimed the right to do so under the contract reopening provision of the 1945 accord, which he maintained had been carried forward into the Lewis-Krug agreement. Under this provision, either party could serve notice that it wanted talks resumed within ten days. If the other party refused, the contract was cancelled.

The announcement of Lewis's action set journalists to speculating on the meaning of this latest move. Was Lewis gluttonously seeking greater gains from the government, they asked, or was he pressuring the operators to come to terms with the union before the government granted the miners more concessions? Some felt Lewis sought to embarrass Truman on the eve of the 1946 congressional elections. Other envisioned an attempt to steal Philip Murray's thunder by winning a sizable advance while the CIO held its convention.

In responding to Lewis's letter, Secretary Krug and Coal Mines Administrator N. H. Collisson insisted that the agreement signed in May prevailed for as long as the government controlled the mines; they pointed to a clause in the contract that seemed to justify their view. As the days passed and the deadline neared, however, the president and others in the administration began to reconsider Krug and Collisson's initial reply. In particular, Secretary of Labor Lewis B. Schwellenbach and War Mobilization and Reconversion Director John R. Steelman both counseled the president to reopen negotiations. With Truman heeding this new advice, on October 27 Krug resentfully informed Lewis that his staff would meet with UMW representatives. Lewis accepted this as an acknowledgment of the validity of his interpretation of the existing contract.

On November 1, Coal Mines Administrator Collisson and his associates assembled with a delegation from the UMW. Because only Interior Department underlings attended, Lewis sent his own lieutenants while he stayed behind in his office. Naturally, the ensuing session accomplished little until both Krug and Lewis appeared on November 11. Ready for business, Lewis spelled out a series of proposals calling for a reduction in hours, a sharp increase in hourly wages, a hike in the amount of royalty paid into the welfare and retirement fund, recognition of the foremen's union, and other demands.

While the Interior Department's staff analyzed the union's demands, Krug concentrated on developing a plan to thwart Lewis. He was aided in this effort by the reverses suffered by the administration on Election Day, when the voters turned both houses of Congress over to Republican control, because now Truman began paying closer attention to General Counsel Clark Clifford and others who advised an aggressive stand against Lewis as a means of improving his prestige.

By the evening of November 12, Krug had plotted his strategy. "The Government," he informed the president, "must now choose between two major alternatives: Reaching a new agreement with Lewis or forcing him into negotiations with the operators." Krug opposed the first course. "It would be uniformly interpreted in all quarters as another surrender to Lewis. It would be Government sponsorship of a second round of inflationary wage increases. . . . It would, finally, postpone for an indefinite period the time when the Government might get out of the coal business." The better approach, Krug recommended to the president, was to "accept perhaps an even chance of an immediate coal strike" and compel the union to negotiate with the operators. This would avoid "the even greater disaster of a second Government-sponsored wage increase in the coal mines," and, equally important, it would "put the Government in a position where it has an aggressive program rather than a numbed acquiescence in whatever Lewis should really insist upon."

With Truman's consent, on Wednesday, November 13, Krug began executing his scheme. That morning Lewis received a call from the secretary requesting a private meeting. He willingly agreed but insisted that first the joint negotiators should meet and hear the government's response to the union's proposals. When the negotiators gathered at midday, Krug announced that at a morning meeting with operators, they had indicated their willingness to resume contract talks with the union. Lewis became incensed, criticized the secretary for dealing with a party that had no standing under the prevailing agreement, and stormed back to his office without keeping the planned private conference. When tempers cooled and the two men finally met in the late afternoon, Krug informed Lewis that although the government would not negotiate, it would agree to return the mines within sixty days of the UMW's resumption of talks with the private operators. He also produced a "formal" opinion by Attorney General Clark upholding the secretary's stand that the Lewis-Krug agreement prevailed for as long as the government possessed the mines.

On the morning of November 15 Lewis rejected Krug's proposal. "You now, at the last hour, of the last day, yield to the blandishments and soothing siren voice of the operators and seek to place the United Mine Workers of America and its members between Scylla and Charybdis," he berated the secretary. In line with Krug's strategy, at 2:30 in the afternoon the president sought to mobilize public opinion with a press release describing Krug's proposal as "fair and equitable" and calling on the mine workers to reconsider their stand. Informed of this move, Lewis officially notified the Secretary of the Interior that in accordance with the UMW's interpretation of the contract reopening provision, the Lewis-Krug agreement would terminate at midnight November 20.

While Lewis kept silent, Truman, Krug, Clark Clifford, and Tom Clark spent the next forty-eight hours plotting the government's next move. During their deliberations they persistently referred to the events of 1919: the Anderson injunction, the citation of Lewis and his colleagues for contempt, and the UMW acting president's surrender with the declaration, "we cannot fight our Government." Finally, on the afternoon of November 17, a White House spokesman informed the press of Truman's orders to "fight John L. Lewis on all fronts."

Administration officials moved quickly to dramatize the crisis. Although the nation possessed a thirty-seven day coal supply, the Solid Fuel Administration froze all bituminous coal in transit or storage, and the Office of Defense Transportation ordered railroads to curtail the use of coal. Truman and his family journeyed to Key West for a vacation, a gesture that both communicated to the public the president's confidence that the situation was under control and implied that Lewis no longer rated his personal attention. Behind this front, however, Truman kept close watch over developments in Washington.

On November 18, Attorney General Clark obtained from Judge T. Alan Goldsborough a temporary injunction against the union and its officers that instructed Lewis to cease giving effect to the November 15 notice of termination. Apparently Goldsborough agreed with Clark that given the union's no contract–no work policy, the notice constituted "in fact and in effect" a strike call.

Lewis ignored the injunction and remained silent as the termination deadline drew near. News of Goldsborough's order, however, provoked thirty-three thousand miners to strike prematurely, and when midnight, November 20, passed without word from UMW headquarters, the entire bituminous industry closed. In the nation at large, memories of the disruptive spring coal strike blended with administration projections of doom to generate a state of panic. After only one day of the walkout, even the normally restrained *New York Times* bore the dramatic headline "25,000,000 MAY BE IDLE IF COAL STRIKE IS PROLONGED."

On November 25, Lewis appeared in federal district court to argue why he and the UMW should not be held in contempt of court. During the hearings, he tried to project an image of confidence and good humor, but occasionally the mask fell, disclosing a tired, pale, and frustrated figure. Lewis's legal staff contended that Goldsborough's injunction had no force because it violated the Clayton and Norris-LaGuardia acts which sharply restricted the issuances of injunctions. But on December 3 Judge Goldsborough ruled that Lewis and his union were guilty of civil contempt of court.

Early the next morning, a dour Lewis accompanied by his legal retinue returned to the courthouse. For an hour or two they moved from one conference room to another as Judge Goldsborough sought a formula that would bring peace to the coalfields. Finally, word arrived from the White House that it would talk with Lewis only after the miners returned to work. Faced with a choice of surrender or defeat, Lewis chose the latter and marched into the courtroom, where the judge fined the UMW $3,500,000 and its president $10,000.

The nation now waited to see if the vanquished Lewis would yield and send the miners back to work. The pressures upon him were great. Each day that the strike continued could cost the union an additional fine of $250,000. The president, moreover, had scheduled a news conference for Sunday evening. At 2:00 p.m., Saturday, December 7, Lewis summoned reporters and dramatically called off the strike. He was doing so, he informed the press, to protect the nation from a coal shortage and to enable the Supreme Court to consider his appeal free from pressure.

Shortly thereafter Lewis vanished to "somewhere in Florida," where, until mid–February 1947, he nursed his ailing health and wounded pride. On March 6, the Supreme Court upheld the conviction of Lewis and the union. The justices reduced the UMW's fine to $700,000 but sustained the $10,000 penalty against Lewis. Pleading poverty, Lewis used union funds to pay his fine.

The outcome of the 1946 coal crisis provided the Truman administration the boost it desperately needed. As Truman's first major domestic triumph, the coal victory restored, in the words of Robert Allen and William Shannon, "a dash of vigor to the flabby spiritual tone of the executive office." It also marked Truman's emergence from the shadow of Roosevelt. "There was a big difference in the Old Man from then on," Clark Clifford recalled. "He was his own man at last."

The crisis also brought into full public view the feud between the UMW chief and the Truman administration. For the next several years, the nation listened as the protagonists hurled undignified insults at one another. The president labeled Lewis a "headline hunter," and when someone jestingly suggested that he appoint the labor leader ambassador to Moscow, Truman publicly quipped that he would not make that man chief dog catcher of this country. Lewis, in turn, pronounced Truman "totally unfitted" for the presidency. "His principles are elastic and he is careless with the truth," the labor leader snarled. "He has no special knowledge on any subject. And he is a malignant, scheming sort of an individual who is not only dangerous to the United Mine Workers of America but dangerous to the United States."

Although exchanges between Truman and Lewis filled the headlines, Lewis actually considered Secretary of the Interior Julius A. Krug the administration villain. This animosity derived in part from Krug's role in the UMW's 1946 conviction for contempt of court. But it also stemmed from Lewis's belief that the secretary was insensitive to the miners' welfare and unconcerned with the health of the coal industry.

In the spring of 1947, Lewis seized upon an explosion at the Centralia Coal Company in Illinois where 111 were killed as a means of publicly dramatizing his case against Krug. In testimony before a House subcommittee investigating the tragedy, Lewis expounded upon both the inadequacies of prevailing laws and the failure of government agencies to execute their responsibilities even when they possessed authority. Of the 3,345 mines inspected in 1946, he related, only two fully complied with the safety code. Lewis used such data to attack Secretary Krug, to whom he assigned major responsibility for the disaster. He harped on the fact that the UMW's agreement with Krug made him "the exclusive agency" charged with enforcing the Federal Mine Safety Code and correcting all violations. The bodies at Centralia, Lewis stressed, proved that the secretary had failed to meet this moral and legal duty.

Lewis also battled Krug over the directorship of the Bureau of Mines. Two weeks before Centralia the secretary had convinced Truman to nominate for the post James Boyd, dean of the Colorado School of Mines. Boyd's background in metal mining suited the administration's concern with developing stockpiles of vital minerals. Until his nomination, however, Boyd had never ventured down a coal shaft. This fact alone would have warranted Lewis's opposition to Boyd's selection, but Krug added insult to injury by failing to follow the customary form of soliciting the UMW's president's advice.

Under lobbying pressures by Lewis, the Senate recessed in July 1947 without acting on Boyd's nomination. During the break, Truman appointed Boyd interim director in the belief that the Senate would approve the nomination once it reconvened. Yet for another year and a half Lewis mobilized enough political support to stall confirmation. As a result, Truman cooled to the nomination in late 1948, however both the nominee and his backer wanted to fight Lewis to the finish. In the end Krug won; on March 22, 1949, the Senate finally confirmed Boyd. Lewis dramatized his defeat by calling a two-week memorial stoppage, which also served a second purpose of reducing the extensive coal supply then above ground.

At the same time he was jousting with Fair Dealers in the White House, Lewis vied with conservatives in Congress. Since the formative days of the CIO, Republicans and southern Democrats had united to seek stringent regulations of organized labor. In this campaign, they pointed to John L. Lewis as the personification of the evils that they wished to wipe out. In the reconversion era, the conservatives vowed to replace the Smith-Connally Act with new legislation. The UMW's battle with the government in late 1946 in conjunction with the most massive strike wave in United State's history stimulated public support behind their antiunion drive.

As could have been expected, Lewis first maneuvered to protect the UMW against any adverse legislation. With the government's authority to manage the collieries expiring on June 30, 1947, Coal Mines Administrator Collisson summoned all parties to private contract bargaining beginning on April 29. Lewis treated these negotiations both as an opportunity to demonstrate the superiority of free collective bargaining over government intervention and as a chance to write into the contract clauses circumventing some of the restrictions on unionism being considered by Congress. Throughout May and early June, Lewis acted in conciliatory fashion, presenting the operators with "proposals" rather than "demands." He delayed serious bargaining until he was certain of the fate of the Taft-Hartley Act. The prosperity of the coal industry put most operators in a cooperative mood, for they realized their bonanza would end if the miners struck once the government relinquished the mines. Finally, after Congress passed the Taft-Hartley Act over Truman's veto on June 23, the parties hammered out an agreement that all segments of the industry approved by mid-July.

The 1947 contract represented a solid advance on the issues of wages, hours, and fringe benefits for the miners. Most important, the operators agreed to establish a welfare and retirement fund comparable to the one created by the Lewis-Krug agreement. The contract also contained provisions designed to protect the union from the Taft-Hartley law. Lewis had negotiated the agreement subsequent to the enactment of the bill but before the effective date of certain of its sections. This would enable him, he hoped, to place in the contract conditions that, if executed a few days later, would have been illegal. To prevent civil suits against the union for unauthorized work stoppages as mandated by the Taft-Hartley Act, the new coal agreement was to apply to miners only "during such time as such persons are willing and able to work." Likewise, a clause found in earlier contracts imposing penalties on the union for wildcat strikes was omitted from the new document out of concern that Taft-Hartley would weaken the UMW leadership's ability to exert discipline over the rank and file.

The achievement of a new coal contract enabled Lewis to direct his energies toward undermining that "despotic, damnable, reprehensible, unwholesome, vicious slave statute," the Taft-Hartley Act. For several years he would be among the most outspoken foes of the measure, just as the law would be used most effectively against Lewis and his union. Unlike other labor leaders who privately preferred to amend the statute's more reprehensible features, Lewis was committed to repeal of the act itself.

Perhaps intoxicated by his own reputation as a strategist, Lewis believed he had found a tactic to debilitate the law. The act required labor officials to file affidavits affirming that they were not members of the Communist party in order for their unions to utilize the services of the National Labor Relations Board. Lewis's strategy called for labor leaders collectively to refuse to file the requested affidavit and thus force the board into a position where it served only the employers. Such action, he hoped, would arouse "the sense of fair play of the American people," and they would demand Taft-Hartley's repeal.

When the NLRB ruled, in the fall of 1947, that all officers of the A. F. of L. had to file anticommunist affidavits in order for the organization's federal locals to enjoy the privileges of the board, Lewis—one of the fifteen vice-presidents—refused to comply. To circumvent his refusal, the other officers proposed an amendment to the Federation's constitution that technically demoted the vice-presidents to the status of council members and reclassified the president and secretary-treasurer as the sole officials of the organization.

When the proposed amendment came before the October 1947 A.F. of L. convention, Lewis subjected it to some of his finest oratory. For a half hour he treated the delegates to a scorching diatribe against the Taft-Hartley Act—"the first ugly, savage thrust of Fascism in America"—and the failure of the A.F. of L. leaders to do their duty to the membership. "I am reminded of the Biblical parable," he intoled, "Lions led by asses." At the conclusion of his speech he refused to be a candidate for the "debased" board if the delegates approved the amendment. "Perhaps that makes no difference; perhaps you will say 'John Lewis is trying to hold a gun to the head of the convention.' That is not true. I don't think anyone can hold a gun to the head of this convention. . . . As far as that is concerned, on this particular issue, I don't think the Federation has a head. I think its neck has just grown up and haired over."

Lewis's parting sarcasm amounted to an admission that he had failed to sway the delegates, who promptly passed the amendment. True to his word, Lewis declined to be a member of the reconstituted council, and, indeed, he resolved that the time had arrived for the UMW again to depart from the Federation. No doubt it would have done so quickly had Lewis not been hospitalized for two weeks following the convention. Although the newspapers claimed he was only undergoing a checkup and enjoying a rest, Lewis likely suffered another heart attack. Thus six weeks passed before Lewis consulted with his executive board on December 12, after which he scribbled in pencil a memo to the Federation's president:

> Green, AFL
> We disaffiliate
> Lewis

Lewis continued his fight to repeal the Taft-Hartley Act after the miners left the A.F. of L. As a result of the UMW's 1948 campaign, forty-one congressmen and six senators residing in coal-mining areas who had supported the law were defeated for reelection, and in 1950 two of the four Ohio counties lost by Senator Taft were heavily populated by UMW members. The series of defeats that the UMW experienced in the late 1940s and early 1950s reinforced the aging labor leader's ideological disposition against federal action and led him to recommend to a Senate committee in 1953 the repeal not only of the Taft-Hartley law, but of the Wagner Act as well. "This would give to this country, its employers and employees," he argued "an opportunity. . . to practice for a season true, free and genuine collective bargaining without government interference, free from the brooding shadows which presently hover over all bargaining tables." Lewis was now convinced that another historical cycle had begun: That the federal government that had stimulated trade unionism during the 1930s now preferred to protect corporate interests.

By 1948, Lewis and the UMW confronted opposition on all fronts. Press and public opinion condemned them. The labor leader's relations with the Truman administration had soured so badly that he lacked meaningful influence with the Bureau of Mines, an agency important to the union's day-to-day business. A conservative Congress sought to paralyze militant unionism as represented by the UMW. And Lewis's and the union's conviction for contempt in 1946 seemed to indicate that the courts were willing to help Congress in its drive. Even the A.F. of L., after the 1947 convention, joined the CIO in criticisms of Lewis. Naturally, the coal operators resisted the miners' demands.

In the spring of 1948, another in the decade-long series of labor-management crises erupted in the coal industry. This dispute and the others that followed over the next two years were vividly colored by the Truman-Lewis feud and the efforts of operators and government officials to apply the Taft-Hartley Act to the UMW. Yet although fre-

[handwritten marginal note: Lewis as anti-regulation]

quently obfuscated by clashes of personalities and assertions of legal rights, monetary issues were at the core of these disputes, with the fate and scope of the welfare and retirement fund the primary source of contention.

Although the 1947 contract had included provisions for a welfare and retirement program, for seven months after its signing the three trustees—Ezra Van Horn for the operators, Lewis for the union, and Thomas E. Murray—failed to agree on terms to activate the fund. Then, on January 16, 1948, Murray threw the fund into a crisis by resigning his trusteeship. Neither Lewis nor Van Horn was willing to approve a new neutral trustee if any likelihood existed that the person would support the other side on the pension issue. Yet without a third trustee, Van Horn needed only to sit tight to prevent the program from becoming a reality.

More than a month passed, during which the operators made no gesture toward activating the fund. Angered at their intransigence, on Friday, March 12, Lewis informed the union's membership that "the Bituminous Coal Operators, through their trustee . . . have dishonored the 1947 Wage Agreement and defaulted under its provisions affecting the Welfare Fund." He also implied that the UMW would take action to force the operators "to honor their agreement." When a reporter asked Lewis if his comments alluded to a strike, he dismissed the question as being "more or less hypothetical."

To the miners, however, Lewis's choice of words "dishonored" and "defaulted" carried more than hypothetical implications. On Sunday, March 14, two hundred thousand miners commenced an "unofficial" strike, which by Tuesday had closed a substantial portion of the bituminous coal industry. Lewis insisted that the Taft-Hartley Act was inapplicable in this situation because he had not ordered the strike, and the law guaranteed the right of individuals to act on their own. He also contended that the walkout did not violate the union's 1947 contract because the document clearly stipulated that its provisions applied to the miners only when they were "willing and able" to work.

With the closing of the coal mines, the federal government moved onto the scene. First, the director of the Mediation and Conciliation Service, Cyrus S. Ching, unsuccessfully sought a way to resolve the dispute. Then, on March 20, President Truman created a board of inquiry to determine whether the situation warranted an eighty-day Taft-Hartley injunction. Lewis initially refused to appear before the board—challenging its legality and charging prejudice against two of its members—but finally testified under the compulsion of a court order. Finally, on March 31, the board of inquiry informed Truman that the coal dispute did threaten the nation's welfare and three days later Attorney General Clark approached Judge Matthew F. McGuire, who issued an injunction ordering Lewis to "instruct forthwith" the idle miners to return to work. In a second injunction, the judge also directed the UMW to resume negotiations with the operators on the pension issue.

The injunctions placed Lewis in a delicate position. To recognize them as valid would weaken his legal challenge to the Taft-Hartley Act. Yet he knew that to ignore the orders would result in the union and himself being convicted of contempt of court. In an effort to escape this predicament, on April 3 he again circularized the union membership. "I . . . now repeat that you are not now under, and have never been under, any orders, directions or suggestions, expressed or implied, from me or any of the union officers to cease work or to continue to cease work in protest to the present dishonoring (as we see it) of the 1947 Contract."

As could have been expected, the coal miners did not return to work, nor did the Truman administration view Lewis's circular as compliance with the injunctions. On Wednesday, April 7, Judge T. Alan Goldsborough, acting on a petition from the attorney general, ordered Lewis and the United Mine Workers to show cause on the following Monday why they should not be found in contempt for failing to call off the strike.

Fears of a repeat of 1946 now mounted for Lewis, as he searched for a way to avert the impending verdict. To fulfill Judge McGuire's second order, he delegated a squad of lieutenants to bargain with the operators. Meanwhile, he spent the weekend struggling to extricate himself from his legal predicament by playing presidential primary politics.

Lewis reportedly used the good offices of Alf Landon to contact the speaker of the House of Representatives, Joseph W. Martin, about arranging a settlement to the coal dispute. Martin hoped to win the 1948 Republican presidential nomination as a compromise candidate, and apparently he envisioned settling the coal crisis as a coup that would give him national recognition. At Martin's suggestion, both Lewis and Van Horn accepted New Hampshire Senator Styles Bridges as the fund's new neutral trustee.

On Monday morning Senator Bridges proposed a "tentative" solution to the pension crisis which Lewis approved and Van Horn rejected. Under the plan, an annuity of $1,200 would go "to those members of the UMWA who attain the age of 62 years and complete 20 years in the coal industry on or after May 29, 1946." True to form, Lewis announced the settlement a glorious union victory and wired all bituminous locals: "Pensions granted. The agreement is now honored." Lewis then set off for court to answer the contempt charges.

Judge Goldsborough proved unresponsive to the argument that Lewis and the union had purged themselves of contempt by settling the pension dispute that morning, and he ordered the accused to stand trial. After several days of proceedings, a "gray and grimvisaged" Lewis listened as the judge ruled the UMW and its president guilty. On April 20, Goldsborough fined the union $1,500,000 and Lewis $20,000—double the penalty imposed on them in 1946. Seeking to avert further court action, Lewis wired all bituminous district presidents instructions to "convey to each member my wish that they immediately return to work." This gesture still did not satisfy Judge Goldsborough, who granted the government's petition for an eighty-day injunction despite the union's insistence that the dispute had been settled.

To the contrary, the pension fight continued. At the very moment that Judge Goldsborough was issuing the injunction, Ezra Van Horn was in another courtroom filing a petition to suspend the Bridges pension plan until the courts determined its validity. Then, a week later, while a judge pondered Van Horn's request, Lewis and Bridges voted to activate the fund and named the miners' leader as administrator and his friend Josephine Roche as director. To nullify this action, Van Horn notified all banks serving as depositories for the fund that the removal of monies without his signature would be at their risk. Again, Lewis saw his goals frustrated.

At this point, the pension issue became inextricably involved with the 1948 contract negotiations, for on April 30, Lewis notified the bituminous operators that talks would begin on May 18. This action permitted him legally to call a strike at the expiration of the 1947 contract on June 30. Indeed, the probability of a work stoppage seemed high; besides the pension issue, this would be the first agreement written since the Taft-Hartley Act went into force, and the operators wanted to restrain the union.

After a three-week delay while the union and the operators fought in court over who had to participate in the bargaining, the 1948 national wage conference began with Lewis insisting that the operators "honor" the welfare and pension provisions of the 1947 contract as a "condition precedent" to a new agreement. Under pressure, the operators finally offered a plan, but its terms were clearly unacceptable to the union. The talks rambled on for a week. Then, on June 15, the northern and western operators declared the sessions "futile" and walked out of the conference.

Within hours, Federal Mediation and Conciliation Director Ching requested both sides to meet with him the next day as the administration began to move through the steps for an eighty-day injunction. By June 19, Ching had referred the deadlock to Truman, who proceeded to

name a board of inquiry to investigate the dispute. The nation tensed
for another showdown between Lewis and the courts.

Then the unexpected happened. On June 22, Justice Goldsborough
upheld the legality of Bridges's pension plan and dismissed the suit filed
by Van Horn. In his decision, Goldsborough concurred with Lewis that
all members of the union could be covered by the fund and not just
employees of the signatories of the 1947 contract. He also supported
Lewis's contention that the business of the fund required only a majority
vote of the trustees. Goldsborough's ruling undermined the operators'
case against the fund, leading them promptly to seek a truce. Within
forty-eight hours the commercial operators and the union agreed on a
new contract granting the miners a dollar-a-day increase and doubling
to twenty cents the operators' payment to the welfare and retirement
program.

Strikes in the coalfields subsided for eight months. The board of
inquiry appointed by Truman declared the 1948 contract dispute settled
and adjourned. During the summer, Josephine Roche assembled an
administrative staff for the welfare and retirement fund, and on September 9, Lewis ceremoniously awarded the first pension check.

The routine nature of union life during these months, however, veiled
a growing awareness by leaders of labor and management of the changing
fortunes of the coal industry. From reports for the first quarter of 1949,
they learned that coal production had fallen 11.4 percent from the same
period the year before and that prices had declined substantially. Actually, some observers had noted signs of the industry's waning prosperity toward the end of World War II, as diesel engines replaced coal-
burning steam locomotives and homeowners converted their coal-burning furnaces to cleaner and more convenient fuels.

Again, as in the 1920s, the operators attempted to meet the downturn
in business by cutting costs. In particular, their gaze fell upon the
multimillion-dollar welfare and retirement fund, which under the 1948
contract drained from their purses twenty cents for each ton of coal
dug. In their drive to curtail the fund, moreover, they were encouraged
by the steel industry, for the United Steelworkers of America also wanted
such a program and the industry's policymakers feared that they could
not grant their mill workers fewer benefits than their captive miners
received.

The Southern Coal Producers' Association (SCPA) made the first
move in the coal drama of 1949–50 when it summoned the UMW to
separate contract negotiations in May. Lewis insisted that the talks be
held in Bluefield, West Virginia, away from the political influences of
Washington and in a community whose lack of renown communicated

his contempt for the association. From the start of the conference, Lewis refused to make demands and cunningly asserted that he would consider any improvements the operators wished to suggest in the prevailing contract. When SCPA proposed terms that actually restricted or eliminated many of the old contract's provisions, Lewis ordered an industrywide "stabilization period of inaction" to run from June 13 to June 20.

Because the SCPA had compelled the UMW to enter separate negotiations, Lewis decided further to divide the bituminous industry; on May 18 he notified the captive mine operators of his desire to begin talks and then waited until late June before initiating negotiations with the northern and western commercial operators. This group represented more than 55 percent of the nation's annual tonnage and dominated the industry. Under the leadership of George Love of Pittsburgh Consolidated Coal Company, moreover, it frequently aligned with the steel corporations. Over the ensuing months, Lewis haggled with this group and with Harry Moses of the captive mines while UMW Secretary-Treasurer John Owens dealt with the South.

From July 1 to mid-September, participants in the three conferences parleyed without notable progress. When the old contract expired on June 30, Lewis broke the union's tradition of "no contract, no work," and instead imposed a three-day work week on the industry. In response, the southern operators withheld payments to the welfare and retirement fund. By mid-September, their failure to pay, combined with the reduced income of the fund owing to the three-day week, placed the welfare and pension programs in jeopardy and led the board of trustees to halt the disbursement of benefits. When the miners were informed of the "default" of the southern operators and the suspension of payments, they engaged in a wave of work stoppages.

The coal dispute, having simmered along for six months, began to boil once the steel corporations settled their pension dispute with the steelworkers in late November, and the captive mine operators became more willing to talk seriously with the UMW. So, too, did George Love of the northern commercial operators, who on December 28 proclaimed his readiness to effect a welfare and retirement plan with the miners "equal to the program which settled the recent steel strike." Because the steelworkers' settlement was inferior to the miners' current arrangement, Lewis ignored Love's offer. To make him more cooperative, the SCPA, backed by the captive and northern operators, filed with the NLRB unfair labor practice charges against the UMW and pleaded for an injunction. Provoked by this action, groups of miners again initiated a wave of wildcat strikes, which further increased pressures for federal intervention.

Lewis searched vigorously for a way to checkmate both a possible court injunction and imminent action by the White House. When George Love made a publicity-oriented overture to renew negotiations, Lewis seized it and cornered the operators into renewing talks on February 1. Yet even before the parties met, Truman assured the failure of the conference. On January 31, he sent identical telegrams to Lewis and the operators asking the miners to return to work for seventy days while an all-citizen fact-finding board investigated the issues. At the end of this period, the disputants would consider the board's recommendations, although they were not bound to accept them. This procedure clearly favored the operators, because it guaranteed them full production during the peak winter season without requiring from them any sacrifice. In light of the recent steelworkers' settlement, moreover, the board's report could be expected to lean toward the operators' side.

The operators naturally found little reason to bargain with the union when a fact-finding board might recommend even better terms. Therefore, on February 2 they walked out of negotiations and accepted Truman's plan. Lewis, on the other hand, rejected the president's proposal, leading Truman to create a board of inquiry that quickly confirmed that the dispute now posed a danger to the nation's welfare. Within hours of receiving the board's report, the administration obtained from Judge Richard B. Kleech an injunction directing the miners to return to work and the union to resume talks with the operators. At the same time, Judge Kleech upheld the operator's contention that some of the UMW's demands constituted unfair labor practices under the Taft-Hartley Act.

Lewis, desiring to avoid a repeat of his contempt convictions of 1946 and 1948, immediately ordered an end to the strike. His words, however, failed to move the miners off the picket line, committed as they were to the union's program and annoyed by the operators' obstinance and government intervention, nor did they heed his second directive, issued a week later, "to cease forthwith all stoppages and return to work without delay." The continuation of the strike, therefore, led the Truman administration to obtain from Judge Kleech an order directing the UMW to show cause why it should not be held in contempt. Significantly, this time the judge refused to name Lewis in the citation and after considering the case for two weeks, he ruled that the government had failed to prove the union in contempt despite the fact that most of the membership remained away from work.

The not-guilty verdict created the preconditions for a rapid settlement of the nine-month dispute. With the miners having successfully frustrated a Taft-Hartley injunction, Truman immediately asked Congress for authority to seize the collieries. Both the union and the operators viewed Truman's plan with alarm and objected to the further interjection of government into their affairs. Undermining Truman's seizure plan now became more important to the disputants than the differences between them. Within hours of the president's petition to Congress, they announced the settlement of major points in contention. Two days later, on March 5, they signed the National Bituminous Coal Wage Agreement of 1950, leading Congress readily to abandon Truman's seizure proposal.

The new agreement constituted a compromise. The operators received reassurance that the union would respect their right to control their facilities and that labor and management would work together to reduce the extent of government involvement in industry affairs. In return, the operators agreed to cooperate with the union in administering the welfare and retirement fund. Most particularly, they consented to replacing Senator Bridges as the neutral trustee with Josephine Roch. This move guaranteed that the fund would always reflect Lewis's will. The operators also agreed to pay their employees an extra seventy cents a day and to increase their contribution to the welfare and retirement fund from twenty to thirty cents per ton.

The most important aspect of the 1950 contract, however, was its spirit rather than its content. "We have had a good fight, but we are all glad it's over," George Love informed newsmen after the signing. Lewis concurred, adding that the new agreement provided "assurance that for a substantial period of time the industry can abate its labor warfare and apply itself—both management and labor—to the constructive problems of producing coal in quantity for the benefit of the American economy at the lowest possible cost permitted by modern techniques."

The abrupt termination of the 1949–50 coal dispute also concluded many years of turbulence in the mining industry. The rise of competitive fuels, the threat of intensified and continuous government intervention in the industry, and the increase in small "gopher hole" nonunion mines led the combatants rapidly to become allies. Although Lewis would remain president of the UMWA for another decade, he had led his last great strike. The public's personification of an irresponsible union leader now began to transform himself into a labor executive.

20

A Prisoner of Change, 1950–60

The 1950s was a period of trial for John L. Lewis. The decade began with the sixty-nine-year-old union boss leading a major strike that he did not foresee as his last. His name still evoked editorial criticism; his actions continued to warrant presidential attention. Yet with coal's declining importance and his own increased isolation from the labor movement, Lewis gradually came to sense the end of an era. At first, he responded by trying to recapture some of his old dash. Unsuccessful, he then spent the remainder of the decade establishing himself as a coal industry statesman, a labor executive, and a noble humanitarian.

Each year during the 1950s, Lewis witnessed the death of family members, associates, and adversaries, and he also experienced failing health. Sorrowfully, too, he experienced frustration as the new generation in power treated his cherished values as outdated. By 1958, he had concluded that the time had come for new leadership to develop in the UMW, and two years later he voluntarily abdicated his throne. Such action was unprecedented among labor leaders of his stature: Samuel Gompers, William Green, Phil Murray all died in union office, and George Meany retired only when death was near. It is a measure of the change Lewis underwent that he, whose life centered so much on amassing power, considered relinquishing it to others.

Few events communicated as clearly to Lewis his waning importance as did the reunification of the A.F. of L. and CIO without him. Even before his dramatic break with the CIO in 1942, he had dreamed of being the person who would reunite the two federations. In the mid-1940s he strove to attain a position with the A. F. of L. from which to lead a unity movement. Spurned by his associates, Lewis then sought to create a new vehicle for unity independent of the two federations.

In the fall of 1952, Lewis and William Green were again exploring the possibility of the UMW rejoining the A.F. of L., when the Federation's president died. His successor, George Meany, seldom agreed with Lewis, so the discussions were never resumed. Nor did Walter Reuther's advancement to the presidency of the CIO after Murray's death improve Lewis's chances for an accommodation on that front. The UMW president loved to taunt the autoworkers' head for his former socialism, his fascination with "big" ideas, and his use of "fancy" phrases. Lewis now sought to bring together those union heads who felt slighted in the transfer of power.

For help in this matter, he called upon David B. Charnay, the head of the Allied Public Relations Association, which the UMW had been employing since the late 1940s to improve its public image. Charnay began lining up allies for Lewis. One natural candidate was Charnay's client, Dave Beck, president of the million-member International Brotherhood of Teamsters, who feared losing his union's independence and jurisdiction in the possible A.F. of L.–CIO merger. David McDonald, the new head of the United Steelworkers, seemed another potential ally, as he was brooding over his union's declining influence in the CIO since Walter Reuther became president.

On April 30, 1954, Charnay set up the first in a series of luncheon meetings involving Lewis, McDonald, and Beck and released enough publicity to create some concern within the two houses of labor that a third dwelling might be built. Lewis hoped that the talks either would lead to the formation of a new federation or would scare the leaders of the A.F. of L. and CIO into inviting him to their unity negotiations. Neither Beck nor McDonald, however, shared such desires. For them, the "Lew McBeck" discussions were part of a strategy to enhance their own influence within their respective federations. Both men represented larger memberships than Lewis, and neither needed UMW money. By the end of 1954 Beck and McDonald discarded Lewis and excluded him from future luncheons.

When, in 1955, it became clear that the A.F. of L. and CIO would reunite without the miners, Lewis was outwardly critical but inwardly hurt. Appearing on CBS's "Face the Nation," he grumbled about the UMW being "stipulated" out of the talks and characterized the unity arrangements as "particularly unfortunate" because they placed in "a small group of men in the merged organization, the sovereignty and jurisdiction and welfare of all the lesser unions in both groups."

Lewis could not repress his personal feelings. On November 30, 1955, in the petty manner in which he customarily responded to slights, Lewis instructed John Owens to demand repayment of $1,685,000 that he contended the UMW had loaned the CIO back in the 1930s. Only resentment can explain the resurrection of a dead issue. Upon receiving Owens's message, James Carey wrote back directly to Lewis: "The CIO owes you no money." And then he added: "You have achieved the momentary ripple of publicity which you sought to relieve the boredom of your isolation from the democratic labor movement."

Lewis's loss of national prominence involved far more than his isolation from the labor movement. From beginning to end, his career was shaped by the fortunes of the coal industry—and in the years following World War II, coal's importance as a national energy source dwindled. Intense competition from oil, natural gas, and hydroelectricity rapidly reduced the anthracite industry to slow death and placed bituminous producers in grave economic straits.

The operators sought to protect profits by cutting labor costs. For most large and middle-sized companies, increased productivity through mechanization accomplished this end. By 1950, mining technology had changed greatly from what it had been when Lewis first went underground. Coal was no longer dug with picks, the traditional symbol of the trade. Now miners participated in a highly mechanized operation or, as Harry Moses described it in 1952, "the only assembly-line mass production industry carried on underground." Power-driven machines cut the black rock from the seam, loaded it onto shuttle cars, and transported it to the surface. In the most modern collieries even this equipment had been outmoded by the continuous mining machine, which coordinated the entire operation. Strip-mining, moreover, which produced only 1 percent of the total tonnage when Lewis first became a national union officer, accounted for nearly one-quarter of the annual output by the mid-1950s and seemed likely to grow.

Coal companies could also cut labor costs by operating on a nonunion basis. The demand for coal during World War II, followed by the emergence of the Tennessee Valley Authority as a major coal consumer, fostered hundreds of small mines in traditionally antiunion areas of Kentucky and Tennessee. These marginal mines generally resorted to nonunion production in order to win a competitive advantage. Even if a nonunion operator granted his employees the UMW wage, he still realized tremendous savings by escaping royalty payments to the welfare and retirement fund. And without the UMW to police safety practices, small nonunion operators could reap further cost savings because the federal mine laws did not apply to companies with fewer than sixteen employees. The government also bolstered nonunion mines through the coal purchasing policies of the TVA, which granted contracts to the lowest bidder. Hence, the number of nonunion mines grew until, by the early 1960s, they accounted for almost 25 percent of the annual coal production.

Such economic changes in the coal industry weakened the United Mine Workers of America. The increase in productivity, the decline in markets, and the rise of nonunion pits interacted to reduce the size of the work force Lewis represented. Whereas in 1945, four hundred thousand UMW members dug coal, a decade later this figure fell by half. For families of unemployed miners, this translated into a life of poverty in Appalachia; for Lewis and his organization, it meant a decline in stature in an era of million-member unions.

More ominous from an institutional perspective was the union's loss of its strategic position in the economy. With coal's waning importance and the industry's tendency to exceed demand, a miners' strike no longer immediately threatened the nation's well-being. Coal disputes could continue for months or even a year before arousing alarm. In fact, now they actually hurt the union, because they forced coal consumers to seek alternative fuels. The situation struck Lewis as a replay of the 1920s and as proof of his cyclical theory of history. Clearly the economics of coal demanded a new mode of action from the UMW and its chief.

The operators, not the union, however, pioneered in adapting to the new conditions. Coal's decreased proportion of the energy market, the rise of price-cutting nonunion producers, the disruptive impact of strikes on markets, and the constant threat of government intervention all caused leading operators to recognize that they could not allow the contentious pattern of labor relations to prevail and still operate profitably. During the 1950s, electric power companies became the foremost consumers of coal, with the steel industry occupying second place. By 1957, these two industries burnt more than 60 percent of domestic coal output. Because both required steady deliveries of the mineral and electrical utilities possessed the capability of switching to other fuels, both industries demanded multiyear contracts with operators, again reinforcing the need for labor peace and predictable production in the coalfields.

The rise of new leadership among the operators facilitated the implementation of a new approach to labor relations. In place of the melodramatic Charles O'Neill and the dour Ezra Van Horn—veterans of two decades of warfare with Lewis—emerged genial but forthright George Love. A Pennsylvania blue blood replete with a Princeton degree, Love had entered the coal business in 1926 after a brief career as an investment broker. Skilled at high finance and corporate administration, he sought to create a prosperous coal industry through "farsighted" management. "We had a dream," Love told a writer for *Fortune* mag-

azine. "The trouble with the coal industry was that it was fragmentary
in its organization, and wasteful in its technology. We reasoned . . . that
if we could get our hands on enough properties, we could close down
or sell off the bad mines, [and] exploit only the good ones." Following
this plan, in 1945 Love merged three large firms into the Pittsburgh
Consolidation Coal Company. The new colossus, popularly known as
Consol, was the world's largest commercial producer of bituminous
coal. As president of this giant—and with the behind-the-scenes aid of
Secretary of the Treasury George Humphrey, whose business connections linked Consol to the captive mines—Love dominated the coal
industry during the 1950s.

The strikes of the postwar era, culminating in a long, bitter struggle
in 1949–50, threatened Love's plans for the industry. Love concluded
that such strife stemmed as much from the way the parties engaged in
collective bargaining as it did from clear conflicts of interest between
labor and management. The employers, he noted, lacked sufficient unity,
which meant that too often a small band of obstinate producers provoked a strike that threatened the best interests of a majority of the
firms. The designation of a fixed expiration date for each contract also
promoted needless strife, because Lewis, responding to rank-and-file
pressures, felt compelled to make demands regardless of the health of
the industry. The practice of conducting negotiations at public joint
mass meetings transformed collective bargaining into a spectator sport
in which both parties broadcasted half-truths, vilified their adversaries,
and locked themselves into untenable positions in an effort to enlist
the power of public opinion. Inevitably, such conduct led to government
intervention and the settlement of the industry's economic problems
on a political basis or at the whim of a judge.

In July 1950 Love initiated a major step toward restructuring labor
relations in the industry by organizing the Bituminous Coal Operators
Association (BCOA). Essentially an alliance among northern commercial operators and the captive mines, BCOA was headed by U.S. Steel's
Harry Moses, although Love remained its guiding spirit. The new association accounted for roughly 50 percent of the coal mined in the
country and out-produced its southern counterpart, SCPA, by better
than two to one. Such strength enabled BCOA to shape policy for the
remainder of the industry. Love intended to use his association to
persuade the country's coal operators that strikes were ruinous and
should be avoided, that the government and public should be eliminated
from dealings with the union, and that labor and management should
work together to solve mutual problems in a businesslike way.

BCOA's leadership faced a major task—convincing Lewis of the operators' commitment to developing more harmonious relations with

the union. Fortunately for them, Lewis had no ideological qualms about collaboration and was well practiced at it. Moreover, he, too, sought a way to cope with the political, economic, and technological forces that concerned the mine owners. In particular, Lewis, as much as any employer, sought to minimize government intervention in the industry. Yet Lewis approached BCOA cautiously. After three decades of bickering with coal barons, the aging labor leader doubted their ability to adopt a new attitude toward the union. Most particularly, he remembered the breakdown of cooperation in the 1920s, when the coal industry faced a similar economic plight. Thus, he initially treated Love's labor strategy as a delicate, temporary arrangement dictated by external forces. It was not until the middle of the decade that he abandoned circumspection and became an apostle of the "new look."

Lewis first tested Love's labor relations system in December 1950. Although the March 1950 agreement still had almost a year to run, Lewis nonetheless indicated to Moses of BCOA and Moody of SCPA his desire for a new contract. Clearly, the UMW sought an advance in wages in anticipation of the national government imposing controls to curtail inflation during the Korean War. Through December and early January, Lewis, Moses, and Moody engaged in a new style of casual, quiet negotiations, with no fanfare, no public spectacles, and no meddling by "bureaucrats." Few people even knew of the contract talks, least of all the miners. Despite appearances, however, Lewis played his old game of pitting the South against the North and also kept the threat of a strike always present. Finally, on January 18, a surprised public learned that the parties had reached a new accord, that gave coal miners $1.60 more a day in pay. Thus far, Lewis indicated to the press, he was satisfied with BCOA's performance.

Yet the operators still had not won Lewis's full confidence. He respected the 1951 accord until mid-1952, when he again notified them that he wished to formulate a new agreement. And in the ensuing negotiations, he applied steady pressure, including a "memorial" work stoppage to reduce coal stockpiles. When, on September 10, BCOA rejected the terms of an agreement arranged by Lewis and Moses, the mine workers' president threatened to disrupt the association. All nonmembers of BCOA, he proposed, could continue producing coal when the present contract expired if they agreed to accept any new accord once negotiated. Attracted by the prospect of large profits while much of the industry lay idle, a number of BCOA members indicated their intention of becoming independent. Soon Love and the other major operators, afraid that labor relations would revert to the old, turbulent pattern if BCOA collapsed, acquiesced to the original Moses-Lewis terms. The 1952 agreement, signed by BCOA on September 29 and by SCPA the next day, provided miners with a wage increse of $1.90 a day and added ten cents more a ton in royalty payments to the welfare and retirement fund.

Before the 1952 contract could be implemented, however, it required the approval of the Wage Stabilization Board that Truman had established to combat inflation during the Korean War. Since the start of the Asian conflict, Lewis had opposed government controls, and now he had an opportunity to press his point. Lewis's behavior in the ensuing events betrayed a pathetic attempt to recapture his World War II notoriety. His battle against Washington bureaucrats, moreover, sorely tested BCOA's commitment to ameliorating union-management relations and to eliminating government interference in the industry. The association's willingness to cooperate, and even to do his bidding, helped convince Lewis that a new era of labor policy had truly dawned.

On October 1, the operators alone submitted the new contract to the Wage Stabilization Board for its approval. The majority, composed of all the public and industry members, approved $1.50 of the $1.90-a-day wage increase, but it denied the additional forty cents on the ground "that it is inconsistent with the economic stabilization program." The miners' hourly wage rates and annual earnings, they contended, compared favorably with employees in manufacturing industries and did not warrant special treatment.

The WSB's decision angered the workers in the coalfields. As soon as they heard the news, miners walked out of the pits without Lewis's formal approval. Disturbed by these shutdowns, Harry Moses reminded Lewis that BCOA "unilaterally and without reservations has urged the Wage Stabilization Board to approve the $1.90 increase called for in this agreement." The association's willingness to pay the full amount "is restrained only by legal limitations imposed by the Board." In light of such cooperation, Moses pleaded, could not Lewis urge the miners to return to work?

Although not calling off the strike, Lewis nonetheless joined Moses on October 24 in requesting the economic stabilization administrator, Roger L. Putnam, to review the case. They based their appeal on two points. First, they contended that the miners should receive the higher pay because they had not received added fringe benefits. Second, they asserted that the total contract should be approved because it ensured "the maintenance and furtherance of the American way of life." "The principal contribution to the stabilization policy that this contract makes, . . ." Lewis and Moses jointly maintained, "is the fact that agreement was reached, after concessions on each side, without a shutdown in the industry. Failure of approval by competent authority defeats this purpose."

As the coal walkout provoked public discontent only weeks before a presidential election, Harry Truman summoned Lewis and Moses to the White House on October 26. There they explored the issue, with Moses no doubt repeating his belief that the government's policy threatened the new, harmonious labor relations in the coal industry. After the conference, the president announced to the press that Putnam would give "serious and prompt" consideration to the case and that in the meantime Lewis would order the miners back to work.

Increasingly the coal situation became a major headache for Truman. On the one hand, the majority of the Wage Stabilization Board, the administrator of the Economic Stabilization Agency, and the director of defense mobilization all endorsed the WSB's rejection of the forty-cent increase. To ignore their advice would emasculate what remained of Truman's economic control program. On the other hand, the director of the Federal Mediation and Conciliation Service warned the president of the likely adverse consequences if Putnam sustained the board's decision, and he urged Truman personally to approve the 1952 contract.

On December 3 Truman ordered Putnam to reverse the WSB's ruling and to approve the disputed forty cents. Truman's order to uphold the 1952 coal contract terminated the economic control program, as Chairman Archibald Cox and all industry members of the wage stabilization board resigned in protest. Lewis, of course, was pleased with his victory and ranked it as "one of the greatest triumphs of our Union." Yet in truth Lewis had slain no giant. Truman's action merely disclosed that the government would not hold the line against labor when corporate interests desired otherwise. By December it was clear that the control program would end as soon as Eisenhower assumed the presidency.

The Bituminous Coal Operators' Association's support of Lewis in his battle against controls stimulated cooperation between the union and the large producers. Henceforth, the UMW chief spoke more and more of partnership for the good of the industry and less and less of labor-management conflict. He allowed the 1952 contract to remain in force until 1955 and requested a new accord only when coal's financial fortunes seemed to improve. Although the ensuing negotiations involved months of shadowboxing between Lewis and Moses, the prospect of a strike was absent. By late 1956, labor relations had become so "normalized" that Tom Kennedy negotiated that year's agreement without Lewis's aid. Likewise, the 1958 contract talks, the last Lewis participated in, lacked any excitement whatsoever—a far cry from the hectic scene that had existed when he took over the union almost four decades before.

Lewis publicly justified collaboration as necessary for the preservation of free enterprise capitalism and free collective bargaining. Yet when translated from ideology to actuality, Lewis's and the large operators' plan was simply to promote the profitability of an industry in whose future both workers and owners had a stake. Despite odes to unrestrained competition, Lewis freely called upon the government for special favors. Among other things, he solicited a tariff on residual oil, a foreign aid program that promoted coal exports, and a floor under the wages paid to miners producing coal sold to the TVA. His pet cause was the establishment of a federal fuel policy to "determine the line of demarcation for the uses of the liquid and solid fuels of this country."

The UMW and the large operators built their marriage on economic necessity, not interclass love. Management conceded to labor a series of agreements that the union's officials viewed as "equal, if not better than any wage contract now in existence anywhere in the world." By 1958, working UMW members earned between $23 and $27 dollars a day. The operators also provided them improved vacation benefits and, from 1952, paid forty cents on each ton of coal mined to the welfare and retirement fund, which they left Lewis free to administer.

Further, BCOA worked with the union in securing from the government various policies of direct benefit to the miners but also advantageous to the large operators. In the late 1950s, for instance, they jointly agitated for a stricter mine safety law. Indeed, here was a classic case of corporate liberalism, for although the overt purpose of the law was to save miners' lives, the covert aim was to force small companies out of business by imposing on them the same expensive safety standards required of larger producers.

Finally, in return for the union's cooperation, the large operators granted Lewis a role in determining industry policies. In the early and mid-1950s, for instance, the miners' chief fervently argued that the industry could offset the loss of domestic markets by active foreign trade. Then, in 1956, leading mine owners and representatives of coal-carrying railroads joined with him in forming the American Coal Shipping Company. Symbolizing his new standing as a constructive force in the industry, Lewis spoke for the new company—one-third owned by the UMW—when it applied to the federal government for use of thirty mothballed Liberty ships to transport coal throughout the world.

The operators' ultimate recognition of Lewis as an industry statesman came on May 5, 1958, when, for the first time in his life, he addressed many of his former bargaining foes at the coal convention of the American Mining Congress. In introducing Lewis, George M. Humphrey—former Secretary of the Treasury, chairman of National Steel, and a behind-the-scenes power in the bituminous industry—proclaimed his "great respect and admiration" for the UMW president and knighted him "a friend of coal." Lewis, in his speech, called for the creation of a body that would coordinate the policies of the various coal interests so that the industry could confront the government and the public with a united front. In less than a year, his idea became reality as coal operators, the union, thirty-two coal-carrying railroads, seven power companies, and a number of mine equipment manufacturers formed the National Coal Policy Conference. Appropriately, George Love became the group's first chairman, with Lewis succeeding him in 1962.

The UMW, of course, had to reciprocate for the blessings bestowed on it by the operators. Most obviously, Lewis assured management that work stoppages would not disrupt production, and throughout the decade he dealt harshly with wildcat strikes. He also vowed to avoid actions that might provoke government interference in the industry. Finally, he consented to use the union's resources to advance the industry's productivity, to find new markets for coal, and to eliminate nonunion mines. Because Lewis believed that the miners' standard of living could advance only if the coal industry prospered, he did not perceive any of these activities as injurious to his members' interests.

This was certainly his reasoning on the issue of mechanizing the mines. "We've encouraged the leading companies in the coal industry to resort to modernization in order to increase the living standard of the miner and improve his working conditions," Lewis told an interviewer for *U.S. News & World Report*. Failure to mechanize, he maintained, would have meant intense pressures from the operators to reduce the miners' wages.

But modernization made large numbers of miners unemployed by technology and caused the union's roster to shrink. Yet this reality never vexed Lewis. "The United Mine Workers of America has never undertaken to oppose modernization or progress from the standpoint of compelling the retention of uneconomic employment in the industry," he contended. "From a policy standpoint, it is immaterial to us whether the Union has a million or a half million members." (Actually, by then the issue was two hundred thousand or one hundred thousand members.)

Lewis so prided himself on being an economic realist and so much believed that the primary goal of unionism was higher and higher pay that he never truly grasped what modernization meant to the unemployed coal miner. When questioned on the fate of the technologically displaced miners, he replied with the economist's formula of individuals being reabsorbed into the economy rather than with a realist's picture of the squalor and degradation of Appalachia. The young, he envisioned, would go off to Pittsburgh or Detroit to work in steel or autos, while the old would live pleasantly on Social Security and their UMW pension checks. He knew this was not true, but he seemed unable to force himself to admit that the union had become a prisoner of conditions under which some members had to suffer so that others would prosper. Lewis, the opponent of "creeping socialism," increasingly suggested that displaced miners seek relief from the state.

The large operators also urged Lewis either to organize or drive out of business the rising number of nonunion mines. The advantages of mechanization—low labor cost per ton yet high daily wages—could only benefit the large operators and working UMW members if other producers could not attain the same result—low price per ton—by simply working on a nonunion basis. In June 1953, BCOA spokesman Harry M. Moses publicly criticized the UMW for failing to organize the entire industry.

By Moses's estimate, in 1953 20 percent of the working miners were not UMW members. Nonunion miners could be found throughout the coalfields, but they were concentrated in Kentucky and Tennessee. Here, the Tennessee Valley Authority, rapidly becoming the nation's largest consumer of coal, encouraged the development of hundreds of "truck" mines, whose aggregate annual production added up to a sizable tonnage. Before 1947, Lewis had used the NLRB's procedures to organize the area, only to find that antiunion sentiment and pressures from operators made this approach futile.

Finally, Lewis instructed his field staff to organize the area "and damn the lawsuits. We'll take care of them." There soon followed a reign of violence against persons and property—a labor guerrilla war. From the late 1940s on, people were killed, property was destroyed, and threats and intimidation abounded. Union miners, fighting for their livelihood, resorted to the strong-arm tactics that had been used against them not many years before. And the nonunion operators met force with force. Unlike the 1930s, however, liberals and radicals now viewed the union as the giant monopoly and sided with the price-cutting, nonunion operators, whom they treated as simply little guys trying to make good.

Lewis apparently made a point of keeping poorly informed about events in Kentucky and Tennessee. He wanted to become known as a labor statesman and so turned the "embarrassing" problems of the union over to his assistant, William Anthony "Tony" Boyle. Boyle was already familiar with "rough stuff" from his tenure as president of the Montana coal miners before 1948. Now, as assistant to the UMW president, he executed a host of ill-defined, covert duties.

By 1959, the mounting number of lawsuits against the union and the adverse publicity they generated finally led Lewis to order most of the "rough stuff" stopped. He now felt he could eliminate the nonunion producers through the protective wage clause of the 1958 contract. This provision, which prohibited unionized firms from allowing unorganized collieries to use their services, hindered truck mines from marketing their coal. Eventually, the propriety of the protective wage clause would be challenged in court, but then legalisms did not bother Lewis.

Lewis, in fulfilling the UMW's obligations to the operators and, indeed, in endeavoring to extend his influence throughout the economy, increasingly resorted to using his organization's financial might. No longer could he act as spokesman for the toiling masses as he had in the 1930s. Nor could he command attention, as he had through most of the 1940s, by threatening to paralyze the national economy with a miners' strike. Lewis, at times unintentionally and unknowingly, acted to transform the UMW's primary concern from the welfare of its membership to the preservation of its purse.

This process was most apparent on the issue of mechanization. Lewis promoted modernization principally because he felt it better for the industry to support two hundred thousand well-paid miners than five hundred thousand destitute ones. Yet his arrival at this policy was eased by the realization that the UMW's strength would not suffer with a decline in membership. Lewis recognized that increased productivity would actually increase the income of the welfare and retirement fund, because it was based on a per-ton royalty and not a payroll tax. Moreover, he knew that well-paid miners could afford higher dues and more assessments than poor men. And finally, even if fewer miners worked, the union would still retain control of all the jobs in and around the mines. Modernization, in short, did not threaten the UMW's power base.

With the establishment of the welfare and retirement fund in the late 1940s, Lewis gained access to a multimillion-dollar treasury that he decided to invest in the banking business. This decision was perhaps inevitable given his personal fascination with high finance, the counseling of such friends as Cleveland tycoon Cyrus Eaton, and his belief that financiers controlled the economy. Lewis saw no reason why the welfare and retirement fund should sit in other people's banks and not be put to work for the union. In this exploit, as well as in his other entrepreneurial activities, Lewis was not seeking personal financial profit but rather trying to strengthen the union and, consequently, his own position of power. Unfortunately, activities advantageous for the institution were not necessarily beneficial to the membership.

Apparently, in the spring of 1949, Lewis secretly employed the investment firm of Johnston, Lemon and Company to purchase controlling interest in the National Bank of Washington for the UMW. By April, the firm had completed the arrangements. Over the next thirteen months the union transferred the welfare and retirement fund into the bank's vaults, which increased the institution's total deposits from

$22,610,346 to $83,676,875. By June 1950, the National Bank had become fourth largest among nineteen banks in the city. Even then, Lewis refused to acknowledge his connection to the institution, although he had personally chosen Barnum L. Colton to be the bank's president and his brother Dennie and UMW attorney Welly K. Hopkins sat on the board of directors. In 1956 they would be joined by Lewis's son, John Jr., and then later by the comptroller of the welfare and retirement fund, Thomas Ryan, in an appointment that seriously raised the issue of conflict of interest.

The scope of the UMW's banking activities, as with most of its financial adventures, increased as Lewis became further isolated from the labor movement. Shortly after the A.F. of L. and CIO made their merger plans known, Lewis directed the National Bank to outbid all competitors for controlling interest in the Hamilton National Bank. This accomplished, the National Bank of Washington subsequently absorbed the Liberty National Bank and the Anacostia Banks so that by 1964 it was the second largest bank in Washington, with eighteen units and total assets of $432 million. By 1964, Secretary-Treasurer John Owens proudly boasted that the union's $23 million investment in bank stocks over the previous fourteen years was worth $72 million.

The deposits in the National Bank of Washington provided Lewis with tremendous financial leverage. Full details on the actual use of the bank's resources are unavailable, but it is clear that the institution responded to Lewis's will. It made loans to coal operators wishing to modernize their properties, and it bought heavily in the electric power field, where it then used its position to convince companies to burn union coal. Like all financial institutions, it made loans to people of influence when the need arose. Perhaps because of the possibility of government scrutiny of the bank's affairs, Lewis generally relied directly on the UMW treasury in delicate situations.

The UMW hierarchy intentionally cloaked the disposition of the union's monies. For years. the officers had reported the union's assets at approximately $30 million. Then the passage of the Labor-Management Reporting and Disclosure Act in 1959 compelled them to reevaluate the organization's worth at more nearly $110 million. This dramatic disclosure, combined with a series of legal cases, created enough of a stir among the membership and the press to force the officials to offer more detailed information on the UMW's financial empire.

At the 1960 convention, John Owens presented a murky report on the union's financial resources that named names and cited figures at least, even if it did not measure up to the standards of intelligible accounting. According to Owens, the $21,646,174.72 tied up in the National Bank of Washington was the union's largest outright investment. Next came Lewis's 1951 investment of $9,421,518.45 in securities of the coal-carrying Chesapeake and Ohio Railway, which was managed by his close friend and economic counselor, Cyrus Eaton. "I am only sorry to report to you," Owens gloated to the delegates, "that we have made just a few million dollars out of that investment for which no coal miner worked in the coal mines." Finally, since 1956, when the union allied with business interests to sell coal abroad through the American Coal Shipping Corporation, Lewis invested $8,346,489 into that venture and, through it, into the Bull Steamship Line.

By 1960 such outright investments amounted to a sum conservatively estimated by Owens to be $17,688,329; but the union's secretary-treasurer reported a far larger amount—$56,743,337—tied up in loans and notes receivable. Since 1950, Lewis loaned union money to several parties, unnamed by Owens, who offered as collateral stock in such enterprises as the Tampa Electric Company, the Union Electric Company of Missouri, the Illinois Central Railroad, the Cleveland Electric Illuminating Company, and the Tri-Continental Corporation (Eaton Investment Company). Each of these firms was linked to the coal industry in one way or another. The loans did more than advance the industry, however, for according to Owens the union itself received $14,623,200 in "profits and dividends" over the decade from these deals.

The most opaque section of Owens's report concerned the UMW's financial ties with actual mining properties. He told of advancing $5,200,000 to the Coaldale Mining Company in an effort to keep at least one segment of the decaying anthracite industry alive. He also defended the union's $26 million investment in the West Kentucky and Nashville Coal companies. Yet on all other arrangements he was incredibly fleeting, asserting something about bringing stability to the Pittsburgh Midway properties and blurting out that the union had attained mines in Kansas under contract. "We brought about hundreds and thousands of other tons of production on which men are receiving the wage scale, and the 40 cents a ton is going into the Welfare and Retirement Fund," he concluded without further elaboration. Nonetheless, he had said enough to substantiate the *New York Times'* conclusion that the United Mine Workers was "the wealthiest union in the land."

One reason Owens said as much as he did was the increasing publicity given to Lewis's collaboration with Cyrus Eaton. Lewis and Eaton first became friends in the 1940s, when they discovered that they shared a desire to stabilize the coal industry, a fascination with financial power, and a love of classical lore. Gradually, the Nova Scotia–born, Rockefeller-trained capitalist became Lewis's unofficial financial consultant, instructing the labor leader in his specialty, the art of leverage. The UMW's purchase of the National Bank of Washington met with Eaton's full approval, for the institution proved of great value to the two men as they united to strengthen their respective empires.

The two men mapped out a plan to unionize major Kentucky and Tennessee nonunion mines. In 1951 Lewis lent Eaton about $6 million from the National Bank and the UMW treasury. The union also purchased West Kentucky Coal Company stock and assigned its proxy to Eaton. By 1953, the Cleveland industrialist had become chairman of the company's board of directors, and shortly thereafter West Kentucky Coal recognized the union. More UMW money, funneled through Eaton, enabled the company to improve its competitive position and attain an ever larger share of the TVA's business. During its first few years, the venture looked so promising that in 1955 Lewis provided Eaton with at least another $7 million in order to purchase the Nashville Coal Company, another large nonunion coal mining and sales operation. Together West Kentucky and Nashville produced 12,500,000 tons of coal annually, which, when combined with the output from other properties controlled by the Cleveland industrialist and the union in 1960, made the Eaton-Lewis empire the third largest bituminous producer in the country.

Lewis and Eaton collaborated in other business ventures, particularly in investing in electrical utility stocks. Some of these power companies, such as Tampa Electric, also purchased West Kentucky and Nashville Coal. Of all the UMW's investments, however, the involvement in coal-mining properties placed the union in the most awkward position. Lewis had to drive out of business all marginal properties regardless of their union standing. And in the area of the TVA, the union-backed West Kentucky and Nashville companies enforced the rules of competition, often to the detriment of UMW members employed at small mines. When in the autumn of 1955, union and nonunion miners from the small collieries of the Sequatchie Valley struck for higher pay, the West Kentucky Coal Company moved in and captured the business of the area's main consumer—the TVA's Willow Creek steam plant—and in the process broke the strike. More frequently, the union-backed coal companies combined with other large operations to force marginal, unionized mines first into a nonunion status and then completely out of business. Although slight rumbles of discontent over these activities could be heard in the 1950s, it would not be until after Lewis retired in 1960 that the full story of such business manipulations would unfold.

Privately, Lewis enjoyed his standing as the head of a great financial empire and gloated when a tycoon such as Eaton referred to him as "the giant in Washington who has been my silent but stalwart coadjutor."

With his belief in capitalism, free enterprise, and the myth of the self-made man, Lewis's financial adventures proved to him that he had indeed made it—albeit with mineworkers' money.

Of all his activites in the 1950s, Lewis wanted to be remembered most for his work with the sick and the aged, the orphaned and the lame, through the welfare and retirement fund. He was truly dedicated to ameliorating the conditions of the miners, but he also wanted to build a monument to himself. Subconsciously, it seems, the elderly general of labor sought to emulate the senior captains of industry who engaged in philanthrophy in their declining years.

In establishing the details of the welfare and retirement fund Lewis had allowed his idealism to transcend practical hard-headedness. He refused, for instance, to heed actuary reports that recommended the creation of a large trust fund to guarantee the promised benefits for the lifetime of the recipient. Rather, he insisted on his own pay-as-you-go scheme, in which benefits came directly out of income. Although this approach permitted workers to receive higher monthly payments, it also tied the program's future to fluctuations in the industry. Again, he refused to follow the customary procedure of first determining the amount of money available and then dividing it among the beneficiaries. Instead, he insisted on a liberal benefit program and expected to wrest from the operators the money needed to cover the costs through his collective bargaining skills. As a result of these decisions, the welfare and retirement fund was a noble venture fated for financial troubles.

To cover the cost of benefits and to meet inflation, Lewis successfully increased the royalty paid per ton of coal from five to forty cents between 1946 and 1952. Under the provisions prevailing by 1952, a retired union miner received $100 a month at the age of sixty if he had put in twenty years of service in the industry, regardless of his income from other sources. In comparison with similar pension programs, the UMW's was quite generous, partly to encourage older miners to retire in order to reduce the extent of technological unemployment.

The welfare aspects of the fund, which accounted for some 55 percent of the expenditures in fiscal 1952, consisted of two small programs—rehabilitation and maintenance aid cash benefits and aid to widows, dependent children, and orphans—and the much larger medical and hospitalization program. By 1956, ten years after the establishment of the fund, more than seventy-five thousand retired miners had received pensions and almost forty thousand widows and orphans had obtained some form of aid. The fund's hospital and medical program had enabled six hundred thousand patient cases to benefit from more than seven million days of hospitalization and six million visits by physicians. In addition, the fund financed some four hundred thousand office consultations for beneficiaries by specialists and outpatient clinics.

Lewis took particular pleasure from praise of the fund's low operating costs—roughly 3 percent of expenditures each year. He strove for administrative efficiency in part to prove the superiority of an industry-run free enterprise welfare system over socialized government operations. But more important, efficiency was dictated by the necessity of making Lewis's pay-as-you-go scheme work under the adverse conditions facing the coal industry in the 1950s. In the fiscal year 1952, for instance, the fund took in only $166,000 more than it expended in benefits, and the next year it actually went into the red by spending $7,500,000 more than it received. The difference came from the $100 million the fund kept in reserve, which was not enough to meet benefit payments for a year if all income stopped. Indeed, Lewis was lucky that the operators had insisted back in 1946 that the fund be financed by royalty on tonnage mined rather than the more common methods of a per-capita tax on a percentage of the payroll. Although coal production dropped substantially in the 1950s, the decline in the number of miners working and the industry's labor costs were even more dramatic because of mechanization.

Clearly, economic realities demanded a revision of Lewis's expectations of the fund. In 1951 and 1952, the fund had tried to provide dental care for its beneficiaries but had to drop it as too expensive. For the same reason it stopped assuming the cost of thousands of tonsil and adenoid operations for miners and their children. The failure of revenues to cover costs in 1953 led Lewis and his associates on the board of trustees to tighten the eligibility requirements for pensions from any union miner over sixty with more than twenty years in the industry to any UMW member who accrued twenty years of service within the thirty years before his application for a pension. Until the trustees reversed this rule in 1965, it created injustice in some unique cases involving old-timers and long-disabled individuals, which Lewis and his associates seemed too inflexible to correct. For the most part, however, the new rule assured those miners who had spent their lives in the industry and had fought with the union in the 1930s and 1940s first access to the funds.

In 1954 the trustees again cut the number of beneficiaries in order to enable expenditures to balance receipts. By rewriting the eligibility rules, they denied thirty thousand disabled miners and twenty-four thousand widows and children further benefits from the fund. The inclusion of these unfortunates in the first place dramatized Lewis's idealistic attempt to have the fund alleviate all suffering linked to coal. Their exclusion demonstrated the inadequacies of his industry-financed free enterprise system. Such retrenchment enabled the fund to meet expenses for the next few years, but by 1958 it was again operating at a deficit, leading the trustees to reduce benefits further in the early 1960s.

Lewis's critics felt that he should have solved the fund's financial problems with transfusions from the UMW's treasury. They saw little reason for the union to make loans to the longshoremen's union or purchase stock in coal and power companies when the fund reduced benefits to the miners. Lewis contended that Taft-Hartley and other laws prohibited the intermingling of the two treasuries, although occasionally he funneled UMW money to operators so that they could pay it back in the form of royalties to the fund. For the most part however, he felt that it was best to invest the union's resources in building up the strength of the industry, which would eventually improve the fund's position.

Actually, during the 1950s most union members overlooked the fund's retrenchment policies and continued to praise Lewis. At the 1956 convention, for instance, a delegate from Gary, West Virginia, resolved that the union begin building a monument to Lewis, who humbly ruled the motion out of order. But he had already executed its spirit by spending almost $30 million from the welfare and retirement fund on the construction of a chain of ten hospitals. The chain ran through Virginia, West Virginia, and Kentucky and brought high-quality medical and health service to an area pitifully lacking such care.

The dedication of the hospitals in 1956 was a momentous occasion for the seventy-six-year-old union leader. He saw the project as proof of his commitment to the miners and as the crowning achievement of his long career. The UMW even hired a special train to convey the guests from Washington to Beckley, West Virginia, where the dedication occurred. There, on a drizzly June 2, a crowd of thousands participated in Lewis's moment of glory. And before them stood a well-equipped brick and glass building that gave the sense of having been constructed around a portrait of John L. Lewis.

At the beginning of the 1950s, Lewis had few reasons to feel generationally out of date. Although new faces appeared, individuals with whom he had interacted for years still held key positions in the nation's social, political, and economic life. As time passed, the old faded away and a new generation emerged. The Republicans who took over Washington in 1953 were neither personally nor ideologically akin to the GOP leaders that Lewis had related to for most of his career. He now felt more comfortable with old-timers from the party of Roosevelt—Alben Barkley, Oscar Chapman, Averell Harriman, and even Harry Truman—and apparently voted Democratic in presidential elections for the rest of his life. And in the coal industry such men as George Love and Martin Fox replaced such longtime adversaries as Charles O'Neill, Ezra Van Horn, Harry Moses, and William W. Inglis. Lewis watched the most sweeping transition in leadership occur within the labor movement. Here, Daniel Tobin, William L. Hutcheson, Matthew Woll, John Frey, George Berry, and others of their breed—men who had dominated unionism for nearly a half century—passed from the scene.

The deaths of William Green and Phil Murray in 1952 had particular meaning for Lewis. So much of his career had involved these two men, first in their roles as his faithful lieutenants and then as heads of the national federations that Lewis alternately courted and cursed. Since the mid-1940s, the miners' chief had rekindled a personal fondness for Green. When Green died, Lewis felt real sadness, and at the next miners' convention he magnanimously listed the A.F. of L. president as among the UMW's "Departed Brothers." Lewis proved unable to make a similar gesture for Phil Murray and to the end could not forgive the CIO chief for his "betrayal."

Perhaps Lewis could control the psychological sense of aging as long as his mother survived, but on January 12, 1950, Ann Louisa Lewis died at the age of ninety-one. For two years she had been in poor health. When his mother finally died, the coal situation was at such a critical state that he had little time—physically or emotionally—to adjust to his loss.

Time also took a heavy toll of other members in Lewis's circle of family and faithful associates. A little more than a month after his mother's death, he received the tragic news that his brother, Tom, painfully ill for an extended period, had ended his suffering by committing suicide. Many of Lewis's "union brothers" also died during the decade. No longer could he call upon W. Jett Lauck for advice or be entertained by the sarcasm of K. C. Adams. Gone, too, were William Sneed, Sam Caddy, O. E. Gasaway, William Brennan, Frank Hefferly, John T. Jones, William Blizzard, A. T. Pace, and other fellow union warriors.

For Lewis, the deaths of family, associates, and adversaries constituted one part of the totality of experiences that ultimately led him to recognize the passing of his era. On another level, he increasingly feared that the American people no longer revered his generation's values and principles. True, since his break with Roosevelt he had been protesting the direction in which the country seemed headed; but now, in the 1950s, his cry approached a lament: "Can we keep this nation of ours?" he asked. "Can we retain free enterprise? Can we offset and resist the rising, threatening tide of world Communism? Can we resist the tendency in a Republic such as our own, to adopt the device of the more absolute forms of government, seeking to justify ourselves in so doing that we are saving the basic concepts of the Republic?"

Most disturbing to Lewis was the tendency of the government to investigate and regulate unions. To him, the McClellan Committee, established by the Senate to investigate corruption in labor-management affairs, was but "a re-establishment of the principle of the star chamber of the Tudor and Stuart kings—with a slight touch of the Spanish Inquisition." He contended that there were enough laws on the books to punish wrongdoing by labor leaders and that efforts to attain special legislation constituted nothing more than a drive to cast aspersions upon the labor movement. Lewis's opposition to the Landrum-Griffin Act and other measures rested upon his vision of a pluralistic society of voluntary associations threatened by the rise of the corporate state. "I do not believe," he told Senator John F. Kennedy's subcommittee on welfare funds, "that the Republic, through its central powers, can regulate those voluntary associations either in whole or in part without of necessity expanding its powers as a central government to the point where it will become a police state in truth and in fact."

Yet although opposed to government regulation of labor unions, he also rejected the idea that the organizations themselves should police the honesty of their officers. He viewed unions as simply vehicles to attain better physical conditions for their members. "The question of sin and morality and the hunting down of sin and immorality and its eradication," he declared, "is not an enterprise within the purview of the province of labor unions and the members of those labor unions didn't pay in their money—whatever it may be for membership—to have it used for that kind of a purpose."

It now made little difference what Lewis believed, for few people outside of the miners' union paid attention to him. Senators would flock into a committee room to gaze at him as they would a museum piece; he was a living bit of history and a great theatrical show. More and more, he was the recipient of patronizing courtesies granted elders rather than the blunt respect offered to a person of power. His appointment to Eisenhower's Citizens Advisory Committee on Foreign Aid was just such a gesture because it was known that his health and age would limit Lewis's role.

As a response to aging, Lewis, under the coaxing of Josephine Roche, sought to forge closer bonds with his children and their offspring. In the mid-1940s, Kathryn had made another attempt to escape her father's domination by moving to an isolated cottage near Scarborough-on-Hudson in New York. By the early 1950s however, she was again by his side. Together they took a South American vacation in 1952, and

Lewis—in his fatherly way—appointed her UMW specialist for foreign labor relations. As his administrative assistant for the rest of the decade, she saw her job as protecting him from others.

A far wider gap separated Lewis and his son, although it was closed somewhat by the young psychiatrist's attentiveness during his father's wave of heart attacks in the 1940s. In June 1948 Lewis was delighted when he became a grandfather for the second time and disrupted a negotiating session to celebrate. Perhaps Lewis's interest in building hospitals and medical facilities was in part an attempt to win his son's favor. In 1956, he did appoint John Jr. to the board of directors of the National Bank of Washington. Despite such overtures, however, the distance between the house on Orinoco Street in Alexandria and the son's residence near Baltimore remained greater than one of mere miles.

By 1958 Lewis began to speculate about whether he should retire. The realities of his isolation in the labor movement, the weakening of his union, the decline of the coal industry, and the obsolescence of his politics all weighed heavily on his mind. Retirement, too, could be that ultimate gesture to certify that his aim in life was not simply amassing and holding power. And by stepping down, Tom Kennedy could end his own career as UMW president as a reward for faithful service. More directly, Lewis confronted the condition of his health. In 1955 he entered Emergency Hospital in Washington with another heart attack, and in 1957 poor health forced him to cut short a world tour as a member of Eisenhower's commission to investigate foreign aid programs.

Then in January 1959, another heart attack sent him back to Georgetown Hospital. He spent three weeks there and several more recovering in Alexandria. Lewis could have retired then, but apparently he wanted to stay in office a little longer, perhaps in order to match Samuel Gompers's forty years as a leader in the labor movement. Finally, on December 15, 1959, Lewis informed the membership of his intent to resign soon after the beginning of the new year.

21

Twilight and Darkness, 1960–69

On January 14, 1960, John L. Lewis retired as president of the United Mine Workers. The union marked the occasion with some ceremony, but not with the pomp and pageantry that reporters had anticipated. Even Lewis's speech at the dinner in his honor was "without histrionics and, for him, quiet." The entire day's activities emphasized that although Lewis was retiring from formal leadership in the union, he intended to remain active in coal industry affairs for some time to come.

The official transfer of power from Lewis to Thomas Kennedy occurred at an afternoon meeting of the UMW executive board. The order of succession at his retirement followed bureaucratic lines. Seventy-three years old, Vice-President Kennedy automatically moved into the presidency. Secretary-Treasurer John Owens declined the vacant vice-presidential post, however. Unaware that Kennedy had cancer and would die shortly, Owens saw no reason to master new duties at the age of seventy. Consequently, the vice-presidency went to the next person in line, Lewis's assistant W. A. "Tony" Boyle. The executive board sanctioned this arrangement and then appointed Lewis to the new position of president emeritus with an annual pension of $50,000.

For the first few years of retirement, Lewis played an active but diminished role in coal industry affairs. For the most part, Lewis conducted his activities out of the public's view. In consultation with Cyrus Eaton, he continued to oversee the UMW's far-flung financial empire.

Lewis's primary responsibility in the 1960s was as chairman of the welfare and retirement fund, a post he held until his death. Although the fund's staff assumed greater discretion as Lewis aged, the octogenarian dictated the program's basic policies. His decisions displayed increasing insensitivity, poor judgment, and manipulation, yet neither

Josephine Roche, the neutral trustee, nor Henry G. Schmidt, the operators' representative, challenged his verdicts. As a consequence, the fund that Lewis had once envisioned as a monument to his humanitarianism became a symbol of dictatorial rule.

Through the 1950s and early 1960s, the depressed state of the coal industry greatly reduced the fund's income. By 1961 royalties amounted to only $114 million—the smallest figure in the program's history. At the same time, the number of pensioners had reached a record 66,759, forcing the fund to expend nearly $16.5 million more than it received. In meeting this crisis, the UMW refused to demand a larger per-ton royalty from the operators out of fear of both placing unionized mines at a greater competitive disadvantage and driving marginal producers to a nonunion status.

Consequently, Lewis sought to solve the fund's financial problems by cutting expenditures. In mid-1960 the trustees revoked the medical and hospital coverage of all miners unemployed for more than a year. At the same time, they denied coverage to working UMW members if their employers had not signed the national wage agreement. A few months later, in December 1960, the trustees reduced pension payments from $100 to $75 a month. Again, in 1962, they canceled the health cards of miners employed by operators making only token royalty payments. This last policy generated a wave of wildcat strikes against the reneging companies and a letter to Lewis from his brother Raymond, president of District 17, criticizing him for arbitrary and illegal action.

Lewis also put the fund's ten "miners" hospitals up for sale in order to free the millions of dollars tied up in noninterest-bearing mortgages for income-generating investments. Apparently, he lost interest in the hospitals when declining employment in the coal industry reduced the proportion of miners as patients.

By the mid-1960s, the growing demand for electrical energy improved coal sales and generated larger royalties for the fund. Some of this money went toward improved benefits for miners, but Lewis also used it in the UMW's battle against nonunion coal. In February 1965, for example, the trustees raised pensions, previously cut from $100 to $75, to $85 a month. They could have restored the full amount but instead decided to lower the qualifying age from sixty to fifty-five in order to encourage older unemployed miners to retire rather than to take jobs at nonunion pits. In another attempt to reduce the work force available to nonunion operators, the trustees ruled that a miner's last year of work had to be in a union colliery in order for him to qualify for a pension. This policy harshly punished those old-timers who had labored for years in organized mines only to be forced by the vicissitudes of age to accept nonunion employment.

Under Lewis's domination the faults apparent in the fund's benefit programs also characterized its investment policies. The fund lost nearly $4 million, for example, when the trustees sold almost $46 million worth of government securities before their maturity date. Lewis and his associates argued that they had accepted this loss in order to obtain capital for investment in higher-yield ventures. Yet if the trustees wanted capital, they could have tapped the fund's general checking account, which contained millions of dollars not earning interest. Indeed, from 1961 to 1967 the nonyielding deposits in the general account climbed from $12 million to $72 million, or 44 percent of the fund's resources. The UMW-owned National Bank of Washington, where the fund did its business, had use of this money at no cost.

Although Lewis remained a trustee until his death, he no longer seemed to view the fund as the crowning accomplishment of his career. Rather, he took greater pride in his role in initiating the National Coal Policy Conference (NCPC) to coordinate the industry's affairs and was elated at becoming NCPC chairman in 1962. To Lewis, attainment of this post symbolized his arrival as a peer of the captains of industry.

For several months Lewis served as coal's spokesman in demanding benefits and subsidies from the government equal to those provided other fuels. Surgery and prolonged hospitalization in late 1962, however, curtailed Lewis's work as NCPC chairman. And then, on January 19, 1963, while he recuperated, his longtime associate and successor as UMW president, Thomas Kennedy, died of cancer. Kennedy's death symbolized to Lewis the departure of all his old comrades and the end of the UMW that he knew best. These thoughts, along with his erratic health, led Lewis to limit his activities.

On April 3, 1963, when Lewis retired as NCPC chairman, the conference honored him with a luncheon. Accepting praise graciously — indeed, concurring with it — Lewis uttered appropriate thoughts. This occasion, and not the 1960 UMW ceremonies, marked Lewis's retirement from a central role in the coal industry. "The shadows are gathering on all of us," he philosophized. "We only make such contributions as we can while we are here." As if granting absolution, he disclaimed any animosity toward those operators who fought him so viciously before 1950. "They moved as they saw the light," he conceded. "They acted within the limitations that were upon them as so do we now."

Although Lewis proved able to announce the end of his era, he still seemed incapable of evaluating his life or fathoming his personality. When the members of the NCPC presented him with a painting of himself, he thanked them for the gift. "I value this portrait," he said. And then looking down at his likeness, he added: "although I am going to have a hard time reading all the facets of his character."

During his first few years of retirement, Lewis vacationed in the West and in Florida and journeyed to New York City to be with Kathryn, who was under psychiatric care. He also collected numerous honors that had evaded him during his active career. It was as though proper society chose to wait until the volcanic man became inactive before offering him the homage paid most prominent individuals earlier in their lives. Lewis did not receive his first honorary degree, for example, until 1957, when the University of West Virginia granted him an LL.D. Three years later Georgetown University made him a "Doctor of Humane Letters, *Honoris causa,*" but not commencement speaker. No other university came forth with similar recognition, although in 1966 Buena Vista College, observing its seventy-fifth anniversary, gave Lewis one of seventy-five Honor Iowans' Awards.

Some tributes clearly amused Lewis. Upon receiving the Freedom Medal from President Lyndon Johnson in 1964, Lewis chucked, "So they gave me a medal for doing all those things they fought me for doing all those years." Even more irony lay behind his acceptance of the Eugene V. Debs Award in 1965. Not only had Lewis opposed Debs when the socialist was alive, but in 1962 he also forbade the UMW from participating in a memorial to the man. Now, perhaps moved by a vain drive to accumulate recognition, Lewis took the award and forwarded $50 to the Debs Foundation.

When not traveling, Lewis still lived in his Alexandria house, where the black couple who had served him for many years continued to wait upon his needs. On weekdays he would be chauffeured to the UMW building, where he would spend a few hours in his sixth-floor office. Actually, his quarters consisted of a suite of rooms filled with overstuffed leather sofas and chairs, where mementos decorated the walls and a wagon-wheel chandelier obtained during one of his western vacations hung above his desk. At noon, Lewis usually strolled to the Sheraton-Carlton Hotel, occasionally with company, but most often alone.

After lunch, Lewis occasionally granted an audience to a reporter, foreign labor dignitary, or old acquaintance. He could be quite charming and generally treated his guests to a delightful time. Labor reporter John Herling enjoyed one such interview in late 1963. Herling anxiously waited in the sixth-floor anteroom for a few minutes before Lewis strolled out of his office with his hand extended. "His look is sharp and seems to fold back on itself," Herling recalled.

> He looks you over and, as you return the look, he seems to be trying to guess your thoughts about him.
>   "It must be a dull day on the rialto that brings you to this humble abode," he rumbles softly. It's an old line of his and he utters it

with relish. Then he settles back in an armchair. He stares at you and you stare back, faint-heartedly. His eyes, always deep, now seem more cavernous. His eyebrows grow hugely. They flare out luxuriantly. He picks up a long cigar, bites the end, lights up, and waves it like a scepter.

"How are all your heroes?" he says derisively. "Heroes?" I reply defensively, bristling a little, "Whom do you mean?" Then he mockingly intones the names of several great and near great—in and out of the labor movement. After he gets through with this elephantine caper, I say: "Mr. Lewis, you do yourself an injustice. You know, sir, even those who are reluctant to admit it consider you something rather special. They are only great. You are most great, you are maximus." We are trading extravagances. His eyes light up.

"Aha," says Mr. Lewis, "we know you as being most gracious, even though you are not always perceptive." To which I reply, "On this subject of yourself, you can hardly be objective. By profession, I can only tell the truth."

He waves, as if granting that this round must end somewhere. And then, as is his wont, he interviews you. He asks you a question, and doesn't always wait for your inadequate answer. Most of his questions are rhetorical. They punctuate the reality around you and the world beyond. His talk is filled not only with generalizations about men and motives, but like a cigar wrapper, it encloses layers and layers of detail.

People continually prodded Lewis to write his memoirs, and several publishers offered him lucrative book contracts. But Lewis unhesitatingly rejected such pressures. Infrequently, he would reminisce with reporters, but even these talks were not for repeating. Students of the past approaching him for an interview almost always met a negative reply. "The moving finger has made a record," he wrote to one scholar. "It is available in every library and newspaper morgue across the land. Not all my 'piety nor wit shall lure it back to cancel half a line, nor all your tears wash out a word of it'."

Lewis undoubtedly recognized that it had been his own "moving finger" that had "made the record" through his control over everything the UMW put into print. Understandably, Lewis displayed a love for history but suspicion for historians. Although he avidly read *American Heritage* and prided himself on being a student of classical culture, he also doubted that the "true" past could be recreated. Himself devious, he believed that all historical actors maneuvered in secret and conspiratorial ways that historians could never penetrate. Nor did he like to have his own mysteries probed by someone he could not dominate because Lewis characteristically sought to control all events in which he participated, even those that had already occurred.

At night and on weekends, Lewis engaged in little socializing, partly to preserve his waning strength and partly because he found cocktail parties to be "an abomination." He preferred spending his evenings at home reading a novel or article on business and listening to the radio.

Josephine Roche became Lewis's most comforting friend during his retirement years. In addition to looking after most of the routine welfare and retirement fund business that came across Lewis's desk, Roche provided the octogenarian with cheerful companionship that brightened his otherwise lonely existence. In the last few years of his life, when infirmities often kept him confined to his Alexandria home, Roche served as both a link and a protective buffer between the fading Lewis and the outside world. Among other things, Roche helped satisfy Lewis's almost insatiable desire for worship. He thrived on adulation and purposely sent her the eulogistic correspondence he received in order to evoke her praise.

Like Roche, Cyrus Eaton heaped unqualified acclaim on his old friend. When the labor leader extended Eaton birthday greetings in 1964, the Cleveland financier lauded: "To be the recipient of such generous praise from one of the world's great citizens of all times gives me new inspiration for the busy years ahead." "The pride of my own 84 years," Eaton extolled on Lewis's eighty-eighth birthday, "is my long and cherished friendship with history's greatest labor statesman."

Lewis thought that such formality and pomposity communicated deep affection. Yet in reality, Lewis's Victorian stiffness tended to hinder warm interaction with those he loved. He gloated over his grandson, Tom, for example, but corresponded with the youngster in business letter format. Formality also stood between John L. and Kathryn, who, while emotionally tied to him, seemed unable to penetrate his defenses and share his innermost life. Ever since the 1930s, she had been either working intensely by his side or fleeing from his domination. Frustrated, in the early 1960s Kathryn again sought to end her submissiveness to her father and fled to New York, where she underwent treatment for depression. Then, mysteriously, on January 7, 1962, she died at the age of fifty in Wickersham Hospital. Her death deeply grieved Lewis, who had tried to be a good father even if he did not know how. As always, he kept his sorrow to himself.

A few weeks after Lewis suffered the loss of Kathryn, Dennie Lewis died. Of all the Lewis brothers, Dennie had fought longest by John L.'s side and had remained the most faithful. Lewis lost other members of his family over the next few years: his sister, Hattie, on January 18, 1963; his brother, Howard, on April 5, 1968.

The remaining relatives proved unable or unwilling to meet Lewis's emotional needs. Most painful to the aging leader, John Jr. continued to have little to do with him and kept the grandchildren from visiting the old man too frequently. Lewis spent the last years of his life almost isolated from his offspring when his son moved his family from Baltimore to Milwaukee. His brother, Raymond, moreover, showed few indications of affection for his brother and at times criticized him harshly. But for Josephine Roche and a few other UMW staff members, Lewis would have been depressingly lonely in his declining years.

W. A. "Tony" Boyle's ascent to the UMW presidency in 1963 placed the retired Lewis in an awkward position. Although Boyle had served as Lewis's assistant, the new president enjoyed no special rapport with the elderly labor leader. The UMW patriarch kept Boyle, as he did all his lieutenants, at a social distance, and he could not envision anyone adequately replacing him as head of the union. Yet publicly, the president emeritus supported his former assistant, occasionally with kind words but most often with silence. After Boyle took over the union, Lewis avoided involvement in UMW affairs except for welfare and retirement fund business and even failed to attend the miners' 1964 convention. In a sense, the aged Lewis became subject to the code of loyalty he had originated, because now Boyle expected him to suppress his personal opinions just as for decades Lewis had demanded the same from others.

Boyle needed Lewis's acquiescence in order to strengthen his control over his inherited union. In an effort to capitalize on the miners' allegiance to Lewis, on June 12, 1963, the executive board elected his brother, Raymond, UMW vice-president. Although this might have pleased union members in the coalfields, it caused Boyle alarm. As an official in District 17, Raymond had exercised family liberties and harshly criticized his brother. He now felt little reason to submit to Boyle, and perhaps he even thought of obtaining the union presidency for himself. All was not harmony between the two men; on at least one occasion Raymond charged Boyle with acting unconstitutionally. Soon after the episode, Raymond received a letter from George Titler, Boyle's strongest ally and head of the union's violent southern West Virginia district. "What would John L. Lewis have done with a maverick of your ilk?" Titler asked. "The answer is simply: a kick in the pants with a hard-toe shoe." Faced with such blunt opposition—and apparently unable to enlist his brother's backing—Raymond Lewis resigned the vice-presidency in November 1965.

By the late 1960s, the decay of the UMW under Boyle began to disturb Lewis. He felt sadness at seeing his kingdom weakened by a rank-and-file revolt from within and legal challenges from without. The appointment of Boyle, he reportedly told intimates, was "the worst mistake I ever made." Perhaps old age and cognitive dissonance prevented Lewis from recognizing his responsibility for the state of union affairs. Lewis, not Boyle, had initiated collaboration with large operators, sweetheart contracts, and the drive to wipe out marginal and nonunion mines. He had created the UMW's financial empire and repressed rank-and-file democracy. And as chairman of the welfare and retirement fund, Lewis was responsible for most of the manipulations and misdeeds condemned in Judge Gerhard Gesell's 1971 decision, *Blankenship* vs. *Boyle*. In short, entrepreneurism, despotism, and a contempt for the law ranked high among the legacies that Lewis passed on to his successors.

Lacking Lewis's political skills and petrified of losing control of the union, Boyle did everything heavy-handedly, from transforming the UMW *Journal* from a subtle to a blatant house organ to allowing an army of his supporters to intimidate convention-goers indiscriminately. Boyle also lacked Lewis's insight into the miners' minds and consequently could not satisfy their emotional needs. When, on November 20, 1968, an explosion at the Consolidation Coal Company's No. 9 mine near Farmington, West Virginia, killed seventy-eight men, Boyle did not understand what the bereaved relatives psychologically needed to hear. "As long as we mine coal," he told them, "there is always this inherent danger." And then he added that Consolidation Coal was "one of the best companies to work with as far as cooperation and safety are concerned." Clearly, in the same situation, Lewis, concealing his personal beliefs, would have shouted at the operators for their greed and insensitivity and at the government for its failure to enforce the law.

The Farmington disaster and Boyle's cold response to it transformed the disjoined and weak opposition to his regime into an increasingly stronger and purposeful revolt. The rebellion leaders recognized that an endorsement of their cause from Lewis would help wean the rank and file from its traditional loyalty to the incumbent administration. On May 22, 1969, therefore, consumer and safety crusader Ralph Nader sent Lewis a letter, which he also released to the press to make sure that its contents reached the average miner. Nader charged Boyle with trying to oust Lewis from the chairmanship of the welfare and retirement fund and called upon the eighty-nine-year-old labor giant to lead a rank-and-file revolt against his "incompetent" and "authoritarian" successor. Through his letter, Nader cleverly attempted to link Lewis and the rebellion in the miners' minds, even though Nader did not really expect Lewis to reply. The letter created consternation at the UMW's headquarters, with Boyle's supporters wanting Lewis to lash out at Nader for breeding division within the union. But Lewis refused to cooperate.

"They built that cesspool over there," he reportedly remarked to Josephine Roche. "Let them drown in their own slime."

When Joseph "Jock" Yablonski decided to challenge Boyle for the UMW presidency, he thought that he stood a chance of winning Lewis's support. As a devoted Lewis lieutenant in the 1950s, Yablonski had earned some of the patriarch's strongest praise. "He's my right-hand man," Lewis had declared. "Whenever I have trouble in the coal fields, I need him." On May 25, 1969, three days before he formally announced his candidacy, Yablonski telephoned Lewis at his home in Alexandria and asked for an appointment. Lewis was too ill to see visitors, but suggested that the insurgent approach him at another time. A week later, on June 1, Yablonski talked to Lewis's confidant Josephine Roche and learned that she at least enthusiastically greeted his candidacy. Encouraged by this news, Yablonski called Lewis in Alexandria. Lewis was still too ill to receive visitors, but suggested that they meet the following week. Yablonski interpreted Lewis's willingness to confer as a favorable sign.

Lewis's meeting with Yablonski never occurred. On Sunday, June 8, the labor giant entered Washington's Doctors Hospital with acute internal bleeding from some unknown cause. Three days later, on June 11, 1969, John L. Lewis died.

Just as Lewis had spent his life hiding his personal affairs from the public, so now his family kept the details of his death private. Doctors performed an autopsy but, obeying the family's wishes, made no report to the newspapers. The family also declined a public funeral service and requested that mourners send donations to the welfare and retirement fund instead of flowers. Lewis's body was cremated in Washington and then entombed in Springfield, Illinois.

Miners across the coalfields felt a genuine loss at Lewis's death and for four days remained away from work as a memorial. Other labor leaders and politicians uttered expected eulogies, with even David McDonald, one of the most passionate Lewis-haters, admitting that "in the field of labor he was the greatest Roman of them all."

Index

MELVYN DUBOFSKY is a professor of history at the State University of New York at Binghamton. He is the author of many articles appearing in *Labor History, The Nation, The Progressive,* and other publications. His books include *When Workers Organize: New York City in the Progressive Era; We Shall Be All: A History of the IWW;* and *Industrialism and the American Worker, 1865–1920.*

WARREN VAN TINE is professor of history at Ohio State University. A contributor to *Monthly Labor Review, The Historian,* and *Labor History,* he is the author of *The Making of a Labor Bureaucrat.*